Analyzing Politics

SECOND EDITION

Analyzing Politics

Rationality, Behavior, and Institutions

SECOND EDITION

Kenneth A. Shepsle
HARVARD UNIVERSITY

W · W · Norton & Company
New York · London

In memory of my parents,
Philip and Edythe Shepsle

Manufacturing by Courier Companies, Inc.
Book design by Jack Meserole
Production managers: Chris Granville and Christine D'Antonio

Library of Congress Cataloging-in-Publication Data
Shepsle, Kenneth A.
Analyzing politics : rationality, behavior, and institutions /
Kenneth A. Shepsle.—2nd ed.
p.   cm.
Includes bibliographical references and index.
ISBN 978-0-393-93507-3 (pbk.)
1. Political science.   I. Title.
JA71.S435   2010
324.072—dc22   2010014477

W. W. Norton & Company, Inc., 500 Fifth Avenue, New York, N.Y. 10110
www.wwnorton.com
W. W. Norton & Company Ltd., Castle House,
75/76 Wells Street, London W1T 3QT
2 3 4 5 6 7 8 9 0

Contents

Part III
COOPERATION, COLLECTIVE ACTION, AND PUBLIC GOODS

Part IV
INSTITUTIONS

Acknowledgments for the Second Edition

The first edition of *Analyzing Politics* appeared more than a decade ago. It is an elaboration of the lectures I give in Social Analysis 46 at Harvard University, a course still offered all these many years later. I owe a debt to the many students over the years who have caused me to think hard about analyzing politics and about how best to encourage others to do so. I hope the fruits of this reconsideration make this new edition not only new but improved as well.

I also owe a debt to the teaching fellows who have collaborated with me in Social Analysis 46. Many are now prominent scholars in their own right. They include Christopher Afendulis, Alison Alter, Matthew Blackwell, Mark Bonchek, Ethan Bueno de Mesquita, Eric Dickson, Sven Feldmann, James Fowler, Sean Ingham, Miriam Jorgensen, Michael Kellermann, Steve Kafka, Iain Osgood, Shana Rose, Alexander Schuessler, Gilles Serra, Melissa Thomas, and Robert Van Houweling. Iain Osgood has done a splendid job in helping me add discussion questions and problem sets to chapters of this new edition. A password-protected instructor website provides an answer key (wwnorton.com/instructors). In addition he and I have worked together to produce the "Experimental Corner" sections found in many of the chapters of this edition.

Let me also thank the many readers who have contacted me over the years with questions and suggestions, many of which have found their way into the present volume. I have tried to acknowledge them in footnotes at the relevant places.

Harvard's Department of Government and its Institute for Quantitative Social Science have been my homes for more than two decades. In addition to being intellectually stimulating settings, filled with intelligent, ambitious, and supportive people, they have provided me with many instances and occasions in which to "analyze politics" as a participant-observer (especially when I served as chair of Harvard's Department of Government). I've learned much about politics (sometimes the hard way) by being here.

My wife, Rise, has always been by my side. Her support and love are the essential ingredients of my life, allowing me the privilege to write, think, and teach, for which I am ever grateful.

—Kenneth A. Shepsle, Harvard University

Analyzing Politics

SECOND EDITION

Part I

INTRODUCTION

1

It Isn't Rocket Science, but . . .

This book pretends to be modest, but it really isn't. Although the prose will be sprinkled with qualification and "on the one hand this, but on the other hand that," I shall in fact be describing a sea change in the study of politics. Since the end of World War II, changes in political studies have been numerous and many-splendored, but I shall concentrate on two of the most significant shifts of emphasis—from describing to explaining, and from judging to analyzing.

A SCIENCE OF POLITICS?

Consider this illustration. We are all familiar with reproaches in the popular press and in everyday coffee-break conversations about *politicians*. Their sins are routinely depicted; their persons are often held in contempt; and their actions are regularly alleged to border on the venal, the immoral, and the disgusting. In nearly every culture, politicians are taken as scoundrels of one sort or another—sometimes charming, even enchanting; necessary evils at best, but scoundrels nonetheless.[1] These characterizations, in both oral and tabloid traditions, are rich in description and unforgiving in judgment.

[1] Why else was *Profiles in Courage*, John F. Kennedy's book about politicians who sacrificed their own personal well-being for a greater good, so short?

Rarely, however, are they more than exercises in storytelling and hand-wringing.

Political science at the end of World War II was much more than this. It consisted, first and foremost, of detailed contemporary description and political history writing. Any of the major books on the U.S. Congress, for example, was both a compendium of facts about current legislative practice and an account of how that practice had evolved over the entire history of the institution. The same could be said about scholarly tomes on political parties, elections, the presidency, the courts, interest groups, state and local institutions—in short, about studies of nearly every facet of American political life. The anthropologist Clifford Geertz refers to this mode of analysis as *thick description*.[2] Thick description is typically careful, detailed to a fault, and comprehensive, in contrast to "mere" storytelling. But it is also indiscriminate, and the accumulation of detail does not always add up to much more than a pile of facts.[3]

Postwar political science is also more than normative hand-wringing. The evaluative emphasis of postwar political science consisted chiefly of reformist sentiments. Thus, in the very same thickly descriptive books on Congress there typically were objections to the overbearing nature of the Speaker of the House, concerns about the dominance of congressional committees, and general unhappiness with the antidemocratic nature of the filibuster in the Senate, the inordinate influence of lobbyists, and the intolerance of the majority party for diversity of opinion within its ranks (not to speak of the outright

[2] Thick description and political history writing, it should be added, were not unique to the study of *American* politics of the time; they were the primary methods of political analysis of politics in nearly every country in the world.

[3] This is true of quantitative data as well as of qualitative facts. A detailed census of some particular population is just a bunch of numbers until it is analyzed. The numbers do not speak for themselves. Indeed, a humorist once described statistics as a tool of analysis in which the numbers are grabbed by the throat and beseeched, "Speak to me! Speak to me!"

contempt of the majority for opinions of the minority party). Reforms were advocated to cure the legislature of these ills.

But in these descriptions, judgments, and reform suggestions, attention was given by scholars and commentators neither to explaining the evils they described nor to defending how their alleged reforms would play out. A codification of historical minutiae about congressional committees, for example, was not accompanied by any consideration of *why* committees were used in legislatures in the first place. That is, why is there a division of labor in legislative bodies, and why does it take the particular form that it does? Likewise, the advocates of reform for various disapproved-of practices paid scant attention to *why* these practices existed in the first place, why an existing legislature would be moved to adopt the proposed reform, *why* the proposed reform would cure the problems, and *why* the reformed institutional arrangement would itself not be subject to further tinkering (or even regression to its pre-reform condition).

In short, the political science that a college student at the end of World War II might have encountered was primarily *descriptive* and *judgmental*. It was much less oriented toward *explanation* and *analysis*. Over the next twenty years, political scientists got even better at description. They learned data-collection skills, more precise measurement, and statistical techniques allowing more precise inferences about causal relationships. But it was not until the 1960s that systematic attention began to focus on questions of "why." "Why?" is the principal interrogative of science; answers to it are explanations, and getting to explanations requires analysis.

The transformation of the study of politics from stories and anecdotes, first to thick description and history writing, then to systematic measurement, and more recently to explanation and analysis, constitutes significant movement along a scientific trajectory. Stories and anecdotes are part of an oral tradition most commonly found in the communities of journalists, public-affairs commentators, and politics junkies. There is often little presumption of anything more than the wisdom that attaches (sometimes) to those who accumulate juicy detail. While almost everything is anecdotal and idiosyncratic for the storyteller, those who measure carefully and describe systematically are engaged in activity essential to the conduct of scientific inquiry. From systematic description comes the possibility of identifying empirical regularities. This requires separating wheat from chaff, so to speak, but this cannot be done until measurement and description have been carefully conducted.

It is empirical regularities, especially those that are robust in the sense that they seem to recur often and under a variety of different circumstances, that pique our curiosity. Why do incumbent legislators seem to get reelected so frequently (known as the "incumbency effect")? In modern democracies, why do countries that use proportional representation have so many political parties, while those that use alternative voting arrangements (for example, district-based systems in which the candidate with the most votes is elected) have fewer parties (known as Duverger's Law)? Why do democratic states rarely go to war against other democracies (known as the "democratic peace" hypothesis)? Why have the countries of the Pacific Rim developed their economies more successfully than those of Africa or Latin America in the absence of resource advantages or other conspicuous differences?

Obviously I will not answer here the wide range of questions associated with the empirical regularities identified by a generation of careful measurement and description. But I will definitely focus quite intently on the "why" questions and on how to think through to answers. This is one of the major ways political science is practiced in the twenty-first century, and is a harbinger of a maturing social science. Political science isn't rocket science, but an emphasis on explanation and analysis moves it closer in form to the physical and natural sciences than was the case in an earlier era.

MODELS AND THEORIES

Let's pause now and see where we are heading. The main purpose of this book is not to expose students to specific details about political life—details you undoubtedly study in other courses in history, political science, and sociology—but rather to introduce you to some theoretical tools you will find useful in making sense of these details. We will be intent especially on becoming acquainted with elementary *models*. These are stylizations meant to approximate in very crude fashion some real situation. Models are purposely stripped-down versions of the real thing. Events in the real world are complex bundles of characteristics, often far too complicated to understand directly. We depend on a stylized model to provide us with insights and guidance that will shape our analysis of these events.[4]

In the next chapter, for example, we construct a simple model of human choice. It contains no more than a shadow of any real flesh-and-blood human being. Instead, in an utterly simple way, it considers a person exclusively in terms of the things he or she wants and the things he or she believes. We want to get a feel for how a person makes choices when confronted with alternatives. Since political behavior is often about making choices, our model will provide us with hunches and intuitions about how a generic or representative individual confronts these circumstances in the abstract.

In Chapters 3 and 4, to take another example, we expand our focus from the individual to a group of individuals. Although politics is often about making choices, only in the world of Robinson Crusoe do individuals make choices entirely in isolation from others, and that is hardly a very political sit-

---

[4] I have described here how I use the term *model* in this book. A model of something is (or should be) recognizable as a highly stylized simplification of the real thing. A sphere to represent a planet or the nucleus of an atom is a good example.

uation. We thus expand upon our elementary model of individual choice by constructing a more elaborate model of a group decision setting. In the remaining chapters of Part II, we embellish this group setting, taking into account more and more features of the decision-making context. Our model starts out being simple but begins to take on, a step at a time, some of the complexity of real groups and the decisions they confront. Along the way our intuitions about "how the world really works" become increasingly sophisticated.

Part III requires some new, but still basic, models. Whereas the groups we study in Part II make their decisions, at least part of the time, by voting (we may think of these groups as committees or legislative bodies), other kinds of groups operate in different ways. A group of farmers, for instance, faced with the problem of a mosquito-infested marsh adjacent to their respective properties, may decide to cooperate with one another in order to rid themselves of the nuisance. The question that arises here is why any farmer would cooperate. If the others manage to eradicate the mosquito population, then the noncooperator benefits as well (and doesn't have to pay any of the costs, to boot); if, on the other hand, the others don't manage to solve the problem, then only if the one presently not cooperating would make a difference would he or she bear any of the cost (and maybe not even then). The issue to be studied here hinges less on how the group makes decisions—whether by voting or by some other method—and more on the mechanisms by which these individuals capture the dividends of cooperation by creating the group in the first place. We need a model that allows us to study the logic of participation and collective action. I elaborate on this in the chapters of Part III.

I endeavor throughout these parts of the book to enliven things a bit with cases in point drawn from the real world. Sometimes the cases are simply concrete instances of what we're talking about. Thus, in Chapter 2, I illustrate the role of uncertainty in individual choice by talking briefly about the

risky career choices of politicians. On other occasions, I play a
bit fast and loose with history in order to give an account of
some real historical occurrence to illustrate an important
idea. Thus, in Chapter 3, I provide some concrete examples of
the manipulation of group choices by looking at how the
strategic maneuverings of congressional leaders influenced
tax policy during the Civil War, the Great Depression, and the
Reagan years. These cases would hardly pass a historian's
muster, since I have quite consciously abbreviated the presentation and stripped the stories of all but what is essential to illustrate a specific theoretical point. Remember, it is not thick
description we're after but theoretical principles.

These stripped-down historical cases come close to transforming a specific model into a *theory* of something real. A theory, as I plan to use the term, is an embellishment of a model
in which features that are abstract in the model are made
more concrete and specific in the theory. To move from an abstract formulation of group choice to a more concrete application involving a specific group (the U.S. Congress) at a specific
time (1862 or 1932 or 1986) on a specific issue (raising national revenue) requires us to nail our colors to the mast on a
whole variety of matters. What is the specific size of the
group? How many members does it take to pass a motion? Can
the motion be amended? Who gets to make motions? If a motion is defeated, can a new proposal be made? A theory, then,
is a specialized elaboration of a model intended for a specific
application.[5]

We get even closer to theory in the chapters of Part IV.
There we look at institutions, often in the abstract but occasionally in specific detail. The discussion of legislatures and
their relationships with bureaucratic agents, for example, is

---

[5] *Model* and *theory* are terms used in various ways depending upon which
philosopher of science you wish to consult. Since there is no uniformity of
usage, I can do no more than state clearly my own practice, in no sense
claiming superiority or seeking converts.

based on the conduct of intergovernmental relations between
the U.S. Congress and its committees on the one hand, and
between Congress and executive branch officials and regulatory bodies on the other. Likewise, the discussion of cabinet
government is based on real-world experiences, mostly in continental Europe, with multiparty parliaments and coalition
governments.

In this new edition, I have added two features that bring
some of the abstraction associated with models and theories a
bit more to life. The first is *problem sets and discussion questions*. In most chapters, I provide a series of problems or questions to give the reader some experience at putting the
principles of the chapter to work—sometimes on real-life matters, other times on interesting puzzles of a more abstract
quality.[6] The second is the *Experimental Corner* sections. In
many of the chapters, I describe in some detail a social science
experiment, drawn from the new but growing literature in experimental economics and political science, that seeks either
to discover how real people (e.g., college sophomores) behave,
or to test some proposed theory about individual or group behavior against data generated experimentally. I hope you find
that these additions enrich the chapters of this book.

POLITICS

Now that you know where I'm heading, it's time to get on. My
purpose in writing this book is to provide some tools to enable
you to conduct your own analysis of the political events that
affect your life. I believe that an understanding and application of the concepts contained in this book will help you to predict and explain political events. My job is to present the
concepts clearly and to communicate how they can be applied

---

[6] An answer key is provided to instructors at wwnorton.com/nrl.

to real-world situations. Your job is to engage the material, understand the concepts, observe how they may be applied to real-world situations, and try them out in coming to terms with events in your own life and the world around you. If we do our respective jobs properly, I think you will begin to see the world differently. You will understand why certain groups have difficulty cooperating or reaching decisions. You will understand why people grumble about problems but don't do anything to solve them. You will understand why political candidates and political leaders do some of the crazy things they do. And you will begin to appreciate why some problems may be solvable and others not. In short, you will be able to analyze politics.

I haven't yet hazarded a definition of exactly what I am analyzing when I analyze politics. As a final preliminary, then, I need to demarcate our subject somewhat. In one of the most famous definitions, David Easton defined *politics* as "the authoritative allocation of values for a society."[7] This useful definition has been around for more than fifty years, but it leaves out more than I would like. Imagine an exhausted breadwinner returning home worn out by a dreary day of "office politics." There is nothing "authoritative" about, say, the fact that Smith was trying to impress the boss in order to improve his chances of getting the regional manager post that would soon be opening up. Moreover, the intrigues of the workplace surely do not embrace the allocation of values for an entire society. Office politics, university politics, church politics, union politics, clubhouse politics, family politics, and many other instances besides, all seem to involve what, in ordinary parlance, I include under the rubric of "politics," yet seemingly are excluded by Easton's definition. For the purposes of our discussion, I will take politics to be utterly indistinguishable from the phenomena of group life generally. It consists of indi-

[7] David Easton, *The Political System* (New York: Knopf, 1953).

viduals interacting, maneuvering, dissembling, strategizing, cooperating, and much else besides, as they pursue whatever it is they pursue in group life.

One of the real benefits of attaching politics to all facets of group life is to demystify politics. Our enterprise concerns not only the "capital P" politics that takes place in the White House, the Kremlin, 10 Downing Street, Capitol Hill, Whitehall, the Supreme Court, and other places of official activity. It also includes the "small p" politics of the workplace, the faculty meeting, the student government committee, the union hall, the kitchen table, the corporate boardroom, the gathering of church elders, and other less formal group settings. This hardly defines our subject comprehensively, but I am content to leave it at this. If you can live with this bit of ambiguity, then I invite you to read on.

2

Rationality: The Model of Choice

In analyzing politics I shall take what has come to be known as the *rational choice approach*. It also goes by other names: formal political theory, positive political theory, political economy. Indeed, in a genuine (but failed) attempt at intellectual imperialism, some economists like to think of it as the economic approach to politics.[1] They are right in one sense. The rationality assumption has been used most extensively and has seen its fullest flowering in economics. But there is nothing distinctly economic about rational behavior, as we shall see.[2]

The term *rationality* has a long history and, in ordinary language, often means something entirely different from what I have in mind. If a friend of yours does something that you would not have done were you in the friend's shoes—say, go to the movies the night before a final exam—you might say, "Jeez, that's really irrational." By that you might mean: Given what *your friend* wants, that is not the best way to go about getting it. Or perhaps you mean something different: Given

---

[1] For an excellent essay on positive political theory as a failure of economic imperialism, see Peter C. Ordeshook, "The Emerging Discipline of Political Economy," in James E. Alt and Kenneth A. Shepsle, eds., *Perspectives on Positive Political Economy* (New York: Cambridge University Press, 1990), pp. 9–31.

[2] Even in economics, rationality is undergoing revision under the rubric of "behavioral economics." For a fine review of this revisionst interpretation, see Norman Frohlich and Joe A. Oppenheimer, "Skating on Thin Ice: Cracks in the Public Choice Foundation," *Journal of Theoretical Politics* 18 (2006): 235–66.

what *I* want, I would not do what she is doing (and she ought to want what I want). In either case, you are claiming that what your friend is doing is crazy. Crazy it may well be, but I shall reserve *irrationality* for something quite specific.

The term *rationality* as I shall use it does not mean brilliant or all-knowing. The men and women whose behavior we wish to understand are not gods, so we certainly do not want to characterize any deviation from omniscient, godlike behavior as irrational (for then nearly all behavior would fall in this category). The people we model are neither all-knowing nor worldly wise; they are ordinary folks. As such they have *wants* and *beliefs*, both of which affect their behavior.

PRELIMINARIES

Individual wants, which I refer to as *preferences*, can be inspired by any number of different sources. Clearly we humans come hardwired with a number of wants related to survival and reproduction: food, protection from the elements, sexual desires. Other wants may be socially acquired and only indirectly related to such large and weighty matters as survival of the species—a preference for the latest fashion in jeans or the most recent jazz CD. Modern man and woman are economic and social animals. While one cannot deny the strong influence of material, economic wants on individual preferences, additional important sources of preference include religious values, moral precepts, ideological dispositions, altruistic impulses, and a sense of common destiny with a family, clan, tribe, ethnic group, or other community.

The individuals who populate our model world are assumed to have preferences derived from any and all of these various sources. We do not pretend to know why people want what they want—we leave that to evolutionary biologists, psychologists, and sociologists. Nor do we need to know why in order to proceed. For us, preferences are one of the givens of a situation and, for purposes of analysis, we assume that they don't change much in the short run. In short, we take people as we find them.[3]

I shall occasionally say that people who act in accord with their preferences are *self-interested*. Hindmoor has cleverly noted that "most of us have no difficulty in accepting that some people are self-interested all the time and that everyone is self-interested some of the time, but we balk at the notion that everyone is self-interested all of the time."[4] As already noted, however, I do not require a pinched view that people are selfish in the ordinary sense of that word, but rather that people are selfish only in a less self-absorbed sense: People pursue the things they regard as important, to be sure, but this may include empathy for family, friends, whales, trees, or random strangers. An individual's conception of self is reflected in his or her preferences and priorities. Pursuit of those preferences and priorities is self-interest in this weaker sense at work.

The world of preferences and priorities is an *interior* world. Indeed, because a person does not wear her preferences on her forehead, and sometimes, for subtle reasons, may not be all that she seems, we often have to make *assumptions* about her preferences. That is, in trying to figure out what someone might do, we have to start somewhere, and entertaining hunches and intuitions about that person's motives is often a useful point of departure.

---

[3] Methodologically, this is very similar to the approach of economists, who take tastes for goods, services, labor, and leisure as fixed in the short run and determined outside the boundaries of their inquiry. However, let us reemphasize that preferences in our discussion are construed more broadly than in conventional economic models—they should not be equated with material well-being. And we should leave room for preference change arising from learning, experience, persuasion, or deliberation.

[4] Andrew Hindmoor, *Rational Choice* (London: Palgrave-Macmillan, 2006), p. 5.

But preferences, tastes, and values are not all there is to rational behavior. Complementing this interior world is an *external environment* in which people find themselves. This environment is filled with uncertainty—about how things work, about the preferences of others, about random events over which individuals have neither control nor sometimes even knowledge. This uncertainty is of interest to us because it affects the way people express their preferences. Individuals have preferences, as already stated, and I assume they have a behavioral repertoire or behavioral portfolio available as well. They may do any of a number of things in pursuit of whatever it is they want (things like going to the movies or studying on the night before a final). They often cannot choose the thing they want directly (like getting an A on the final), but instead must choose an instrument—something available in their portfolio of behaviors. If each instrument leads directly to some distinct outcome, then the job of the rational person is simple: choose the instrument that leads to the outcome preferred the most. If you want an A on the final, and studying the night before produces it while going to the movies does not, then by all means study.

Enter uncertainty. More often than not, individuals may not have an exact sense of how an instrument or behavior they might adopt relates to the outcomes they value. That is, they may have only the vaguest sense of "how the world works," may not quite appreciate how the choices of others influence the final outcome, and may not be able to anticipate random events (like the virus that arbitrarily picks you on the morning of the exam). Consequently, the effectiveness of behavioral instruments for the things an individual wants is only imperfectly known. Personal knowledge and wisdom take one only so far. But one must use what he or she has available. We describe the hunches an individual has concerning the efficacy of a given instrument or behavior for obtaining something he or she wants as that person's *beliefs*. Beliefs connect instruments to outcomes. Acting in accord both with one's preferences and one's beliefs is called *instrumental rationality.*

Beliefs, like preferences, come from a variety of sources, and we need not resolve their origins in order to take them as part of what defines an individual at any moment in time. Indeed, beliefs may change as the individual acquires experience in his or her external environment. Learning takes place, causing the individual to revise initial opinions about the effectiveness of a specific instrument for achieving some particular objective. To be on the "steep" part of a learning curve means for you to be in a relatively novel situation of high uncertainty in which each new bit of experience causes you to revise your views about how the world works in this situation. As bits of experience accumulate, your beliefs begin to settle down, your opinions begin to firm up, and you revise your opinions less frequently and dramatically; you are in the "flat" part of the learning curve—you've learned most of what there is to know and have squeezed out most of the uncertainty (that is squeezable).

I've done a fair bit of throat-clearing to this point. To sum up this preliminary discussion, the conception of rationality employed in this book incorporates both preferences and beliefs. A rational individual is one who combines his or her beliefs about the external environment and preferences about things in that environment in a consistent manner. Since we have no time to spare, I can only note in passing that the rational choice approach is a form of *methodological individualism.*[5] The individual is taken as the basic unit of analysis. In contrast, many sociological theories take the group as the basic building block. Marxist approaches begin with economic classes as the actors in their models. Most theories of interna-

---

[5] For readers interested in pursuing this theme further, see Geoffrey Brennan and Michael Gillespie, eds., "Special Issue: Homo Economicus and Homo Politicus," *Public Choice* 137 (2008): 429–524.

tional relations aggregate all the way up to the nation-state as the unit of analysis. Indeed, even some economic theories treat aggregates like a firm or an entire industry as the unit of analysis. The most important thing to know about method- ological individualism is that it is taken as fundamental that individuals have beliefs and preferences. These things are the stuff of human cognition and motivation. Groups, classes, firms, and nation-states do not have minds, and thus cannot be said to have preferences or hold beliefs.

Now it is time to make these ideas more precise.

MOTIVATION

To motivate a rational model of political behavior, let's begin with a glimpse of how economists practice their craft. I sim- plify shamelessly in advancing the view that economics is con- cerned mainly with how four different classes of actors choose to allocate what's theirs. For the *consumer* the choice is one of how to spend his or her monetary endowment so as to achieve a maximum of contentment (or utility, as the economist likes to say). *Producers*, on the other hand, possess various produc- tive inputs and must determine how best to combine them so as to maximize their profits. The endowment of a *worker* con- sists of time. To keep things simple, suppose that workers toil at a fixed wage rate so that once they decide how much time to spend at work, both their total wages (and hence monetary endowment from which they derive contentment when they transform themselves into consumers) and the amount of time left over for leisure are determined. Workers, then, pick an amount of time to work in order to acquire purchasing power and leisure time, each of which contributes to their content- ment. Finally, *investors* are providers of capital. They allocate their wealth across alternative investment opportunities with

DISPLAY 2.1		
Actor	**Endowment**	**Objective**
consumers	budget	contentment
producers	inputs	profits
workers	time	purchasing power/leisure
investors	wealth	long-run return

an eye on the overall long-term financial return. This is laid out in Display 2.1.

Now, there is surely ambiguity in each of these ideas, but it is fair to say that economists, in one fashion or another, firmly commit themselves to what it is that animates various economic actors. This is not because they think their assumptions—and Display 2.1 is one very simple set of assumptions—are verifiable as descriptive statements. Start asking some obvious questions and you will quickly determine that these assumptions are seriously flawed as descriptive statements. Don't consumers care about anything except their own consumption? Are producers driven entirely by the profit motive, or do they give some weight to other things, like the welfare of their workers or the quality of their products, even if these sometimes come at the expense of profits? Don't workers get any satisfaction from the job itself, or do they only care about how much effort they must expend (and indirectly about their wages)? Is investing for long-run return the only thing an investor can do with her wealth? Can't she devote some of it to finance a tropical vacation in the dead of winter, or a new wing on the local children's hospital?

It is evident that descriptive accuracy is not the point or purpose of the economist's assumptions. The reason is *scientific*, not substantive. The idea is this: Can we explain variations and regularities in economic performance, outcomes, and behavior with a simple set of assumptions? The modern theory of economics is a grand intellectual edifice precisely because it has succeeded, as no other social science has, in constructing explanations logically, rigorously, and in empirically meaningful ways. At the foundation of this edifice is a scientific commitment to explanation, not description.[6]

This does not mean there is no controversy in economics. What it does mean is that over the past two centuries, a *corpus of scientific knowledge* has accumulated, a corpus different from either an encyclopedia of descriptive detail or even a body of wisdom (by which we mean serviceable commonsense notions). It is, instead, a logically integrated collection of principles, a set of tools of inquiry—a methodology, if you will—for prediction and explanation. Of great importance is the fact that this scientific knowledge is *cumulative*, something that distinguishes it from wisdom, which is intuitive, implicit, and often nontransferable (it dies with its possessor).

Is it possible, in a manner precisely analogous to what has occurred in economics, to create a science of politics? That is, is it possible to begin with a simple set of premises or assumptions and, from these, derive principles of political performance, outcomes, and behavior? This is a daunting challenge, but it is the objective that has motivated the body of work in positive political theory that is the focus of this book.

The Simple Logic of
Preference and Choice

Our first building block is the notion of preference. We must begin by defining terms, explaining notation, and making assumptions. Since the machine we are building must serve in a

---

[6] For an elaboration of this issue as a philosophical matter, see Frank Lovett, "Rational Choice Theory and Explanation," *Rationality and Society* 18 (2006): 237–72.

variety of contexts, our building blocks must be developed in an abstract and general fashion (for which I beg the reader's indulgence). To give the reader something concrete to hold onto, however, consider the dilemma that Claire McCaskill, state auditor of Missouri, confronted after the 2004 election.

CASE 2.1
CLAIRE MCCASKILL'S ELECTORAL OPTIONS

Claire McCaskill graduated from law school in 1978 and went on to become a very successful state politician in Missouri. After several years of judicial clerking and private practice, she was a local county prosecutor, a county representative, a state representative, and, in 1998, was elected statewide as auditor, a position to which she was reelected in 2002. Along the way she broke down barriers for women in politically conservative Missouri. In 2004 she defeated Governor Bob Holden in the Democratic gubernatorial primary, becoming the first person in Missouri history to defeat a sitting governor in a primary election. She lost the general election to Secretary of State Matt Blunt, a Republican, with 48 percent of the vote to his 51 percent. This was her first losing effort in a twenty-year political career.

What would her next career step be? Talking heads and political insiders assumed that her close loss for governor in a year when circumstances favored Republicans would propel her candidacy for governor four years later—a rematch against Blunt, the only politician who had ever beaten her. However, there was the possibility of 2006. Jim Talent, the incumbent Republican senator was up for reelection. He had come to the Senate in the 2000 election cycle in a most peculiar way. Mel Carnahan, then Democratic governor of Missouri, died in an airplane crash while campaigning for the Senate seat only days before the election. His name remained on the ballot and he actually *won* the election! A special election was then called, and Talent defeated Carnahan's widow, Jean.

McCaskill had a choice to make. She could challenge the incumbent Talent for the Senate seat in 2006, or wait and challenge the incumbent Blunt for the governorship in 2008. If she ran and won the Senate seat in 2006, she would not enter the governor's contest in 2008. If she ran and lost the Senate seat in 2006, her prospects, as a two-time loser, of succeeding in 2008 would have been rather dim.

Thus, the career outcomes facing McCaskill were these:

x: a term as senator
y: a term as governor
z: out of politics for the near term

We can be reasonably confident that McCaskill preferred x to y and y to z (and, as will be shown later in this chapter, if she weren't "incoherent" she would also certainly have preferred x to z). But she could not literally choose from $\{x, y, z\}$. Her behavioral options were "run for senator," "run for governor," and "run for both." Since I've assumed she would not choose to run for governor if she won the Senate seat, and she could not expect success if she ran for governor after *losing* the Senate race, it is reasonable to suppose that McCaskill focused only on {"run for senator in 2006," "run for governor in 2008"}.

We can think of her decision problem as that of choosing between two *lotteries*. If McCaskill chose to run for the Senate in 2006, she would obtain outcome x with some probability p and outcome z with probability $1-p$. If she held off to run for governor in 2008 on the other hand, she could obtain outcome y with probability q and outcome z with probability $1-q$. The keys to her decision are how much she prefers x to y and how good are her chances for the former (p) as opposed to the latter (q).

McCaskill ended up running for (and winning, as it happens) a Senate seat in 2006 because her outright preference for x over y was reinforced by a belief about her chances of victory. In either case she would be running against an incumbent, so that factor was more or less a wash. The reason she thought 2006 would be a better year to run than 2008 was her fear that Hillary Clinton would win the Democratic presidential nomination in 2008. (Recall that back in 2005 and 2006, people believed that Clinton as the Democratic nominee was a *fait accompli*.) In her view, no Democrat would win statewide office in relatively conservative Missouri with Ms. Clinton at the head of the ticket.*

*For a wonderful essay on Claire McCaskill's decision making, see Jeffrey Goldberg, "Letter from Washington—Central Casting: The Democrats Think About Who Can Win in the Midterms—and in 2008," *The New Yorker* (May 29, 2006).

In the remainder of this section I abstract from the specific features of this case in order to develop a general logic of rational choice. We begin with a situation in which there are three objects over which a typical actor, named Mr. i, has preferences. We call the objects *alternatives*, and label them x, y, and z. Mr. i, in a manner we make precise below, has the capacity to make statements like, "I prefer x to y," or "I am indifferent between y and z." The alternatives may be career paths (as in McCaskill's choice problem), or political candidates, or potential marriage partners, or laptop computers. It does not matter, for our purposes, what comprises the choice situation or the set of alternatives. Nor does it matter how Mr. i arrived at his preferences. What does matter is that Mr. i is rational in the sense that his preferences have coherence and that his ultimate choice bears a logical relationship to his preferences.

Symbolically, "$xP_i y$" means Mr. i (whose name appears as a subscript) prefers x to y. In words, the symbols in quotation marks state that "x is better than y according to Mr. i's preferences." Similarly, "xI_iy" means Mr. i is indifferent between x and y. Thus P_i is i's *strict preference relation* and I_i is i's *indifference relation*.[7]

If Mr. i is given the opportunity to choose among x, y, and z, then we say that his choice is *rational* if it is in accord with his preferences. Thus, a choice is rational if the object chosen is at least as good as any other available object according to the chooser's preferences. Put differently but equivalently, an object is a rational choice if no other available object is better according to the chooser's preferences.

So far this is pretty straightforward and, once you get used to the notation, pretty commonsensical. Now we must determine what must be true about the preference and indifference relations just described so that choosing in conformity with them accords with our intuitions about rational choice. What we are seeking, in effect, are properties of preference relations that allow the chooser to *order* the alternatives in terms of preference (and enable him, being a rational soul, to choose the top-ranked alternative in the ordering). It turns out that two underlying properties capture the commonsensical notion of rationality as ordering things in terms of preference:

> *Property 1: Comparability (Completeness).* Alternatives are said to be *comparable* in terms of preference (and the preference relation *complete*) if, for any two possible alternatives (say, x and y), either xP_iy, yP_ix, or xI_iy. That is, the alternatives are comparable if, for any pair of them, the chooser either prefers the first to the second, the second to the first, or is indifferent between them.[8]

---

[7] Putting strict preference and indifference together yields i's *weak preference relation*, R_i, so that "$x R_i y$" means that Mr. i either strictly prefers x to y or is indifferent between them. In words, "x is at least as good as y according to Mr. i's preferences."

[8] Equivalently, the alternatives are comparable if, for any pair of alternatives like x and y, either $x R_i y$ or $y R_i x$ or both. In words, a person has complete preferences if either x is at least as good as y, or y is at least as good as x, or both (that is, each is as good as the other). If the latter, then $x I_i y$.

Property 2: Transitivity. The strict preference relation is said to be *transitive* if, for any three possible alternatives (say, x, y, and z), if xP_iy and yP_iz, then xP_iz. That is, if Mr. i strictly prefers x to y and y to z, then he strictly prefers x to z. Likewise, the indifference relation is transitive if xI_iy and yI_iz imply xI_iz (if i is indifferent between x and y and between y and z, then he is indifferent between x and z, too).[9]

As Case 2.1 makes clear, Senator McCaskill possessed complete and transitive preferences over the alternatives $\{x, y, z\}$. She preferred a Senate seat (x) to the governorship (y); a term as governor (y) to being out of politics altogether (z); and, of course, the Senate seat (x) to the political wilderness (z).

If i's preferences satisfy comparability and transitivity, then i is said to possess a *preference ordering*. As noted, the rational choice is the alternative at the top of the ordering. Note that P_i and I_i are exactly like > (greater than) and = (equal to), respectively, as applied to real numbers. For real numbers x and y, either $x > y$, or $y > x$, or $x = y$; hence, they are comparable. Similarly, for any three numbers, x, y, and z, if $x > y$ and $y > z$, then $x > z$; and if $x = y$ and $y = z$, then $x = z$; hence the relations are transitive. In consequence, real numbers can be ordered in terms of magnitude. (The reader can check for himself or herself that the weak preference relation, R_i, is analogous to ≥ [greater than or equal to] as applied to real numbers.)

This is all pretty simple. Preferences that permit rational choices are, in effect, *ordering principles*. They are personal— P_i is Mr. i's particular way of ordering alternatives, which may differ from P_j, Ms. j's way of ordering the alternatives. They allow comparisons of alternatives a pair at a time (compara-

---

[9] Finally, the weak preference relation is transitive if $x\,R_iy$ and $y\,R_iz$ imply $x\,R_iz$.

bility). And the comparison they permit are internally consistent (transitivity).

Before concluding that all is well and moving on, however, we must satisfy ourselves about exactly what we are assuming. We need to ask if *all* relations satisfy properties 1 and 2. If so, then we haven't made very hard demands at all. If not, then we need to know precisely what is excluded from consideration by our assumptions.

In fact, not all relations are complete or transitive (or both). Some relations satisfy transitivity but not completeness.[10] Others satisfy completeness but not transitivity.[11] And still others satisfy neither.[12]

---

[10] The relation "is the brother of" applied to the set of all males satisfies transitivity but not completeness. It violates completeness since neither "John is the brother of Bob" nor "Bob is the brother of John" is true if they are not brothers! However, if John is the brother of Bob, and Bob is the brother of Charles, then John and Charles are also brothers, so the relation is transitive.

[11] Suppose Ms. i prefers Bill Clinton to George H. W. Bush ($C \, P_i \, B$), Bush to Ross Perot ($B \, P_i \, P$), and Perot to Clinton ($P \, P_i \, C$) in the 1992 presidential election. The alternatives clearly satisfy comparability, but they violate transitivity. You may think Ms. i quite daffy in this case, but we know people like her and expect you may, too. For example, whenever i thinks about the Clinton-Bush comparison, domestic policy issues are triggered in her mind ("It's the economy, stupid!" was the Clinton campaign war chant in 1992, after all), and she prefers the Democratic candidate on these issues. Whenever she thinks about the Bush-Perot comparison, foreign policy issues loom large and she worries about the ship of state in the hands of a businessman with no diplomatic or political experience, like Perot. Finally, whenever Ms. i makes the Perot-Clinton comparison, she can't help thinking about the character issue on which the businessman with no political skeletons in his closet dominates someone who has been nothing but a politician his entire adult life. Intransitivity or inconsistency may arise when different criteria are used for different pairings. When this happens, it is not possible to order all three alternatives in terms of preference. Ms. i ranks Clinton ahead of Bush, Bush ahead of Perot, and Perot ahead of Clinton.

[12] The relation "is the father of" satisfies neither completeness nor transitivity. Suppose we take the population of males and draw two at random. It is entirely possible, indeed highly probable, that neither one is the father of the other; thus, not all pairs of alternatives are comparable according to this relation. On the other hand, even if, for three selected males, the first is the father of the second and the second is the father of the third, it is obvious to any five-year-old that the first is not the father of the third, but rather is the *grandfather*. That eliminates transitivity.

So I have actually said something of substance when I assume properties 1 and 2. The issue now is whether I can defend what's been said. Regarding comparability, clearly you could push things far enough so that making a comparison in terms of preferences would be absurd. *Sophie's Choice* is author William Styron's literary invention for this absurdity. In his novel, a concentration camp prisoner in Poland is permitted to save one of her two children from the gas chamber, but she must choose whom to save; in the absence of a choice, both will die. It is a horrible, inhuman choice. Nevertheless, Sophie does indeed choose (for not to do so is far worse), even though she does not regard her children as comparable. Horrible choices may be painful to make, and some of us may ultimately lack the courage to do what we must. But, as in Sophie's case, even the failure to choose is a choice with its own consequences.

The real problem for the comparability property comes in situations in which the comparison doesn't make sense to the chooser. If objects do not connect up in the mind of the chooser as competing alternatives, then you are likely to get shrugs, puzzled looks, and, if given the option, a response of "don't know." If pollsters, in late 2007 or early 2008, were to have asked a random sample of voters whether they preferred John McCain or Barack Obama in the 2008 presidential contest, they would have obtained many don't-know responses, for that far in advance of an election, most candidate pairings really don't connect in the mind of the average voter. This is not a critique of rationality-based models so much as a warning label advising appropriate use. Choices must have meaning to the choosers if they are to be guided by principled considerations such as those associated with rationality.[13]

[13] Although peripheral to the main line of argument, it is nevertheless interesting to ask what it means for someone to say "don't know" when confronted by a pollster with one of these puzzling choices. It could either mean "this comparison is loony and I cannot make a choice," or "the alternatives

Transitivity requires that the chooser not be confused in a different sense. It requires consistency, something in short supply at times. Psychology professors have, since time immemorial, imposed saline-solution and shades-of-gray experiments on captive sophomores in introductory psychology classes. The typical experiment begins with ten bottles of water of varying salt content (or ten pictures of a triangle colored white, black, or some shade of gray). A student is asked, when presented with two bottles (or triangles), which tastes saltier (or is darker). Her answer is recorded and then a different pair is presented. This continues for some time as alternative pairs are presented and answers recorded (there are forty-five distinct pairs). Because the different saline solutions shade into one another (as do the gray triangles), invariably the student, sometime during the experiment, answers that bottle 2 is saltier than bottle 9, that bottle 9 is saltier than bottle 7, but that bottle 7 is saltier than bottle 2—a clear violation of transitivity. It is hard to be consistent in the manner property 2 requires when the comparisons are so difficult, when there are potentially consequential random events for which the experimenter does not control (such as how thirsty the subject is or how much sunlight is coming into the room), when so little is at stake, and when the answers of a particular subject aren't likely to make much difference.

This, too, is less a critique of rationality than a warning about the domain over which it is likely to be more or less relevant and useful. When the stakes are low, uncertainty is high, and individual choices are of little consequence to the chooser, then inconsistencies are likely to be common. Behavior is likely to be more random than rational, more arbitrary

---

are so close in my mind in terms of preference that it is a matter of indifference to me." Which one it is is a judgment call that the researcher needs to make. In terms of predicting behavior, however, it may not make any difference. Whether a person is indifferent or confused, if a choice is forced, his or her behavior is likely to be random.

than principled. But when the choices *matter* to the chooser, he or she is likely to be more intent on being consistent. As in the case of comparability, whether transitivity is appropriate or not is a judgment call to be made by the investigator. The kind of consistency required by this property is demanding, to be sure, even in more significant situations. But we need it to get on with our business and must content ourselves with the knowledge that, as in other sciences, simplifying assumptions are necessary in order to make progress.[14]

THE MAXIMIZATION PARADIGM

The assumptions of comparability (completeness) and transitivity yield an "ordering principle"—they permit an individual to take a set of objects and place them in an order, from highest to lowest (with ties permitted), that reflects personal tastes and values. Rationality is associated with both this capacity to order *and* an aptitude to choose from the top of the order.

The very existence of a "top" to a preference ordering, and individuals with sufficient sense to choose it if given half the chance, is the reason that most of us working in this tradition think of rationality as consisting of *maximizing* behavior. Individuals in social situations are thought to be seeking some goal, pursuing some objective, aiming to do the best they can according to their own lights. Indeed, instead of describing an individual in terms of his or her preferences, we may write down the principle that led the individual to order alterna-

---

[14] Transitivity strikes me as an assumption like that of perfectly spherical atomic particles in particle physics, perfectly spherical planets in astronomy, and frictionless planes in mechanics. All were known to be contrary to fact, even as they continued to be used; all nevertheless proved essential to move the science forward; all ultimately were relaxed as later generations of scientists subsequently saw how to strip away the offending parts.

Rat choice
1) wants
2) beliefs

1) comparability
2) Transitivity

tives as he or she did. We may, in other words, state what it is that the person is seeking to achieve or trying to maximize.

The earlier economic example (Display 2.1), in fact, did this. Consumers are interested in maximizing contentment, producers want to maximize profits, workers want the best division of their time between labor and leisure, and investors want the highest long-term return on investment. In the various political models that are examined in the next three parts of the book, political actors are similarly intent on maximizing. Elected politicians, for example, are interested in maximizing their votes at the next election. Legislators seek to maximize the amount of pork and other policy satisfaction they can deliver to the folks back home. Bureaucrats are interested in maximizing their budgets or their turf. The language in the remainder of this book will often reflect this maximizing perspective.

ENVIRONMENTAL UNCERTAINTY AND BELIEFS

Rational individuals choose from the top of a set well ordered according to preference. In many circumstances, however, the individual doesn't get to choose outcomes directly, but rather chooses an instrument that affects what outcome actually occurs. Claire McCaskill (Case 2.1), for example, could not simply *choose* to be the senator from Missouri in 2006. All she could choose was the option to run for that office. So we should revise our idea of rationality, saying now that a rational individual chooses the instrument or action he or she believes will lead to the best outcome.

I slipped the word "believes" into the reformulated definition of rationality. Just as I was precise about preferences earlier, I need now to be precise about beliefs. A belief is a probability statement relating the effectiveness of a specific action (or instrument) for achieving various outcomes. If an

People maximize

individual is highly confident that he knows what will happen if he does some particular thing (for example, if I turn the handle the door will open), then he is operating under conditions of *certainty*. An incumbent politician's choice to seek reelection against a "sacrificial" opponent is made under conditions of (near) certainty. If, on the other hand, a person is not so confident that she knows what will happen, but nevertheless has a pretty clear sense of the possibilities and their likelihoods (if I turn the handle, there is a fifty-fifty chance that the door will open or be locked), she is operating under conditions of *risk*. Thus, McCaskill's choice to oppose the incumbent Jim Talent was a gamble made under conditions of risk. Finally, if in the mind of the chooser the relationship between actions and outcomes is so imprecise that it is not possible to assign likelihoods, then she is operating under conditions of *uncertainty*.

To see what is meant by certainty, risk, and uncertainty, consider the following example in which there are three possible outcomes—x, y, and z—and three actions—A, B, and C. Our chooser has preferences over the outcomes; suppose she ranks x first, then y, then z—written xyz, but she must make a choice from among the actions. If she knew for certain that C led to y, that B led to z, and that A led to x, then her decision is one of certainty (and, as the reader can ascertain, a pretty simple one—choose A). If, on the other hand, she knew that A led to a fifty-fifty chance of x or z, that B led to a fifty-fifty chance of y or z, and that C led to an even chance of x, y, or z, then the choice involves risk (and is a bit more complicated). Finally, if she weren't sure how to put probabilities on the odds of various outcomes from specific actions, then she would be uncertain (and, without further analysis, the appropriate choice would be quite illusive).

When there is certainty, rational behavior is pretty apparent: Simply pick the action or instrument that leads to your highest-ranked alternative. When beliefs about action-outcome

relationships are more complex, the principle of rational behavior requires more explanation. You need to assign a numerical value to each outcome, called a *utility number*. The
utility numbers for x, y, and z, respectively, are $u(x)$, $u(y)$, and
$u(z)$; they reflect the relative value you associate with each
outcome. If you like x a whole lot better than y and z, and
there is not much difference between the latter two in your
mind, then $u(x)$ will be a much larger number than $u(y)$ and
$u(z)$, and the latter two numbers will be close in magnitude—
for example, $u(x) = 1$, $u(y) = 0.2$, $u(z) = 0$. On the other hand, if
x is only barely your first choice, with z trailing badly, then the
utility numbers would be on the order of $u(x) = 1$, $u(y) = 0.9$,
and $u(z) = 0$.

In effect, we have "quantified" preferences by moving from
ordered preference information to numerical preference information. There is nothing magical about the particular numbers we wrote down—they are gauged, by you, to best reflect
your relative valuations of the alternatives.[15] Now let's do the
same for beliefs. For each action or instrument, we can write
down the probability that it will lead to one of the final outcomes. In the example above, action A led to a fifty-fifty
chance of x or z; that is, $Pr_A(x) = 1/2$, $Pr_A(y) = 0$, and $Pr_A(z) =$
$1/2$. The probability numbers must all be between zero and
one, and they must add up to one. As you can see, these beliefs
about action A effectively make A a *lottery*—one in which y is

---

[15] It is the relative numerical values, not their absolute values, that convey
this kind of information. Consequently, it is typical to "normalize" the utility numbers, setting your most-preferred alternative to a utility value of
one, your least-preferred to a value of zero, and intermediate alternatives at
utility levels between zero and one. It would have done just as well to set
most-preferred and least-preferred alternatives at 100 and 0, respectively,
or 1000 and –1000, respectively. The normalization values are arbitrary. We
report on all this only for the rare reader who wishes to delve more deeply.
A standard, accessible reference for further details is Howard Raiffa, *Decision Analysis* (Reading, Mass.: Addison-Wesley, 1968). Readers will not
need very much detail to digest the materials in the remainder of our book,
so breathe easy!

an impossibility and x and z are equiprobable. We can write $A = (1/2\ x,\ 0\ y,\ 1/2\ z)$. Each of the other actions is a different lottery over final outcomes.

Making a decision under conditions of risk involves choosing from among alternative lotteries. A rational choice entails choosing the "best" lottery. The rule of rational choice is known as the *Principle of Expected Utility*. It provides a method for assigning a single number to each action-lottery and then choosing the one with the largest number. The expected utility of action A of the previous few paragraphs is

$$EU(A) = Pr_A(x) \cdot u(x) + Pr_A(y) \cdot u(y) + Pr_A(z) \cdot u(z)$$

That is, the expected utility of action A is simply the sum of the utilities of all the outcomes that could result from A, weighted by the likelihood that each outcome will happen. If we make the same calculation for actions B and C, then we have a basis for comparing them. Rationality requires a chooser to select the action that *maximizes expected utility*.

Under conditions of uncertainty, a chooser is sufficiently confused that he or she cannot even figure out the likelihoods of various outcomes associated with each action. Needless to say, it is hard to be rational, however you might define it, if you are utterly confused. It turns out, however, that many people do have hunches about likelihoods that they can associate with various actions. So, if pushed a bit, they can give some quantitative precision to their beliefs. They, too, can be treated as if the expected utility principle covered their behavior.[16]

---

[16] There are many theories of decision under uncertainty that cover the circumstances in which choosers cannot assign probabilities of outcomes to alternative actions. We do not review them here. Still one of the best presentations of this material is to be found in R. Duncan Luce and Howard Raiffa, *Games and Decisions* (New York: Wiley, 1957), Chapter 13.

CONCLUSION

I have covered quite a bit of ground in this chapter and the last. But everything can be summarized with a few simply stated ideas. First, our general enterprise is that of explaining social and political events and phenomena. Second, the individual is our basic explanatory building block. Third, because we are interested in prediction and explanation rather than description, we characterize individuals in a very abbreviated form, namely in terms of their preferences and beliefs. Fourth, the individuals in our analysis are rational. This means that they act in accord with their preferences for final outcomes and their beliefs about the effectiveness of various actions available to them. The cause-and-effect relationships between actions and outcomes may be well defined (certainty), probabilistic (risk), or only crudely known (uncertainty). Fifth, acting rationally requires ranking final outcomes, assigning utility numbers to them if necessary, determining the expected utility of actions by weighing outcome utilities by action probabilities, and then selecting the action that has the highest expected utility. Sixth, and perhaps most controversial of all, rational political choices—whether career paths chosen by politicans, candidates chosen by voters, decisions to go to war made by kings or presidents, or something as banal as pizza toppings chosen by a group of friends—all are premised on the same comparability-and-transitivity foundation. Aristotle, Hobbes, Rousseau, and other great political thinkers and philosophers have suggested that there is something special about politics—that the collective choices for a nation, for example, are altogether different from choosing pizza toppings. Perhaps. Indeed, certainly this must be the case. But the process of choosing *rationally* bears characteristic markings in all these contexts and so may be analyzed with the same intellectual framework.

In what follows, this rationality machinery is used repeatedly while keeping technical matters to an absolute minimum. So, having covered the preliminaries, let's move on to the study of groups and their politics.

PROBLEMS AND DISCUSSION QUESTIONS[a]

1. How is rationality defined in this chapter? Answer with reference to both preferences and behavior, and then concoct an example of a violation of each of these aspects of the rational actor model, explaining carefully which assumption has been violated.

2. Rational choice models generally start with a well-defined set of actors ($N = \{1, 2, \ldots, n\}$), a number outcomes over which actors hold preferences ($X = \{x, y, z, \ldots\}$), a set of behaviors or instruments with which to achieve preferred outcomes ($I = \{A, B, C, \ldots\}$), and some rule which links actors' instrumental choices to outcomes (R). For example, each of n voters may vote for A, vote for B, or abstain. A candidate wins if he or she gets more votes than any other. Thus, $N = \{1, 2, \ldots, n\}$, $X = \{A$ wins, B wins, tie$\}$, and $I = \{$vote A, vote B, abstain$\}$. The rule, R, is plurality rule, implying that a vote for A (or B) increases the likelihood A (B, respectively) wins. Give simple characterization of each of these model foundations for the following political actors: campaign contributors, political activists, and candidates. In what forms do these actors confront uncertainty in making their behavioral choices?

---

[a] In this and succeeding chapters, I provide some problems and discussion questions to elaborate ideas in the chapter and to allow the student to test his or her mastery. Difficult questions are marked with an asterisk.

3. Rational choice is a methodology defined by instrumental action toward a goal, where the goal itself is determined by individual values. Given this definition, is it possible for rational individuals to undertake altruistic acts? Provide an affirmative response that a dyed-in-the-wool rat choicer would offer, as well as the perspective of a critic.

4. Mr. i holds the following preferences over outcomes w, x, y, and z: xPw, xPy, zPx, yPz, wPy, and wPz. When presented with a choice over any subset of these outcomes (e.g., x, y, and z; or all four outcomes), for which subsets can Mr. i identify his most-preferred choice? Do any of those subsets contain a preference intransitivity among all outcomes in the subset? Now consider Ms. j, who holds preferences: xIy, xPz, xPw, yPz, yPw, wIz. Answer the same questions as before. What does this exercise suggest about the relationship between transitive preferences and maximizing behavior?

5. In November 2008, a couple of weeks after the election of Barack Obama, Hillary Clinton was offered the job of Secretary of State of the United States. It was generally assumed that she faced the following trade-off: joining the new administration, in perhaps the highest-profile cabinet position, which offered the chance of enhanced prestige and policy-making clout in the executive branch, or continuing in the Senate, an option that promised less power (she would still be only one of a hundred) but greater autonomy. The other wrinkle was that most commentators assumed that taking an administration job would preclude a primary challenge against Barack Obama in 2012, and thus meant giving up on a life-long dream to be president of the United States. Thus, Hillary Clinton faced three possibilities: Remain in the Congress and not win the presidency in 2012 (C), remain in the Congress and win the presidency in 2012 (P), or join the administration as secretary of state (S). State what you think Hillary Clin-

ton's preference ranking was at that time. If the probability of winning the White House in 2012 if she had remained in the Senate is p, then use an expected utility argument to determine the smallest p that would have induced Clinton to remain in the Senate in order to run in 2012. In your opinion, did Hillary Clinton's decision make sense?

*6. Imagine that you are confronted with two pairs of lotteries over the following three outcomes: $x = \$2.5$ million, $y = \$.5$ million, and $z = \$0$. The first pair pits P_1 against P_2, where $P_1 = (p_1(x), p_1(y), p_1(z)) = (0, 1, 0)$ (i.e., you are certain to win $500,000) and $P_2 = (p_2(x), p_2(y), p_2(z)) = (.10, .89, .01)$. The second pair is a choice between $P_3 = (p_3(x), p_3(y), p_3(z)) = (0, .11, .89)$ and $P_4 = (p_4(x), p_4(y), p_4(z)) = (.10, 0, .90)$. Empirically, most individuals express a strict preference for P_1 to P_2, and P_4 to P_3. Is this behavior consistent with the theory of expected utility? In order to solve this problem, rephrase each of the expressed opinions in terms of expected utility (e.g., $EU(P_3) = .11u(x) + .89u(z)$) and then use basic operations on the resulting inequalities to see if a contradiction emerges. No knowledge of the actual utility function is necessary to solve this problem.

Part II

GROUP CHOICE

3

Getting Started with Group Choice Analysis

A WARM-UP EXERCISE

Andrew, Bonnie, and Chuck are friends who have decided to cut class on a pleasant spring afternoon in Boston. Andrew, an intellectual snob, suggests going to see a fabulous collection of Impressionist paintings at the Museum of Fine Arts. Bonnie, a bit more political, wants to go down to the Boston Common to attend a rally to raise funds and consciousness in support of preserving Walden Pond, which is threatened by commercial development. Chuck, a jock, thinks an afternoon at Fenway Park watching the Red Sox would be just fine. Display 3.1 supplies each group member's rank order of the alternatives. In terms of the notation in Chapter 2, Andrew's preference ordering is $MFA\,P_A\,WP\,P_A\,RS$. Similar expressions may be written down for Bonnie and Chuck. Each member of the group, $\{A, B, C\}$, has preferences over the alternatives, $\{MFA, WP, RS\}$, satisfying completeness and transitivity—properties 1 and 2 of Chapter 2.

It becomes evident after the briefest of times that this group of friends does not have an obvious course of action. It suffers from a common group affliction, an affliction with no known cure short of authoritarian measures—*preference*

	DISPLAY 3.1	
A	**B**	**C**
MFA	*WP*	*RS*
WP	*RS*	*WP*
RS	*MFA*	*MFA*

diversity.[1] If Andrew, Bonnie, and Chuck are going to hang out together as a group, they must come to a choice in spite of their heterogeneous preferences. Not realizing that the decision on how a group should arrive at collective decisions is something over which much blood has been spilled throughout human history, our three friends rather casually decide to take "a" vote and let "the" majority rule. (We put the indefinite and definite articles of the previous sentence in quotation marks, since two of the main points of this chapter are that there are many ways to take a vote and there are many different majorities.)

Our group has a problem, it seems, because the three friends do not unanimously share the same first preference; if they did, there would be no problem. In the present circumstance, then, one commonsense way to "take a vote" is to poll the group members on whether a *majority* shares a first preference in common. A quick inspection of the preference orderings in Display 3.1 reveals that this method fails to resolve the group's problem. In terms of first preferences, our group is heterogeneous in the extreme. As a fallback, then, a more bothersome but still commonsensical plan for resolving problems of group choice is to conduct a *round-robin tournament*. Each alternative is pitted against each other alternative

---

[1] Although collections of individuals often consort together because of shared interests, this does not mean that they share identical preferences on all manner of things. Moreover, many collections of individuals of interest to political scientists consort together *not* because of shared interests, but more often for exactly the opposite reason—they are *representative* bodies reflecting the diversity of a larger population.

DISPLAY 3.2

MFA vs. *WP*:	*WP* wins 2-1 {**B,C**}
MFA vs. *RS*:	*RS* wins 2-1 {**B,C**}
WP vs. *RS*:	*WP* wins 2-1 {**A,B**}

---

and, if one is preferred by a majority to all the others, then it is declared the group choice. (If this condition fails to materialize, then we go back to the drawing board.) Consulting the preference orderings above, we see that this tournament produces the results of Display 3.2.

Several things are worth noting about this little exercise. First of all, going to the Common for the Walden Pond political rally is the majority preference of this group: *WP* wins the round-robin tournament by beating all the other alternatives in pairwise contests. The vote in each case is 2–1, and the particular friends on the winning side in each instance are listed in brackets in the display.

But notice that *different* majorities prefer *WP* to each of the other alternatives; Bonnie is the only common member. So, second, groups are composed of many majorities: {**A,B**} {**A,C**} {**B,C**} and {**A,B,C**} are all majorities of our group of friends. Letting "the" majority rule is not unambiguous and, as we shall see, can get you into trouble.

Third, we have interpreted the taking of a vote here as having each individual reveal his or her preference honestly. When confronted with a pair of alternatives, each group member voted for the one that he or she ranked higher. This is known as *sincere* preference revelation. It is entirely possible, of course, for an individual to vote contrary to preference, perhaps because by doing so a person paradoxically makes out better than if he or she had voted sincerely. This latter maneuver, known as *strategic* or *sophisticated* preference revelation, does seem a bit like cheating, especially among friends, and involves some disingenuous, if not dishonest, behavior.

We will explore strategic behavior more systematically in Chapter 6, but let's briefly and casually examine the possibilities of strategic behavior in this example. What we want to determine is whether any of the friends has an incentive to *misrepresent* his or her preferences by voting strategically. A person might consider doing this if he or she could produce a more preferred final outcome. In our example this is a very real prospect because each outcome in the round-robin was decided by a single vote. Thus, there are two things to determine—feasibility and desirability: (1) *Can* someone shift the outcome by shifting his or her vote? and (2) Given the possibility, would such a person *want* to shift the outcome?

It is clear that any one in the majority in each pairing above could, by misrepresenting preferences, change the outcome in that pairing. This answers the first question about feasibility. As to desirability, one thing is clear: Bonnie has absolutely no incentive to change her vote in any pairing since she is the great beneficiary of sincere voting by members of the group—her first preference wins the round-robin. Poor Andrew is pivotal only in the comparison between Walden Pond and Red Sox and, if he were to change his vote to favor *RS*, then he would make the latter the overall winner of the round-robin. But the latter is the worst thing for him, so he certainly has no incentive to switch votes. This leaves Chuck as the only one with a possible motive to behave strategically. It is clear that he could change the result of the pairing between *MFA* and *RS*, but this would not change the overall outcome so there is not much point to his doing that.[2] However, what if he voted against *WP* (his second preference) and for *MFA* (his last preference) in the first pairing in Display 3.2? Then the

---

[2] He could simultaneously change his votes in each of the first two ballots, in which case *MFA* would be the round-robin winner. But this is Chuck's least-preferred outcome, so he hardly has an incentive to behave strategically in this fashion.

round-robin tournament would have *no* winner. Before we can determine whether it is rational for Chuck to vote strategically in the first ballot above, we would need to know (and certainly *he* would need to know) what transpires in the event of no winner (something I neglected to arrange for in describing this tournament above).[3] I shall not pursue this here, though I promise to take it up more systematically in the chapter after next. It has been sufficient to have demonstrated that one of the friends *may* have an incentive to behave strategically.

Several lessons emerge from this little exercise. The first is that there are multiple majorities, rather than "the" majority. A second lesson is that there are multiple forms of preference revelation—at the time of balloting a person may vote sincerely or strategically. A third lesson of this example, one I pursue a bit further now, is that there are multiple ways for groups to decide by voting.

We have already seen that *rule by unanimity* is one way for a group to proceed, but that in this particular case it fails to produce a solution to our group's problem since preferences are just too heterogeneous. Likewise, we have determined that *first-preference majority rule*, in which each person votes

---

[3] We actually have been purposeful in our "neglect," since this allows us to point out that larger societies often neglect to arrange for all possible contingencies in their constitutional deliberations. Sometimes the neglect is done knowingly; some events are regarded as so improbable or farfetched that it simply isn't worth designing arrangements for them. Often, however, the neglect is not by design, in which case a group may find it has to freelance. Kids playing baseball in a wooded area, for instance, add to the rules of the game as unanticipated events occur, e.g., a ball hits an overhanging branch. Grown-ups playing baseball, to take another example, add to the rules of the game (for instance, establishing a "designated hitter" rule for pitchers) in response to unanticipated market circumstances. (Major League Baseball team owners, I am informed, worried thirty-some years ago that baseball was getting too dull for the go-go American public; some of the owners—those of the American League—decided to jazz the game up. This incredibly stupid move, supported only by people ignorant of the subtleties of the game, and by the players' union in its effort to save the jobs of aging sluggers, is a matter of great debate best left to another forum. Needless to say, the author is a fan of the National League.)

sincerely for his or her first preference, fails to resolve the issue of what the group should do, and for the same reason— too much preference diversity. Finally, we have discovered that the preferences of individuals in the group do lend themselves to *majority rule by round-robin tournament*, at least as long as everyone votes sincerely. Fortunately for our friends, there were only three of them and only three alternatives so that, given their preferences, a round-robin tournament was both easy to administer and decisive. Had there been more friends, more alternatives, or more diverse preferences, a round-robin tournament may not have suited the needs of the group as well as some alternative method. Indeed, there are many ways in which to decide by voting. Often the institutional features of the voting system will be absolutely essential in determining which alternative wins.

A REVISED EXAMPLE

This will not be the last time you hear me say, "Institutions matter." In this case I want to claim that the institutional procedure for conducting a vote to resolve a problem of group choice dramatically affects that group choice. To show this, I alter our "warm-up exercise" slightly. Suppose that Andrew, Bonnie, and Chuck have the same preferences with which they were endowed in Display 3.1. But now let us suppose that, before any votes are taken, there is an intervening stage of debate and deliberation (otherwise known as arguing). While debate and deliberation may often seem like window dressing, it is entirely possible that, from time to time at least, some persuasion, reconsideration, conceivably even coercion, takes place that results in someone changing preferences.

Thus, while our friends are deliberating, suppose Chuck becomes convinced that a trip to the museum might be brief and he might, at the very least, catch the last few innings of

DISPLAY 3.3		
A	**B**	**C**
MFA	*WP*	*RS*
WP	*RS*	*MFA*
RS	*MFA*	*WP*

the Red Sox game on the tube afterward. The Walden Pond rally, on the other hand, would go on all afternoon. As a consequence, suppose he elevates *MFA* in his preference ordering (and lowers *WP*). Thus, before the voting but after deliberation, the preferences of the group members now are as given in Display 3.3. A round-robin majority rule tournament does not produce a winner in this new situation (as shown in Display 3.4). Each alternative is beaten by one of the other alternatives: *MFA* loses to *RS*, which loses to *WP*, which loses to *MFA*. If we were to write the *group* majority preference relation as P_G, then we would have *RS* P_G *MFA* P_G *WP* P_G *RS*. But this doesn't look like a preference ordering at all. Indeed, it is not![4] Whereas the individuals of the group possessed coherent—that is, transitive—preferences, the group does not. The group preference relation is *intransitive* or, to put it more colorfully, the group's preferences *cycle*, with a different majority coalition supporting the winner in each pairwise comparison.

Since round-robin voting doesn't solve our group's problem in this circumstance, we need to think about other institutional schemes. One arrangement that is found in official institutions is called the *agenda procedure*.[5] For a given set of alternatives, some individual (or subcommittee)—called the *agenda setter*—is charged with assembling an order of voting

---

[4] Notice that *RS* is simultaneously (!) at the top and bottom of this list—something not characteristic of an *ordering*.

[5] This procedure is also used in many sports competitions, under the rubric of *single-elimination tournament*.

DISPLAY 3.4		
Contest	**Winner**	**Supporters**
MFA vs. *WP*	*MFA*	{A,C}
WP vs. *RS*	*WP*	{A,B}
RS vs. *MFA*	*RS*	{B,C}

for the larger group. The alternatives, themselves, are usually generated by the larger group, although in some organizations an especially powerful agenda setter both proposes items for the agenda and puts them into a voting order. Once this *agenda* is formed, the group votes on the items a pair at a time. Specifically, the first two items on the agenda are voted on by majority rule, with the losing item eliminated and the winning item paired with the next item on the agenda. A majority vote between these two follows along the same lines. This procedure is repeated as often as necessary to work through the agenda. Whichever alternative survives the entire gauntlet is the winner.

Returning to our example, suppose Andrew, because he is the oldest member of the group, is charged with proposing an agenda. What are his options? Generally speaking, for a set of k agenda items, there are $(k) \times (k-1) \times (k-2) \times \ldots \times 3 \times 2 \times 1$ ways to order an agenda. In the example, where $k = 3$, there are $3 \times 2 \times 1$, or six, orderings. But really there are only three substantively distinct agendas, since what is really being chosen is which of the three alternatives goes last and which pair, as a consequence, is voted on first.[6] So, Andrew may choose one of the agendas in Display 3.5. If he chose agenda I, for instance, then *MFA* would be voted against *WP* with the winner then voted against *RS* and the survivor declared the group choice.

---

[6] That is, in this circumstance it really doesn't matter which of the two items in the initial pair is first and which is second.

DISPLAY 3.5		
Agenda I	**Agenda II**	**Agenda III**
MFA	*RS*	*WP*
WP	*MFA*	*RS*
RS	*WP*	*MFA*

If Andrew knows his friends' preferences and is prepared to believe that they will vote honestly once he chooses an agenda (both of which we will assume here for the sake of argument), then he can actually figure out what will transpire for each agenda selection he makes. All he needs to do is consult Display 3.4. If he chooses agenda I, then *MFA* is paired against *WP*. From Display 3.4, *MFA* wins and advances to the next round of voting, pitted against *RS*. *RS* prevails in this pairing and thus in the entire contest, so Agenda I ⇒ *RS*. In a similar fashion, he determines that agenda II ⇒ *WP* and agenda III ⇒ *MFA*. Thus, by choosing agenda III, Andrew can produce his most-preferred alternative as the outcome of group choice. Agenda power is powerful indeed! And the institutional norm that says, "If there is no round-robin winner, then let the oldest in the group select an agenda," sure makes a difference, too. Had the norm given that power to the tallest (Chuck) or the lightest (Bonnie), and each of them had gone through the same exercise, then agenda I and agenda II, respectively, would have been chosen with altogether different group choices.

SUMMARY

I've wandered a bit astray, but I hope the reader has been sensitized to the fact that even when individuals honestly reveal their preferences, it is nevertheless entirely possible for a group's preferences to be "badly behaved" (read: intransitive) in comparison to those of the individuals who comprise it. This is an instance of what the political philosophers Brian Barry and Russell Hardin call "rational man and irrational society."[7] As a consequence, what is best for the group, or even what a majority thinks is best for the group, is not at all evident. Even more important, the precise institutional procedures by which the group determines what it shall do are absolutely critical in making that choice.

In the next several chapters I make these matters, and more besides, a bit more precise. In Chapter 4 the focus will be on the method of majority rule and the problem of group preference intransitivity. Chapter 5 continues on this theme by investigating the method of majority rule from the perspective of the *spatial model* of group choice. Chapter 6 turns attention to the issue of *manipulation*, in terms of both the misrepresentation of preferences and agenda stratagems. Finally, in Chapter 7 the theme of alternative ways for groups to make choices is taken up.

PROBLEMS AND DISCUSSION QUESTIONS

1. Five members of a committee are voting over four proposed spending plans, abbreviated as *A*, *B*, *C*, and *D* (you can assume that the committee members vote sincerely). Two of the committee members have the preference *ABCD* (*A* is preferred to *B* is preferred to *C* . . . and so on). The other three have preferences: *BCDA*, *DBAC*, and *CBDA*. Does any spending plan win under a system of *plurality rule*, in which the outcome with the most first-place votes prevails? Which plan

---

[7] *Rational Man and Irrational Society?* (Beverly Hills, Calif.: Sage, 1982).

would win in a round-robin tournament? Suppose that the committee members determine that there is a fatal flaw in plan B, and only vote over A, C, and D. Would there be a clear winner under the round-robin tournament method? Why or why not?

2. Three individuals, i, j, and k, are voting over four outcomes q, r, s, and t. Their preference orderings are

$$qP_isP_irP_it, \ rP_jqP_jtP_js, \text{ and } tP_krP_ksP_kq.$$

If they vote honestly using a round-robin tournament, are there any group preference cycles? Now k changes his mind, and switches his preferences to $tP_ksP_krP_kq$. Are there any group preference cycles? How does this problem illustrate the idea of "rational man, irrational society?"

3. Using the same preferences as above (before k changes his mind), can i fashion a sequential agenda (i.e., each outcome introduced sequentially and only retained if it beats the existing winner) such that her top choice wins? What about after k changes his mind? Then, identify agendas that j and k could design to secure their top choices (for both before and after k changes his mind, *if possible*). In general, can an agenda be fashioned that leads to the defeat of an alternative favored by a majority over each other alternative?

*4. Now using the preferences after k has changed his mind, show that if player j proposes the agenda $tsrq$,[a] then player i has an incentive to strategically misrepresent her vote if she assumes the others vote honestly. Now suppose k proposes the

---

[a] First t and s are voted on, then the winner of that contest faces r, then the winner of that contest faces q. The winner of that final contest is the overall victor.

agenda *rqst*. Can *j* do better than the expected outcome under honest voting by misrepresenting his preferences?

5. In Chapter 2, we argued that complete and transitive preferences at the individual level were a fundamental part of a rational-actor model of politics. Why are transitive preferences so important? Are transitive preferences similarly important at the level of group decision making? Why or why not?

4

Group Choice and Majority Rule

In the previous chapter I introduced three subjects, though only in the most casual of fashions: cycling majority preferences, manipulation of agendas and of the way preferences are revealed, and alternative voting methods for making group choices. In the next several chapters I take these subjects up one at a time and in considerably more detail. By the end of our intellectual tour, I hope the reader will have come to appreciate (if not admire) the expertise politicians must acquire in order to master the arcane procedural details of group choice.

CYCLICAL MAJORITIES

Condorcet's Paradox

We saw in the last chapter that a group of rational individuals can collectively produce irrational results. Even though each *individual* in the group has preferences that are consistent (complete and transitive), this need not be true of the *group's* preferences. This puzzle has come to be known as *Condorcet's paradox*, named after the eminent scientist, philosopher, and mathematician of late eighteenth-century France who (re)dis-

DISPLAY 4.1
CYCLICAL MAJORITY PREFERENCES

1	2	3
a	b	c
b	c	a
c	a	b

covered it.[1] Although not actually a paradox in the strict logical sense, the disjuncture between group preferences and the preferences of individuals always seems to surprise and puzzle students when they first encounter it. Its general format is given in Display 4.1, where a group $G = \{1, 2, 3\}$ must choose by majority rule from among the three alternatives, $\{a, b, c\}$, which could be political candidates, public policies, or places to go in Boston on a sunny spring afternoon. A majority, $\{1, 3\}$, prefers a to b; another majority, $\{1, 2\}$, prefers b to c; but (contrary to transitivity) still another majority, $\{2, 3\}$, prefers c to a. For members of a group with these preferences, majority rule produces alternatives that are said to cycle. More formally, a group preference relation, P_G, is said to be cyclical if it violates transitivity (property 2 of Chapter 2). In the example given in Display 4.1,

$$aP_Gb$$
$$bP_Gc$$
$$cP_Ga,$$

which violates transitivity. (A *transitive* group preferring a to b and b to c would prefer a to c.)

---

[1] For the longest time, Condorcet was credited with inventing this voting paradox. Only recently it has come to light that, in fact, he had rediscovered something that had been known five hundred years earlier. For a general historical overview of this subject, see Iain McLean and Arnold B. Urken, eds., *Classics of Social Choice* (Ann Arbor: University of Michigan Press, 1993).

DISPLAY 4.2
ALTERNATIVE PREFERENCE ORDERINGS
OF THREE ALTERNATIVES

(1)	(2)	(3)	(4)	(5)	(6)	(7)	(8)	(9)	(10)	(11)	(12)	(13)
a	a	b	b	c	c	ab	ac	bc	a	b	c	
b	c	a	c	a	b							abc
c	b	c	a	b	a	c	b	a	bc	ac	ab	

This raises both a normative and a positive question—what *should* the group *G* do? and what *will* the group *G* do? In more general contexts, in which G is a legislature, a town meeting, or indeed possibly an entire electorate or society, these questions take on a broad significance.

However, before we get up a head of steam on "broadly significant" questions, and with all due respect to Monsieur Condorcet, a prior question naturally arises: just how important is this puzzle of group intransitivity? Is it merely an arcane logical possibility, a trick foisted upon the unknowing student by professors, philosophers, and textbook writers? Or is it a profound discovery, the stuff from which important insights about political philosophy and social life are made? In my opinion, the answer lies much closer to the latter.

The general issues raised in the preceding paragraph may be approached by thinking first about the likelihood of Condorcet's paradox in the simplest of all settings, namely, the three individuals and three alternatives given in Display 4.1. Any one individual may rank order the three alternatives in thirteen different ways (see Display 4.2). Preference orderings (1) through (6) involve no indifference and are said to be *strong*. Orderings (7) through (12) involve some indifference, while (13) represents total indifference; these latter orderings are *weak*. Each member of the group thus may adopt any one of thirteen orderings, so that there are 13 × 13 × 13, or 2197, combinations of three individuals with preferences over three alter-

---

DISPLAY 4.3
ANOTHER SET OF CYCLICAL MAJORITY PREFERENCES

1	2	3
c	a	b
b	c	a
a	b	c

---

natives. That is, there are 2197 different "societies." To keep things simpler still, let's focus on the $6 \times 6 \times 6$, or 216, societies of three persons with strong preferences (preference ordering 1 through 6 in Display 4.2). It is now possible to calculate how many of these societies are afflicted with Condorcet's paradox.

Notice in Display 4.1 that the cyclical group preferences are produced by a situation in which each alternative is ranked first by exactly one person, second by exactly one person, and third by exactly one person. This produces the "forward cycle" $a\,P_G\,b\,P_G\,c\,P_G\,a$. (Recall that P_G means "is preferred by a majority of the group.") There are actually six different ways to produce this forward cycle, since Mr. 1's preference ordering in Display 4.1 could be held by any one of the three individuals, Ms. 2's by any one of the two remaining, and Mr. 3's by whoever is left. There are also six ways to produce the "backward cycle," $c\,P_G\,b\,P_G\,a\,P_G\,c$, generated by the individual orderings given in Display 4.3, as well as by any reassignment of them among group members.[2] So, taking forward and backward cycles together, there are exactly 12 of 216 (strong-preference) societies that generate group preference cycles.[3]

---

[2] Display 4.3 is Display 4.1 with everyone's preference ordering reversed.

[3] I am claiming here that only the preferences given in Displays 4.1 and 4.3, and their reassignments, produce group preference cycles. These twelve preference configurations are the only ones in which each alternative appears exactly once at each rank level. It is relatively easy to show that if any alternative shows up at the same rank for *more than one* individual, then the group preference will not cycle. The reader may like to try his or her hand at establishing this fact.

So we now know that in the world of three-person groups choosing among three alternatives, the odds are extremely good that majority rule will work smoothly. In 204 of the 216 possible configurations there will be a *Condorcet winner* rather than a Condorcet cycle.[4] If each of the preference configurations (societies) that cause majority rule cycles is no more likely than each of the 204 for which majority rule works smoothly, then majority rule will generate consistent group preferences most of the time. In short, majority rule is normally a splendid way to conduct business, when the number of individuals is small and the alternatives are few.

If only life were so simple! Alas, it is not. And as soon as we start complicating things, the case for majority rule needs re-examination. There are really only two ways in which to make this pure majority rule setting more complicated: increase the number of individuals (n) or increase the number of alternatives (m). (Of course, we can increase both at the same time, too.) We are interested in deriving a probability or proportion that gives the likelihood of a majority rule preference cycle, given the number m of alternatives and the number n of individuals in the group. We write this probability as $Pr(m,n)$. We already know, for example, that $Pr(3,3) = 12/216$, or .056. Generally,

$$Pr(m,n) = [\text{\# of "problem" preference configurations}]/(m!)^n$$

This formula states that the probability of intransitivity in the majority preferences of a group of size n voting on m alternatives is the ratio of two numbers. The numerator is the number of "societies" with cycling group preferences, like those presented in Displays 4.1 and 4.3. This number is 12 for $m = 3$ and $n = 3$, as we saw in the discussion surrounding those

---

[4] A *Condorcet winner* is the alternative that can defeat all others in pairwise majority contests. If three alternatives do not cycle, then it must be the case that one of them is a Condorcet winner. It is the one at the top of the majority preference relation, P_G.

TABLE 4.1

PROBABILITY OF A CYCLICAL MAJORITY, $Pr(m,n)$

Number of Voters (n)

Number of Alternatives (m)	3	5	7	9	11	limit
3	.056	.069	.075	.078	.080	.088
4	.111	.139	.150	.156	.160	.176
5	.160	.200	.215			.251
6	.202					.315
limit	≈1.000	≈1.000	≈1.000	≈1.000	≈1.000	≈1.000

SOURCE: William H. Riker, *Liberalism Against Populism* (San Francisco: Freeman, 1982), p. 122

displays. The denominator gives the total number of possible societies, computed as follows: With m alternatives, any individual in the group may choose any one of $m \times (m - 1) \times (m - 2) \times \ldots \times 3 \times 2 \times 1$ (or $m!$ in mathematical symbols) different ways to order his or her preferences over the alternatives. Since there are n individuals, this means there are $m! \times m! \times \ldots \times m!$ (n times), or $(m!)^n$ different societies. This number, for $m = n = 3$, is $(3 \times 2 \times 1)^3 = 6 \times 6 \times 6 = 216$, as we also saw in the discussion of Display 4.2. Fortunately for us, computationally talented scholars have determined $Pr(m,n)$ from the formula given above for various values of m and n. A partial summary of their calculations is presented in Table 4.1.[5]

The columns of this table give groups of different sizes, ranging from three to some extremely large number (which I call the "limit"). The rows give sets of alternatives of different sizes, again ranging from three to a limiting (very large) num-

[5] A very accessible discussion of this entire subject is found in William H. Riker, *Liberalism Against Populism* (San Francisco: Freeman, 1982), Chapter 5. The literature on estimating $Pr(m,n)$ is cited there in footnote 3.

ber. The entries of the table give the probability that majority preferences cycle, $Pr(m,n)$. Thus, if we look at the first row ($m = 3$ alternatives), the probability of a cyclical majority rises slowly from the $12/216 = .056$ computed above for three-member groups to .088 in the limit as the number of group members becomes very large. Increase the number of alternatives to four and the probability of a cyclical majority roughly doubles for each group size; that is, it starts at a higher level and smoothly increases to a limiting probability of .176. As the number of alternatives grows very large, $Pr(m,n)$ approaches 1.0—it becomes nearly certain that there will be preference cycles among majorities.

So, the good news of the small-group/few-alternatives situation does not extend to more general situations. As the number of group members increases, and especially as the number of alternatives increases, the probability of badly behaved majority preferences—that is, cycles—grows, becoming nearly certain as we approach the limit. In general, then, we cannot rely on the method of majority rule to produce a coherent[6] sense of what the group wants, especially if there are no institutional mechanisms for keeping participation restricted (thereby keeping n small) or weeding out some of the alternatives (thereby keeping m small).

This is a troubling state of affairs for anyone trying to analyze politics. We have just concluded that, most of the time, when we employ majority rule, we must tolerate either group incoherence, a highly compressed franchise (small n), or highly restricted agenda access (small m). That is the gist of Table 4.1. There is, however, an important qualification.

In computing the entries of Table 4.1, a very specific assumption was made about the likelihood of various preference configurations. We assumed that, for any size group (n), each

---

[6] Throughout this text, we shall use "coherent," "consistent," and "transitive" interchangeably.

of the strong preference orderings is as likely as any other to characterize the preferences of an individual. Moreover, one person's "selection" of a preference ordering is entirely independent of some other person's. Thus, for $m = 5$ for example, there are $5 \times 4 \times 3 \times 2 \times 1 = 120$ ways to strongly order the five alternatives. Each of the group members is assumed to have his or her preferences represented by any one of these 120 preference orderings with equal probability. Thus, for $n = 7$ persons for example, there are (120) equally likely seven-person societies. And, as the appropriate entry in Table 4.1 reveals (the one for $m = 5$ and $n = 7$), 21.5 percent of these societies generate cyclical majority preferences. That is, more than one time out of every five, a group of seven choosing among five alternatives by majority voting will produce group incoherence.

However, almost any *real* conception of society is bound to be more all-embracing than a collection of equiprobable preference-orderings; indeed, most conceptions of society emphasize *inter*dependence rather than *in*dependence among individuals. Individuals often choose to join groups, for example, precisely because they have preferences in *common* with other group members. This would lead one to expect correlation, not independence, between the preferences of group members. The conception of society as a collection of independently chosen preference orderings provides no more than a baseline assessment of majority-rule methods. So, our concerns about cycles in majority rule as reflected in Table 4.1 are probably exaggerated—but only somewhat. Even if the feasible "societies" are not equally likely, as long as either n or (especially) m is large, the odds of majority preferences cycling is sufficiently large to be of concern. Moreover, in other circumstances quite common in politics—circumstances described momentarily as "distributive politics"—majority cycles are inevitable. Condorcet's paradox cannot be lightly dismissed. I hammer these points home in concluding this section, first with one last abstract example and then with a couple of real-world cases of cyclical majorities.

Cyclical Majorities and "Divide the Dollars"

So many interesting political fights involve a group deciding how to share something. Usually it is something desirable and the fighting is about getting the most favorable distribution. Manna from heaven is wonderful, but how should it be divided up? The same logic, however, applies to things people want to avoid. For the past decade or so, reducing the federal deficit has been of great political import in the United States. Everyone agrees that hundreds of billions of dollars of public expenditures need to be cut (or revenues raised), but from where and from whom? Divvying up program cuts or tax burdens, just like sharing the revenues from newly discovered oil or some other windfall, involves group conflict over distribution.

Suppose a small town has lucked into a windfall of $1,000, because the state had made an earlier error of overcollecting fees from the town. The town's three-person board of selectmen[7] must decide how to spend this "found" money, this manna from heaven. The politicians on the board represent the East, Central, and West districts of town, respectively, and, like most representatives, they want to hang on to their jobs by taking care of their respective constituents. By this it is meant that each politician—whom we shall name E, C, and W—believes that the more money he or she can land for the district, the better his or her chances are for reelection. The board operates by simple majority rule. Is there a division of the spoils that a board majority prefers to any other division?

---

[7] "Board of selectmen" seems to be a New England thing. In other parts of the United States, the local legislature is called a city or town council or board of aldermen.

That is, is there a Condorcet-winning sharing scheme or, instead, do the sharing schemes cycle?

Let us write a share of the $1000 for each district as s(E), s(C), and s(W), respectively. A sharing scheme, [s(E), s(C), s(W)], is feasible if (1) each of its components is nonnegative (you can't give one of the districts a *negative* share of $1000)—s(E), s(C), s(W) ≥ 0; and (2) if the components sum to no more than $1000—s(E) + s(C) + s(W) ≤ $1000. In this feasible set, (1000, 0, 0) is the most-preferred distribution for E, (0, 1000, 0) is most-preferred by C, and (0, 0, 1000) is W's first choice. Generally speaking, a selectman prefers one distribution to another if and only if his or her component is larger in the one distribution than in the other.

My claim is that "divide the dollars" is a game that produces cyclical majorities. No distribution is preferred by a majority to every other distribution; there is no Condorcet winner. Before showing this generally, let's consider some cases. Consider first what many would consider the fair distribution—[333⅓, 333⅓, 333⅓]. A majority consisting of E and C prefer [500, 500, 0] to it; another majority consisting of E and W prefer [500, 0, 500] to it; and, finally, the coalition of C and W prefer [0, 500, 500] to it. In each of these instances two of the three selectmen do better than with the fair distribution in the sense that they bring home more revenue to their constituents. The fair distribution is thus vulnerable to some majority coalition of selectmen ganging up on the excluded selectman.

But what about these latter distributions? It turns out that they, too, are vulnerable. And the distributions to which they are vulnerable are also vulnerable. In fact, majority preferences over various distributions cycle. To see this, consider the distribution [500, 500, 0] that E and C prefer to the fair distribution (since 500 > 333⅓ for both E and C). Against [500, 500, 0], E and W prefer [700, 0, 300] (since 700 > 500 for E and 300 > 0 for W); and then C and W favor the fair distribution to

---

DISPLAY 4.4
MAJORITY CYCLE IN "DIVIDE THE DOLLARS" GAME

Distribution 1	Distribution 2	Majority Coalition Preferring 2 to 1
[333⅓, 333⅓, 333⅓]	[500, 500, 0]	{E,C}
[500, 500, 0]	[700, 0, 300]	{E,W}
[700, 0, 300]	[333⅓, 333⅓, 333⅓]	{C,W}

[700, 0, 300] (since 333⅓ > 0 for C and 333⅓ > 300 for W), thereby producing a majority cycle (Display 4.4).[8]

I have claimed that "divide the dollars" represents a generic kind of politics. I have just proved that sharing out benefits and burdens, or what is known as "distributive politics,"[9] is inherently cyclical in majoritarian settings. Any proposed distribution is open to amendment as different majorities jostle with one another for advantage. Final outcomes, whatever they happen to be, are extremely sensitive to other institutional features of the group decision-making setting. They will depend, for example, on someone's exercising agenda power, on some arbitrary time limit on deliberation,

---

[8] Generally speaking, consider an arbitrary feasible distribution, $d = [x, y, z]$. This can be any distribution whose components are greater than zero and which sum to no more than \$1000. Take two small positive amounts, δ and ε (where $\delta + \varepsilon \leq z$), and reallocate them away from W to E and C. This new distribution, $d' = [x + \delta, y + \varepsilon, z - \delta - \varepsilon]$, is also feasible as long as we don't take too much away from W (which is what the inequality in the parenthesis above guarantees). Now, since δ is positive, E prefers d' to d and, since ε is positive, C prefers d' to d. (Of course, for exactly these same reasons, W prefers d to d'.) Since a majority of the selectmen prefer d' to d, the latter is not a Condorcet-winning sharing scheme. But d was an *arbitrary* scheme. It could have been *any* distribution and the same logic would have applied. So, what we have proved is that *no sharing scheme is a Condorcet winner*, since any scheme is subject to reallocations like the one constructed above.

[9] This term was popularized by Theodore J. Lowi in his classic paper "American Business, Public Policy, Case-Studies, and Political Science," *World Politics* (July 1964): 677–715, and developed further in his book, *The End of Liberalism* (New York: Norton, 1969).

on procedural features like who is permitted to make motions, or whatever. In sum, in this very important class of political activity, the only way to avoid preference cycles like the one in Display 4.4 is to impose some form of *antimajoritarian restriction*. This is the principal content of Arrow's Theorem, the subject of the next section. Before turning to that, I illustrate my main point one more time with some illustrations drawn from American political history (Case 4.1).

CASE 4.1
CIVIL WAR TAXES, GREAT DEPRESSION
TAXES, 1980S TAX REFORM

Tax politics is distributive politics par excellence; it is certainly a good example of "divide the dollars." Various social groups want to avoid paying more taxes, and this leads to unstable coalitions and preference cycles. The question to be asked, then, is how we in the United States have been able to pass tax reform legislation at all (reforms either to increase taxes, decrease taxes, or redistribute the burden). In this case I have chosen three episodes to demonstrate the dynamics of preference cycles as they play out in the U.S. Congress. In the first episode, uncertainty played a critical role. In the second, institutional features restricted the ability of groups to offer amendments to a proposed bill.* In the final episode, organizational problems prevented a coalition from uniting to block proposed legislation.†

The very first income tax in (what remained of) the

---

* The institutional features emphasized here are procedural rules that are common in most legislatures. They will be discussed more systematically in the next chapter.
† The organizational problems, known as *collective action problems*, will be more fully analyzed in Chapter 9.

United States was passed in 1861 as part of the effort to finance the Civil War. The interesting thing about the income tax is that it resulted from a preference cycle (and was not even part of the original suggestion for raising revenue). There was a motion in the House of Representatives to raise federal revenue by taxing *wealth*. To this motion was offered an amendment to raise revenue instead by taxing *land*. And, of course, if neither the original motion nor the amended version passed, the status quo of *no taxes* would prevail. Different majorities preferred the land tax to the wealth tax, the wealth tax to no tax, and no tax to the land tax. There was much confusion and to-and-fro during the debate as this majority preference cycle wreaked havoc. Finally, someone introduced the idea of taxing *income*. This swept to victory primarily because, unlike each of the other taxes (in which politicians knew exactly whose ox would be gored), there was much uncertainty about how an income tax would impact various constituencies. Politicians preferred the "lottery" of an income tax to no tax at all or a tax on either land or wealth.‡

A legislative bill to raise, lower, or redistribute taxes is a proposal to alter the status quo in some fashion. One way to prevent preference cycles is to restrict the right of anyone to amend a proposal. Then there are, in effect, only two alternatives—the proposal and the status quo—and a majority prefers either the proposal to the status quo or the status quo to the proposal, or there is a tie (in which case, by convention in nearly all legislatures, the status quo prevails). At various times throughout its history, and especially in the first half of the 20th century, Congress has restricted the rights of legislators to offer amendments to tax bills. When it has not, preference cycles often emerged.

---

‡ The details are provided in the fine essay by James E. Alt, "The Evolution of Tax Structures," *Public Choice* 41 (1983): 181–223.

The Revenue Acts of 1932 and 1938, for example, were pieces of legislation in which Congress *did* permit members to amend the legislation on the floor, and scholars have identified the majority preference cycles that resulted from this activity. From experiences like these, members of Congress have often agreed in advance to impose institutional restrictions on one another's legislative rights—in this instance, a restriction on the right to offer amendments—in order to avoid preference cycles.§

The Tax Reform Act of 1986 provides still another episode in which preference cycles were overcome. What happened? Against the status quo of doing nothing—always an option, of course—Senator Bill Bradley (D-N.J.) took advantage of various "supply-side economics" arguments to fashion a proposal that attracted a majority from both parties. As initially introduced by Bradley, the bill eliminated hundreds of billions of dollars in tax *breaks* in return for a lower individual tax *rate*. At this point it was expected that so-called special interests (whose tax breaks were being eliminated) would band together to offer a proposal (essentially an amended bill) that would woo Republicans away from the Bradley bill. This proposal, while protecting special-interest tax breaks and "bribing" Republicans in various ways, would nevertheless be sufficiently offensive to the majority that they would rather have no bill at all. That is, the so-called special-interest bill would defeat the Bradley proposal but then would itself be defeated by the status quo. The result would be no bill at all, even though the Bradley bill was preferred to the status quo. In short, the special-interest proposal would generate a preference cycle that would have the effect of killing tax reform alto-

§ The argument that Depression-era revenue bills were haunted by majority preference cycles is found in John C. Blydenburgh, "The Closed Rule and the Paradox of Voting," *Journal of Politics* 33 (1971): 57–71.

gether. But this special-interest proposal did not materialize. Like hogs around a trough, the individual groups in the
special-interest camp were so focused on preserving their
own tax breaks that they failed to coalesce to produce the
proposal to split the Bradley coalition. Deputy Treasury
Secretary Richard Darman, the Reagan administration's
tax reform strategist, had said at the time that an organized effort by the special interests would have been a "killer
coalition." Darman went on to say that the lobbyists were
"brought down by the narrowness of their vision. Precisely
because they defined themselves as representatives of single special interests, they failed to notice their collective
power."**

** The politics of the 1986 tax reform process, and the specific quote from
Darman, are found in Alan S. Murray and Jeffrey H. Birnbaum, "Lawmakers, Lobbyists and the Unlikely Triumph of Tax Reform," *Congress
and the Presidency* 15 (1988).

Arrow's Theorem

I have looked both theoretically and practically at the puzzle
of Condorcet's paradox. The choices of rational individuals
(based on complete and transitive preferences) do not necessarily translate through majority voting into a well-defined
group preference. Condorcet's paradox is problematic for majority rule in theory because its probability in natural groups
is not trivial and grows both with the size of the group and
with the number of possible alternatives for choice. It is problematic for majority voting in practice because in very real political settings, especially those dealing with the distribution
of a fixed pie, voting cycles do emerge.

Nevertheless, it may be that we aren't looking at the problem properly. Maybe the problem of group incoherence is a pe-
culiarity of round-robin tournaments, or of specific features of

majority rule, but not of voting more generally. If we employed some alternative way of arriving at a group choice, the problem might be less severe, or might possibly even go away altogether. That is, it might be possible to overcome the theoretical and practical problems of group incoherence by structuring the institutional arrangements of group choice differently. Arrow's Theorem, one of the most profound insights of twentieth-century political thought (and one that won its originator a Nobel Prize in economic sciences), indicates that these hunches, these hopes that the problem of group incoherence will go away if only we think about it in the right way, are wrong. Arrow's Theorem asserts that Condorcet's paradox is a problem for *any* reasonable method of aggregating individual preferences into group preferences.

Arrow's Theorem: Assumptions

Kenneth Arrow, in his seminal *Social Choice and Individual Values*,[10] assembled a set of general conditions that he claimed any reasonable method for aggregating preferences would satisfy. He did not *equate* these conditions with "reasonableness." Rather, in a much more powerful argument, he suggested only that his conditions were *minimal*; any reader is free to add additional reasonable requirements that the method by which a group makes choices should satisfy. Arrow concludes that *no* method of aggregating individual preferences into a coherent group preference can simultaneously satisfy even his minimal conditions.[11]

Arrow sets the problem up in an abstract fashion. There is a group of individuals, $G = \{1, 2, \ldots, n\}$, where n is at least three. (Rather than naming group members, I shall simply call them by numbers.) There is also a set of alternatives, $A =$

[10] (New York: Wiley, 1951).
[11] Therefore, the conclusion extends to any collection of conditions beyond the minimal ones proposed by Arrow: If no method satisfies the minimal conditions, then certainly it will not satisfy any expanded set of conditions.

{1, 2, . . . , *m*} where *m* is also at least three. A typical individual is called Mr. or Ms. *i*. Likewise, alternative *h* or *j* or *k* identifies a typical alternative. All of this will be apparent in context.[12] The individuals in *G* are assumed to possess preferences over the alternatives of *A*, written R_i for $i \in G$, which satisfy:

Rationality assumption. R_i is complete and transitive.

This is just property 1 and property 2 from Chapter 2. Completeness is the assumption that Mr. *i* is capable of saying, for any pair of alternatives, which he prefers (or that he is indifferent between them). Transitivity is the requirement that Mr. *i*'s preferences are coherent—that if he prefers *h* to *j* and *j* to *k*, then he prefers *h* to *k*.

To the rationality assumption for group members, Arrow adds four conditions to be taken as minimal requirements for the method by which the group makes choices:

Condition U (Universal Domain). Each $i \in G$ may adopt any strong or weak complete and transitive preference ordering over the alternatives in *A*.

Condition P (Pareto Optimality or Unanimity). If every member of *G* prefers *j* to *k* (or is indifferent between them), then the group preference must reflect a preference for *j* over *k* (or an indifference between them).

Condition I (Independence of Irrelevant Alternatives). If alternatives *j* and *k* stand in a particular relationship to one another in each group member's preferences, and this relationship does not change, then neither may the group preference between *j* and *k*. This is

---

[12] For the reader unfamiliar with mathematical notation, I will occasionally make use of the set-theoretic symbol $\in$, which means "is an element of." Thus, $i \in G$ means "Mr. or Ms. *i* is a member of group *G*." Similarly, $h, j, k \in A$ means "*h, j,* and *k* are all alternatives in *A*."

true even if individual preferences over other (irrelevant) alternatives in A change.

Condition D (Nondictatorship). There is no distinguished individual $i^* \in G$ whose own preferences dictate the group preference, independent of the other members of G.

Condition U makes sense if we are interested in designing a mechanism of group choice that responds to the preferences of group members. Although we assume that the individuals in G are rational, we do not want to restrict their preferences in any other manner. Rather, we want the mechanism to be universally applicable. Thus, if $A = \{a, b, c\}$, then Ms. i may select as her preferences any one of the thirteen preference orderings given in Display 4.2.

The rationale for condition P is also driven by a concern for linking group preference to individual preferences. Surely if the group preference ordering ranked alternative k ahead of alternative j, even though *every* member of G had the opposite preference, then we would be correct in describing the choice mechanism as perverse. It would certainly be the case that the group preference ordering was not a "positive" reflection of individual preferences, and this Arrow wanted to prevent.

Condition I states that the relative positions of alternatives j and k in the *group* preference ordering should depend only upon their relative positions in *individual* orderings. Suppose an expert group of American historians in 2010 sought to rank American presidents. Some in this group ranked Thomas Jefferson ahead of Andrew Jackson while others had the opposite view. The decision rule—whatever it happened to be—combined these various views into a group preference, say for Jefferson over Jackson. Suppose all initially had Barack Obama below these two. Suppose, however, that Obama's brilliant leadership during the financial crisis of 2009 caused some members of the group to elevate Obama in their respective preference orderings. Condition I states that it still should be the group's assessment that Jefferson ranks ahead of Jackson—that in the comparison between Jefferson and Jackson, *the group's (changed) assessment of Obama is irrelevant and therefore should not affect this comparison.*

Condition D is an extremely minimal fairness condition. It says that if *j* is preferred to *k* by some specific person—say Ms. *i**—and if *k* is preferred to *j* by everyone else, then it cannot be that the group preference is *j* $P_G k$. There cannot be some privileged person in the group (Ms. *i**) whose preferences become the group's preferences, no matter what the preferences of the other members of the group, even if this person is an expert, a philosopher-king, or a megalomaniac.

As I noted above, these four conditions are rather sparse and minimalist. There is a range of other things, both procedural and substantive, that many thinkers would want to include as additional "reasonable" conditions on the mechanism for group choice. As well, the four conditions are stated in an especially weak form. For example, condition D only precludes the most extreme form of dictator—one who gets her way against any opposition; it does not preclude weaker forms of social and political inequality—oligarchies, power elites, exclusive committees, and so on. The theorem I am about to state, as applied to the minimalist conditions, will apply with a vengeance to any more elaborate set of conditions one might want to impose on the method for making group decisions.

The Theorem and Its Meaning

I have emphasized how weak, reasonable, minimalist, and sparse the Arrow conditions are because Arrow's Theorem is of the "even if" form: Even if we insist only on conditions as weak, reasonable, minimalist, and sparse as these, something horrible may still happen. The theorem, known as an *impossibility result*, follows:

Arrow's Theorem. There exists no mechanism for translating the preferences of rational individuals into a coherent group preference that simultaneously satisfies conditions U, P, I, and D.

Put more dramatically, any scheme for producing a group choice that satisfies U, P, and I is either dictatorial or incoherent: the group is either dominated by a single distinguished member or has intransitive preferences. This restates the Arrow Impossibility Theorem in terms of the great trade-off it implies: *There is, in social life, a trade-off between social rationality and the concentration of power.* Social organizations that concentrate power provide for the prospect of social coherence: the dictator knows her own mind and can act rationally in pursuit of whatever it is she prefers. Social organizations in which power is dispersed, on the other hand, have less promising prospects for making coherent choices. Though these organizations may appear fairer and more democratic to the person in the street, they may also be more likely to be tongue-tied or inconsistent in ordering the alternatives under consideration.[13]

Does this mean that any particular mechanism for aggregating preferences is always either inconsistent or unfair? Absolutely not. Earlier, for example, we saw that in the three-voter/three-alternative situation, the method of majority rule yielded coherent group preferences in 204 of 216 configurations. It is easy to see (and I shall show this more formally below) that majority rule satisfies conditions U, P, I, and D. *It is just that this method cannot guarantee group coherence in all situations* (as the twelve "troublesome" configurations give testimony to). That is, the Rationality Assumption is violated on some occasions.

---

[13] An alternative interpretation of the trade-off is that we cannot insist on coherence universally—that the Rationality Assumption and condition U are in tension. As we shall discuss later in this chapter, the tension goes away if we relax our insistence on a universal domain.

Perhaps, as discussed earlier, we are overracting to this problem. The doubtful reader might say, "Sure, coherence and fairness in preference aggregation cannot be guaranteed, but perhaps this conflict only arises occasionally. Nothing is perfect, after all." This is an overly optimistic view. The very fact that *some* social situations produce either incoherence or unfairness means that it will be possible for clever, manipulative, strategic individuals to exploit this fact.

Before turning to an illustration of how this theorem should affect the way we think about social life, let me make one last abstract observation. Although I have claimed that Arrow's conditions of reasonableness are rather weak and unexceptional (and that, if anything, one might wish to impose additional and more demanding conditions on the method for producing group preferences), some may claim that Arrow's conditions are already too demanding. That's fair enough. But I can report that in the sixty years since Arrow's Theorem first appeared, social choice theory (as the field created by Arrow has come to be called) has become something of an academic light industry. Somewhere close to 10,000 books and articles have been written on Arrow's Theorem.[14] Scores of new theorems—variations on Arrow's original result—have been proffered in which one or more of Arrow's conditions has been weakened or altered.[15] Short of actually *eliminating* one of the fairness conditions—for example, by permitting dictators—the Arrow result does not evaporate. Fairness and consistency in decision making by social groups must be traded off. This

[14] Google Scholar reported in mid-2009 that Arrow's book had been cited nearly 7,500 times. Two other books on closely related themes had each been cited nearly 2,500 times. See Amartya Sen, *Collective Choice and Social Welfare* (San Francisco: Holden-Day, 1970), and Duncan Black, *The Theory of Committees and Elections* (Cambridge: Cambridge University Press, 1958).

[15] Several surveys cover this broad literature. An accessible point of entry is provided by Riker, *Liberalism Against Populism*, especially Chapter 5. The more advanced reader may consult Jerry S. Kelly, *Arrow Impossibility Theorems* (New York: Academic Press, 1978) in addition to those cited in the previous footnote.

forces us to think about political life in new ways, as Case 4.2
illustrates.

CASE 4.2
LEGISLATIVE INTENT

A piece of legislation cannot possibly cover all conceivable
contingencies for which it might be relevant. So, in any
specific instance a bureaucrat, judge, or lawyer must determine whether a specific statute is applicable in a given
situation. Because differences of opinion can arise over
whether or in what manner a statute is applicable, the appellate courts are often called upon to render a judgment.
Judges, lawyers, and legal scholars often give priority to the
following question in making this determination: What did
Congress intend in passing this law? In discovering congressional intent, appellate courts hope to discern the class
of circumstances covered by a statute, even if not explicitly
mentioned in the statute.

Often the specific instance in question is a novel circumstance that could not possibly have been anticipated in advance in legislative deliberations. For example, do the laws
from the 1930s affecting and regulating the propagation of
radio waves also apply to television, satellite, or cellular
telephone transmissions? To answer in the negative is to
say that because the statute neither explicitly addressed
nor could conceivably have anticipated these novel developments, the statute does not apply. According to this view,
congressional intent can only be discovered in the "plain
meaning" of the language in the statute. To answer in the
affirmative, on the other hand, is to acknowledge that lawmaking is a costly undertaking, that a legislature cannot be
all-knowing, and thus that legislation should be interpreted

broadly, and reasoning by analogy should be encouraged, in order to minimize the occasions in which the legislature has to revisit subjects.

Especially in the context of New Deal politics in the 1930s and civil rights politics in the 1960s, 1970s, and 1980s, liberals have tried to define legislative intent broadly so as to permit the federal courts to expand the domain over which congressional statutes applied. By arguing against a broad interpretation of intent and in favor of the "plain meaning" doctrine, conservatives have sought to limit what they regard as judicial imperialism—a judiciary that, in effect, uses its power to interpret laws in order to extend or rewrite them. Thus, liberals have developed principles of statutory interpretation to enable broad meaning to be read into acts of Congress, whereas conservatives have insisted on canons of interpretation that require judges to stick to the plain meaning of the statutory language.*

Who is right here? Short of appealing to our own personal prejudices and policy preferences, we can provide an analytical perspective by means of Arrow's Theorem. The theorem cautions against assigning individual properties to groups. Individuals are rational, but a group is not, since it may not even have transitively ordered preferences. If this is true, then how can one make reference to the *intent* of a group? That is, a legisla*tor* may have intentions; a legisla*ture* does not. Indeed, in passing a statute, there may be as many different intentions as there are legislators voting for the bill. And some of these may not even be consistent with one another. Former Senator John Danforth (R-Mo.) has

---

* While it is often the case that liberals seek broad interpretive principles and conservatives prefer narrow ones, it does not always play out that way. On matters of "police power," for example, conservatives often incline toward a more permissive reading of a statute to justify greater state activity.

said, "Any judge who tries to make legislative history out of the free-for-all that takes place on the floor of the Senate is on very dangerous grounds. . . . It is a muddle."†

I thus sympathize with the advice given by one of the most eminent jurists in American legal history, Justice Oliver Wendell Holmes: "The job of this Court is not to ask what the legislature intended, but rather what the statute means." This may not require an extremely literal reading of all legislation (an extremely restrictive notion of "plain meaning"), but it leaves no room for legislative intent. Indeed, because groups differ from individuals and thus may be incoherent, legislative intent, like jumbo shrimp and student-athletes, is an oxymoron! Arrow's Theorem warns us not to attribute individual characteristics, like rationality, to groups.‡

---

† Consequently, Antonin Scalia, associate justice of the Supreme Court, has declared, "We are governed by laws, not by the intentions of legislators." The Danforth and Scalia quotes are both found in Joan Biskupic, "Scalia Sees No Justice in Trying to Judge Intent of Congress on a Law," *Washington Post*, May 11, 1993, A4.
‡ The connection between legislative intent and Arrow's Theorem is developed in more detail in Kenneth A. Shepsle, "Congress Is a 'They,' Not an 'It': Legislative Intent as Oxymoron," *International Review of Law and Economics* 12 (1992): 239–257.

ARROW'S THEOREM AND MAJORITY RULE

I have been careful to state Arrow's Theorem as applying to any process or mechanism by which individual preferences are combined, or aggregated, or added up to produce a group preference ordering. From the perspective of democratic theory, however, we are most interested in the applicability of Arrow's Theorem to the method of majority rule. In this section I explicitly link the two.

First, I need to define terms. The *method of majority rule*

(MMR) requires that, for any pair of alternatives, j and k, j is preferred by the group to k (written: $j\,P_G\,k$) if and only if the number of group members who prefer j to k exceeds the number of who prefer k to j. We can characterize this method explicitly and then see that it is clearly a special instance of the methods satisfying Arrow's conditions. That is, I first show that MMR is actually composed of several essential building blocks or properties. Then I show that these properties are all special cases of the general conditions in Arrow's Theorem.

Consider, then, some additional (so-called) "reasonable" conditions on preference aggregation methods:

Condition A (Anonymity). Social preferences depend only on the *collection* of individual preferences, not on who has which preference.

Condition N (Neutrality). Interchanging the ranks of alternatives j and k in each group member's preference ordering has the effect of interchanging the ranks of j and k in the group preference ordering.

Condition M (Monotonicity). If an alternative j beats or ties another alternative k—that is, $j\,R_G\,k$—and j rises in some group member's preferences from below k to the same or a higher rank than k, then j now strictly beats k— that is, $j\,P_G\,k$.

Like Arrow's conditions, conditions A, N, and M embody notions of fairness in a prospective method of group choice. Anonymity is just what it sounds like. It is a condition that requires only that we know *what* an individual's preferences are, not *who* the individual is holding them. Thus, if, in a group setting like the one involving the group of college friends described in Chapter 3, Andrew and Bonnie swap preference orderings, condition A requires that the group's choices are unaffected by this. Condition A requires that each individual's preferences be fed into the group decision-making machinery with his or her name omitted—as, for example, is done with a secret ballot.

Neutrality is for alternatives what anonymity is for individuals. Condition N says that it does not matter how we label alternatives; all that matters is the alternatives' respective ranks in individual preference orderings.

Finally, monotonicity requires that the method of group choice respond "nonperversely" to changes in individual preferences; moreover, it requires that the method satisfy a very specific "knife-edge" property. The first feature of condition M requires that if one alternative is strictly preferred by the group to another ($j\,P_G\,k$), and then rises in someone's preferences, it *still* is strictly preferred; that is, the method of preference aggregation does not respond to this change in a perverse or negative manner. The second feature of condition M states that if two alternatives, j and k, are judged to be "socially indifferent" ($j\,I_G\,k$), and j then rises in an individual's preferences from below k to above k, j would now be *strictly* preferred to k by the group—$j\,P_G\,k$; in effect, this says that the decision procedure must be sensitive to changes in individual preferences (a knife-edge property).

We can now report two results. The first characterizes the method of majority rule (MMR):

May's Theorem. A method of preference aggregation over a pair of alternatives satisfies conditions U, A, N, and M if and only if it is MMR.

Kenneth May, a mathematician interested in social choice issues at about the time Arrow proved his famous theorem, established this especially clean and clear way of describing MMR. The theorem states, in essence, that if a group uses "counting noses" as its method of deciding between any pair of alternatives, then it necessarily satisfies the four conditions of May's Theorem. These four conditions *are* the method of majority rule.

Consequently, if in some circumstance you believe MMR is

inappropriate, then it must be because you think one of May's conditions should not hold. Should grades in the class for which you are reading this book be determined by a majority vote among the students? Should amendments to the U.S. Constitution be decided by majority rule? Should the captain of a pirate ship be elected by a majority of the pirates?[16] Should my breakfast cereal tomorrow morning be decided by a majority vote of my neighbors? Should family decisions be put to a majority vote? In each of these cases, there is bound to be some diversity of opinion. What May's Theorem permits each of us to do is to *defend* our opinion by saying why (if in the affirmative) we believe the four conditions in the theorem are apt or why (if in the negative) we believe at least one of the four conditions is unsuitable. Tell us why, for example, most of you believe MMR is inappropriate as a means for selecting an individual's morning repast.

There is more to the story, as given in the next theorem. Display 4.5 will allow you to keep track of the conditions upon which the theorems of Arrow and May are based (which by this point are probably overwhelming you if you never encountered them before). The theorem below shows that May's conditions, which are equivalent to the simple majority-rule group decision process, are but a special case of Arrow's conditions. This allows us to draw an obvious conclusion—majority rule must be a process vulnerable to the afflictions described by Arrow.

May's Corollary.[17] The conditions of May's Theorem are special cases of those of Arrow's Theorem:

May Condition		Arrow Condition
A	→	D
N	→	I
M	→	P

---

[16] Apparently this was the case on many pirate ships. Arrow's Theorem would lead one to believe either that there were many revolts against captains, or that an existing captain managed to control the agenda of subsequent votes.

[17] The "→" symbol means "logically implies."

DISPLAY 4.5
CONDITIONS CHARACTERIZING GROUP
DECISION-MAKING METHODS

Arrow	**May**
U (Universal Domain)	U (Universal Domain)
P (Unanimity)	A (Anonymity)
I (Independence from Irrelevant Alternatives)	N (Neutrality)
D (Nondictatorship)	M (Monotonicity)

It is pretty easy to see why the first implication in the corollary is true. If there were a dictator, then the condition of anonymity could hardly hold, since the group preference is produced by an *identifiable* individual; consequently if some procedure is anonymous, then it must be nondictatorial. The second and third implications are a little trickier to establish and so I implore the reader either to take the claims on faith or to consult May's original paper or Riker's discussion of it.[18]

Stringing together May's Theorem, Arrow's Theorem, and May's Corollary yields the result that MMR is but a special case of the aggregation mechanisms covered by the Arrow conditions and, therefore, is subject to the same vulnerabilities. Symbolically, we have:

MMR ↔ {U, A, N, M}   (May's Theorem)
{U, A, N, M} → {U, P, I, D}   (May's Corollary)
{U, I, P, D} → P_G violates the Rationality
                Assumption (Arrow's Theorem).

---

[18] Kenneth O. May, "A Set of Independent Necessary and Sufficient Conditions for Simple Majority Decision," *Econometrica* 20 (1952): 680–84; Riker, *Liberalism Against Populism*, chapter 3.

MMR is "equivalent"[19] to {U, A, N, M} from May's Theorem; these four conditions, in turn, imply the Arrow conditions from May's Corollary; and these latter conditions imply incoherent group preferences from Arrow's Theorem. Hence, MMR cannot assure coherent group choice—something we have already seen in practice several times.

Restrictions on the Arrow Conditions

What is to be done? I have claimed that the Arrow conditions and the May conditions—which are special cases of the Arrow conditions—are mild and innocuous requirements of fairness. But it may be somewhat misleading to suggest that *all* the conditions are, in fact, criteria of fairness. Condition P certainly is, since its claim is that it would be unfair if P_G failed to reflect whatever (unanimous) consensus exists among group members. If everyone thought j was better than k, then shouldn't the social preference be $j P_G k$? Likewise, condition D is a fairness requirement—allowing for a dictator is unfair prima facie. Condition I is intuitively less clearly a fairness requirement. It effectively requires that the group preference between any pair of alternatives, say j and k, depends *only* on the individual preferences between j and k. It is claimed that it would be "inappropriate" if individual preferences for irrelevant alternatives like h affected how j and k were ranked. In short, condition I says that the only "sensible" way to determine whether a group prefers j to k, k to j, or is indifferent between them is to ask each group member what his or her preference is between j and k. So, condition I is perhaps more fittingly thought of as a criterion of appropriateness or sensibleness, rather than of fairness. Nevertheless, it qualifies as a procedural requirement.

[19] That's what the double arrow means. That is, "↔" means both "→" (implies) and "←" (is implied by).

I → perhaps the Group Compromises?

It is difficult, then, to alter condition I, P, or D without at least having to present a compelling value-laden argument as to why a fair or procedurally appropriate criterion should be changed. Condition U, on the other hand, is an entirely different kind of condition. It is not a fairness criterion, nor a criterion of appropriateness or sensibleness. It is a *domain* requirement, and an especially wishful one at that. Essentially, it expresses the desire that the group decision mechanism work in all conceivable environments—that the mechanism have the widest possible domain. This is certainly desirable. But if we insist on this, then Arrow's Theorem tells us we will inevitably trade off fairness for consistency. Maybe we can do better by *not* insisting on condition U. That is, it may be possible to obtain *both* fairness *and* consistency, but in a restricted domain of circumstances. This insight, at any rate, provided the basis for several very interesting variations on the otherwise pessimistic conclusion of the Arrow result.

Single-Peakedness

This most famous domain restriction was invented, even before Arrow's Theorem, by the Scottish economist Duncan Black. He believed that minimal forms of consensus well short of unanimity might be sufficient to produce coherent group choice.[20] For example, consider the abortion issue in American politics over the last four decades. Opinion is quite polarized on a woman's options and rights. A sizable bloc of citizens, calling themselves pro-life, believes abortion should be prohibited in all circumstances (**L**). Another sizable group of citizens,

---

[20] Black was unable to serve in the British Army during World War II, so he took on voluntary night-watch duty in Scotland. Spending long nights in a bunker watching for German aircraft, his curious mind toyed with various geometric conditions that would enable majority rule to function smoothly. These ideas appeared in a series of papers at the end of the war. Their fullest statement is found in Black, *The Theory of Committees and Elections*.

calling themselves pro-choice, believes a woman has an absolute right of choice (**C**). In 1973 the U.S. Supreme Court articulated, in its famous *Roe v. Wade* decision, a compromise permitting abortions that are not late term (**R**). A third group of citizens is comfortable with this compromise position. Pro-life and pro-choice citizens have diametrically opposed preferences—**L** P_i **R** P_i **C** and **C** P_i **R** P_i **L**, respectively. Citizens who do not identify with the two extreme positions have either of two preference orderings—**R** P_i **L** P_i **C** or **R** P_i **C** P_i **L**. Notice that neither the two extreme groups nor the one in the middle regard **R** as the worst alternative; the extreme groups rank it second, while the moderates rank it first. Now, this sort of "consensus" is hardly earth-shattering, but in its most general form it is sufficient to assure that a group preference based on majority rule will be transitive.

> **Black's Single-Peakedness Theorem. Consider a set A of alternatives from which a group G of individuals must make a choice. If, for every subset of three alternatives in A, one of these alternatives is never worst among the three for any group member, then this is sufficient consensus so that the method of majority rule yields group preferences P_G that are transitive.**

The condition that some alternative from every collection of three alternatives in A is "not worst" for all group members is called the *single-peakedness condition*, because it means that there is a way to plot a preference curve for each group member that has a single peak in it. I will show this in the next chapter. Essentially the theorem says that majority rule works perfectly well, even when group members hold wildly divergent views on what the group ought to do, as long as a minimal degree of consensus, captured by single-peakedness, obtains.

Value Restriction

In a brilliant insight, the economist Amartya Sen asked, "What's so special about being 'not worst'?"[21] Consider the set of alternatives $A = \{a, b, c, d, e\}$. What if, for $\{a, b, c\}$, all the members of a group agreed that b was "not best"?[22] What if they agreed that c was "not middling"?[23] Indeed, what if for $\{a, b, c\}$ there was consensus that alternative a was "not worst," whereas for $\{b, c, d\}$ all group members agreed that d was "not best," and in $\{c, d, e\}$ the group members agreed that e was "not middling"? Sen refers to this as the *condition of value restriction*. A group's preferences are value restricted if, for every collection of three alternatives under consideration, all members of the group agree that one of the alternatives in this collection either is not best, not worst, or not middling (with all members agreeing on which quality the alternative in question was not). He proved a remarkable result, generalizing Black's Theorem:

Sen's Value-Restriction Theorem. The method of majority rule yields coherent group preferences if individual preferences are value restricted.

Both single-peakedness and value restriction circumscribe Arrow's universal domain condition, U. True enough, majority rule won't work in all situations. But in a surprisingly large number of such situations (204 of 216 in the three-person/three-alternative situation, recall), the kind of consensus required may, in fact, exist.

---

[21] "A Possibility Theorem on Majority Decision," *Econometrica* 34 (1966): 491–99.

[22] In terms of Display 4.2, agreement by group members that b was "not best" means that no member of the group had preference ordering 3, 4, 7, 9, or 11.

[23] Likewise, agreement by the group that c was "not middling" means that no group member had preference ordering 2 or 4 in Display 4.2.

Conclusion: The Illusiveness of Collective Clarity

There is much to digest in this chapter, and you should not be particularly alarmed if much of this material remains somewhat alien and unfamiliar to you. Since Arrow's famous theorem, social choice theory has become a technical language and style of analysis with which to explore features of group decision making with great care and precision. It also permits the careful consideration of significant facets of political philosophy concerning what democratic, majoritarian, institutional arrangements are capable of, as well as what meaning should attach to the outcomes they produce. In short, the literature on social choice is quite sophisticated and covers, in an entirely more analytical style, much of the same ground as the more qualitative work on democratic political philosophy.

As a practical matter, I hope the reader now appreciates the fact—probably not at all obvious or transparent before you read this chapter—that combining individual preferences into a group choice, by majority rule or some other method, is not a straightforward undertaking. One thing should be clear from even a quick and dirty read of the chapter: No method, no procedure, and no institutional arrangement that is *fair* in the most spartan, minimalist sense of this term is capable all the time of manufacturing the silk purse of group coherence from the sow's ear of individual coherence. Rationality may inhere in the tastes and values of individuals, but there is no magic wand that transforms this individual clarity about preferences into a collective clarity, especially when the group size is large, when individual preferences are heterogeneous, or when there is a large number of alternatives for group members to consider. This is the content and import of Arrow's Theorem. However, certain kinds of consensus—single-peakedness (Black) and value restriction (Sen)—lubricate the institutional gears of group choice processes.

These are not the last words on these subjects in this book. Indeed, they are only the first. Although this brief summary hardly covers the territory of social choice, don't hang up yet; the conversation continues in the next chapter.

PROBLEMS AND DISCUSSION QUESTIONS

1. Rational individual preferences can aggregate into irrational group preferences characterized by majority preference cycles. Are these preference cycles likely to be common according to social choice theory? If so, under what circumstances? Are such cycles frequent and visible occurrences in practice, or are there features of decision-making institutions that have reduced the apparent prevalence of group preference cycles? Describe some of these institutions and explain how they might provide "order" to an otherwise chaotic group decision-making process.

2. Consider the following two sets of individuals and their group preference rankings, aggregated using the same voting rule.

1. individual preferences: $x>y>z>w$, $y>z>w>x$, and $z>w>x>y$
   group preferences: $x>_G y$, $z>_G x$, $w>_G x$, $y>_G w$, $y>_G z$, and $z>_G w$
2. individual preferences: $y>z>x>w$, $y>w>x>z$, and $y>w>z>x$
   group preferences: $y>_G x$, $y>_G w$, $z>_G y$, $x>_G w$, $z>_G x$, and $z>_G w$

Which of Arrow's conditions (P, D, I, or Transitivity) is violated by their group preferences? (Hint: checking I requires *comparing* the outcomes in the two different groups to find a violation.)

3. For each of the following voting rules determine if it violates one of Arrow's conditions (P, D, or I): the method of majority rule, a round-robin tournament, the unanimity rule ($x\ P_G\ y$ if and only if at least one member of society strictly prefers x to y, and no members of society strictly prefer y to x), and the lexicographic rule (society adopts the preferences of the individual whose name comes first alphabetically). If not, give a simple example to show that it can generate preference cycles.

4. May's theorem suggests that any deviation from majority rule must be justified by a reasonable departure from one of four conditions: U, A, N, or M. For each of the following cases, explain which of these conditions is violated by the electoral rule, and suggest a possible justification: (a) the proposal of an amendment to the U.S. Constitution requires two-thirds support in each chamber of Congress; (b) the International Monetary Fund (IMF) uses a system of weighted voting where weights are determined by contributions to IMF operating funds. The United States also holds a veto in some circumstances; (c) a guilty verdict in a criminal case usually requires unanimity, or a large supermajority on the jury; (d) the French president is elected under two-stage majority rule. In the first stage, all parties' candidates compete against one another. A second stage takes place between the top two vote getters from stage one only if no candidate secured an outright majority in stage one.

*5. For each of the following societies, state whether the preferences satisfy Sen's value-restriction criterion, that is, that for any three outcomes, all voters agree that at least one of the outcomes is not first, middle, or last. If not, identify the tuple(s) of preferences that violate value-restricted preferences. Assuming that the voting rule is majority rule, are the group preferences in societies without value-restricted preferences transitive or intransitive?

Society 1:
$$y \, P_1 \, x \, P_1 \, z \, P_1 \, w$$
$$w \, P_2 \, y \, P_2 \, x \, P_2 \, z$$
$$z \, P_3 \, y \, P_3 \, w \, P_3 \, x$$

Society 2:
$$y \, P_1 \, w \, P_1 \, z \, P_1 \, x$$
$$w \, P_2 \, x \, P_2 \, y \, P_2 \, z$$
$$z \, P_3 \, w \, P_3 \, y \, P_3 \, x$$

Society 3:
$$y \, P_1 \, w \, P_1 \, z \, P_1 \, x$$
$$z \, P_2 \, x \, P_2 \, y \, P_2 \, w$$
$$x \, P_3 \, y \, P_3 \, w \, P_3 \, z$$

6. Explain the relevance of Arrow's Theorem for the following individuals: a social scientist trying to predict how a legislature will vote to divide up some new tax revenue; a committee trying to identify the perfect voting rule to avoid committee cycling and deadlock; a political theorist who defends democracy on the grounds that it is the only way to determine society's true preferences; and a jurist attempting to interpret the "legislative intent" of the coalition which passed a particular bill in Congress.

7. Arrow's Theorem suggests that there is a trade-off between the concentration of power and collective rationality. Explain this trade-off, and then provide a brief example using three individuals voting over three outcomes to illustrate. An alternative formulation is that Arrow's Theorem suggests a trade-off between fairness and consistency. Explain this trade-off, carefully describing the meaning of fairness and consistency under these circumstances.

5

Spatial Models of Majority Rule

The story line to this point has emphasized a trade-off in group decision making between the coherence of group choices on the one hand and the fairness of the method of decision making on the other. If we consider a limited domain of circumstances, then we may be able to avoid the pain of this trade-off. Put somewhat differently, if individual preferences happen to arrange themselves in particular ways—that reflect a consensus of a specific sort—then group decisions (certainly those made by majority rule) work out quite nicely. In the previous chapter, I described single-peaked preferences as one kind of consensus that facilitated coherence in majority-rule decision making. In this chapter I want to give an intuitive geometric characterization of this condition.

Frankly, however, all this gets pretty boring pretty quickly. The author, and perhaps some of the readers, may enjoy technical riffs and philosophical discourses, but most readers are more impatient and anxious to see some payoff. I think this chapter constitutes an important investment. Once I give single-peakedness a geometric representation I will be able to apply it to some interesting political situations—namely, two-party electoral competition and legislative committee decision making.

SPATIAL FORMULATION

The Simple Geometry of Majority Rule

Suppose a group's problem is, in effect, to pick a point on a line: the group must select some single numerical parameter. For example, a bank's board of directors must decide each week on the week's interest rate for thirty-year home mortgages. In effect, the relevant interest rates are points on a line, one endpoint being 0 percent and the other being some positive number, say 10 percent. This interval is written as [0, 10]. In this and other circumstances, I want the reader to imagine a group of individuals each of whom has a most-preferred point on the line and preferences that decline as points further away in either direction are taken up.

In Figure 5.1 the preferences of the five-person board of bank directors, $G = \{1, 2, 3, 4, 5\}$, are displayed. The board is meeting on Monday morning to decide the interest rate to

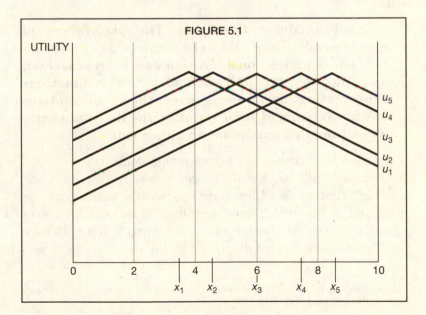

FIGURE 5.1

charge for home mortgages this coming week. Each individual $i \in G$ has a most-preferred point (also called *bliss point* or *ideal point*), labeled x_i, located on the [0, 10] interval (drawn as the horizontal axis), representing his or her most-preferred interest rate.[1] Thus, director 1 has a most-preferred interest rate (x_1) of just less than 4 percent, director 2's (x_2) is just more than 4 percent, and so on. On the vertical axis I have written the label "utility" to measure preferences. For each individual I have graphed a *utility function,* which represents the director's preferences for various interest rate levels in the [0, 10] interval. Naturally, the utility function, labeled u_i for Mr. or Ms. i, is highest for i's most-preferred alternative, x_i, and declines as more distant points are considered. Thus, Ms. 5 most prefers an interest rate a little higher than 8 percent, with her preference declining either for higher or lower rates. For obvious reasons (just look at the graphs) the preferences of these individuals are *single-peaked*, which is defined as follows:

> **Single-Peakedness Condition. The preferences of group members are said to be *single-peaked* if the alternatives under consideration can be represented as points on a line and each of the utility functions representing preferences over these alternatives has a maximum at some point on the line and slopes away from this maximum on either side.**

Is there any connection between this definition of single-peakedness and Black's definition given in the previous chapter? That is, do utility functions with a single peak, as displayed in Figure 5.1, have anything to do with all voters agreeing that some alternative is "not worst"? You bet! Take any three interest rates displayed in Figure 5.1—say, 3 per-

---

[1] Recall that "$i \in G$" means "the element i in the set G," where i stands for any one of the five bank directors.

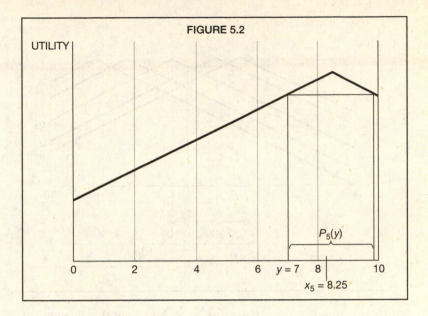

FIGURE 5.2

UTILITY

$P_5(y)$

0   2   4   6 $y = 7$ 8   10

$x_5 = 8.25$

cent, 5 percent, and 9 percent. It is pretty easy to see that
5 percent is not the worst among these three rates for any of
the five members of the group. Indeed, for any three interest
rate levels the reader chooses, one of those is not worst for any
of the five bankers. That's what single-peakedness means!

In order to develop some tools that will be used in subsequent analysis, let's look at one of these individual bankers in
isolation (by which we *really* mean let's look at an isolated
utility function). In Figure 5.2 we show the most mean-
spirited of the bank's directors, Ms. 5, who most prefers a
fairly high interest rate: x_5 = 8.25%. Consider an alternative
rate, y = 7%. The set of points Ms. 5 prefers to y is described by
the set labeled $P_5(y)$ in Figure 5.2. This is Ms. 5's preferred-
to-y set: if y were on offer, then $P_5(y)$ describes all the points
she would prefer to it, given her preferences. As the figure
shows, $P_5(y)$ is computed by determining the utility level for y

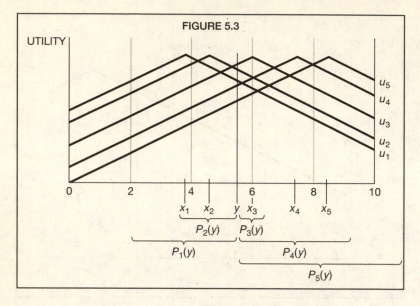

FIGURE 5.3

and then identifying all the interest rates on the horizontal axis with utility levels greater than the utility for y.[2]

In Figure 5.3 I display the preferred-to-y sets of all five bank directors (note that y, in this figure, is just below 6 percent). Notice that these sets overlap to some degree—there are points in common to $P_4(y)$ and $P_5(y)$, for example. This means that there are specific points that *both* Mr. 4 and Ms. 5 prefer to y.[3]

Of great interest to us is the set of points a majority prefers to y. This is called the *majority winset of y*, written as $W(y)$. We define it as follows. Let M be the set of majorities in our group of bankers, G; it is the collection of three-person coalitions (there are ten such coalitions), four-person coali-

---

[2] The endpoints of the preferred-to-y set are included even though, technically speaking, the group member ranks these endpoints at the *same* utility level as y.

[3] In set-theoretic notation, we can write these common points as the *intersection* of the two preferred-to-y sets: $P_4(y) \cap P_5(y)$. ($\cap$ is the intersection symbol, so that A$\cap$B means "the points in both set A and set B.")

DISPLAY 5.1
THE MAJORITY COALITIONS OF G = {1,2,3,4,5}

Size of Coalition	Coalitions
3	{1,2,3}, {1,2,4}, {1,2,5},
	{1,3,4}, {1,3,5}, {1,4,5}
	{2,3,4}, {2,3,5}, {2,4,5}
	{3,4,5}
4	{1,2,3,4}, {1,2,3,5}, {1,2,4,5}
	{1,3,4,5}, {2,3,4,5}
5	{1,2,3,4,5}

---

tions (there are five of these), and the coalition-of-the-whole. So, there are sixteen different majority coalitions in M; they are listed in Display 5.1. For each of these sixteen majority coalitions, consider the common intersection of preferred-to-y sets (if there is any); these are the points that this particular majority prefers to y. Thus, the members of the majority {3,4,5} in Figure 5.3 share points each prefers to y. Determine this set for each of the majority coalitions. Then take the union of these sixteen sets. This is $W(y)$.[4]

It is now rather straightforward to describe the coherent choices of groups. If some alternative, x, has an empty winset (written: $W(x) = \varnothing$, where $\varnothing$ means "empty" in set notation), then it is a clear candidate for the group choice. Why? Simply because $W(x) = \varnothing$ means there is no other alternative that any of the sixteen majority coalitions prefers to x. It's hard to deny choosing x if there is nothing any majority agrees on in its

---

[4] In Figure 5.3 it turns out that members of only *one* of the sixteen majorities, {3,4,5}, has overlapping $P_i(y)$ sets. Members of the remaining fifteen majorities (listed in Display 5.1) cannot agree on any points they jointly prefer to y. For any one of those fifteen, say, {1,2,4}, some members prefer only points to the left of y while others prefer only points to the right of y. As a group they cannot agree. Thus $W(y) = P_3(y) \cap P_4(y) \cap P_5(y)$.

place. On the other hand, if the winset of x is not empty ($W(x)$ $\neq \varnothing$), then it is hard to justify the choice of x. How can you choose x when some majority of the group clearly wants some other specific alternative? And if the winset is nonempty for *every* alternative, we have a problem: the group's preferences are incoherent, since some majority prefers something to every alternative available.

The question of the moment is whether, or in what circumstances, an x possessing an empty winset exists. If any complete and transitive preferences may be held by the individuals in G—Arrow's "universal domain" condition—then, as we have seen, the answer is "not necessarily." Why? Because under Arrow's condition U, it is possible for majority preferences to cycle, in which case $W(x) = \varnothing$ for *no* alternative. But if preferences are restricted, then a different answer is possible.

> **Black's Median-Voter Theorem. If members of group G have single-peaked preferences, then the ideal point of the median voter has an empty winset.**

One such group consisting of individuals with single-peaked preferences is pictured in Figure 5.3'. The median voter ideal point in this group is x_3 of Mr. 3.[5] The claim of Black's Theorem (the same Duncan Black, by the way, as in the previous chapter) is that $W(x_3) = \varnothing$, and that x_3 is the majority choice.

We can prove this theorem using the example of the five bank board members. Consider any arbitrary point in the feasible set of interest rates, [0, 10], to the left of x_3—say the point labeled α in Figure 5.3'. Notice that α is preferred to x_3 by members 1 and 2, since x_3 is not in either $P_1(\alpha)$ or $P_2(\alpha)$, but x_3 is preferred to α by members 3, 4 and 5. Thus, x_3 is

---

[5] The median of a set ordered from left to right is the point such that at least half the points are at or to its right and at least half the points are at or to its left.

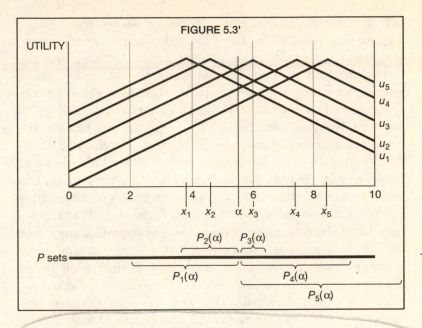

FIGURE 5.3'

majority-preferred to α. But α is any arbitrary point to the left of x_3. For any such point, we know at the very least that members 3, 4, and 5 will prefer x_3 to it. (It is possible that some of the remaining members will share this preference, too.) Next, consider any arbitrary point to the right of x_3 (not pictured). Members 4 and 5 may prefer it to x_3, but members 1, 2, and 3 hold the opposite preference, so that x_3 is majority-preferred. The argument is exactly the same as with α above, since we selected an arbitrary alternative to the right of x_3. To sum up, we now know that the ideal point of the median voter is preferred by a majority to *any* arbitrary point to the right or to the left of it, that is, to all remaining points. Hence, it has an empty winset and is the majority choice.

Before complicating this key result, I should mention that there are three hidden assumptions, and probably more besides, that warrant some discussion. First, in the example, the group G of bankers is *odd* in number. Thus, in Figures 5.3 and

Please explain further

5.3' the displays of five group members possessed a unique median—x_3. What if the size of the group were *even*? Suppose, for instance, that Ms. 5 in either figure is ignored and the focus is instead on the truncated group $G' = \{1, 2, 3, 4\}$. Now members 2 and 3 are both medians. Moreover, since it takes three votes to constitute a majority, it is true that $W(x_2) = \emptyset$ and that $W(x_3) = \emptyset$, too. Indeed, the winset of *any* point in the interval between the two, $[x_2, x_3]$, is empty. Technically, then, Black's Median-Voter Theorem is true whether the group size is odd or even. But, as has just been shown, when a group has an even number of members, then more than one alternative can have the property that it cannot be beaten. This follows because of the possibility of tie votes. For example, suppose x and y each defeat every other alternative in $\{x, y, z, w, u, v\}$ by a simple majority, but tie when paired against each other. Then neither x nor y can be beaten. This absence of a unique winner is a pain in the neck. It is a bit like more than one pre-tender to the throne, or more than one person claiming to be king of the mountain. It is for this reason that groups estab-lish some procedure for breaking ties *well in advance* of any substantive deliberations or, better yet, that they make sure that the group is odd in number.[6]

Second, *full participation* is assumed. Everyone with the franchise is assumed to exercise it. Of course, in any particu-lar instance of group choice this need not happen. If bank board members 4 and 5 oversleep one week, then Ms. 2 be-comes the median voter of the now reduced three-person board; if members 1 and 3 are out of town the following week, then Mr. 4 becomes the median. In each of these cases, as well

---

[6] For example, the U.S. Constitution *requires* the Senate to have an even number but establishes a tiebreaking procedure. The vice president of the United States, sitting as the president of the Senate, is allowed to vote only in case of a tie. Likewise, the standing rules of the House of Representatives, which has an odd number, provide a tiebreaking rule, asserting that a mo-tion *fails* if it obtains no more yeas than nays—it fails on a tie.

as in the case of the full board, the median-voter result applies. *Who* the median is, however, depends upon who the participants in the group are. We may forecast the group decision if we make *assumptions* about participation (for example: assume everyone votes), or we may make forecasts *contingent* on participation (for example, if 4 and 5 oversleep, then we predict x_2 will be the group's choice; but if everyone votes, then x_3 is the predicted choice).

Third, it is assumed that those exercising the franchise do so *sincerely*. But as we have seen in earlier chapters, group members will have occasion and incentive to misrepresent their preferences and not reveal them honestly. This is a subject of great interest that we take up on its own in Chapter 6.

The (Slightly) More Complicated Geometry of Majority Rule

One-dimensional models of choice with the single-peakedness condition permit rather sophisticated ways to think about real politics. They generate very crisp expectations about how politics in these settings gets played out. But many social situations cannot be reduced to one-dimensional affairs.

Recall the game of "divide the dollars." If the game were played by a group of three individuals, then it is necessary to have *two* dimensions in which to represent outcomes. The first dimension gives the amount that player 1 receives, while the second dimension gives the amount that player 2 receives. (Subtract the sum of these two numbers from the total number of dollars to be divided and you get the amount that player 3 receives.[7]) I hope I convinced the reader earlier that games of division, like "divide the dollars," are commonplace in political life. So it must be conceded that as crisp and as sophisti-

---

[7] Generally, when dividing a fixed pie among n categories (or people), we need only $n-1$ dimensions to display all outcomes.

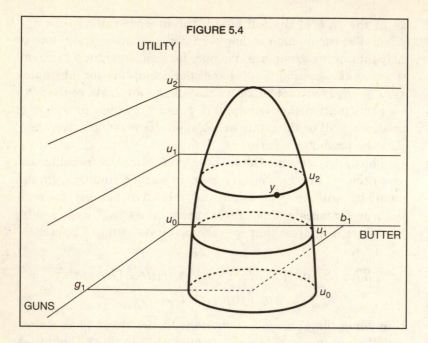

FIGURE 5.4

cated as the one-dimensional models are, they are *special cases* of a more general multidimensional arrangement. We need to see what this more general arrangement is like.

Most of what needs to be said is covered by focusing on a two-dimensional circumstance, like that pictured in Figure 5.4. (There are actually *three* dimensions in this figure, but this will be clarified shortly.) Let's consider a problem in budgeting, in which a group of legislators, perhaps an appropriations committee, must decide how to divide expenditures between "guns" and "butter" (symbolizing the competition between defense and other domestic programs). Outcomes, then, are described by two numbers: dollars spent on butter and dollars spent on guns. The set of outcomes, or simply the "policy space," is two-dimensional, and this is the domain over which preferences are expressed.[8] The third dimension of Figure 5.4, marked "utility," permits us to draw three-dimensional graphs of legislator preferences. As earlier, a legislator is assumed to have an ideal point in the policy space. His preference function, or utility function, is at a maximum over this point. It is assumed further (in most of the applications) that preferences decline with "distance" from the legislator's ideal point. A typical legislator, with a typical ideal point and preference function, is displayed in Figure 5.4. The legislator's preference function is a "hump" that reaches its highest utility level just over his ideal point in which b_1 dollars are spent on butter and g_1 dollars on guns. This ideal point, (b_1, g_1), is located in the plane of the butter-guns policy space.

A more convenient way to represent precisely this same information, however, is given in Figure 5.5. In this figure the reader is looking down directly onto the plane of the butter-guns policy space. It is as though you are hovering in a helicopter above the peak of the preference hump in Figure 5.4. The location of our typical legislator's ideal point is exactly the same as in Figure 5.4. But instead of adding a third dimension (coming out of the page toward you) in order to graph his preference function, we instead overlay "slices" of his utility function onto the policy space, producing the set of nested circles called *indifference curves*. Each circle is a slice of the policy hump in Figure 5.4. It is a locus of policy outcomes among which the legislator is indifferent (since all the points on a circle lie on the same slice and hence at the same height on the utility function of Figure 5.4). Since distance from an ideal point is a measure of preference, points on a circle centered on

---

[8] If the size of the budget were fixed in advance, then by the argument in the previous paragraph and footnote, only *one* dimension would be needed, say, dollars for defense; once this is established, dollars for domestic programs is strictly determined—it's what is left over. When the budget is *not* determined in advance, then we need *both* dimensions to display all outcomes.

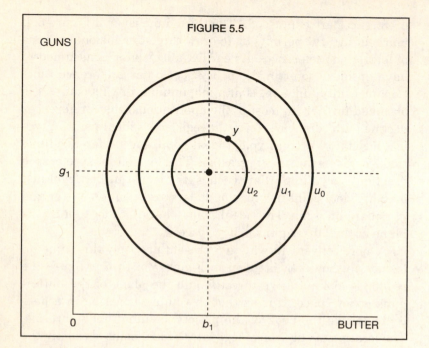

FIGURE 5.5

GUNS

g_1

y

u_2 u_1 u_0

0   b_1 BUTTER

her ideal, being equidistant from that ideal, are equally preferred by her. The logic is the same in comparing a point on
one circle to that on another. A legislator prefers a point on a
circle with a *smaller* radius to one on a circle with a larger radius, because this means the former point is closer to her ideal
than is the latter point.[9]

Notice the point labeled y in Figure 5.5. The circle through

[9] In this simplest of multidimensional setups, in which the policy space is
two-dimensional and preference is measured by distance, indifference
curves will be circles centered on the legislator's ideal point. In more than
two dimensions, the indifference "contours" will be spheres or (in four or
more dimensions) hyperspheres. A second sort of complication, which applies
in the (simplest) two-dimensional as well as higher-dimensional situations,
is to allow preferences to be related to distance, but in a more complicated
way. One dimension of policy may be "more important" to a legislator than
another dimension. Thus, movement away from her ideal point along one dimension will have a greater impact on utility than an identical movement

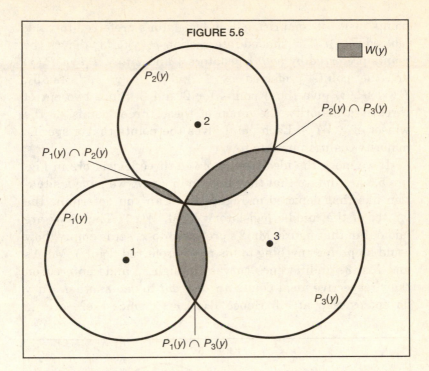

FIGURE 5.6

y centered on our legislator's ideal point, as we just determined above, contains all the points of legislator indifference
to *y*. This means that all the points *inside* the circle, being
closer to her ideal, are actually *preferred* by her to *y*. That is,
we can call the points inside the circle our legislator's
preferred-to-*y* set, a natural generalization of that same concept in the one-dimensional development earlier in this chapter. Figure 5.6 displays three legislator ideal points and each
legislator's indifference curve through *y* (the curve plus all

---

along the other dimension. Put differently, preference is said in this instance
to decline with *weighted* distance from the ideal (where the weights reflect
the salience of each dimension to the legislator). In this instance, indifference contours will no longer be circles, but will be *ellipses* instead. I will
stick with the most basic formulation.

points inside it comprising each legislator's preferred-to-y set, labeled $P_i(y)$). The shaded intersection $P_1(y) \cap P_2(y)$ gives the points preferred by *both* legislators 1 and 2 to y; $P_1(y) \cap P_3(y)$ are the points preferred by 1 and 3 to y; and, finally, $P_2(y) \cap P_3(y)$ give those points for 2 and 3. Since two out of three is a majority, the union of these three "petals" is the winset of y, $W(y)$. Each petal gives the points that a specific majority coalition prefers to y.

If we move the ideal points of the three legislators in Figure 5.6 around, so that they line up in a row, we have a situation like that depicted in Figure 5.7. Can you determine the winset of the middle legislator's ideal, $W(x_2)$? The steps are laid out in that figure. Mr. 2's preferred-to-x_2 set is empty (how could he prefer anything to his most-preferred point?). Ms. 1's and Ms. 3's indifference curves through x_2 and centered on their respective ideal points are *tangent* to one another. They do not overlap at all. Hence $W(x_2) = \varnothing$, since there are no

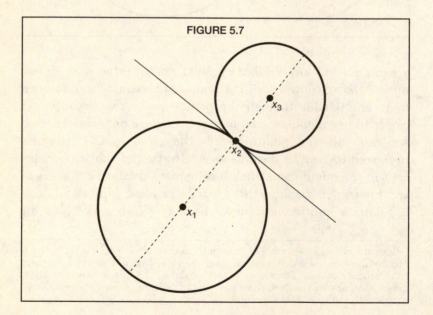

FIGURE 5.7

points preferred to x_2 by majority {1,2}, {1,3}, {2,3}, or {1,2,3}. That is, the members of no majority coalition have preferred-to-x_2 sets that intersect. Thus, x_2 is the majority choice.

Another look at Figure 5.7 should show why this happened. Consider the bold line through x_2 perpendicular to the dashed line. On the x_1 side of this bold line, for any selected point off the dashed line, x_2 is closer to x_3 than the selected point is. So a majority, {2,3}, prefers x_2 to any such point. From a precisely parallel argument, a majority, {1,2}, prefers x_2 to any point off the dashed line on the x_3 side of the bold line. So, the only points that remain are those *on* the dashed line. That is, even though the group choice problem is *actually* two-dimensional, individual preferences line up so as to make the problem *effectively* one-dimensional. On this line individual legislators have single-peaked preferences (the reader should convince herself of this), with x_2 the median ideal point. Hence, Black's Median-Voter Theorem applies, which is precisely what Figure 5.7 demonstrates.

Having the legislator ideal points line up is pretty convenient, isn't it? Pretty unlikely, too. Certainly it seems more unlikely than arbitrary configurations such as that in Figure 5.6. Thus, while we have tools like Black's Median-Voter Theorem with which to analyze majority rule in one-dimensional settings, it is probably fair to say that many interesting political circumstances are genuinely multidimensional. Can we say anything about the prospects for a majority choice in multiple dimensions? The answer is yes, but the news is not very good.

The highly unlikely distribution of individual preferences in Figure 5.7 provides a basis for generalization. What allows the ideal point of Mr. 2 to emerge as the majority choice is the fact that the ideals of the others are "symmetrically" distributed about 2's ideal. From Mr. 2's ideal, any movement away from it is obviously opposed by Mr. 2 himself; but it is also always opposed by at least one of the other guys. In fact, as we saw when considering the bold line through x_2 perpendicular to the dashed line containing all three ideal points, any point on Ms. 3's side of that line is less preferred than x_2 by 1 and 2, and any point on Ms. 1's side of the line is less preferred than x_2 by 2 and 3.

Now let's add two more voters to the picture that are symmetrical in precisely the same way (Figure 5.8). Voters 2, 4, and 5 lie on a line, just as 1, 2, and 3 do. It is still the case that $W(x_2) = \varnothing$, because any departure from x_2 is opposed by at least three of the five voters. You may test this proposition out for yourself by laying a straightedge through x_2 at any angle. There are always two voters who would like to move to some point on one side of the straightedge, two who would like to move to points on the other side of the straightedge, and one (Mr. 2) perfectly content to stay at x_2. Since no majority favors moving in any direction (there are always three votes against), the winset of x_2 is empty. Something about distributing voters symmetrically around a common point seems to be producing a coherent majority choice.

Indeed, we can be very specific here. Let us consider a set of m voters (where m is any number, which we will take to be odd to simplify the presentation), whose ideal points are x_1, x_2, . . . , x_n. These m ideal points are in a multidimensional policy space, like the one pictured in Figure 5.8 (although the results presented below apply to policy spaces of more than two dimensions as well). These ideal points are distributed in a *radially symmetric* fashion if the following conditions hold: (1) There is a distinguished ideal point, labeled x^*; (2) the $n-1$ remaining ideal points can be divided into pairs (since n is odd, $n-1$ is even and this is possible); and (3) the two ideal points in any pair, say x_i and x_j, plus x^* all lie on a line with x^* "between" x_i and $x_j$yj. In Figure 5.8, x_2 is the distinguished point, x_1-x_3 and x_4-x_5 are the pairs of remaining ideal points, and x_2 lies on a line "between" the ideal points in each pair. Notice that radial symmetry does not require the two ideal

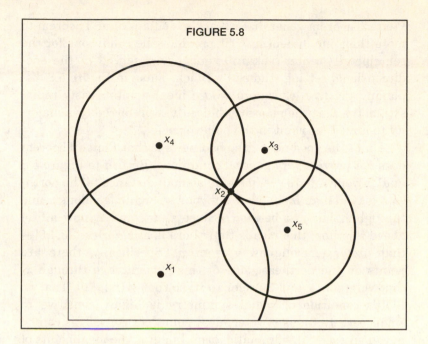

FIGURE 5.8

points of a pair to be equidistant from the distinguished point (x_3 is closer to x_2 than x_1 is); they must simply line up.

The economist Charles Plott noticed that radial symmetry of ideal points captured in higher dimensions a property that single-peaked preferences possess in one-dimensional policy spaces. In a famous paper in 1967,[10] he established the following result:

> **Plott's Theorem.** **If voters possess distance-based spatial preferences, and if their ideal points are distributed in a radially symmetric fashion with x^* the distinguished ideal point, and the number of voters is odd, then W(x^*) = $\varnothing$.**

[10] Charles R. Plott, "A Notion of Equilibrium and Its Possibility under Majority Rule," *American Economic Review* 57 (1967): 787–806.

Plott's Theorem generalizes Black's Median-Voter Theorem to more than one dimension.[11] It provides the conditions for the centripetal ("center-seeking") tendency observed in the one-dimensional setting studied by Black. Thus, in Figure 5.8 displaying the five legislators whose ideal points satisfy radial symmetry, x_2 is the majority choice. It is preferred by a majority to any other point in the policy space.

That's the good news. The bad news is that Plott's Theorem does not provide very general conditions. Return to Figure 5.8 and, in your mind's eye, move x_4 a small distance to the northeast (say half an inch). Now lay your straightedge along a line through x_2 but just below x_5. Since x_3, x_4, and x_5 now all lie above this line, this means that there is a majority—{3,4,5}— that prefers moving away from x_2. Specifically, there are points on the northeast side of this straightedge through x_2 that voters 3, 4, and 5 prefer to it, so that $W(x_2) \neq \varnothing$. That is, Plott's condition of radial symmetry is highly sensitive to small perturbations of voter ideal point locations. This can be put in an especially dramatic form. Imagine the ideal points of 1,000,000 voters radially distributed around the ideal point of the 1,000,001st voter. So, $W(x_{1,000,001}) = \varnothing$, in accord with Plott's Theorem. Now suppose two new voters move into the community, *and their ideal points are not radially symmetric about* $x_{1,000,001}$. This small perturbation in the voting situation—after all, how much effect can the introduction of two new voters have in a voting population of more than one million?—completely destroys the previous equilibrium.[12]

---

[11] One result is said to "generalize" another when the latter is a special case of the former. Thus, Black's median-voter result is the one-dimensional version of Plott's Theorem, in which the median voter's ideal is the distinguished point and pairs of voter ideal points, one from each side of the median, are distributed around it in a radially symmetric fashion.

[12] The sensitivity is not quite so severe when the number of voters is even. In this case the distinguished point is *not* a voter ideal point. Some shifts in voter ideal points are possible without disturbing the empty winset property of this distinguished point.

If departures from radial symmetry were relatively unusual events, then this sensitivity to ideal point distributions
in Plott's Theorem would not really be bad news. But, as the
reader may grasp intuitively, the requirement of radial symmetry is actually quite restrictive; one would not expect groups
"naturally" to have their preferences distributed in so elegant
and uniform a manner as this. So departures from this condition take on a greater significance. In what is one of the most
remarkable theoretical statements in this entire field, Richard
McKelvey demonstrated exactly how significant these departures from radial symmetry are.

McKelvey's Chaos Theorem.[13] **In multidimensional
spatial settings, except in the case of a rare distribution of ideal points (like radial symmetry) that
hardly ever occurs naturally, there will be no majority rule empty-winset point. Instead there will be
chaos—no Condorcet winner, anything can happen,
and whoever controls the order of voting can determine the final outcome.**

I started out by seeking ways to restrict Arrow's universal-
domain condition to see if there were narrower domains in
which majority rule worked tolerably well. In one-dimensional
choice situations, we saw that single-peakedness is sufficient.
In multidimensional situations, a radially symmetric distribution of ideal points is sufficient. But small departures from the
latter throw everything into chaos. No point is the "king of the
mountain" in the sense that it is preferred by a majority to all
contenders, so it is difficult to justify any particular group
choice (since for any proposed choice there is some alternative
a majority prefers to it). This, in turn, means that there will
always be majority cycles.

[13] Richard D. McKelvey, "Intransitivities in Multidimensional Voting Models,"
Journal of Economic Theory 12 (1976): 472–82.

Indeed, McKelvey establishes that all the points are in one great big cycle. What this means, practically speaking, is that the situation is ripe for manipulation by whoever controls the agenda. What McKelvey shows is this: Pick any two points in the policy space—call them s (starting point) and t (terminating point). Then there is a sequence of points— $z_1, z_2, \ldots, z;zk$ (for some finite number, k) such that $z_1 P_G s$, $z_2 P_G z_1$, $z_3 P_G z_2$, $\ldots$, $z_k P_{G\ k-1}$, and $t\ P_G\ z_k$. That is, from any starting point, there is a sequence of votes by which a majority will move the outcome to *any* terminal point (including, say, the ideal point of the agenda setter).

This is illustrated in Figure 5.9 for a three-person legislature. The ideal points of the three legislators are x_1, x_2, and x_3. The point s is the status quo ante. If Mr. 3 were the agenda setter empowered to make motions and order them in a voting sequence, then he could, in a small number of steps—in fact, in only *three* steps—drive the outcome to x_3, his ideal point. First he proposes z_1, which both Mr. 1 and Ms. 2 prefer to s. So $z_1 P_G s$. Then he proposes z_2, which both he and Mr. 1 prefer to z_1; so $z_2 P_G z_1$. Then, in the final step, he proposes his ideal point, x_3, which both he and Ms. 2 prefer to z_2. Voila! He has driven the legislative process, by artfully choosing the alternatives upon which to vote, to a terminal outcome located at his ideal policy: $t = x_3$.[14]

APPLICATIONS

Applications of the spatial model are so plentiful and rich that it is hard to know where to start. I begin at the beginning, so

---

[14] It should be noted that the members of each majority coalition in this example blindly vote their preferences, like lambs following the judas goat to slaughter. The legislators seem like putty in the hands of the wily agenda setter, Mr. 3. In the next chapter, we will endow "followers" with some sophistication by which they might be able to control their "leader."

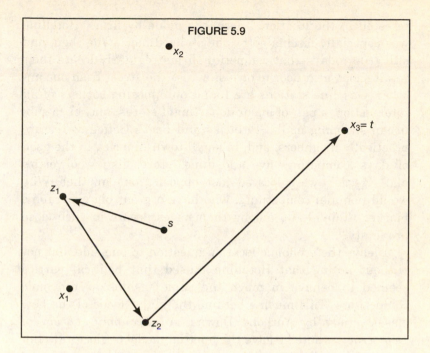

FIGURE 5.9

to speak, with Downs's model of electoral competition. Anthony Downs was one of the first scholars to use the spatial model for political analysis. This application also demonstrates both the strengths and weaknesses of the simplifying assumption that the political world can be modeled as one-dimensional. Then we will turn our spotlight on institutional analysis, looking at both a one-dimensional and multidimensional analysis of legislative politics.

Spatial Elections

The real origins of the spatial model are found in a famous paper written in 1929 by Harold Hotelling.[15] An economist in-

---

[15] "Stability in Competition," *Economic Journal* 39 (1929): 41–57.

terested in the locational decisions made by firms, Hotelling was especially fascinated by the stylized fact—true then, and still true today—that competitor firms regularly locate their retail shops next door to or just across the street from one another. Gasoline stations are found on opposing corners of an intersection, a pair of major department stores "anchor" a suburban shopping mall, Starbucks and Peet's Coffee & Tea are practically neighbors, and, in small-town America in the good ol' days, competing "five and dime" stores like Woolworth's and Kresge's were located just opposite one another. Why would nominal competitors, who have a great big geographic market to divide up among themselves, locate in such close proximity?[16]

I leave the economic location question to one side, but not without noting that Hotelling mused that political parties seemed to behave in much the same fashion as economic competitors. This musing became the major focus of the now classic study by Anthony Downs, *An Economic Theory of Democracy*, where he gave the "spatial model of electoral competition" its fullest development and exposure.[17]

The "spatial" part of Downs's spatial model consists of a one-dimensional ideological continuum, [0, 100]. The continuum is scaled by the proportion of economic activity left in the hands of the private sector, so that the left endpoint reflects a fully socialized economy, while the right endpoint is identified with a totally private-enterprise economy. While political competition in real life consists of taking positions on and articulating visions about a host of political issues, Downs supposes that, when all is said and done, political debate boils down to ideology—do you want some good, service, or purpose provided

---

[16] Even more spectacular in many cities is a small stretch of a major highway along which dozens of automobile dealerships locate.

[17] Anthony Downs, *An Economic Theory of Democracy* (New York: Harper & Row, 1957).

by government or by the private sector? Political competition, then, is a contest between politicians intent upon capturing control of government by appealing to voters with offers of alternative plans, platforms, programs—indeed visions. These appeals are identified with different points on the left-right ideological continuum.

As a first approximation for the hurly-burly of campaigning, electioneering, and voting, this is not a bad one. Politicians are conceived of as single-minded seekers of election. They are graduates, so to speak, of the Vince Lombardi School of Politics, whose motto is, "Winning isn't everything; it's the only thing."[18] Downs assumed politicians seek to maximize *votes*, although in variations on his model, politicians alternatively maximize their vote plurality (the difference between their vote and that of their closest competitor) or their probability of winning. In any event, most early spatial models of electoral competition took votes to be the coin of the realm, regarded politicians as focused exclusively on winning elections, and suggested that they did so by promising policies, platforms, and programs that attracted voters. In this spatial context, a candidate is represented by some location on the ideological continuum, some point in the [0, 100] interval. This is his or her political position.

Voters, Downs assumed, were single-mindedly interested in policy: the goods and services produced by government (or left to the private sector); the form and content of government regulation of the private sector; the distribution of tax, unem-

---

[18] For those too young to remember, Vince Lombardi was the legendary football coach of the Green Bay Packers and, at the end of his career, the Washington Redskins. To Lombardi, nothing was more important than winning. While not exactly an uplifting imperative, Lombardi's maxim is a pretty good first approximation for what it takes to succeed in the national politics of most countries, the business world, and the National Football League. (By the way, though associated with Lombardi, it is not clear he really ever said this!)

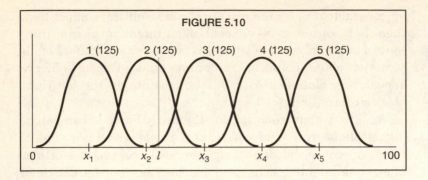

FIGURE 5.10

ployment, and inflation burdens; government policies on social issues like abortion and divorce; and matters of war and peace. Voters care mightily about these matters and base their assessments of candidates accordingly. Voters, however, are heterogeneous in their tastes so, just as there are left-wing and right-wing politicians, there are left-wing and right-wing voters. Specifically, each voter is identified with some point in the [0, 100] ideological space—the voter's ideal point—and his or her preferences are assumed to decline for points more and more distant from this ideal. That is, the set of voters may be represented by single-peaked preferences. Figure 5.10 displays an electorate of 625 voters (actually, five different voter "types" with 125 voters of each type). A voter of type i (i = 1,2,3,4,5) has ideal point x_i, and preferences declining in distance from x_i.

The most famous version of the Downsian model involves two-candidate competition. The question Downs asks is: Given a distribution of voters like that in Figure 5.10, where will two single-minded seekers of election locate themselves? We can gain some insight into this question by fixing the position of one of the candidates. Let's fix the position of L, the leftie candidate, at l as shown in the figure. What position, r, should R, the rightie candidate, adopt so as to maximize his votes? To answer this question we need a rule of calculation. The Downsian rule is that each voter votes for the candidate whose location is closest to his or her ideal point.[19]

We can now answer the questions posed in the previous paragraph. Candidate R should snuggle up infinitesimally close to the right-hand side of L. That way, R gets all the votes to the right of l and, since l is to the left of the midpoint of the voter distribution, that means that R gets more than half of all the votes.[20] That is, R gets the 375 votes from voters of types 3, 4, and 5; L gets the 250 votes of types 1 and 2. Put more generally, L's location divides the electorate into two groups: those with ideals less than l and those with ideals greater than l. R's optimal response is an r just next to l on the side of the larger group. We have thus figured out how R will respond to any move made by L. L thus knows that her position will divide the electorate into two groups and she will get the *smaller* group. Given that she, too, wants to maximize votes, she should try to make this smaller group as large as possible. She can do this, the reader may have guessed, by setting l equal to the ideal point of the median voter, since the groups to the left and right would then be equal in size. If l and r just straddle the ideal point of the median voter, x_3, then each location is optimal against the other's and the election ends in a virtual tie.

We draw precisely the same conclusion if we fix R's position first and let L respond optimally. For any r chosen by R, L will set l just next to r on the side of the larger group. Under

[19] For any two candidate positions, say, α and β in [0, 100], where α is to the left of β, the midpoint is $(\alpha + \beta)/2$. The candidate located at α receives the votes of all voters with ideals to the left of this midpoint, whereas the candidate located at β gets the votes of all voters with ideals to the right of this midpoint. Voters at the midpoint are indifferent between the two candidates, since their positions are an identical distance from these voters' ideals; these voters flip coins to decide for whom to vote.

[20] If l happened to be to the right of the midpoint of the voter distribution, then R would maximize his votes by squeezing up against L on its left side, thereby getting a majority of the votes.

these circumstances, the best R can do is to "move to the median."

Finally, suppose L and R must announce their policy platforms simultaneously. Once a policy is announced, if a candidate is "stuck" with the position for the duration of the campaign, then he or she is likely to worry that his or her position is vulnerable. A position is vulnerable if the opponent's position lies between it and the median of the voter distribution, since, by the Downsian rule of calculation, the opponent will then get more than half the votes.[21] The only position that *cannot* be vulnerable is one that actually is at the median ideal. If, on the other hand, candidates are not stuck with their announced positions but can revise their policy platforms during the course of a campaign, one of two patterns will be observed. If both initial announcements are on the same side of the median ideal, then there will be a "leapfrogging" converging pattern as the vulnerable position (as just defined) leapfrogs over her opponent's position in order to be closer to the median, that position in turn is leapfrogged over by the now vulnerable opponent, and so on until there is no more leapfrogging to do—namely when both positions have converged upon the median. If, on the other hand, initial announcements are on opposite sides of the median ideal point, then there will be a homing in on the median from each side as the one more distant moves closer.[22]

In all of these circumstances, each a slightly different modeling assumption about the sequence in which various events take place in the course of a campaign, there is a common convergence on the ideal point of the median voter. And this *centripetal* tendency is precisely what is predicted by Black's

[21] Indeed, a position is vulnerable if the opponent's position is *closer* to the median. The position closest to the median wins more than half the votes.

[22] Of course, if politicians are perfectly informed about voter preferences, they won't need to proceed tentatively toward the median, whether by leapfrogging or homing in; instead, they can move directly to the median.

Median-Voter Theorem. In effect, Downs's model provides a rationale for why majoritarian politics is centripetal.[23]

The logic of Black's theorem, as elaborated in the electoral context by Downs, reminds me of those occasions when someone says something very intelligent and quite obvious (once it is said!), causing you to reflect, "Now why didn't I think of that?" Downs was motivated by the fact that so many foreign observers of American life had, since practically the beginning of the Republic, noted how similar America's political parties were: "Tweedledum and Tweedledee," empty bottles differing only in their labels.[24] More recently, observers of British politics have begun to notice that the losing party ultimately transforms itself to look at least a bit like its more successful opponent. Thus, in the postwar period, British Tories have accepted a good deal of the welfare state championed by the Labour Party, whereas, in the latter part of the twentieth century, Labour has trimmed its more socialist sails in order to look to voters a bit more like Margaret Thatcher's and John Major's Conservative Party. In the twenty-first century, both parties struggle toward the center, neither bearing the extremist trappings that once described them.

The centripetal forces Downs identified are certainly plau-

---

[23] Notice that the rationale is not that the middle is "where the votes are." Certainly this may be true; in many circumstances the middle of the spectrum is where most persons' preferences lie, with the numbers getting smaller as one moves toward the more extremist tails of the distribution. But go back to Figure 5.10 and suppose that the extremists are the more plentiful. That is, suppose types 1 and 5 have 250 voters each, types 2 and 4 have 62 voters each, and type 3 consists of a single voter. Will the Downsian logic recounted above be any different here? No. The centripetal pull is the same, even though the "center" is *least populated* with voters!

[24] It might interest the reader to know that Downs's book originated as a doctoral dissertation in economics at Stanford University, where a member of Downs's dissertaion committee was Kenneth Arrow. So, Downs had both cycles and instability à la Arrow's Theorem on one side and their opposite— stylized facts about stable party configurations—on the other. His research sought to make sense of these seemingly incompatible matters. Single-peakedness did the job.

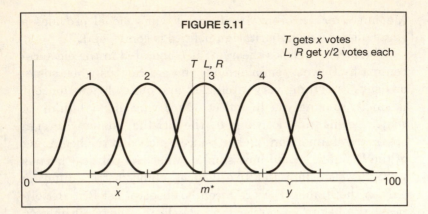

FIGURE 5.11

T gets x votes
L, R get y/2 votes each

sible, yet it is clear that parties do not converge all the time. Why might this be? Downs's spatial model is quite user-friendly as a "discovery tool," so we can vary some of its assumptions and see what happens. Suppose, for example, we do not foreordain that there are two candidates. What if Leftie (*L*) and Rightie (*R*) are not the only two kids on the block? There is a third candidate—call her Trey (*T*)—who may enter the race if she thinks she has a chance. Well, if *L* and *R* locate at the median (call it m^*)—$l = r = m^*$—and if, when there are more than two candidates, the one with the *most* votes (not necessarily a majority) wins the election, then *T* certainly does have a chance. She can locate close on one side or the other of the median, win nearly all the votes on that side, and thus defeat *L* and *R*, who end up splitting the remaining votes (Figure 5.11). On the other hand, if the positions of *L* and *R* are sufficiently widely dispersed, then *T* can enter *between* them at some position *t*. She will get the votes of voters whose ideal points lie in the interval $[(l + t)/2, (t + r)/2]$. The left boundary of this interval is the midpoint between the positions of *L* and *T*, whereas the right boundary is the midpoint between the positions of *T* and *R*. By the same Downsian rule of calculation, L gets all the voters in the interval $[0, (l + t)/2]$, and R gets all the voters in $[(t + r)/2, 100]$. If there are more voters in the first interval than in the second or in the third, then *T* wins. So, when there is the possibility of entry, *L* and *R* can locate neither too closely together nor too far apart.

In fact, there may be a set of *entry-deterrence* locations for *T* and *R*, with these two getting roughly the same number of votes, and no third candidate able to locate in any place that would give her a victory (thereby discouraging her from entering at all). The point here is that when we broaden Downs's initial model to take account of some factor he had omitted—the possibility of entry by a third candidate—we discover that there may be occasions and circumstances in which the established parties (*T* and *R*) are ill-advised to converge toward the median.

Research has, in fact, been conducted on precisely the issue of Downsian candidate competition with (prospective) entry.[25] As noted, it is clearly one extension of the original Downsian assumptions that produces the possibility of nonconvergent candidate locations. But there are other possibilities. Candidates, for instance, may have their own policy preferences, ones often known to the voters. Thus, suppose *T* and *R* have their own policy ideal points at l^* and r^*, respectively (shown in Figure 5.12). They may declare policy programs at other locations, say, $l \neq l^*$ and $r \neq r^*$. But why should the voters believe these policy declarations? It's not necessary to be altogether cynical to believe that once one of them wins, she or he will be sorely tempted to implement her or his preferred policy (l^* or r^*), not declared policy (l or r); politicians cannot be trusted to do what they say when they have preferences of their own. Effectively, then, candidates once again will not converge, this time because there is no point in doing so (they

---

[25] The interested reader may consult Kenneth A. Shepsle, *Models of Multiparty Electoral Competition* (Chur, Switzerland: Harwood, 1991), for a summary of much of this research.

Down$S$ = Political candidates →
Median Voter

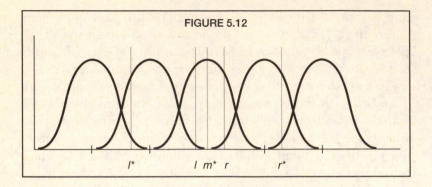

FIGURE 5.12

won't be believed by voters), even if they were willing to implement what they promised. The "commitment technology" is simply not up to the task.

What if it were? What if candidates had policy preferences, as in the previous paragraph, but had available to them means of making promises stick. Perhaps all they need to say is "Cross my heart," and the voters will believe them. Perhaps voters believe policy promises because they know that politicians know that a reputation for deception and misrepresentation is a serious electoral obstacle in future electoral campaigns. So, for any of a number of reasons, suppose that candidates' promises are credible on the one hand, but that candidates still care about what policies are implemented on the other hand. What will the candidates do in this circumstance? In a lovely paper, Randall Calvert[26] demonstrates that, just as in the case where candidates didn't care a whit about policy, these two candidates will converge to the median voter's ideal. Referring again to Figure 5.12, *L* wants an outcome closest to *l** and *R* wants the final policy to be closest to *r**. If these two points happen to be equidistant from *m**,

[26] Randall Calvert, "Robustness of Multidimensional Voting Models: Candidate Motivations, Uncertainty, and Convergence," *American Journal of Political Science* 29 (1985): 69–95.

and if each candidate (credibly) announced his or her ideal policy, respectively, then the election would end in a tie (and, presumably, the winner would be determined by something like a flip of a fair coin). But *L*, by moving just a tad toward the center, could win the election outright at a very small cost to herself in terms of policy. But this would be terrible for R— not that he lost the election but that a policy near *l** is so awful. He could avoid all this by moving in toward the center a bit more than *L* had, which, in turn, encourages *L* to move in a bit more, and so on. In the end, *even though both candidates had policy preferences and, in fact, did not care at all about who won the election but only about what policy would be implemented,* they converge to the median voter's ideal anyhow.

Needless to say, we could play with Downs's model in a variety of interesting ways. Many have.[27] What has been shown in this section is that the stripped-down spatial model of Downs, with competition on an ideological dimension between two election-oriented candidates, leads to policy convergence. The policy that emerges from the competitive forces captured by this model is the ideal point of the median voter. This result, to the casual observer, describes what often happens in real elections, as candidates try to smooth down their more extremist edges in order to curry favor with voters in the center of things. Thus, once Bill Clinton vanquished his liberal opponents within the Democratic Party in 1992 (Jesse Jackson and Mario Cuomo), he headed toward the ideological center, running in the general election as a more conservative

[27] For two early summaries of the extensive literature the interested reader may turn to James M. Enelow and Melvin J. Hinich, *The Spatial Theory of Voting* (New York: Cambridge University Press, 1984); and James M. Enelow and Melvin J. Hinich, eds., *Advances in the Spatial Theory of Voting* (New York: Cambridge University Press, 1990). A more recent review is Torun Dewan and Kenneth A. Shepsle, "Economic Models of Elections," *Annual Review of Political Science*, forthcoming 2011.

"new Democrat." The incumbent president, George H. W. Bush, on the other hand, tried to shed some of his hardline conservative attributes, also moving toward the center as he compromised on his "no new taxes" pledge. In 2000, the Republican, George W. Bush ran as a "compassionate conservative" against the centrist Democrat Al Gore. In 2008, the Democrat, Barack Obama moderated his views in the general election, after securing the nomination in a close contest with Hillary Clinton; the Republican Party nominated its most moderate candidate, John McCain. In many other elections one sees a similar dynamic—partisan candidates of the left and the right hedging, qualifying, and compromising in order to appear more centrist.

This convergence is not always complete, however. Sometimes a candidate applies brakes on convergence for fear of alienating his or her base, or even stimulating a third-party entrant. Thus, civil rights activists, unions, and government workers—elements of the Democratic base—made it virtually impossible for Walter Mondale to converge toward the center as a candidate in the 1984 presidential election. Elements of the conservative movement kept Ronald Reagan ideologically true in that same election. Third-party candidates entered the presidential races of 1968, 1980, and 1992 (George Wallace, John Anderson, and Ross Perot, respectively), sometimes because the candidates were thought to have converged too much,[28] sometimes because they were thought to have stayed too close to their more extremist supporters.[29] Thus, both too much convergence and too little convergence may provide the impetus for a third-party challenge.

---

[28] In 1968, Wallace entered on the right, thinking "there's not a dime's worth of difference" between the Democrat Hubert Humphrey and the Republican Richard Nixon.

[29] Both Anderson and Perot sought to capture the center, which they believed had been conceded by Carter and Reagan in 1980 and Clinton and Bush in 1992, respectively.

I have clearly only scratched the surface of Downs's spatial model of party competition and only covered some of the many mechanisms and rationales according to which competitors converge toward the median voter's ideal policy on the one hand, or maintain distinctive policy profiles on the other. This, in sum, suggests the richness of Downs's approach.

Electoral phenomena, however, are not the only focuses of the spatial model. A twin enterprise, a kind of "elections writ small," has employed the spatial model to study the selection of policy in legislative settings. I turn to those now, and examine both one-dimensional and multidimensional versions of the spatial model.

Spatial Models of Legislatures

There will be a much more thorough look at legislatures in Part IV, so here I am interested primarily in seeing what the spatial model can do. It turns out to be quite a powerful analytical tool for representing the ways in which preference-based (rational) behavior and structural features of institutions interact to produce final outcomes. It suggests that legislative outcomes depend in essential ways not only on what legislators want but also on how they conduct business in the legislature.

To keep things as simple as possible, the legislature is taken to be a set of n individuals, where n is an odd number, and where everyone casts a vote. It makes decisions by majority rule. The most elementary situation, one that is examined first, is the unidimensional case in which the legislature must choose a point on a line. Each legislator, i, has an ideal point x_i, and single-peaked preferences. The median voter is legislator m with ideal point x_m. We know in this circumstance that x_m can defeat any other point on the dimension in a majority contest (Black's Theorem). Perhaps more amazing is the fact that the median preferences prevail in a comparison between *any* two alternatives, so that if m prefers x to y then so does a majority for *any* x and y.[30]

In addition to the preferences of the median legislator, x_m, two other distinguishing features of the situation are important. Whenever a legislature faces a decision-making opportunity, there is always a *status quo* in place, labeled x^0. This is the current policy at the time of legislative choice. It remains in place if the legislature chooses not to change it.[31] The second feature of interest common to most legislatures is a division-of-labor arrangement known as a *committee system*. In such a system, a committee is a subset of the n legislators (momentarily, we describe some of its specific powers). The median ideal point of the committee members is labeled x_c. Just as majority preferences in the entire legislature are identical to the preferences of the legislature's median voter, majority preferences inside a committee are a copy of the preferences of the committee's median member. Because of these identities, much of our analysis need only consider x^0, x_m, and x_c. In what follows, then, I put the spatial model through

[30] This may be proved as follows. Suppose x_m, x, and y are all points in the dimension, and that $x_m \leq x \leq y$. Legislator m clearly prefers x to y. But then so does every legislator to the left of m. Together these legislators constitute a majority, so x is preferred by a majority to y. Likewise, by the same reasoning, if $y \leq x \leq x_m$, then both m and a majority (all the legislators to the right of m) prefer x to y. So, it has been shown that whenever x and y are on the *same* side of the median, a majority always agrees with the preferences of the median voter. Suppose, then, that $x \leq x_m \leq y$, and that m prefers x to y. Consider the legislator just to the left of m. Her ideal is closer to x and farther from y than was m's ideal; so if m prefers x to y, surely she does, too. But then, so do all the other voters to the left of m's ideal, and once again they jointly comprise a majority. This establishes that a majority *always* agrees with the preferences of the median voter.

[31] In some circumstances, the status quo policy does *not* remain in place, unless the legislature takes positive action to keep it in place. If the legislature fails to do anything, then the status quo reverts to some specific policy (known, naturally enough, as the *reversion point*). This is true, for instance, in statutes that possess *sunset provisions*, an example explored further in Case 5.1.

its paces in examining the making of policy choices by an n-member legislature possessing a committee system.

Three decision-making regimes, or institutional arrangements, are identified. The first is **pure majority rule**. There is a status quo, and any legislator can offer a motion to change it. A motion, once proposed, is pitted against the status quo. If it wins it becomes the new status quo; if it loses it goes to the place where all losing proposals go (a sort of elephants' burial ground). The floor is once again open for some new motion (against the old status quo, if it survived, or the new status quo, if the previous proposal prevailed). This procedure of motion making and voting continues until no member of the legislature wishes to make a new motion.[32]

The second regime is the **closed-rule committee system**. In this system, a (previously appointed) committee first gets to decide whether the legislature will consider changes in the status quo; that is, it has *gatekeeping agenda power* and can decide whether to open the gates to enable policy change or not. Second, if the gates are opened, only the committee gets to make a proposal (*monopoly proposal power*). Third, the parent legislature may vote the committee's proposal either up or down. If it passes, then it becomes the new status quo; if it fails, then the old status quo prevails. The proposal is closed to amendments. Hence, the proposal is said to be considered under a *closed rule*, and the committee is said to offer its parent body a *take-it-or-leave-it* proposal.

The third regime is the **open-rule committee system**. This system is identical to the one described in the previous paragraph, except for the third feature. Under an open rule, once the committee has made a proposal, the parent legislature may open the floor to *amendments* to the committee's pro-

---

[32] A variation on this "stopping rule" is to allow a motion to be in order at any time to close the floor to new motions (in effect, a motion to take a final vote and then to adjourn the legislature, at least on the subject matter at hand).

posal. Once the committee has opened the gates and made a proposal, it concedes its monopoly access to the agenda.

Each of these systems is explored in both the one-dimensional and the multidimensional setting in order to determine whether there is anything regular or routine that we can expect from these alternative majority-rule regimes. Some brief comparative observations on these regimes are offered, leaving a full-blown consideration for chapters 11 and 12, where institutions are taken up more systematically.

PURE MAJORITY RULE   I start with a legislative choice in a one-dimensional spatial setting. In the pure majority-rule regime there are no committees, so we need to know only the locations of x_m and x^0. A typical situation is given in the top panel of Figure 5.13. From the median ideal and the status quo, we determine the median legislator's preferred-to-x^0 set, $P_m(x^0)$.[33] Since we've established that the median's preferences are the same as a majority's preferences, this interval is the set of motions that would prevail over x^0 in a majority contest. So, if someone is recognized and makes a motion *outside* this set, it will go down in flames, whereas any motion *inside* this set will be victorious and become the new status quo. It is evident that the political process defined this way will produce outcomes that either leave the status quo unchanged or move it closer to x_m (since every point in $P_m(x^0)$ is closer than x^0 to x_m). As the process of motion making and voting is repeated, the winning alternative will ultimately converge on x_m. Moreover, it will not depart once it reaches x_m (since, as shown above, the status quo cannot move further from x_m in any vote). So, just as in the Downsian model of electoral competition, there is a centripetal tendency in the pure majority-rule legislative regime.

---

[33] Since we assume that legislative preferences are distance-based, we know that legislator m prefers to x^0 all points closer than it to x_m. This determines the set $P_m(x^0)$ pictured in Figure 5.13.

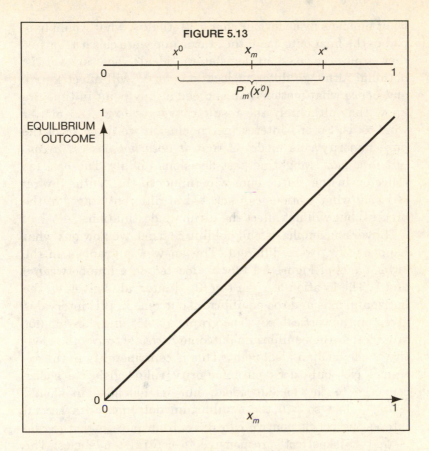

FIGURE 5.13

It is for this reason that we think of pure majority-rule legislative choice as an "election writ small."

The great utility of these spatial models of legislative choice is they permit the analyst to do what in economics is called *comparative statics*—we can ask "what if" questions. Having derived an equilibrium outcome from our basic setup, as I did in the previous paragraph, we may now ask how that equilibrium changes as relevant parameters change. We have already seen that there are really only two relevant parameters—x^0 and x_m. Holding the latter fixed, we first ask what happens if the former changes—that is, what would happen to the final outcome if the status quo were closer to or further from the median legislator's ideal? The answer is: nothing! Although different locations for x^0 will affect $P_m(x^0)$, and hence what motions can succeed at any point in time, we know that ultimately the result converges to x_m, no matter what x^0 is. So one interesting conclusion we draw from the pure majority rule model is that *it does not possess a conservative bias*, weighting past decisions unduly. The past (as reflected in the status quo) will influence the "path" (by restricting what motions can succeed at different stages of the process) but will not affect the ultimate destination.

Reversing emphasis and holding x^0 fixed, we now ask what happens if x_m were different. The answer is graphed in the lower panel of Figure 5.13 for x_m located on a line between 0 and 1. The location of x_m in the [0, 1] interval is given on the horizontal axis and the equilibrium outcome in this interval is given on the vertical axis. The graph is a 45° line showing (for any x^0) that the equilibrium outcome *perfectly tracks* the identity of the median ideal point. This is centripetality in the extreme! Not only does pure majority rule legislative choice converge to the median ideal, but if that median should change, then so will the equilibrium outcome. So a second interesting conclusion we can draw from pure majority rule is that it is perfectly responsive to central tendencies: The median legislator's ideal is, by definition, the central point in the distribution of preferences; pure majority rule produces an outcome at this point; and, were this point to change (as a result, say, of an election), the legislative outcome would "track" it.

CLOSED-RULE COMMITTEE SYSTEM   Most legislatures are not pure majority-rule institutions. Even town meetings and other approximations of pure majority rule about which observers occasionally wax romantic require some mechanism to determine the content of agenda items and the order in which they will be taken up. Some legislatures establish a single agenda committee to decide these matters. However, most legislatures (certainly in the United States) employ a division-of-labor committee system that divides up agenda power by policy area. Subsets of legislators have disproportionate influence over the agenda in specific policy jurisdictions. The committee serves, in its jurisdiction, as an agenda agent for its parent legislature.

I will have much more to say about these things in Part IV. For now, I need focus only on the fact that what distinguishes the closed-rule regime from pure majority rule is that there is, in addition to x^0 and x_m, a third parameter of interest, namely the median ideal point of an agenda-setting committee, x_c.[34] Many of the conclusions drawn about this regime depend on the relative locations of x^0, x_c, and x_m.

The decision-making procedure, as suggested earlier, is for the committee either to make no proposal at all, in which case x^0 remains in place, or to make a motion to change the status quo, which the parent body must accept or reject as is. What will such a committee do? To answer this question, we once again determine $P_m(x^0)$, as in the top panel of Figure 5.13. This is a set whose boundary points are x^0 itself and x^*; it contains the only points a legislative majority prefers to x^0. The committee, as personified by its median voter, c, treats these points as its "opportunity set," picking its favorite as the motion it makes (if it makes any motion at all). We look at three orderings of the relevant parameters (there are six orderings in all, but the omitted ones are simply mirror images of the ones we consider):

[34] Since the one-dimensional model is being elaborated here, we are concerned with the median ideal of only a single committee. In multidimensional contexts, where there are many jurisdictions into which the dimensions of the policy space are arranged, we will need to know the policy preferences of different committees, each responsible for its own bundle of policy dimensions. More on this will be developed in Part IV.

CASE 1 ($x^0 \leq x_m \leq x_c$). Here the median legislator is between the status quo and the median committee member. In this case x^* is the *right* boundary of $P_m(x^0)$, just as shown in Figure 5.13. If $x_c \leq x^*$, then the committee will propose its median ideal point, which then will be approved by a legislative majority (since it lies inside $P_m(x^0)$). If, on the other hand, $x^* \leq x_c$, then the best the committee can do is to propose x^*, which is approved by a legislative majority.[35] In either case, both committee and parent legislature wish to move away from the status quo *in the same direction*. The final outcome will move x^0 in that direction, further than the median voter would want, but not always as far as the committee median wants.

CASE 2 ($x^0 \leq x_c \leq x_m$). Here the median committee member is between the status quo and the median of the whole legislature. In this case $x_c \in P_m(x^0)$ automatically. So the committee can get majority legislative approval for x_c, the committee's best outcome.

CASE 3 ($x_m \leq x^0 \leq x_c$). In this last setting the status quo is between the two medians. This is a particularly interesting case because committee and legislative majority are at loggerheads. The committee wishes to move right, while a majority of the parent legislature wants to move left. The committee's gatekeeping authority pays off for it in a big way here because it will choose simply to keep the gates closed.[36]

---

[35] Actually, a legislative majority is indifferent between x^0 and x^*. I assume that an indifferent voter votes *for* the motion on the floor. (Alternatively, the committee could propose a point just to the left of x^*, which secures a majority outright.)

[36] The committee could move a proposal (some point to the right of x^0), but it would be defeated. So it might as well not bother and simply keep the gates closed (especially if the bother were at all costly). On the other hand, if out-

So, the first thing we learn about the closed-rule regime is that only a very limited number of things can happen—three things, in particular. If x_c is interior to the legislative median's preferred-to-x^0 set, then the outcome is x_c. If it is not, then either of the two endpoints of $P_m(x^0)$ are possible—x^0 if committee and legislative median are at loggerheads; x^* otherwise. In the pure majority rule regime, in contrast, only *one* thing can happen: x_m, something that *never* happens under the closed-rule regime (unless, by coincidence, $x_m = x_c$ or $x_m = x^0$). This suggests that endowing a privileged group with agenda power is not without its consequences: *agenda power discourages centripetal outcomes as it tugs the process in the direction of the privileged group.*

A variety of comparative statics exercises exists that one might do. I focus on one: For a fixed legislative median and committee median, what happens as x^0 changes? (Whoever asks this question doesn't literally mean that the status quo suddenly changes. Rather, it is a question of what would happen if the status quo were more or less extreme.) In case 1, for example, if x^0 were further to the left, then $P_m(x^0)$ would get bigger (x^* moves to the right). At some point it contains x_c (if it doesn't already). So, as x^0 moves away from the chamber median, there will be a discontinuity when x_c jumps from being outside m's preferred-to-x^0 set to inside that set. Put crudely, the worse the status quo, from m's perspective, the more likely c can get her way.[37] The same pattern prevails as x^0 moves to the right. At first it moves toward x_m, so m's preferred-to-x^0 set

---

side interests took heart in the fact that the committee was at least putting up a good fight and rewarded the committee accordingly, then the committee might wish to "bother" (though the result would be unchanged—x^0 would stay in place).

[37] The classic statement of this result, plus a derivation of some of the political consequences of it, is found in Thomas Romer and Howard Rosenthal, "Political Resource Allocation, Controlled Agendas, and the Status Quo," *Public Choice* 33 (1978): 27–43.

contracts. Once it "passes" x_m, the preferred-to set begins expanding again.[38]

CASE 5.1
SUNSET PROVISIONS AND
ZERO-BASED BUDGETING

In the 1970s public policy analysts developed two ideas as an attempt to counter rising budget pressures. The first idea was called a sunset provision. The identified problem was the persistence of expenditures that might have outlived their usefulness. It seemed that once a project was on the books, it never went away. With a sunset provision as part of the enabling legislation, the project would have to be renewed after a specified time period in order to extend its life. In other words, the sun would automatically set on a project unless the legislature took further action.

The second idea was called zero-based budgeting. Also associated with the problem of expenditures that were growing out of control, this concept required bureaucratic agencies to justify a project budget "from zero," rather than merely justifying the *growth* in proposed expenditures over the previous year's budget. It was alleged that this procedure would reduce accumulating and persisting inefficiencies in agency budgets.

For our purposes, sunset provisions and zero-based budgeting are similar because they create situations in which the status quo alternative to a proposal is zero. Consider the case of zero-based budgeting for an agency. The legislative median is at x_m and last year's agency budget is at B. Now we let the agency make a proposal for next year's

---

[38] The reader might try to see what happens as x^0 changes in cases 2 and 3 above.

budget, a proposal which the legislature may accept or reject by majority rule. Under ordinary procedures, we assume that legislative rejection of the agency proposal results in last year's budget, B, continuing in place next year. Under zero-based budgeting, on the other hand, we assume that legislative rejection leads to a zeroing out of the agency budget altogether.

At first glance, it would seem that the zero-based budgeting procedure is pretty tough on the agency. That's the whole idea, since this method was designed to limit an agency's power in budget negotiations. However, zero-based budgeting actually *increases* agency discretion. This is seen in the figure below. If, under ordinary procedures, B is the reversion outcome (the outcome if the legislature rejects the agency proposal), then as long as the agency proposes a budget in the gray region, the legislature will approve it (any such proposal is in $P_m(B)$); that is, under ordinary procedures, the agency could extract a budget as large as B^*. If, on the other hand, the zero-based budgeting procedure were in effect, then the agency could get a budget as large as N (since N is in $P_m(0)$). In their pure form, both sunset provisions and zero-based budgeting provide perverse incentives. Their whole rationale was to *discipline* "out-of-control" agencies and budgets, not *empower* them. (The reader might explore the consequences of a zero-based budgeting regime in which agency proposals may be amended by the legislature.)

0	B	x_m	B^*	N

In concluding this brief treatment of the closed-rule regime, let me reemphasize the fact that the key parameters are x^0, x_c, and x_m. An electoral earthquake that fails to change relationships among these parameters will not change policy outcomes (a fact that may puzzle those not equipped with the theory developed here). If, for instance, a legislative election caused massive turnover in incumbents but did so symmetrically so as to leave x_m unchanged, then "the more things change, the more they stay the same." Likewise, if before an election legislators c and m are at loggerheads, as defined in case 3 above, then electoral change, no matter how massive, that leaves the (possibly newly determined) c and m at loggerheads will simply maintain the status quo ante. The institutional impediments implicit in the closed-rule regime stand in stark contrast to the hypersensitivity of pure majority rule.

OPEN-RULE COMMITTEE SYSTEM   We've seen thus far that although there is an entire continuum of possible final outcomes, only one thing (x_m) can occur under the pure majority-rule regime, and only one of three things $(x_c, x^0, \text{ or } x^*)$ can possibly happen under the closed-rule regime. In the following treatment of the open-rule regime, it will be seen that only two possibilities exist. Either the gates remain closed and x^0 prevails or the gates are opened and x_m is the final outcome. *Nothing else is possible.* We will consider all the cases as we did in the previous regime.

In the open-rule regime the committee once again has the first move. If it makes no motion, then x^0 persists. If it makes a motion, then that motion is open to amendment (hence the term *open* rule). It is assumed here that alternative amendments continue to be offered until no legislator wishes to offer another. So the committee proposal is initially pitted against the first amendment, the winner of that against the next amendment, and so on until all the amendments have been taken up; the survivor of that sequence is then pitted against the status quo (this last vote is often called the "vote on final passage").[39]

---

[39] An alternative procedure would be to allow, after a committee motion, an amendment that is directly voted on. The winner stays on the floor and is

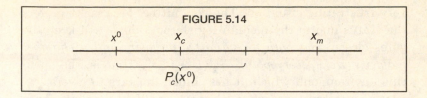

FIGURE 5.14

This procedure looks very much like the pure majority rule regime, *except that the committee has the first move.* Once it opens the gates, we're in the world of pure majority rule. This means that once a proposal is made, it will be amended and amended again, with successful amendments converging the process toward x_m. Indeed, it doesn't even matter what the initial committee proposal is. The reality is:

$$\text{open the gates} \quad \Rightarrow \quad x_m$$
$$\text{keep gates closed} \quad \Rightarrow \quad x^0$$

The committee decision is really pretty simple. If the committee median voter, Ms. c, prefers x_m to x^0, then she makes a motion (any motion); if Ms. c prefers x^0 to x_m, then the committee keeps the gates closed. Thus, all we need to inspect is Ms. c's preferred-to-x^0 set, $P_c(x^0)$, to see whether x_m is in it or not.

Recall the three possible cases in the preceding section. For the parameter ordering of case 1 $(x^0 \leq x_m \leq x_c)$, the committee clearly prefers x_m to x^0, so it will open the gates. For case 3 $(x_m \leq x^0 \leq x_c)$, the committee clearly has the opposite preference, so it will keep the gates closed. It is the case 2 ordering $(x^0 \leq x_c \leq x_m)$ that is the interesting one. If c's ideal policy is less than halfway between x^0 and x_m, then she keeps the gates closed; if it is more than halfway, then she makes a motion.

The first of these case 2 situations is shown in Figure 5.14. What makes this especially interesting is that it represents a

---

subject to another amendment. The process continues until no more amendments are forthcoming, after which there is a final vote between the alternative left standing on the floor and the status quo.

very frustrating situation. The committee, because it prefers the status quo to the median legislator's ideal, will keep the gates closed. *But both a committee majority and a chamber majority prefer every point in $P_c(x^0)$ to x^0.* That is, the open-rule environment, which at first blush appears to give a legislative majority potent authority, in fact penalizes both committee and legislative majorities. It gives the chamber *too much* authority—the right to amend whenever it wants. Its strength is its weakness, because it cannot promise *not* to use its authority; yet, it would be better off if it could credibly promise not to amend some proposal in $P_c(x^0)$ made by the committee (for, if it could precommit in this fashion, then the committee would be prepared to open the gates).

CASE 5.2

THE IMPORTANCE OF COMPROMISE AND
STRATEGIC THINKING

The discussion of the closed-rule and open-rule regimes addresses the general question of how politicians and interested others think about legislative possibilities. In one-dimensional situations, as we have seen, politicians locate a proposal on the policy dimension relative to their own preferences and the status quo that will otherwise prevail if the proposed change is rejected. When faced with a choice between the proposal and the status quo, the politician votes for the alternative closer to his or her ideal. With the open-rule regime, once a proposal is made, the dynamic of amendment activity leads inexorably to a unique outcome—the ideal point of the median legislator. With the closed rule, a proposal wins only if it is closer than the status quo to the median voter's ideal.

Failure to recognize these dynamics can lead to disappointment for principled—that is, stubborn—lobbyists. Advocates of proposed legislation must take into consideration the preferences of the decision maker(s), the rules of procedure in effect, and the relative location of the status quo. An unwillingness to compromise in light of these strategic realities can keep the status quo in place, even though the possibility exists to defeat it with results satisfactory to the lobbyist. This is illustrated in the figure below, where the legislative median is x_m, the status quo is x^0, and a powerful lobbyist's ideal policy is I.

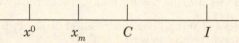

Without going into any of the specifics concerning the way powerful lobbyists exercise their power, suppose that lobbyist I is in a position to undermine any change in the status quo if it finds the change not to its liking (perhaps by "bribing" influential legislators—that is, contributing to their campaign committees). Under the closed rule, the best I could hope for is the compromise point, C—a policy just a little bit closer than x^0 to x_m. If the lobbyist stubbornly refuses to accept C by seeking something more extreme, it loses. Under the open rule, it must be prepared to accept x_m, for this is where the process of amendment will drive the final result. In either of these cases, the lobbyist must be able to anticipate the best deal it can cut and settle for it. In particular, it must be especially sensitive to the fact that "the best deal it can cut" depends upon the procedural rules for amendments. Even though it is powerful enough to *undermine* proposed changes in x^0, it cannot *impose* its own will. It needs a little help from its (legislative) friends.

Some observers have cited the absence of such strategic thinking as a reason for the failure of the Equal Rights

Amendment* and Proposition 174 in California, which would have implemented school choice as a voucher system.† Unwilling to compromise, lobbyists unwittingly kept their proposals further from the status quo than the compromise point required by the strategic realities. Politicians or voters voted against their proposals when more moderate versions very probably would have passed. The importance of such strategic thinking is obvious after the fact but not always in the heat of battle.

---

* Jane Mansbridge, *Why We Lost the ERA* (Chicago: University of Chicago Press, 1986).

† Jack Anderson and Michael Binstein, " 'School Choice' Pitfalls in California," *Washington Post*, November 1, 1993.

MULTIDIMENSIONAL EXTENSIONS Once multiple dimensions come into play, matters get a bit more dicey. In a pure majority-rule regime, the results of the McKelvey Chaos Theorem loom large. Putting to one side the highly unlikely circumstance that legislator preferences are distributed in a radial symmetric manner, we know that $W(x) \neq \varnothing$ for any x in the policy space. Anything can be beaten. In particular, any status quo, x^0, has a nonempty winset, $W(x^0)$. As long as a motion is made from that set, the status quo will be replaced. But then $x^1 \in W(x^0)$, in turn, has a nonempty winset of its own, $W(x^1)$. A motion $x^2 \in W(x^1)$ will replace x^1. Under the assumptions made about legislative voting,[40] an existing status quo is continually replaced.

Suppose the setup is altered ever so slightly. The condition from pure majority rule still holds that anyone is free to make a motion to change the status quo. But let's assume that decision making takes place *one dimension at a time* in some preset order. The first person recognized to make a motion on the

---

[40] Namely, that everyone votes his or her preference rather than voting strategically (which is taken up in the next chapter).

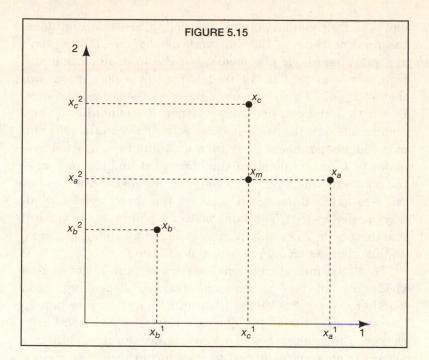

FIGURE 5.15

initially designated dimension states his or her amendment to x^0; this amendment can only change x^0 on the dimension currently under consideration. The group continues to focus on amending the status quo on this dimension until no more amendments are offered. Once it completes its task, the group turns its attention to the next dimension. It continues in this manner until there is no dimension left on which any legislator wishes to alter the status quo level.

It is easy to see in Figure 5.15 that this multidimensional version of pure majority rule mimics the result of the one-dimensional setting. There are three legislators with ideal points $x_a = (x_a^1, x_a^2)$, $x_b = (x_b^1, x_b^2)$, and $x_c = (x_c^1, x_c^2)$. For any status quo (not pictured), $x_0 = (x_0^1, x_0^2)$, motions are entertained, first on dimension 1 and then on dimension 2. At the end of the day, when all motion-making and voting are said and done, the final outcome is the *multidimensional median*, $x_m = (x_c^1, x_a^2)$, since legislator c is median on the first dimension and legislator a is median on the second. This does not mean that $W(x_m) = \varnothing$. There are points to its northeast, for instance, that both a and c prefer to x_m. Rather, it means that on any dimension—say, the first—holding policy *fixed* on the other dimension, no movement away from x_c^1 would be supported by a majority. (For any point on the horizontal line through x_m— the points in which policy on the first dimension changes but remains fixed on the second—two of the three legislators always prefer x_m to it. The same holds for points on the vertical line through x_m. The only points preferred by a majority to x_m require changes on *both* dimensions at once.)

Thus, the multidimensional version of pure majority rule yields one of two possible conclusions, depending upon whether there is additional institutional structure or not. In the pure case, the status quo is continuously vulnerable to change. The group's choices are never very durable, since it is always in someone's interest to introduce a motion to change it, and it is always in some majority's interest to comply. In the case of institutional structure in the form of dimension-by-dimension decision making, the result is both predictable and centripetal. The median ideal point on each dimension prevails under the procedure described above (although it need not be the same median voter on each dimension, of course).

Since I will take up the multidimensional versions of the open-rule and closed-rule regimes in the chapter on legislatures in Part IV, the discussion will be especially brief on this subject now. Imagine, in Figure 5.16 (a reproduction of the spatial positions in Figure 5.13), that Ms. c is an agenda setter and the status quo is x^0. If her proposals are subject to amendment by the parent legislature, then we are back to the wild-and-woolly open-rule majority system. Under a closed rule, however, she can make a take-it-or-leave-it proposal, one that

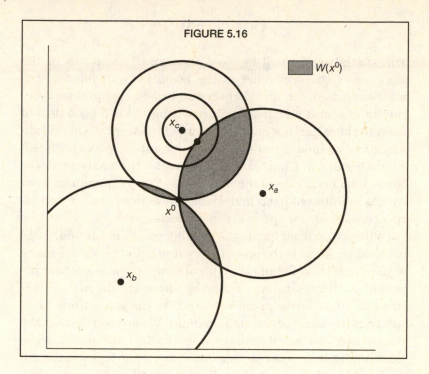

FIGURE 5.16

is *not* subject to amendment but only to an up-or-down vote. The petal-shaped shaded regions comprise c's opportunity set—it is $W(x^0)$. The circles centered on x_c are various of c's indifference contours. Her objective is to move the final policy outcome onto the indifference contour of smallest radius (hence closest to her ideal point) that still lies in $W(x^0)$. The point in this figure (a big black dot!) at the tangency between one of the petals of $W(x^0)$ and the smallest indifference curve of Ms. c is the proposal she will make, which a majority (a and c) will then support. With the closed rule, then, a monopoly agenda setter has considerable power, though constrained by majority preferences.

CONCLUSION

The spatial model will be used time and time again in the analyses of the remainder of the book. I've put forward the basic ingredients in this chapter and briefly explored majority rule in electoral and small group settings. But a good deal of naïveté characterizes voter/legislators (apparently, only candidates and agenda setters are wily). I want to relax this unrealistic feature in Chapter 6. In Chapter 7 the analysis moves beyond majority rule to the multitude of ways human creativity has manifested itself in devising sometimes bizarre and intricate ways for groups to arrive at decisions.

What is exciting about the spatial model to an analytical political scientist is the opportunity it affords to capture many of the interesting details of political competition—whether between candidates in an election or between alternative motions in a legislative assembly—and, at the same time, to do so in a fairly clean and simple manner. We appreciate that the reader may not agree entirely with the last sentiment, since this chapter has required your undivided attention and careful reading. Nevertheless, political scientists over the past fifty or so years have found the model to serve as the principal building block for the analysis of political rivalries of all stripes.

A single chapter in a book, of course, can only portray the spatial model at its simplest. But even the simple formulation possesses nonobvious implications. In the context of one-dimensional pure majority rule with single-peaked preferences, for example, whether in two-party electoral competition or legislative policy choice, the magnetic attraction of the median participant's ideal point is powerful. Majoritarian politics is subjected to centripetal forces, producing outcomes that observers describe with words such as "compromise," "moderate," or "centrist." At the very least, then, the simple spatial model provides a rationale or explanation for the inexorable movement of majority-rule competition toward the center of participant preferences. Its surprise value lies in the fact that this centripetal dynamic is *not* because "that's where the votes are." As we demonstrated earlier, movement toward the median voter's ideal is an equilibrium tendency in a pure majority rule arrangement *even if there are very few voters at the center of things.*

In the legislative realm, where rules of procedure and agenda-setting committees constrain the operation of pure majority rule, there were other surprises. At least in the world of one-dimensional politics, only a limited number of things are possible. A committee system operating under the open rule can produce only one of two possible results. It can, by "closing the gates" and not permitting a motion to be proposed, keep policy at the status quo. Or, if it should make a motion, the sequence of amendments permitted under the open rule will drive the outcome to the median legislator's ideal. These are the only possibilities. Under a closed rule, there are three possibilities. If the gates are kept closed (possibly because the committee and legislature are at loggerheads, with the status quo between their respective median ideals), the status quo remains intact. If the committee median's ideal lies between the status quo and the median legislator's ideal, then the committee's ideal will be proposed and will pass. Finally, if the median legislator's ideal lies between the status quo and the committee's median ideal, then the outcome is the point closest to the committee's median that leaves the median legislator of the full legislature just indifferent between it and the status quo. The details are found in this chapter. The surprise, however, is found in the conclusions: first, that only a small number of items are possible under various legislative procedural regimes and, second, that these small numbers of things differ from regime to regime. Put differently, *institutional arrangements—the political ways of doing business—matter profoundly for the outcomes that emerge from the political process.*

The spatial model also allows us to begin to assemble explanations for why convergence to the center is not always complete. The centripetal tendency is always present, to be sure, but there may be countervailing tendencies as well. In the context of Downs's model of elections, for example, we noted that a politician may fear he will lose his extremist support (to abstention or to a third-party entrant) if he converges too much toward his opponent. In the legislative arena, powerful agenda setters may, through their control of motions and amendments, prevent the process from converging on the median legislator's ideal policy, either because the agenda setter can propose and get passed something she likes better or because she chooses to keep the gates closed.

Thus, the great advantages of the spatial model are its (relative) simplicity, its analytical power, and the "surprises" it produces. Not only do we begin to understand things that we may have long appreciated in an intuitive fashion (like the tendency toward moderation in majority-rule systems), we develop a sophisticated understanding of new things. While surely not a perfect explanatory tool, it's a pretty good start.

One of the matters that I touched on only briefly and unsystematically was strategic thinking. Many applications, especially early in the history of spatial modeling, assume that voters and legislators are "honest" in their voting behavior. When confronted with two alternatives, they simply vote for their favorite, doing so without regard for subsequent consequences. Yet there are many circumstances in which a rational person will think things through in a more sophisticated fashion, sometimes coming to the conclusion that, in a particular voting opportunity, she should *not* vote for her favorite alternative. This is *sophisticated* or *strategic* behavior, the subject of the next chapter.

EXPERIMENTAL CORNER
Group Choice under Majority Rule

Imagine a group that must make a decision. For example, suppose a group of five individuals must choose a point in a two-dimensional space, one that looks like that in Figure 5.8, where each individual values the points in this space differently. Ms. 1 most likes points in the southwestern part of the space; Mr. 3 favors points to the northeast; others prefer points in other regions of the space. In short, there is conflict among the preferences of the members of this group. There are many theories of group choice that attempt to analyze and explain situations like this. In a classic paper, Morris Fiorina and Charles Plott set out to assess these theories by running experiments with real, live groups (mainly of college students, but others have experimented with university employees, business people, townspeople, etc.).[a] In this "Experimental Corner," I will focus on one of their experiments. This is actually a slight variation that I run with my own students.

Begin with an odd number of group members. Each is given experimental preferences by the experimenters. For a five-member group as portrayed in Figure 5.8, member 1 has an ideal or most-preferred point located at x_1, member 2 at x_2, and so on. Their preferences are *Euclidean*, which means that they prefer the final outcome to be a point closer to their ideal point than one further away. Thus, 3, for example, is indifferent among all the points on a circle centered on her ideal point (because they are equidistant from x_3) and prefers any point on a circle of smaller radius to one on a larger radius (because the former is closer to x_3

---

[a] Morris P. Fiorina and Charles R. Plott, "Committee Decisions under Majority Rule: An Experimental Study," *American Political Science Review* 72 (1978): 575–98.

than the latter is). In the experiment, the horizontal and vertical dimensions range from zero to 100. A status quo, x^0, is set at (100, 100) in the extreme northeast of the two-dimensional space. Subjects are paid cash depending on the final outcome—a higher payment for a final outcome closer to their ideal point and a lower payment for an outcome further away. Each subject knows his or her preferences and payment schedule but not those of other subjects.

The procedure for decision making is as follows. A subject is randomly selected by the experimenter to make a proposal. For example, if **1** is recognized, she might say, "I move we change the status quo from (100, 100) to (25, 50)." This motion is put to a majority vote. If a majority approves, then (25, 50) becomes the new status quo; if it fails (with ties constituting failure), then (100, 100) remains the status quo. A new person is recognized to make another motion. This process is repeated, with subjects recognized randomly to make proposals. At any time there is a *privileged motion*: Any subject can move to end the session. This is voted on immediately, and if it passes, the session ends and each subject is paid the value to him or her of the status quo prevailing at that time. Otherwise, motions continue to be made until no subject wants to make a new proposal. (Even if subjects still have motions to make, if a time limit is reached, then the session automatically ends.)

What happens? My experience in running this experiment in classes over nearly two decades is that the spatial theory of majority rule works quite well. To illustrate, return to Figure 5.8, where preferences as displayed there satisfy the Plott Theorem (distance-based preferences, an odd number of subjects, ideal points distributed in a radially symmetric fashion). The theory of majority rule implies that the final outcome should be the ideal point of subject 2, since x_2 can defeat any other point in a majority comparison. As long as someone proposes this point, it will become the new status quo and then it cannot be dislodged by any subsequent proposal. In actual experiments, subjects start off tentatively, partly because they are only just figuring out the setting and partly because they don't know the preferences of other subjects. But once they gain familiarity, things move along at a rapid clip. Subjects seek recognition to make motions; motions are made and approved that move the status quo from the extreme northeast point into the "center of things." Each successive motion, as the theory would predict, moves the status quo closer to x_2, the point the Plott Theorem identifies as the final outcome (the equilibrium of the majority-rule process). Logically, there is always a majority that will prefer a point closer to x_2 to one further away, so motions that move a status quo closer to x_2 should prevail over a more distant status quo, and motions that move the status quo further away should fail. This typically happens in the experiments I've run, though occasionally a mistake is made. But even if this should happen, it is quickly corrected by a new motion. There are intermittent efforts to bring the proceedings to a close (especially when a status quo lands close to some subject's ideal point), but typically a majority rejects this until x_2 is reached. Once x_2 is reached, any subsequent motion is defeated and, ultimately, subjects tire of more motions and finally approve a motion to end the session. A typical experimental session draws to a close quite rapidly; rarely is it ended because it reaches the time limit.

If, however, a distribution of ideal points is not like that of Figure 5.8, violating radial symmetry instead, then majority rule does not have an equilibrium like x_2. The McKelvy Theorem applies. What happens in this experimental condition? My experience in running the experiment in this context is that McKelvey's Theorem captures the situation. Majorities approve proposals moving the status quo around but never settling on any specific point.

More often than in the previous setting, the time limit determines when the session will end. The final outcome is somewhere in the middle of the distribution of preferences, but it does not hone in on a specific point as it did when the Plott conditions were satisfied. It is not exactly "chaos," but outcomes do not display the same regularity they do when preferences are distributed in a radially symmetric fashion.

As a final exercise, I have added a new twist to the original Fiorina-Plott experimental design. In some sessions I tell subjects not only their own ideal points but also those of the other subjects. Does this make a difference? Theory says it shouldn't—either there is a Plott equilibrium point or there is the wandering around of the McKelvey Theorem. The additional information does not alter these facts. And, experimentally, the results are about the same as in the limited-information context, though the chatter among subjects during the experiments does reveal envy and competitiveness when some approved status quo looks to benefit the person sitting across the table.

At least in this rather carefully controlled setting, pure majority rule (with only the most elementary of institutional features) pretty much works the way the theorems of Plott and McKelvy suggest. Indeed, against a large number of theoretical competitors, Plott and Fiorina conclude that this theory of majority rule is superior.

PROBLEMS AND DISCUSSION QUESTIONS

1. Suppose that a society consists of three individuals, 1, 2 and 3, who must choose one among three proposed budgets, x, y, and z. Their preferences over these three possible budgets are as follows: xP_1yP_1z, yP_2zP_2x, and zP_3xP_3y.

- Write down the majority preference relation for this profile of preferences (e.g., indicate which alternatives would beat which in two-way contests).

- Does Black's Median-Voter Theorem support a prediction about which policy will be chosen if the group uses simple majority rule? Why or why not?

- Suppose that the group is going to use a voting agenda v = (y, x, z) to select the budget, where this notation means that the group first votes over y and x, and then votes over the winner of this contest and z, where the winner of this second vote is chosen as the budget. If each individual votes sincerely at each stage of the agenda, what would the outcome be? What would the outcome be if $v' = (z, x, y)$ or $v'' = (z, y, x)$?

2. The Senate Finance committee, in debating a health care reform bill, contains some members who demanded a full government-run insurance scheme ("the public option"), others who were strongly opposed, and a third group who favored a compromise health care cooperative, a kind of government-affiliated nonprofit. Both those in favor of a full public option and those opposed agree that the "co-op" is the second-best compromise outcome. What can you say about this group's preferences? Could you predict the outcome of a vote if you knew the number of members who held each of the three preference profiles?

Some of the committee's more liberal members start to take political flak from interest groups strongly in favor of a full public option, who convince them that it would be better to vote against the "co-op"—and wait for a more propitious time—if the full public option is unachievable. What can you say about this new set of preferences? Could you always predict the outcome of a vote if you knew the number of members who held each preference profile?

3. A famous example of preferences which violate single-peakedness was first presented in Verba et al.'s "Public Opinion and the War in Vietnam."[a] This study found that most individuals identified a specific policy as their ideal point on a one-dimensional policy space varying from a reduction or end to U.S. engagement at one end, continuation of U.S. engagement in the middle, and expansion of U.S. commitment at the other end. Moreover, most stated that policies further away from their ideal points were increasingly less desirable. However, there was a small segment of the population who favored either a U.S. withdrawal or an expansion of the U.S. commitment to a continuation of the present policy. What property of a society's preference profile is not respected in this example? How widespread must non-single-peakedness get before group transitivity is violated? Illustrate this graphically, and then explain whether preferences over policy in the Vietnam War might better be represented using two or more issue dimensions. What might those dimensions include?

4. A seven-member governance committee of a corporation is charged with allocating funds for end-of-year bonuses, and a special subcommittee is appointed to research and then propose to the full governance committee a total value of all bonuses. The corporation's rules state that the subcommittee may bring a proposal before the full committee under a predetermined amendment procedure (either an open or closed rule). All subcommittee and committee decisions are made using majority rule; the minimum the committee may allocate is $0 and the maximum is $12,000. The preferences of each members of the seven-member governance committee over alternative total amounts to allocate for the bonuses are single-peaked and symmetric about each member's ideal points, and are arrayed as follows:

[a] Sidney Verba et al., 1967, "Public Opinion and the War in Vietnam," *American Political Science Review* 61, no. 2 (1967): 317–33.

Bobby and Emma: 0; Amy: 1500; Cathy: 6000; Frank: 7500; Geri: 10,000; and David: 12,000.

Answer the following questions, illustrating pictorially where helpful.

- The subcommittee is composed of Frank, Geri, and David. What is the subcommittee's most-preferred level of funding?

- Last year the governance committee allocated $3000 for bonuses, and under committee rules this is the status quo level of funding (it will be the decision this year, too, if the full committee makes no change). Assuming the subcommittee brings a proposal to the full committee under a closed rule, what is the subcommittee's proposal and what will be the outcome? Why?

- Now assume the subcommittee brings its proposal to the full committee under an open rule. Will the subcommittee "open the gates" and bring a proposal to the floor? If so, what will it propose? What will be the outcome? Explain.

- Now assume that the governance committee follows "zero-based budgeting" in which each year's allocation is initially set to zero, and the committee then proceeds to vote on any new proposals made by the subcommittee. In this case, what will the outcome of the voting be under a closed rule? Under an open rule? Comment on the implications of zero-based budgeting.

5. A legislature is going to vote on a policy that is well represented by a single-issue dimension, on a scale of zero to one. The initial policy proposal will be supplied by a committee (whose ideal point for this exercise can be any point along the x-axis) to a legislature with median ideal point M. The status

quo is currently at point *SQ*. Draw a line showing the equilibrium outcomes for any committee ideal point, when the committee's proposal is considered under a *closed rule*. On a separate set of axes, perform the same exercise when the committees proposal is considered under an *open rule*. Then, do the same exercise for both rules (using a dashed line on the two axes already created), assuming that the legislature operates on the principal of zero-based budgeting, so if no bill is passed in the current session, the policy reverts to *ZB* = 0.

What is the impact of zero-based budgeting under a closed rule? Are equilibrium outcomes closer or further from the legislature's median, on average? What about under the open rule?

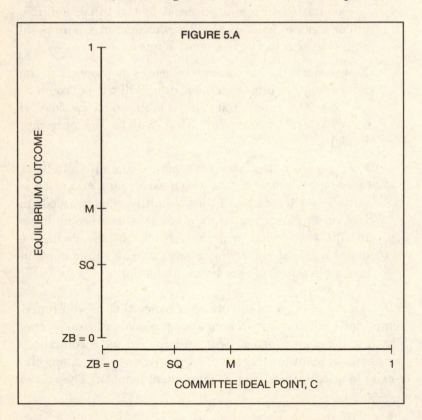

FIGURE 5.A

6. A legislature with three groups similar to that shown in Figure 5.6 is attempting to reach a bargain on some issue which has two policy dimensions. The legislature uses majority rule, and the indifference contours are all circular. Suppose that groups 2 and 3 reach an agreement on some deal where 3 gets its ideal policy on the horizontal dimension and the outcome on the vertical dimension is one-third of the distance from 2's ideal point moving toward 3's. Draw the preferred-to sets for 2 and 3 and show that there are other bargains between 2 and 3 that could leave them better off. Consider the set of bargains that 2 and 3 could make that cannot be altered without making either group worse off; what does this set look like? This is called the "contract curve" for groups 2 and 3. Draw in the contract curve for all other possible majority coalitions. Are any points on these contract curves empty winset points under majority rule?

Now, suppose the legislature operates under a unanimity rule. If the status quo is at the agreement point between 2 and 3 described above, will the three sides be able to find a bill that makes all of them better off? What if the status quo is at 2's ideal point in the horizontal dimension, and halfway between 2 and 3's ideal points in the vertical dimension? What bills have empty winsets when the unanimity rule is employed? Do the existence of these empty winsets contradict McKelvy's Chaos Theorem?

*7. Assume five members of a voting body A, B, C, D, and E. They have ideal points in a two-dimensional issue space, given by A: (1,4), B: (4,4), C: (2,2), D: (1,1), and E: (2,1), where the first coordinate gives a person's ideal policy on the X dimension and the second coordinate gives the ideal policy on the Y dimension. Assume further that each member prefers an outcome closer to his or her ideal point to one further away. All votes are taken over X-Y policy bundles, so all proposals are in the form of ordered pairs (x,y). Is there an equilibrium proposal if the body uses majority rule?

Now suppose that player B has been appointed the sole agenda setter. If the status quo is at C's ideal point, can B construct an agenda that will lead eventually to her own ideal point being approved by the entire legislative body? If so, construct such an agenda (you may assume sincere voting, and that the agenda setter can always persuade legislators indifferent between two policy bundles to vote for the bundle that she prefers). What theorem does this illustrate?

8. Perhaps the most famous political aphorism belongs to Otto von Bismarck: "Politics is the art of the possible." Comment, with reference to Black's Median-Voter Theorem, McKelvey's Chaos Theorem, and the discussion of legislative rules (especially Case 5.2).

9. This question asks you to consider the links between Arrow's Theorem and McKelvey's Chaos Theorem. Do the group preference intransitivities that motivated Arrow's ideas occur in McKelvey's multidimensional, majority-rule settings? Does the "anything can happen" message of McKelvey resonate with any of the lessons of Arrow's Theorem? Does agenda control bestow an ability to determine the outcome in the Arrowian world? In all cases? Develop some small three-person, three-outcome examples to show that the perverse outcomes of the multidimensional spatial model can, but do not always, occur in the discrete world of Arrow.

10. Anthony Downs employed the logic of unidimensional decision making first articulated by Duncan Black in order to understand politics in the largest "committee" imaginable—the electorate. He pointed out that if there were only two parties, and if politicians with extreme views had little inclination to

form parties of their own, then the platforms and campaign promises of the two parties would be very similar.

- Why is that? How does his conclusion follow from Black's Median-Voter Theorem?

- Downs takes politicians to be interested only in winning office. Does a different result (i.e., something other than convergence) arise when politicians have strong policy preferences of their own? Under what circumstances?

- Which other of Downs's assumptions (about the number of candidates, voting behavior, or the dimensionality of the issue space) might explain the apparent differences in party platforms in the United States, and elsewhere?

6

Strategic Behavior: Sophistication, Misrepresentation, and Manipulation

In models of social choice and spatial decision making, voters vote their preferences. To some, this is the essence of rational behavior. To others, however, rationality is more subtle and nuanced. It entails doing the best one can with what one's got, and this sometimes requires making strategic maneuvers, investments, sacrifices, and retreats. It is embodied, for example, in the Protestant work ethic, which encourages deferred gratification in order to harvest later returns. Some might claim that Protestants, in some perverse sort of way, *like* deferred gratification, but the alternative view is that their ethic (an ethic common among Asians, Jews, and others, too) reflects the strategic decision to maximize over the long haul by resisting enslavement to short-term preference satisfaction. Models need to reflect this possibility, for a failure to take strategic capabilities into account may result in disaster (as Case 6.1 demonstrates). This chapter is devoted to elaborating on the multiplicity of ways strategy rears its head.

CASE 6.1
"NEED-BLIND" COLLEGE ADMISSIONS

A prestigious university (which shall remain unnamed), in a spirit of generosity and genuine concern, instituted a need-blind admissions policy for its graduate school. It sought to attract the finest graduate students, independent of their ability to pay the cost of graduate education. But universities, like any other organizations, are faced with a large number of possibilities and a limited number of resources with which to pursue them. Each academic department's entering class had to be limited in number and, to accomplish that, each department was given a fixed budget to spend on graduate students. As we shall see, financial scarcity and need-blindness in admissions compete at the margin, sometimes with perverse consequences.

The admissions procedure works as follows. First, each applicant gives financial data to the central office of the graduate school. Simultaneously, each applicant submits admissions materials (GRE scores, undergraduate grade transcripts, teacher recommendations, essays, and so on) to the academic department in which he or she is interested, but *not* the financial data (which was given to the graduate school). Thus, the department, in ignorance of candidate financial need, constructs a preliminary rank-order of the applicants, along with a cutoff line below which rejected applicants fall. This preliminary list is forwarded to the graduate school, which attaches next to each candidate a *minimum* financial stipend the department must offer. Departments, of course, can make larger offers; but they cannot admit a student and make a smaller offer—that is the rule. This minimum stipend is need-blindness in action—it indicates how much subsidy is required to bring a candidate up to a financial status that would permit him or her to

attend graduate school. These marching orders are transmitted back to the department, which now gets a *second
crack*. Given its limited budget, and its desire to have as
fine a class of entering students as its budget permits, it
may have second thoughts about those it has admitted, now
that it knows the minimum price it must pay from its scarce
resources. For example, an especially needy student ranked
25 may require, by graduate school dictates, $20,000 of sub-
sidy. Candidates 12 and 13 may be less needy, but, the department reasons, if we take the $20,000 from 25 (and
therefore choose not to admit that person after all), and use
it to "top up" the offers we've made to candidates 12 and 13,
we may have a better chance at attracting *two, higher-
ranked* students.

The need-blind admissions procedure inadvertently dis-
criminates against financially needy students who are not
highly ranked (though clearly above the cutoff line). A strategic department will have strong incentives to reallocate
what would have to be spent on these students toward
higher-ranked (possibly unneedy) candidates to enhance
the prospects of the latter accepting an offer.

Need-blind admissions is a noble endeavor; so, too, is producing excellence in graduate education. In Case 6.1, university administrators should have devised a scheme to achieve
need-blind admissions that took into account the possibility
that others on whom they depend—namely, professors on departmental admissions committees—may not share their purposes to the same degree. The scheme described above clearly
did *not* prevent strategic maneuvers that had the effect of un-
dercutting noble purposes. Someone wasn't looking ahead;
someone was failing to anticipate.

RATIONAL FORESIGHT

In politics it is essential to look ahead, to anticipate, to exercise prudence and foresight. The political world is full of purposes, some noble and some ignoble, some competing and some complementary. Rational actors, seeking to enhance the prospects of the purposes they pursue, must think strategically. And one of the fundamental principles for thinking strategically is looking before you leap.[1]

Thinking strategically is not always so easy. Consider a three-person legislature, each of whose members would like a pay raise.[2] But each legislator realizes that constituents will not be pleased with a representative voting to increase his or her own salary. So, the best of all possible worlds for legislator i is for the other two legislators to vote in favor of the pay raise, thereby causing it to pass, with legislator i voting against. In this case, he does not displease his constituents but receives the extra cash anyhow! The worst of all worlds, of course, would be for i to vote yea but for the motion to raise legislative pay to fail. The other two possibilities fall in between, and all three legislators have precisely the same feelings on this issue. That is, they rank-order the outcomes (pass and vote nay) P (pass and vote yea) P (fail and vote nay) P (fail and vote yea).

Now then, the roll is about to be called. Each legislator will be asked for a public declaration on the motion to raise pay. And, being a roll, it lists legislators in alphabetical order—i first, then j, then k. Suppose you are legislator i. How should you vote? Think about your answer, and write it down on a piece of scratch paper before proceeding.

[1] An outstanding book with exactly this title is Avinash Dixit and Barry Nalebuff, *Thinking Strategically* (New York: Norton, 1991). While I can devote only a few paragraphs to this topic in my book, the Dixit-Nalebuff volume is a superb extended discussion of strategic behavior.

[2] This example is drawn from Peter Ordeshook, *Game Theory and Political Theory* (New York: Cambridge University Press, 1986).

The author has tried this out on many student audiences. The typical response is that legislator i ought to vote yea. The following reasoning is offered:

> I don't know how j and k will subsequently vote. And since I don't know I figure it's equally likely that each votes one way or the other. This means there's a 50 percent chance that they will split their votes, making my vote the deciding one. So I'd better vote yea, securing my second-choice outcome, rather than voting nay and ending up with my third-best outcome.

This is not a well-thought-out position. The student whose reasoning we've reproduced has not thought ahead and has not taken into account that legislator i's actual behavior will *affect* what j and k do.[3]

The way to think about this is to put yourself at the end of the process first—in k's shoes—and work backward. There are really only three circumstances for k to consider (2 nay votes, 2 yea votes, or a split in the vote), and in each her preferences provide her with clear counsel on how to proceed. If two nays have preceded, then she will definitely vote nay. If two yeas have preceded, then she will again definitely vote nay. If there is a split vote, then her vote is deciding and she will definitely vote yea. In each contingency we know *definitely* how k will vote.

Specifically, legislator j (who chooses next to last) can forecast with certainty how k will vote (as long as k does what she should!). Suppose, when it comes time for him to vote, i has already voted yea. Then j knows that if he votes yea the bill will pass (and, from the above, k, whose vote will have no effect,

---

[3] What I mean to say here is that most students implicitly assume that j and k have already made up their own minds about how to vote. Students do not appreciate, in general, that the choices j and k will actually make are *reactions* to i's initial choice, so that i can, in fact, affect the thinking of j and k. The true strategist, in contrast, appreciates his or her power to influence the thinking of subsequent movers.

will vote nay and this will be the best outcome for her); on the other hand, if j votes nay, the bill will still pass because k will be forced to vote yea, and this will be best for j. What we have figured out so far, then, is that if i votes yea, then j can afford to vote nay, forcing k to vote yea; the bill will pass, i and k will get their second-preference outcome, while j gets his first choice.

But what if i decides to vote nay? He can think ahead, since he has deduced how the others will react. Legislator i knows that, following his nay vote, if j votes nay, the bill fails (no matter what k does). On the other hand, if j votes yea this will produce a split vote forcing k to vote yea, too. Legislator j is snookered here, since he will reluctantly vote yea to get his second choice rather than vote nay, killing the bill and getting his third choice. We now know what i should do. By voting nay, he *forces* both the other legislators to carry the burden of passing the pay-raise bill.

CASE 6.2
CONGRESSIONAL PAY RAISE DILEMMAS

An examination of actual cases of legislative pay raises provides anecdotal evidence of a logic much like that described in this section. The basic idea is that legislators want to vote no if their vote is irrelevant to the outcome and yes only if they are critical to the outcome. In 1990, the U.S. Senate was debating a major piece of legislation to reform congressional pay. Senator Daniel Patrick Moynihan (D-N.Y.) introduced an amendment to the bill to increase pay. One report recounted the scene this way:

> As opponents nearly defeated the amendment on a 50-50 tie, Moynihan stood in the center aisle of the chamber, hands outstretched. "One more vote!" he pleaded. Laughing, Alaska Re-

publican Frank H. Murkowski switched his vote to support Moynihan, bringing the final tally to 51-49.*

Although we have no direct evidence, we suspect that in the early voting Senator Murkowski understood that voting no would force others to get the bill passed, and thus that he could have his cake and eat it, too. Only when his vote became essential did he switch.†

A similar situation took place in 1992 when the Senate was considering an amendment to transfer funding from military projects to breast cancer research. Senators were reluctant to break the "firewall" between defense and domestic spending, but they also feared being caught on the losing side of an issue like breast cancer, given the salience of women's issues in 1992. If the breast cancer amendment were going to pass anyway, or if it were certain to fail, a senator would want to be recorded as yes. Only if he or she were the decisive vote would an alternative behavior be considered. This created a "pay-raise dilemma." The scene on the Senator floor, as described by the *Washington Post*, demonstrates the argument:

> When votes for the project were safely in hand [that is, the amendment was certain to pass], senators began streaming onto the floor to change their 'no' votes to 'yes.' Minority Leader Robert J. Dole (R-Kan.) was overheard urging the Republican cloak room to alert absent senators to the stampede. An unofficial tally showed 28 senators, including . . . Dole, switching their votes. Several others waited until the last minute before casting votes in favor of the proposal.‡

---

* "Lawmakers' Pay Raised, Fees Curbed," *Congressional Quarterly Almanac* (1990): 74.
† Why he didn't stick to his guns and make some other no voter bear the cost of switching isn't answered here. The reader might wish to speculate. I will discuss such phenomena, known as the "free-rider problem," in Part III.
‡ Helen Dewar, "Senate's New Sensitivity," *Washington Post*, September 24, 1992, p. A1.

These two cases are by no means unique. Watch C-SPAN for other instances of last-minute vote switches as representatives fight to stay on the right side of an issue, giving new meaning to the term "politically correct."

Strategic thinking and rational foresight are general terms for the kind of calculations I've described. They entail a logic that takes advantage of the sequential structure to the decision making. They involve, oddly enough, thinking forward by reasoning *backward*. Indeed, the method is called *backward induction*, and works as follows. Take a generic sequential situation, like the one pictured in Figure 6.1. There are three individuals who must make a collective decision (not unlike the legislative pay-raise example above), each by revealing an individual choice in turn. To complicate things a bit, let's suppose that Mr. I and Mr. III each have three options available in their "action sets"—$\{a_1, a_2, a_3\}$ and $\{c_1, c_2, c_3\}$, respectively—whereas Ms. II has only two options in hers—$\{b_1, b_2\}$. In addition there is a *fictional* fourth player, an androgynous 0 known as Chance. In Figure 6.1 Chance moves first, his/her only responsibility to select the order in which the other players move. Of the six possible choices Mr./Ms. 0 could make, we suppose he/she chooses the order: I, III, II. The "game" now starts.[4]

An outcome of this social circumstance results from the three participants making choices from their action sets.

---

[4] In fact, we are describing what is known as an *extensive form game* in game theory. Game-theoretic ideas run all through this volume, though I don't always take the time to point this out. Political science models are increasingly game-theoretic in spirit if not in fact. A good place to encounter game theory in the context of politics is the Ordeshook volume cited in footnote 2 above. For an outstandingly clean and clear (and brief!) presentation of the essentials of game theory, nothing competes with David M. Kreps, *Game Theory and Economic Modelling* (Oxford, U.K.: Oxford University Press, 1990).

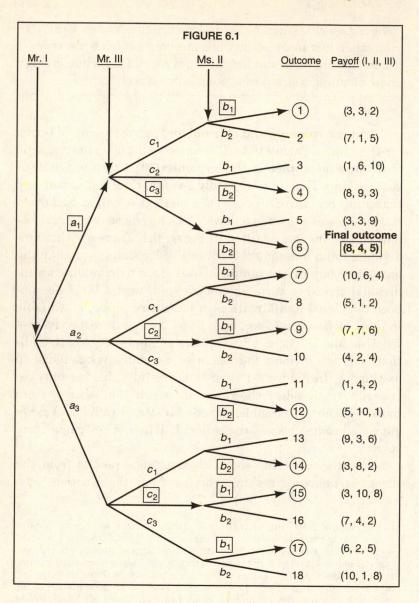

FIGURE 6.1

			Outcome	Payoff (I, II, III)

Mr. I   Mr. III   Ms. II

a_1 c_1 b_1 ① (3, 3, 2)
b_2 2 (7, 1, 5)
c_2 b_1 3 (1, 6, 10)
c_3 b_2 ④ (8, 9, 3)
b_1 5 (3, 3, 9)
b_2 ⑥ **Final outcome** **(8, 4, 5)**

a_2 c_1 b_1 ⑦ (10, 6, 4)
b_2 8 (5, 1, 2)
c_2 b_1 ⑨ (7, 7, 6)
c_3 b_2 10 (4, 2, 4)
b_1 11 (1, 4, 2)
b_2 ⑫ (5, 10, 1)

a_3 c_1 b_1 13 (9, 3, 6)
b_2 ⑭ (3, 8, 2)
c_2 b_1 ⑮ (3, 10, 8)
c_3 b_2 16 (7, 4, 2)
b_1 ⑰ (6, 2, 5)
b_2 18 (10, 1, 8)

There are eighteen different possibilities (resulting from the product of the three possible choices of Mr. I, the two possible choices of Ms. II, and the three possible choices of Mr. III). The method of backward induction begins with the player who moves last—Ms. II in this case. When it actually comes her turn to choose, she will find herself at one of nine choice points. (These are the nine nodes in the game tree in Figure 6.1 that line up below Ms. II's name.) At each node she may decide between two final outcomes (which are determined once she chooses between the two options in her action set). There is nothing fancy for Ms. II to do: once she learns which of the nine nodes the process has arrived at (as determined by choices by the other players), she will choose the option that leads to the outcome she most prefers.[5] At the top node, for example, she will select b_1 or b_2 depending upon whether she likes outcome 1 or 2, respectively, best. The same holds for each of the other eight nodes at which she may have a choice to make. Without bothering to write down complete preference orderings for all three players, I've simply indicated the payoffs to the players in Figure 6.1. For example, if outcome 1 prevails, then Mr. I receives a payoff of 3, Ms. II a payoff of 3, and Mr. III a payoff of 2. We assume, and this is very important, that the three players know one another's payoffs.

For each combination of choices by I and III, Ms. II has a choice between two outcomes, depending upon whether she chooses b_1 or b_2. We have put a *box* around the maximizing choice she will, in fact, make, and *circled* the outcome in each pair that will, in fact, be realized.

Mr. III is the next-to-last chooser. He knows that he will be at one of three choice nodes, depending upon Mr. I's prior choice. Using his foresight—that is, his knowledge of how

---

[5] This is actually an important general principle that I will highlight later in this chapter—namely, that the person moving last behaves pretty much according to her preferences. There are no fancy stratagems at this ultimate stage of the game.

Ms. II *will* choose at each of her subsequent choice opportunities given her preferences over final outcomes—he can determine how he *should* choose, given his own preferences over final outcomes. In effect, he can now erase Ms. II from his mind, replacing her nominal discretion after he chooses with the choice he knows she actually will make (the ones I've already boxed). Mr. III treats the boxed choices of Ms. II as *strategic equivalents* for those nodes. So, at Mr. III's top node he knows the implication in terms of final outcomes of each of the three options available to him there. If he chooses c_1, then outcome 1 is sure to occur; if he chooses c_2, then it will be outcome 4; if he chooses c_3, outcome 6 will be realized. The same will be the case at each of the other two choice nodes for III. He has preferences in each of these instances and, without writing them down explicitly, I simply box his optimal choice at each of his three choice nodes. The reader can check that the boxed choice at each of III's possible decision nodes is optimal for him, *taking account of II's subsequent optimal choice.*

Finally, it comes time for Mr. I to choose. He is now able to suppress the discretion of both Mr. III and Ms. II. He knows exactly what they will do in each contingency in which they might find themselves. Consequently, he knows the effect of each of the three choices he could make. So for him it is simply a matter of deciding which of the three outcomes he likes best.[6]

Working up the game tree via the method of backward induction, we have determined precisely how strategic actors will behave. Each will take into account what has, in fact, preceded their choices, as well as what they forecast will happen after they have made their choices. The final outcome of this

---

[6] If he chooses a_1, he knows Mr. III will follow with c_3 and Ms. II with b_2. Thus a choice of a_1 yields outcome 6 with a payoff of 8 to Mr. I. If he chooses a_2, then the other players will choose c_2 and b_1, respectively, yielding Mr. I a payoff of 7 from outcome 9. Finally, if he chooses a_3, outcome 15 with a payoff of 3 for him results. Of these he prefers outcome 6 and thus chooses a_1.

entire exercise is called the *strategic* outcome or *sophisticated* outcome.[7]

This concept is explored in more detail in the remainder of this chapter. But before moving on, I should point out that we have already seen at least one instance of strategic behavior. In the last chapter, a committee chair operating under an open rule in a one-dimensional legislature "backward-inducted." He asked himself what would happen if he opened the gates and made a proposal, concluding that rational behavior on the floor would lead to amendments ultimately producing x_m. On the other hand, the final outcome would remain at x^0 if he kept the gates closed. His decision on opening the gates, then, depended on his preferences between x_m and x^0. Thus, his own agenda-setting choice was predicated on foresight. We have also seen a failure to exercise this sort of foresight. The graduate school designers of the need-blind admissions policy described in Case 6.1 *failed* to exercise foresight, blithely assuming straightforward compliance of departments with their objectives. They failed to appreciate that there are competing objectives pursued by strategic actors.

CASE 6.3
PRESIDENTIAL VETO STORIES

The ability of the president to veto legislation passed by Congress provides an excellent opportunity to examine strategic behavior and backward induction. Some political observers have taken the infrequency with which presidents have used the veto as an indicator of cooperation be-

---

[7] When the choice is from a fixed sequence of votes, like a legislative agenda, most authors refer to "sophisticated" voting. When the choice is made in a one-shot circumstance, like switching your vote in an election because you believe your favorite candidate is out of contention, it is called "strategic" voting. I will tend to use these terms interchangeably.

tween the legislative and executive branches. In this view, infrequent use of the veto corresponds to a high degree of harmony between the branches. Thus, in his 1994 State of the Union speech, President Bill Clinton proudly announced the end of gridlock and the beginning of a new period of interbranch harmony by pointing to the fact that not once had he vetoed a piece of congressional legislation during 1993. Our backward induction argument suggests that President Clinton did not have logic on the side of his argument. The reason is simple: Rational foresight tells us that Congress should often *change* its behavior in order to avoid stimulating a veto; to do so is a measure of congressional foresight, not an indication of harmony between the branches. For example, in 1992 the Senate was reported to have dropped family planning money from a foreign aid bill in order to avoid a veto from President Bush.

Why would we ever see a presidential veto, if Congress can anticipate this veto and trim its sails accordingly? One answer is procedural: There is the possibility of an override. Congress can nullify the presidential veto if each chamber, subsequent to a veto, re-approves the bill by more than a two-thirds majority. In these circumstances, Congress can push ahead, knowing it can subsequently overcome presidential obstacles if it needs to. But this just pushes the question back a stage, namely, Why didn't the president exercise rational foresight in anticipating the override and therefore desist in using the veto? A second possibility, then, is uncertainty. Congress may not know how the president will respond to the legislation; the president may not correctly guess that his veto will be overridden.

Despite the veto possibility and even without a likely override, it may still be rational for Congress to send a bill to the president. Symbolic or constituent politics is one reason. During the Bush administration public pressure led Congress to consider a series of campaign-finance reform bills. The optimal outcome for each congressperson was to

vote for the bills, thereby appeasing constituents, but somehow to avoid actually having to implement the reforms. A
promised veto by President Bush gave the legislators what
they wanted. According to the *Washington Post*, Congress
was "secure in the knowledge that President Bush would
veto [the bills] and the veto could not be overridden; the virtuous vote was free."* In this case, ironically enough, the
presidential veto was a sign of *cooperation* between Congress and the White House, not *conflict*.

Party politics may also lead Congress to send a bill to the
president knowing it will be vetoed. In 1992 Democratic
Party desires to portray the Republican White House as the
source of governmental gridlock led to a series of bills on a
variety of subjects—cable TV regulation, family leave policy,
most-favored-nation status for China—all of which President Bush, because of previous commitments, was forced to
veto. Because these bills were popular with the general public, and because the vetoes displayed an executive at loggerheads with the legislature, the president's actions came at a
considerable cost to him. In this case the presidential vetoes
were a sign of conflict, not cooperation, with Congress.†

It should be apparent that very little can be inferred
about the degree of conflict or cooperation in a situation
just by observing an outcome. A presidential veto may reflect miscalculation (by Congress if the veto is not overridden, by the president if it is), interbranch harmony, efforts
by one branch to embarrass the other, and many other
things besides. Only by a careful analysis of the strategies,
alternatives, payoffs, incentives, and circumstances can we
form an accurate interpretation of the event.

---

* "Campaign Reform Anyone?" *Washington Post*, February 7, 1993, edito-
rial page.
† Ann Devroy, "Congress Pitching, President Vetoing," *Washington Post*,
September 24, 1992, p. A1.

In what follows, I take strategic behavior to consist of an extended sort of rationality. An individual does not merely assess options in front of her nose, choosing the one that seems best in terms of her preferences. Rather, she takes account of the fact that the choice before her is but one of a sequence of choices in an ongoing process. Strategic behavior requires that she look beyond her nose; the immediate choice before her, therefore, is not merely a one-shot, myopic decision, but instead one with longer-term effects. This leads, in each of the contexts we are about to explore, to the possibility of anomalies in which, at a specific choice opportunity, one ends up choosing what would appear to an outsider as a *less-preferred* option, if taken as a myopic choice. Strategic behavior, in short, taking the full horizon of a process into account, may require individuals to make seemingly less-than-ideal choices at some points in order to secure superior outcomes at the end of the trail. Below, we see this manifested in (1) sophisticated voting and agenda maneuverings in legislative settings, and (2) strategic voting and issue manipulation in electoral settings. First, however, I take up the general issue of strategic manipulation.

Manipulation

Before we go any further, it might be worth taking up an issue that a few doubters may be thinking about. To some, the idea of strategic behavior may be alien and, possibly, morally contemptible. Whether one admires brilliant strategic maneuvers or not, however, we need to know about them and where they are likely to be encountered. One thing we might want to know is whether there are decision-making procedures that encourage only honest, nonstrategic behavior—procedures that are basically *strategy-proof.* This is an abstract question that can be tackled at a fairly general level.

Suppose there are n group members, $G = \{1, 2, \ldots , n\}$, who must choose from a set of m alternatives, $A = \{a_1, a_2, \ldots, a_m\}$. I won't be very specific about the way in which the group makes its choice, except to say that the final choice will be one of the alternatives in A on the one hand, and that it will depend (somehow) on the preferences *expressed by* the group members on the other hand. That is, the social choice is written as $F(Q_1, Q_2, \ldots, Q_n, A) \in A$. In this expression, A is the set of alternatives defined above, Q_i is a preference ordering of the alternatives in A *expressed* by member i, and F is some decision process that transforms these expressed preferences into an outcome in A. Enter strategy.

I italicized the word "expressed" throughout the last paragraph for a reason. In most group choice situations we are not in possession of a fancy "preference meter" that reads people's minds. The group choice procedure, F, can only take the preferences that individuals *choose* to reveal. And where is it written that people are always *honest* in their preference revelation? We have already seen situations where people vote in a deceptive manner. More generally: Might an individual be able to secure a better outcome (according to her true preferences) by revealing untrue preferences—by behaving strategically?

Let's suppose that the *true* preference orderings of the members of G over the alternatives in A are $P_1, P_2, \ldots, P_n$, although no outside observer has any way of knowing or validating this. We say that Ms. i is *sincere* only if, in the group decision setting where she is asked to reveal her preferences, her revealed preference (Q_i) is identical to her true preference (P_i); if $Q_i \neq P_i$, then she is said to be *sophisticated*. So P_i reflects her true tastes, Q_i is what she chooses to reveal, and she is sincere only if the two are the same.[8] A sophisticated indi-

---

[8] I am being a little cagey here because it is quite possible that, sometimes, honesty is the best policy. Thus, $Q_i = P_i$ is a necessary but not a sufficient condition for someone to be said to be sincere. Confused? Don't worry about it. Interested? Then take a look at the piece by David Austen-Smith, "Sophisticated Sincerity: Voting over Endogenous Agendas," *American Political Science Review* 81 (1987): 1323–30.

vidual is someone who may misrepresent her true preferences and, when she does so, she is said to *manipulate F*, the social-choice procedure. Given all this, I now report the bad news:

> **Gibbard-Satterthwaite Theorem. Assume a group *G* of at least three individuals and a set *A* of at least three alternatives. Also assume that any member of *G* may have, as his or her true preferences, any preference ordering over *A* (universal domain). Then every nondictatorial social-choice procedure, *F*, is manipulable for some distribution of preferences.**

Allan Gibbard, a philosopher, and Mark Satterthwaite, an economist, simultaneously established this result about sophisticated behavior in the mid-1970s.[9] For any group (of at least three) and any decision setting (of at least three things to choose among), if the way in which decisions are made does not allow one member of the group to dictate the choice no matter how others feel (Arrow's Condition D), and if individuals are free to have whatever preferences they wish (Arrow's Condition U), then it is entirely possible for circumstances to arise in which at least one individual has an incentive to reveal his preferences strategically. No method of group choice is immune from manipulation.

Two brief examples will illustrate what is meant here and preview the rest of the chapter. In legislative politics, there is something known as a *killer amendment*. It is an amendment to a bill which, if successfully attached to the bill, will cause the bill to be defeated, even though the bill would have passed if it had not been amended. Discovering such amendments, and engineering them through the legislative thicket, thereby

---

[9] Allan Gibbard, "Manipulation of Voting Schemes: A General Result," *Econometrica* 41 (1973): 587–601; Mark A. Satterthwaite, "Strategy-proofness and Arrow's Conditions: Existence and Correspondence Theorems for Voting Procedures and Social Welfare Functions," *Journal of Economic Theory* 10 (1975): 187–217.

snatching defeat from the jaws of victory (often by someone purposely seeking to defeat the bill), is a political gift found in only the most talented politicians (some of whom are profiled in an entertaining little book by the late William Riker, *The Art of Political Manipulation*).[10] Such amendments often require sophisticated voting in which an enemy of the original bill votes for the killer amendment, even though she doesn't like the amendment per se. She does so because she appreciates that the now amended bill will be defeated, whereas the unamended bill would have passed. Thus, conventional legislative decision making is, as the Gibbard-Satterthwaite Theorem suggests, often vulnerable to manipulation.

So, too, is electoral politics. In the section after next, I examine the case of *strategic voting*, a brief example of which will have to suffice for now. It is well known that Anglo-American electoral arrangements, known as *plurality voting systems*, are fertile soil for two-party politics (a subject pursued in Chapter 7). In this electoral order, any number of parties may compete for a single office, with the candidate of the party winning the *most* votes (not necessarily a majority of the votes) declared the winner. The reason this arrangement nearly always reduces to two-party competition is that individual voters are loath to waste their votes, individual contributors are loath to waste their campaign resources, and individual political managers are loath to waste their electioneering skills on hopeless candidacies. They tend to desert such candidacies, *even if they would rather see that candidacy succeed because it is preferable in their view*. That is, people who want to make the most of their strategic endowments (votes, dollars, organizational skills) will prudently deploy them where they think they might make a difference (say, in helping to choose the lesser of evils), rather than deploying them where they serve only to express a preference but have no ef-

[10] (New Haven: Yale University Press, 1986).

fect on the final outcome. In the history of the United States, with some rare but important exceptions, third parties are victimized by strategic voting. Their final vote count *underestimates* their actual support in the electorate, reflecting misrevealed preferences—manipulation—by strategic actors (many of whom are ordinary voters).

SOPHISTICATED VOTING

Sophisticated voting takes the form of voting against one's true preferences at one stage of the legislative process in order to achieve an even better outcome (according to one's true preferences) at the end of the process. There is no law written anywhere that says that a legislator *must* vote his or her true preferences. Consider the history of the Powell Amendment (Case 6.4).

CASE 6.4
AID TO EDUCATION AND THE POWELL AMENDMENT

Probably the most famous and most often reported case of sophisticated voting surrounds the efforts of the Democratic majority in the House of Representatives in the mid-1950s to pass legislation enabling the federal government to provide financial support to local public school districts.* The status quo (x^0) at that time provided for virtually no federal role in public education from kindergarten through the

---

* Fuller versions of this story may be found in William H. Riker, *Liberalism Against Populism* (San Francisco: Freeman, 1982); Riker, *The Art of Political Manipulation*; and Arthur Denzau, William Riker, and Kenneth Shepsle, "Farquharson and Fenno: Sophisticated Voting and Home Style," *American Political Science Review* 79 (1985): 1117–35.

twelfth grade. The Education and Labor Committee of the Democrat-dominated House of Representatives introduced a bill, *B*, to authorize the federal government to subsidize educational efforts by the states. Adam Clayton Powell (D-N.Y.), the second-ranking Democrat on this education committee and perhaps the most prominent black politician in the country at the time, moved an amendment (*A*), now known as the Powell Amendment. If amended, the bill would subsidize elementary and secondary educational efforts by the states, but would restrict any federal funds from flowing to a school district that practiced segregation of the races.

The rules of procedure in the House required that the original bill and the amendment be pitted against each other (*B* vs. *A*). The winner was then subjected to a vote on final passage (effectively, winner vs. x^0). The two votes are displayed in the accompanying table. Reading its last column, it may be seen that the Powell Amendment passed, 229 to 197. From the last row, however, it may be seen that the amended bill failed when pitted against the status quo, 199 to 227. What went wrong?

While I cannot give a complete account here, several things may be remarked upon. The 132 yea-yea voters in the upper left corner of the table are the quintessence of sincerity. They were mostly northern liberal Democrats who both abhorred racial segregation and supported federal aid to education. In the end, as we shall see, they were the ones whose naïveté (if that's what it was) was exploited. The 67 nay-yea voters in the lower left corner are an interesting mix. These are the sophisticated Democrats. They favored school aid, on the one hand, and they saw Powell's motion as a killer amendment, on the other hand. Some may have favored the substance of the amendment, but they voted against it nonetheless. They preferred half a loaf to none. The 97 upper right corner yea-nay voters were crafty Republicans who opposed school aid. They were simply delighted to support Mr. Powell's effort to eradicate racial segregation in the South, not because they cared about that issue but because they saw that it would sink school aid (by peeling off southerners in the vote on final passage who would have supported an unamended school aid bill).

		FINAL PASSAGE		
		Yea	Nay	Total
POWELL	Yea	132	97	229
AMENDMENT	Nay	67	130	197
	Total	199	227	426

In voting against their nominal preferences in the contest pitting *B* vs. *A*, the Republicans assured themselves of a more preferred final outcome; their sophistication paid off. Had the 132 legislators in favor of school aid been willing to settle for half a loaf (in which school aid would not have been denied to segregated districts), they could have voted sophisticatedly against Powell's amendment, even though they preferred it, thereby assuring that *B* would have passed. Why didn't they behave strategically here? Denzau, Riker, and Shepsle speculate that many northern liberals feared explaining to their black constituents that they voted against Powell for "strategic" reasons.

STRATEGIC VOTING

We have just seen that a voter with a sophisticated capacity exercises rational foresight by looking ahead—that is, "down" an agenda that is fixed in advance. He or she may choose, at some stage or other, to vote against his or her nominal preferences for strategic reasons. Sometimes, however, a decision maker exercises rational foresight, though not in quite this same manner (Case 6.5).

CASE 6.5
NOT WASTING ONE'S VOTE

The 1968 national election in the United States found Hubert Humphrey (D) pitted against Richard Nixon (R) for the presidency. There was a third candidate in the race, George Wallace, who ran on the ticket of a new third party, the American Independent Party. Throughout the campaign during the fall of 1968, Humphrey and Nixon ran neck and neck, with polls showing their support in the 40 percent range. Wallace trailed badly, though still acknowledged by nearly 20 percent of the electorate as their first preference. In the "only poll that counts," as politicians like to refer to the actual election, Nixon and Humphrey each captured 43.5 percent of the popular vote, with Wallace coming in third with 13 percent. It appeared that Wallace's strength flagged in the final weeks of the campaign; he apparently lost more than a quarter of his support.

Let's assume that all the Nixon supporters stuck with their man, as did all the Humphrey supporters. Moreover, let's assume that the Wallace supporters—indeed, the entire nation—felt the election was going to be very close, but that their man was out of the running. There are actually three different types of voters preferring Wallace: (1) those who ranked Humphrey second [W-H-N]; (2) those who ranked Nixon second [W-N-H]; and (3) those who were indifferent between the two [W - (N,H)]. (In the type (1) and (2) categories, respectively, we include those who had Wallace tied with Humphrey or Nixon, respectively.) The Wallace campaign tried to transform all Wallace supporters into type (3) voters. His *slogan* emphasized that there was "not a dime's worth of difference between the major party candidates." Undoubtedly, however, some of those in the first and second category, in the privacy of the voting booth, decided not to waste their votes on a hopeless candidate, instead switching to their second preference. As a result, the actual vote totals of both Humphrey and Nixon grew relative to late poll data, whereas Wallace's shrank.

Fast-forward a quarter century to the 1992 presidential election. Once again a winning candidate, Bill Clinton, received only 43 percent of the popular vote. Once again there was a popular third-party candidate, H. Ross Perot. And once again, the third-party candidate's support hovered around the 20 percent mark during most of the campaign. But something was different this time. Perot's strength did *not* diminish at the end (he actually finished with 19 percent). Why did Perot preferrers not desert their candidate as Wallace preferrers had twenty-four years earlier?

Consider the three types of Perot suporters: (1) [P-C-B]; (2) [P-B-C]; and (3) [P-(C,B)]. The wasted-vote argument has clout only with voter types (1) and (2)—that is, with voters who have a decided preference between the major-party candidates, Clinton and Bush. Strategic voting has no allure for type (3) voters. If a higher proportion of Perot preferrers than Wallace preferrers were type (3), then there would be less possibility of falloff in Perot support. An interesting research project (I haven't done it, and don't know of any work in this area at this writing) would be to compare the different voter types for Perot and Wallace to determine whether a preference-distribution argument could account for the different falloff rates.

There is a second argument meriting investigation. In 1968, the election was seen as "too close to call." In 1992, in contrast, by the last week of the election, Clinton was perceived as pulling away from the incumbent president, George H. W. Bush (who ended up with less than 38 percent of the vote). A Perot supporter, even a type (1) or type (2) supporter, could hardly be accused of wasting her vote by casting it for Perot. Neither second-preference candidate would benefit from a Perot supporter's switch if the election weren't close—Clinton didn't need the help and it would be too little too late for Bush. An alternative explanation, then, is not that Perot supporters exercised less foresight than Wallace supporters, nor even that they were differentially distributed across preference types, but that, having exercised foresight, a Perot supporter concluded that a vote for Perot was apparently not a wasteful use of resources.

I have distinguished *sophisticated voting* from *strategic voting*, although each is an instance of rational foresight. Sophisticated voting is made possible by backward induction on a fixed agenda. In the three-person presidential contest, on the other hand, the issue is not one of voting contrary to preference at one node of a fixed agenda in order to achieve a more desirable outcome at a later point; it is one of deciding whether supporting your first choice is a hopeless undertaking. Put differently, *strategic voting* involves weighing two different lotteries. The first lottery (in which you vote for a Wallace or a Perot) gives, in comparison to the second lottery (vote for your second choice), a slightly higher chance of your first choice winning, along with a slightly higher chance of your last choice winning, too. The second lottery gives a higher chance of your middle alternative winning, reducing the chances of either your most-preferred or least-preferred outcome. A strategic voter, in effect, concedes that discretion is the better part of valor.

HERESTHETIC

I conclude the discussion of strategic behavior by claiming that the sort of strategizing just described is "strategizing in the small." For a clearly defined political situation, whether a sequence of votes in a legislature or a national election, manipulation takes the form of not voting for the alternative most highly ranked in terms of preferences. There's no doubt that this is an important form of strategic behavior, as the cases above suggest. But it is a restrictive view of strategic possibilities, because it takes the situation confronting group members as fixed and given. For instance, it does not ask where the agenda came from in the first place. Or, how did the election get shaped the way it did? Asking these questions opens up the possibility of "strategizing in the large," or what William Riker called *heresthetic*.

You will not find this term in a dictionary, for Riker coined it himself. He views heresthetic as the companion to *rhetoric*. The latter—the art of designing an argument—was a standard part of a young man's education in ancient times. Heresthetic—for Riker, the art of designing situations—is a word made up of parts of appropriate Greek words for "choosing" and "electing." Riker felt it should also have been part of that ancient education, for making arguments without attending to the larger strategic context is to strategize in the small, but not in the large.

We have already seen the heresthetician at work in the treatment of agenda-setting bodies, such as wily committee chairs in legislatures. Their jobs consist of structuring the content and sequence of voting—through proposing bills and amendments—so that the result turns out as the agenda setter would like.

Often, heresthetical maneuvers entail making something seem other than what it really is. This is not so much a deception as a "redefinition" of a situation. For example, Senator

Warren Magnuson (D-Wash.), for relatively obvious reasons, sought to get the U.S. Senate to block the Defense Department from transporting potentially lethal nerve gas canisters across his home state.[11] Fearing that his opposition to this national defense activity would be construed as reflecting merely parochial concerns—concerns that paled in significance to the urgency of removing these dangerous military assets from the post-Vietnam Pacific theater—he pursued a strategic tack that did not recount all the potential dangers to which his constituents might be exposed during transit. Indeed, his argument steered clear altogether of the substance in dispute. Instead, he suggested that the issue at hand was really about the constitutional powers of the Senate in foreign relations. He suggested that the decommissioning of the nerve gas, with its subsequent transit across the Northwest, was part of a larger matter in which the president had *failed to consult with the U.S. Senate as was his constitutional obligation.* What was at stake, suggested Magnuson, was the very authority of and respect for the U.S. Senate. This redefinition of the issue, as it happened, contributed to Magnuson's securing an outcome he preferred. The important point here is not so much that the senator won, but that he had the wit to see that reinterpretation was a viable strategic maneuver that promised the possibility of victory, where simply articulating an argument based on his concerns for the welfare of his Washington State constituents would surely have been discounted, even ignored.

The Magnuson maneuver bordered on the rhetorical, because it involved formulating an argument in order to persuade a small number of people on a well-defined issue. Another form of heresthetic involves redefinition on a grander stage. Riker writes extensively about the (strategic) develop-

---

[11] The entire episode is recounted in William H. Riker, *The Art of Political Manipulation*, Chapter 10.

ment of the slavery issue as an electoral heresthetic.[12] Briefly
stated, for much of the first half of the nineteenth century,
American national politics were dominated by the Jeffersonian-
Jacksonian coalition. Certainly by 1820, after the Federalist
Party had disappeared, this coalition was virtually unop-
posed. The coalition was united principally by the issue of
agrarian expansionism and found its greatest strength in the
middle Atlantic states, the South, and the states of the Northwest Territory. Opposition politicians, men like Henry Clay,
who were ambitious for themselves and their causes, searched
and searched for issues that might split this governing coalition. Their substantive opposition to the agrarian expansionism of the Jeffersonian-Jacksonians consisted in their desire
for public policy to encourage commercial development. But
this electoral contest between agrarian expansion and commercial development had already been fought out over the
previous generation, with Jefferson (later Jackson) and his allies winning big. No, the opposition would not win by simply
repeating the old arguments and fighting the old battles. It
needed to find a new issue that would split the currently dominant governing coalition, one that would divide Mid-Atlantic
from Rim South, Northwest from Deep South. And the slavery
issue was the answer.

Riker makes the argument that slavery worked not because of its moral content (although large numbers of Americans in the mid-nineteenth century found slavery abhorrent),
nor even because so many people were animated by abolitionist agitation. There are many morally significant issues float-
ing around at any particular time, but they do not necessarily
bring ruling coalitions down. Slavery worked as a strategic
maneuver because it divided the members of an existing
winning coalition, some of whom tolerated slavery and some
of whom opposed it. Once the northern elements of the

---

[12] This is developed in Riker, *Liberalism against Populism*, Chapter 9.

Jeffersonian-Jacksonian coalition came to fear that support of slavery on which their southern coalition partners depended would be their own personal undoing, the coalition could no longer hold. Subsequent events about which the historians wrote—the Kansas-Nebraska Act of 1854, the Dred Scott decision in 1857, and ultimately civil war itself—put this coalition to an end. But it was the heresthetical maneuverings of losing politicians looking for ways to become winners that set all this in motion.[13]

CONCLUSION

This chapter has covered a number of subtleties of group behavior. It serves as something of an antidote, however, to earlier discussions of group choice, because here individuals are endowed with a capacity to consider the broader implications of their actions. Although I have referred to this as strategic behavior and have occasionally characterized it in emotionally

---

[13] The logic of heresthetic can be understood as the introduction of a new issue, or the redefinition of an old one, in order to destroy a currently winning coalition and replace it with some other. Students of politics should not think that heresthetic is either rare or purely of historical interest. Issues capable of splitting winning coalitions arise all the time. It only takes a master heresthetician (like Warren Magnuson or Henry Clay) to use the issue as a wedge to divide the opposition. Modern issues exhibiting heresthetical traces include the gun-control movement's proposal to ban "cop-killer" bullets and assault weapons in order to split the coalition between the law enforcement community and the National Rifle Association; Ronald Reagan's appeal to anticommunism and conservative social values to create "Reagan Democrats" out of a portion of his former opposition; the use of the abortion issue by Democrats to woo pro-choice Republican women; use of that same issue by pro-life activists to induce Christian fundamentalists to desert the Democratic Party; and finally, the exploitation by antismoking forces of conflict within the tobacco industry between farmers and manufacturers over the matter of tobacco imports. Heresthetical maneuvers do not always succeed. But they constitute the set of activities that those currently out of power employ in an effort to get back on top. See Kenneth A. Shepsle, "Losers in Politics (and How They Sometimes Become Winners): William Riker's Heresthetic," *Perspectives on Politics* 1 (2003): 307–15.

charged terms (misrepresentation, manipulation, and so on), all I have really done is to acknowledge the individual's capacity to look beyond his or her nose, the individual's proficiency in taking a longer-term view of things—in short, the individual's talent for behaving deliberatively and exercising foresight.

Foresight comes in many shapes, and I have covered some of them here. Sophisticated behavior, especially in the context of legislative settings, is the capacity to make voting decisions in a sequential process with an eye to final results. Sometimes this entails voting contrary to nominal preferences—for example, voting against an amendment you like because you know it will damage the chances for the whole bill to survive. For this reason, I have alluded to individuals *misrepresenting* their preferences. Really, though, they are just taking care of business in the most sensible fashion available to them. Likewise, in the electoral setting, voters who elect not to vote for their favorite candidate because he doesn't have much chance of winning are clearly behaving strategically; but here, too, citizens are simply engaging in a perfectly legitimate activity, namely, using the instruments at their disposal (their votes at the very least) to effect outcomes in a direction they prefer.

Sophisticated behavior is also associated with activities other than voting. The committee chair's judgment call on whether to open the gates or not is one manifestation of this kind of exercise in foresight. The opposition politician's injection of new issues into an electoral campaign is another. In each case politicians use the resources at their disposal (control of the legislative agenda and influence over public opinion, respectively) to accomplish goals—policy goals in the case of the legislative chair, electoral goals in the case of the opposition politician. Sophistication resides in their ability to use the assets at their disposal *instrumentally*.

To appreciate fully the strategic options available to individuals, then, it is clear that we must understand the context in which they operate, for it is the context that provides them with opportunities to deploy their resources instrumentally. This is no more apparent than in the world of electoral politics, where different electoral arrangement effectively constitute altogether different contexts in which to deploy resources. This is precisely our agenda for the next chapter.

EXPERIMENTAL CORNER

Agenda Setting and Group Choice

The strategic behavior put on display in the material in this chapter is multifaceted and many-splendored. Most of the instances covered here involve voters or legislators misrepresentating their "honest" preferences by casting strategic or sophisticated votes. Likewise, in Case 6.1, a university department misrepresents its honest evaluation of graduate admissions candidates in order to make the most of its limited resources. In all of these circumstances the actors take the alternatives on offer as given and, based on what's available, figure out how they can best accomplish their personal objectives. In this experimental corner I describe a different kind of strategic behavior—setting the agenda from which choices will ultimately be taken. This is the focus of a wonderful paper by Plott and Levine.[a]

The motivation for this experiment came from a situation of personal significance to Plott and Levine: "As a practical matter, we were involved in an important and complex committee decision. A large flying club in which we held membership was meeting to vote upon the size and compo-

---

[a] Charles R. Plott and Michael E. Levine, "A Model of Agenda Influence on Committee Decisions," *American Economic Review* 68 (1978): 146–60. Also see William H. Riker, *The Art of Political Manipulation* (New Haven: Yale University Press, 1986), Chapter 3.

sition of the aircraft fleet which would be available to the membership for flying. As members we had preferences about the fleet available to us and an opportunity to shape the agenda. Preliminary discussions and meetings had narrowed the range of possibilities greatly. . . . Over these remaining possibilities, however, there were conflicting and strongly held opinions. The group was to meet once and decide the issue by majority vote. . . . The meeting was held. The group used our agenda. The decision was the one we predicted" (p. 146).

Plott and Levine wondered whether their success in manipulating the group's choice by selecting an agenda that yielded the result they wanted was an accidental piece of good fortune or something more general. They set up an experiment to test their hunches. Their experiment involved partitioning alternatives into subsets and having subjects select a subset. The winning subset, in turn, is further partitioned and a subsequent choice is taken. This continues until a unique alternative remains. For example, suppose the issue were one of planning a dinner party in which two choices had to be made: cuisine (French or Mexican) and dress (formal or informal). The four possible outcomes are {French formal, French informal, Mexican formal, Mexican informal}. One *agenda* requires the choice of cuisine to be taken first and dress next. Consequently, subjects choose between two subsets: {French formal, French informal} and {Mexican formal, Mexican informal}. The winner—say, the first subset—then becomes the set of alternatives on offer when choosing dress. Another agenda would have dress chosen first, then cuisine: {French formal, Mexican formal} versus {French informal, Mexican informal}. Other agendas are possible, though they entail choices across these two categories, for example, {French formal, Mexican informal} versus {French informal, Mexican formal}. Thus, the agenda allows group members to cast votes, but *limits the items up for a vote and their order.* The experimenter gets to select the agenda (with an eye to "manipulating" the group into choosing the final outcome he or she likes best).

Plott and Levine focus on three *voting strategies* that participants might adopt: (1) sincere voting—at each partition, vote for the subset that contains the participant's most-preferred alternative (from among those alternatives still alive); (2) avoid-the-worst—at each partition, vote for the subset that does *not* contain the least-preferred alternative among those still possible; and (3) average value—at each partition, treat the alternatives in a subset as a lottery with each having equal probability and vote for the subset with the highest expected utility. Plott and Levine do not know, for any experimental subject, the particular decision rule he or she is using.

Experimental subjects were students from Caltech, UCLA, and USC. They were gathered in a classroom, given a group decision to select a letter from a subset of the alphabet, and were provided with a payoff sheet indicating their particular monetary payoff depending upon which letter was chosen. Thus, each subject had induced preferences over the letters. Decisions were made by majority rule.

The induced preferences of the experimental subjects were such that, from the set {A,B,C,D,E} of alternatives, each of the first four alternatives was preferred to E; A was preferred by a majority to every other alternative; and B, C, and D were part of a majority rule cycle (B preferred to C, C preferred to D, and D preferred to B). Agendas were designed by the experimenters so that if the subjects were of a particular type—(1), (2), or (3) above—and behaved according to the theory, then a specific outcome would prevail. (Actually, Plott and Levine have a more complicated theory in which they assume probabilities for the different types and design an agenda in which the *expected* outcome can be derived from their theory.) For example, consider the parti-

tion {A,B,E} versus {C,D}. If everyone is type (1), a majority
will select the first subset, since a majority prefers A to any
of the other alternatives in the other subset. If the partition
of this winner is {A} versus {B,E}, then A will prevail. If
everyone is type (2), then a majority will select {C,D}, since
E is worst for a majority, and then, from among these, C
will prevail (since C is preferred by a majority to D). If
everyone is type (3), then if their payoff for E is made especially bad, they will opt for {C,D} and then choose C; but if
E is not sufficiently bad, then they might opt for {A,B,E}
and then ultimately for A. More generally, the experimenters can develop expectations for which outcome they
can induce by their strategic choice of agenda.[b]

Running this experiment across many groups of experimental subjects, the experimenters find that their expectations are extraordinarily accurate. Space precludes a
detailed discussion of the results, so readers should consult
the paper on their own. Plott and Levine conclude that, at
least in the laboratory, "the agenda can indeed be used to
influence the outcome of a committee decision" (p. 156).
This provides some empirical support that agenda power is
a manipulable strategic resource—something that legislative committee chairs, academic department heads, and
those who lead meetings undoubtedly discover. Rank-and-
file members, on the other hand, will want to avail themselves of parliamentary protection to reduce the degree to
which they can be exploited by clever agenda setters.

---

[b] If, instead of hypothesizing that *all* group members are of a specific type,
the experimenters assume some distribution of types across the group
members, they can still deduce probabilistic expectations associated with
particular agenda choices.

PROBLEMS AND DISCUSSION QUESTIONS

1. Suppose that strategy c_3 is unavailable to Mr. III in the game displayed in Figure 6.1. Use backward induction to solve this amended game. Now suppose that c_3 is again available to Mr. III, but Mr. I can no longer play a_1. What is the final outcome?

2. Why would supporters of a particular bill ever vote in *favor of* a killer amendment? Some things to consider might include how constituents evaluate their legislators and uncertainty about whether an amended bill will pass.

*3. For this question we return to the setup of Problem 1 in Chapter 5 to see what happens when individuals in an agenda setup vote sophisticatedly.

- It is the last round of a three-item agenda, v, so the society is voting over the option that won the first round and the final option on the agenda. Will any player wish to misrepresent her true preferences? Try out some specific head-to-head matchups (e.g., x vs. y, or y vs. z) to build up your intuition.

- With the agenda $v = (y,x,z)$, first determine what happens in the final round depending on whether y or x wins the first round. Based on this, can player 2 ever do better by supporting x in the first round, contrary to her nominal preferences? What about 3 voting against x? Knowing this, should 1 misrepresent his preferences by playing y in round 1?

- (Bonus) Identify the outcomes (and which player acts strategically) if the agenda is $v' = (z, x, y)$ and $v'' = (z, y, x)$. Compare these answers with the honest voting outcomes.

4. Why do some voters "waste" their vote by supporting third-party candidates who have no chance of winning office? Why do other voters, who may prefer a third-party candidate, nonetheless vote for someone else? Discuss the phenomenon of strategic voting in plurality elections and illustrate your arguments with reference to illustrious third-party candidates in the United States—for example, Ralph Nader (2000), Ross Perot (1992), and George Wallace (1968). Why have the experiences of third-party candidates (in terms of election day dropoffs in support) been so different?

5. In the study of legislatures, political scientists often rely on voting scores to measure the preferences of legislators on policy issues. For instance, the League of Conservation Voters compiles a list of key votes on environmental matters during a session of Congress and then ranks members of Congress based on how often they took the "pro-environment" side. Will we get meaningful results from these types of scores? Under what circumstances? In answering this question, consider the role of the closed rule (which allows committees to make take-it-or-leave-it offers), strategic voting, and sequential voting/minimum winning coalitions (discussed in Case 6.2).

6. Is an assumption of sincere voting ever suitable for analyzing politics? In a legislature? Among voters in an election? On a small decision-making committee?

7. Explain the meaning of the Gibbard-Satterthwaite Theorem in your own words, being careful to define terms like *strategy-proof, manipulable*, and *sophisticated voting*. What are the implications of the theorem for the normative arguments in favor of democracy? Of what significance is the theorem for social scientists trying to make predictions about political outcomes?

7

Voting Methods and Electoral Systems

In the last few chapters an implicit theme has emerged: It is nearly impossible to arrange for the making of fair and coherent group choices. Preference cycles, agenda manipulation, strategic misrepresentation of preferences, heresthetical maneuvers, and so on frustrate our best attempts. The coup de grâce, developed in this chapter, is that "popular sovereignty"— by which we mean any method for allowing individuals in a group to affect their own fates through voting—is not unambiguous either. There are lots of different ways to cast and count votes or "do" majority rule, for instance. If all these methods differed only in the details but not in the final result, then we could relegate the matter of details to politics junkies to chat about. Alas, the devil is in the details. In this chapter, therefore, I explore the procedural context of voting—the rules by which small committees and large electorates make choices.

The discussion is partitioned into two sections according to what it is the group is choosing. The first part of the discussion focuses on how relatively small groups—a set of friends, a club, a committee—choose some alternative from a set of available alternatives. I call these arrangements *voting methods*. The second part of the discussion emphasizes how relatively large groups (called electorates) choose a specific thing (called a legislature). I call these arrangements *electoral systems*. In each part of this discussion, I am not so much interested in conveying specific details about the myriad ways of making group choices as in hammering home the simpler facts that *there are myriad ways of making group choices, that each has merit in some circumstances, but that the rationale for none seems decisive or compelling in all situations.*

VOTING METHODS

The Problem with Methods of Voting—They Matter!

Getting down to business, suppose we have a group of 55 individuals, choosing among five alternatives, {a, b, c, d, e}.[1] Of the 120 possible complete and transitive strict preference orderings an individual might adopt as his or her own,[2] there are only six distinct orderings, or "opinions," represented in this particular group. They are listed in Table 7.1, along with the number of group members holding each. (The underlining in Table 7.1 will be explained later.) For the sake of discussion, six different "reasonable" ways for the group to arrive at a choice among the five alternatives are considered. The reader may well be able to devise others and should rest assured that, in human history, a multitude of alternative methods have been devised.[3]

---

[1] This absolutely evil example was invented by Joseph Malkevitch and is displayed in Figure 2 of his article, "Mathematical Theory of Elections," *Annals of the New York Academy of Sciences* 607 (1990): 89–97. For another example that shows some of the outcome variation that arises in moving from one voting system to another, even with preferences held fixed, see Donald G. Saari, "Chaos, But in Voting and Apportionments?" *Proceedings of the National Academy of Sciences* 96 (September 1999): 10568–71.

[2] Recall that there are five possible first-preference alternatives, four remaining possibilities for second preferences, and so on—or, 5 × 4 × 3 × 2 × 1 = 120 ways to strictly order five alternatives.

[3] A considerably more systematic treatment of alternative voting methods is found in William H. Riker, *Liberalism Against Populism* (San Francisco: Freeman, 1982), Chapter 4. Somewhat more technical, yet quite insightful, is Peter Fishburn, "A Comparative Analysis of Group Decision Methods," *Behavioral Science* 16 (1971): 38–44.

TABLE 7.1
AN EVIL EXAMPLE

I (18)	II (12)	III (10)	IV (9)	V (4)	VI (2)
a	b	c	d	e	e
d	e	b	c	b	c
e	d	e	e	d	d
c	c	d	b	c	b
b	a	a	a	a	a

SOURCE: Joseph Malkevitch, "Mathematical Theory of Elections," *Annals of the New York Academy of Sciences* 607 (1990): 89–97 (Figure 2)

Consider, as a first method, the simplest of them all: *simple plurality voting*. Each voter casts a single vote for a single alternative, and the alternative with the most votes wins. This is one of the hallmarks of the Anglo-American system for electing legislators.[4]

A slight variation is the *plurality runoff*, in which each voter casts a single vote for a single alternative, and the two alternatives with the most votes move to a second stage in which the balloting is repeated between these two survivors according to simple plurality voting.

An even more intricate and general form of runoff is the *sequential runoff*. Here each voter casts a single vote for a single alternative, the alternative with the fewest votes is eliminated, and the balloting is repeated. This procedure continues until there is a single alternative left.

The fourth method we examine allows voters to express preferences about *all* the alternatives. According to the *Borda count*, a scoring system much like that used in international track competitions, each voter expresses personal preferences

[4] When discussed in the latter half of this chapter as an electoral system, it will be called *first past the post*.

over the five alternatives by awarding four points to his or her first choice, three to the second choice, two to the third, one to the fourth, and none to the fifth. These points are totaled and the alternative with the most points wins.

Fifth, the **Condorcet procedure** seeks to determine whether there is some specific alternative that can secure a majority against each of the others in a pairwise round-robin tournament. If so, that is the winner. If not, then we will need to provide some alternative procedure (perhaps one of the others).

Finally, consider the method of ***approval voting***, invented by the political scientist Steven Brams and the operations research scholar Peter Fishburn. It puts no limit on the number of votes an individual can cast. Each individual casts votes for all those alternatives she "approves of." This means that if she wishes, she may cast votes for all the alternatives, none of them, or any number in between. The winner is the alternative that receives the most approval votes.[5] All of the methods are listed in Display 7.1.

With the data of Table 7.1 we can determine how the various forms of popular sovereignty listed in Display 7.1 perform. Voters are assumed to vote sincerely. Display 7.2 provides the results, with the winning alternative given in bold.

The simple plurality method produces a victory for *a*, since it has the most first-preference supporters, though a peculiar victory it is, given that all but the first group *hate* this alternative. This is made all too apparent when we look at the plurality runoff procedure in which *b* triumphs; indeed, *any* alternative that made it to the "finals" against *a* would have

---

[5] An individual who votes for all the alternatives states that all are "above threshold," or acceptable. The impact on the final outcome is exactly the same as the voter who abstains (or, equivalently, states that she approves of no alternative). What matters in approval voting is that an alternative do well *relative to its competitors*; its absolute vote total is less important.

DISPLAY 7.1
SOME VOTING METHODS

Method	Description
Simple plurality voting	Alternative with most votes (plurality) wins.
Plurality runoff	Top two vote getters move to a second round; new balloting determines second-round winner by simple plurality voting.
Sequential runoff	Alternative with fewest votes is eliminated and balloting repeated; elimination procedure continues until one alternative remains.
Borda count	Alternatives assigned points in accord with voter rank-orders. The alternative with the largest sum of points wins.
Condorcet procedure	Pairwise round-robin tournament determines if one alternative defeats each of its rivals.
Approval voting	Each voter casts votes for any alternative he or she approves of. The alternative with the most votes wins.

---

beaten it. The sequential runoff procedure produces c as the final outcome. The Borda count gives the victory to d. And the Condorcet procedure shows that alternative e receives a majority (28 or more of 55 votes) against every other alternative. In short, each of the first five preference-based methods of group choice yielded a *different* winner. The sixth, approval voting, yielded a tie between d and e.

So we must conclude that the rules of preference aggregation matter, and sometimes (as in this example) they matter a lot. It is evident in this example that whoever chooses the method of counting noses determines, finally and decisively,

DISPLAY 7.2
ELECTROAL SYSTEM RESULTS

Simple plurality: **a=18**   b=12   c=10   d=9   e=6

Plurality runoff:
  round 1   **a=18**   **b=12**   c=1   d=9   e=6
  round 2   a=18   **b=37**

Sequential runoff:
  round 1   **a=18**   **b=12**   **c=10**   **d=9**   e=6
  round 2   **a=18**   **b=16**   **c=12**   d=9
  round 3   **a=18**   b=16   **c=21**
  round 4   a=18   **c=37**

Borda count: a=4(18) + 0(12) + 0(10) + 0(9) + 0(4) + 0(20)= 72
                 b=0(18) + 4(12) + 3(10) + 1(9) + 3(4) + 1(2)=101
                 c=1(18) + 1(12) + 4(10) + 3(9) + 1(4) + 3(2)=107
                 d=3(18) + 2(12) + 1(10) + 4(9) + 2(4) + 2(2)=136
                 c=2(18) + 3(12) + 2(10) + 2(9) + 4(4) + 4(2)=134

*Condorcet:**

	a	b	c	d	e
a	—	18	18	18	18
b	37	—	16	26	22
c	37	39	—	12	19
d	37	29	43	—	27
e	**37**	**33**	**36**	**28**	—

Approval:†

a	18+0+0+0+0+0	=18
b	0+12+10+0+4+0	=26
c	0+0+10+9+0+2	=21
d	**18+12+10+9+4+2**	**=55**
e	18+12+10+9+4+2	=55

* Reading across each row in the matrix gives the number of votes that each *row* alternative gets when paired against each of the *column* alternatives. Thus, reading across the second row, alternative *b* gets 37, 16, 26, and 22 votes out of 55 against *a, c, d,* and *e*, respectively.

† Each group is assumed to cast votes for all the alternatives above the line in Table 7.1. Thus, every group but the third votes for three of the five alternatives; the third group approves of four out of the five.

the final outcome. Put somewhat differently, whatever procedure is in place for choosing the method determines the final outcome. But putting procedures in place is the business of constitutions; they either say directly what method will apply or indicate who (or what body) gets to decide. No wonder constitutional politics are such struggles! So much is at stake. And while the example above provides something of a worst-case scenario (what with each method producing a uniquely different outcome), the reader should understand that it is not an altogether extreme instance. As the section title says, the problem with voting methods is that they matter!

Thinking about Voting Methods

At present there is no generally accepted way to think about voting methods. There are so many different ways to vote, and so many potentially useful criteria to bring to bear on alternative systems, that it is easy to become quickly confused. Here I want only to suggest a couple of directions for thought. Generally speaking, a voting method may be thought of in terms of (1) the inputs required, (2) what the procedure does to those inputs, and (3) the output or outcome produced. That is, the final *outcome* is a *function* of the *inputs* (written: outcome = F(inputs)), and we can think about each of the three italicized components separately.

1. In terms of inputs, plurality voting makes the simplest demands on voters (and perhaps for this reason, it is a commonly used method of group choice); each person must simply name an alternative (his or her first preference if a sincere voter, something else otherwise). On the other hand, the demand on voters in a runoff plurality election depends upon how it is administered. If voters are expected to show up for two separate rounds, then less information at each round is required (but the cost of showing up both times is greater). In round one, the same data as in a simple plurality contest is re-

quired. In round two, relative preference between the two highest vote getters in round one is needed. If voters wish to economize on trips to the polls, showing up only once, then they must provide more information on that one occasion. Specifically, they must provide information on every possible pairwise comparison (if there are five alternatives, then there are ten comparisons), since it is not known in advance *which* pair will advance to the second round. However, all this comparison data is contained in a voter's preference ordering, so that's all a voter need provide at the outset. This is precisely the same data required for a sequential runoff election, a Borda count procedure, and a Condorcet procedure, too. Approval voting requires as much information about preferences as each voter wants to reveal.[6]

Allowing these six methods to stand for the many hundreds of voting methods that have sprung from human creativity, the point here is that methods differ as to what they require—a single alternative, a subset (of whatever size each voter wishes), or an entire preference ordering. There may be grounds for preferring one method over another, quite apart from the particular result each may yield, based on the ease of administering it or on the desire to economize on the burden of the voter. On the other hand, the necessary inputs may depend on what you want to get out of the group choice—something discussed below. Wherever one stands on these or a host of other criteria for thinking about inputs, it is patently clear, on the basis of required inputs alone, that democratic voting, broadly understood, takes on a multiplicity of forms.

2. I won't spend much time on the procedures themselves and what they do, since I described a few of them already in Display 7.1. I do want to point out, however, that these proce-

---

[6] That is, the voter can either submit a subset of the full set of alternatives (the "approved of" alternatives) or, as in Table 7.1, he or she can hand in a preference ordering with a line drawn below the "approved of" alternatives.

dures (and any others you can think up) have their peculiarities. Plurality rule, for instance, is especially odd. Alternative *a* was the plurality winner in the example above, yet *it loses to every other alternative in pairwise comparison*. Additionally, the Condorcet winner, *e*, which many would take as a strong normative candidate for the group choice, actually got the *fewest* votes in the plurality contest. Runoffs, whether simple or sequential, have the perverse possibility of eliminating an alternative that can beat every other in a pairwise contest (*e* never made it very far in these runoffs). The Borda count method (indeed, this is true of all the methods) is very vulnerable to strategic behavior. Notice that the twelve voters of group II or the ten voters of group III in Table 7.1, who prefer *e* to *d*, can actually give *e* a victory by misrepresenting their preference ranking for *d* (pretending it is lower in their ranking).[7] The Condorcet procedure does not always produce a winner—and then what do you do?

Finally, there is an issue that applies to each of the voting methods we have described, but we will discuss it in terms of approval voting, since its proponents seem so unperturbed by it.[8] In the example above there are five alternatives. Those alternatives might be various motions (say, what movie the fraternity house should rent this evening) or candidates (say, which of the sorority sisters should be the representatives on the Greek Council). However, which motions are moved or which candidacies are activated depends intimately on the voting method, *F*. You might figure, for example, that *The Hurt Locker* would get a lot of second-choice votes from your

---

[7] Borda, a member of the French Academy of Sciences in the late eighteenth century, was informed by one of its other members, Condorcet, that the Borda count could be manipulated. Borda is reported to have sniffed, "My method is only for honorable men."

[8] See, especially, the various writings of Brams and Fishburn on the merits of approval voting, including "Approval Voting," *American Political Science Review* 72 (1978): 831–47, and their book *Approval Voting* (Boston: Birkhauser, 1983).

frat brothers, and thus have a good chance of winning if the voting method were the Borda count. But you also believe it wouldn't get many first-preference votes, so you probably wouldn't even bother proposing it if the decision rule were plurality voting. To look at a *fixed* set of alternatives and compare the outcome under plurality against that of approval or the outcome under Borda against that of Condorcet, for example, misses this point. In the jargon of the field, the set of alternatives or candidates is *endogenous*—that is, highly dependent on the method of counting heads. In this regard, my hunch is that approval voting encourages a larger number of alternatives to be brought forward (so to speak) than many other voting methods. Candidates know they do not have to be the top choice of a voter, but merely *among* the "approved of" set, and thus may find it easier to rationalize their prospects of victory. Likewise, a motion need not be the favorite of many voters but only *among* the favorites to prosper under approval voting, a fact that may give encouragement to potential motion makers. So, the question comes down to whether it is better or worse for a group to have a rich set of items from which to choose or a more spartan set. Is more always better than less? This question will take on an interesting political significance in the second part of this chapter when we examine proportional representation versus other systems for electing legislatures.

3. It may seem odd that we even need to discuss the output of a voting method, since it is no more than the thing that is chosen. But exactly what is that "thing"? We have somewhat abstractly described alternatives by letters, suggesting that the thing the group must choose is some unitary entity, some element of the set $\{a, b, c, d, e\}$. But we can quickly complicate matters quite a bit. Shortly, for instance, I will talk about ways of choosing members of a legislature. The "thing" here could be a single legislator, a group of legislators from a multi-member district, or the legislature in its entirety. Or, to give an example with a different emphasis, imagine that what we,

as a group, are doing is choosing *instructions* to give our agent. Imagine that our agent must choose among the five letters for us, but she will not know in advance (nor will we) whether all five are available or only some subset thereof. She will need to know more than the group's favorite, since that alternative may turn out to be unavailable. Thus, the group, in this instance, needs to choose a *collective preference ordering* to guide its agent. The point here is that one set of criteria to evaluate a voting method is relevant when all the group needs to do is choose a letter, but an entirely different set may come into play when the group needs to come up with a full preference ordering. The nature of the output, then, should affect the way we think about voting methods.

This entire discussion produces a serious philosophical puzzle. If the "wish of the group," or the "collective will," or the "public interest"—whatever you want to call the output of group deliberation—is to be ascertained from the inputs that the individual group members bring to the voting method (and those inputs vary from method to method), then how are we to give meaning to "wish of the group," "collective will," or "public interest"? Using one method may yield one conclusion about what the group wants, while using a different method yields a different conclusion because it operates on some new set of alternatives. This is crazy! But it is even worse. Suppose, as in the example associated with Table 7.1, the alternatives under consideration remain constant, and that voter preferences have also remained fixed. Then, with alternatives and preferences fixed, it seems only natural to presume the wish of the group is well defined—it is whatever it is. The only thing that might change is the way in which those wishes are revealed or ascertained by the voting method. Yet we have seen that the outcome *does* change (most evilly displayed in the example at the beginning of this chapter). But surely it seems perverse to conclude that the group wish has changed just because the method we have used to ascertain it—and *only* the method—has changed. Are we driven to this conclusion? We ask the reader to think hard about this question, for it has motivated much of the discussion of the last five chapters. I know of no definitive answer to it, although I shall examine some in the summary that follows this chapter.

This part of our discussion is in a woefully incomplete state. Our principal purpose, however, has been less to provide a broad summary of the myriad methods of conducting group voting than to convey by illustration a sense of fragility in group life. The decisions a group reaches, as the last few chapters have suggested, depend not only upon the options made available, not only on the order in which some agenda setter presents them, not only on the degree to which group members reveal or misreveal their preferences, but also on the way they conduct the actual decision making. And all those other things, likewise, are influenced by the voting method we adopt. A group decision surely reflects member preferences. *But it also reflects much more*, a theme to which I will return in the summary.

ELECTORAL SYSTEMS

Just as there are many voting methods, there also is an incredible variety of electoral systems. I restrict consideration to systems for electing legislatures, using these institutions to represent a broad class of elected governance arrangements.[9] I claim here that electoral systems may be thought of in terms of the degree to which their "core value" is *representation* or *governance*. By the former I mean an electoral arrangement that places priority on the degree to which the elected reflect

---

[9] In a sense, a legislature *is* a generic elected institution. For example, a president, governor, or mayor may be thought of as a one-person legislature, an elected court as a one- (or more) person legislature, and so on.

(or represent) the beliefs and preferences of the electors. By the latter I mean an arrangement yielding elected representatives capable of acting decisively, of governing. Obviously, both of these purposes are noble. Yet, they often operate at cross-purposes because an arrangement that emphasizes representativeness may make governance more difficult, and vice versa.[10]

Associated with the end of the spectrum giving priority to representation is the broad family of electoral methods known as *proportional representation* (PR). At the other end of the spectrum is the family of *plurality voting* methods (referred to earlier in this chapter). The discussion begins with plurality methods that are common in the United States and Great Britain. This will be followed by a treatment of the more exotic PR methods found in continental Europe. Finally, arguments are offered on why these broad classes of electoral system are seen as either representation-oriented or governance-oriented.

General Remarks

One of the leading contemporary students of the theory of electoral systems, Gary Cox, has defined an electoral system in terms of five bits of information.[11] For Cox, as for us, the critical separation is between plurality and proportional systems, but five bits of information can be used to characterize

---

[10] For an elaboration on this theme, with special reference to the U.S. Congress, see Kenneth A. Shepsle, "Representation and Governance: The Great Legislative Tradeoff," *Political Science Quarterly* 103 (1988): 461–84.

[11] Two especially important papers by Cox are mathematically advanced but well worth examining, if only to get a feel for the kinds of analysis scholars like Cox are able to do. See his "Electoral Equilibrium under Alternative Voting Institutions," *American Journal of Political Science* 31 (1987): 82–109; and "Centripetal and Centrifugal Incentives in Voting Systems," *American Journal of Political Science* 34 (1990): 903–36. These are summarized and extended in Gary C. Cox, *Making Votes Count* (New York: Cambridge University Press, 1997).

each. These five describe the resources given to voters, what the voters can do with their resources, and finally, how the electoral formula produces a final outcome—in effect, the inputs, procedures, and outputs discussed earlier. Generally speaking, Cox maintains the following distinction between plurality and proportional arrangements.[12]

> By a plurality formula, I mean one in which voters cast votes for individuals (rather than party lists) and the top . . . vote-getters win seats. . . . Proportional formulas, on the other hand, are those in which voters vote for parties, and seats are allocated in proportion to the vote polled by each party.

The five bits of information are v (number of *votes* per voter); p (if $v > 1$, whether voters must cast all v votes, or may *partially abstain*); c (if $v > 1$, whether voters may *cumulate* their votes, or must distribute them); k (the number of legislators to be elected per district, known as the *district magnitude*); and f (the *electoral formula*). Electoral systems can be represented by this information, and Display 7.3 lists some common plurality types.

Plurality Systems: First (or More) Past the Post

The most famous of the plurality systems is single-member districts, first-past-the-post (FPP). As Display 7.3 describes, each voter gets one vote, may cast it for any candidate he or she pleases, and the single candidate with the most votes (not necessarily a majority) is elected. The legislature thus consists of legislators elected from separate districts in this manner. This is the electoral system found in Great Britain and many of its former dependencies (including, of course, the United States).

The key feature, it seems to me, is that each district, or constituency, gets but a single representative. This may

---

[12] "Centripetal and Centrifugal Incentives in Voting Systems," 905–906.

DISPLAY 7.3

ALTERNATIVE ELECTORAL SYSTEMS

	v	p	c	k	f
First Past the Post (FPP)	1	no	no	1	Plurality
Single Nontransferable Vote (SNTV)	1	no	no	$k>1$	Plurality
Limited Vote (LV)	$<k$	yes	no	k	Plurality
Cumulative Vote (CV)	$\leq k$	yes	yes	$k>1$	Plurality

---

mean—and this is in fact a common complaint with the system—that the winner is not particularly representative of the district in which he or she is elected. The district may be 60 percent male and 40 percent female; whoever is elected will not represent (in the sense of "reflect") a rather sizable chunk of the electorate. Another (melting pot) district may be 25 percent Roman Catholic, 23 percent Greek Orthodox, 16 percent Jewish, 15 percent Baptist, 11 percent Episcopal, and 10 percent agnostic. Its representative will not share religious and cultural traditions with at least three-fourths of the constituency. If the district magnitude were more generous—if k were larger—then it would be possible to represent more of a district's heterogeneity. But it would also mean a larger legislature, for one thing, and one almost certainly with a greater heterogeneity of views. This might make it more difficult for representatives to *govern*—to debate, deliberate, form coalitions and compromises, and ultimately come to some conclusion on public policy issues facing the society. This is the "great trade-off" between representativeness and governance.

Oddly enough, an ethnically homogeneous society, Japan, until very recently employed a plurality system with a larger district magnitude. It is identified in Display 7.3 as the method of single nontransferable vote (SNTV). In this arrangement each voter is still endowed with only *one* vote, but now the k highest vote getters are elected from the district, where k is given in advance as the district's magnitude.

Just as SNTV is a small alteration of FPP (namely, a change in district magnitude from 1 to some $k > 1$), the method of limited vote (LV) is only a slight alteration of SNTV. Specifically, LV endows each voter with more than one vote (but fewer than k), still allowing for k winners. If, under FPP, *one* representative is to be elected from a district and each voter casts *one* vote, and, under SNTV, *more than one* representative is to be elected from a district and each voter (still) casts *one* vote, then, under LV, *more than one* representative is elected from a district and each voter may cast *multiple* votes. Thus, a district may elect four legislators under LV by giving each voter, say, two votes. This method, however, offers an additional strategic maneuver to voters—"plumping" (as the English called it in the eighteenth century), or voting only for your favorite candidate.[13] Consider the district with $k = 4$ and $v = 2$ as just mentioned. Suppose I am is considering casting my votes for my two favorites in the field of candidates. The latest public opinion poll showed my second-choice candidate running in fourth place and my favorite candidate in fifth. If I proceed to vote for both candidates, my second choice may win, but just possibly at the expense of my first choice, who will finish just out of the running. I might be better advised to cast only a single vote for my first choice, thus foregoing the support I had planned to give to my second choice, but just

---

[13] In *Safire's Political Dictionary* (New York: Random House, 1978), the following entry is found under *plump*:

"One of the English election phrases for which there is no equivalent in the United States," wrote the *New York Tribune* in 1880, "is 'plumping.' Whenever [an English] constituency returns two members, each voter can give one vote each to any two candidates but he cannot give his two votes to any one candidate. If he chooses he can give one vote to only one candidate, and this is termed 'plumping.'"

possibly helping to elevate my favorite into fourth place. The LV method permits this sort of *partial abstention*.

Cumulative voting (CV) goes one step further, permitting voters not only partially to abstain, but also to *cumulate* their votes.[14] In the example of the previous paragraph, where the voter has two votes and there are four candidates to be elected, but the method is now CV, he could cast *both* of his votes for his first-preference candidate. The state of Illinois, until 1980, elected state legislators from multimember districts via CV. Similarly, nearly half of the states permit and more than one-fourth actually *require* CV in elections for boards of directors of publicly traded corporations. The idea behind CV is that well-organized minorities, by cumulating their votes, can assure themselves a modicum of representation. Cumulative voting in multimember districts, for example, has become one of the "methods of choice" for a number of civil rights activists for electing county commissioners, school boards, and other local officials, primarily in the South, in order to assure minority representation.[15]

Equilibrium in Plurality Systems

Scientists and engineers can usually make intelligent remarks about and comparisons among alternative engines. The same is true here regarding the electoral engines just described; thus far, however, man has been much more creative in *inventing* electoral engines than in *understanding* their operating characteristics.

---

[14] Safire, in the entry referred to in the previous footnote, goes on to indicate that the American usage of the term "plump" differs from the English. In the United States, "to plump" means to cumulate your votes for a particular candidate.

[15] For various points of view, see Lani Guinier, "The Representation of Minority Interests," and Kenneth Benoit and Kenneth Shepsle, "Electoral Systems and Minority Representation," both in Paul Peterson, ed., *Classifying by Race* (Princeton, N.J.: Princeton University Press, 1995), pp. 21–49 and 50–84.

The key to understanding the equilibrium tendencies of the alternative plurality systems we have described is the *number of candidates in a district*. But before developing this thesis, I first must say what I mean by *equilibrium* in this context. Restricting analysis to one-dimensional spatial representations (like those described in the first part of Chapter 5), each voter is assumed to have a unique ideal point and single-peaked preferences on the one dimension. Candidates compete for votes by identifying with specific locations on the dimension. Qualitatively, two equilibrium tendencies may be identified. A *central tendency* is one in which the candidates tend to converge on the median voter's ideal point location. A *dispersed tendency* is one in which the candidates tend to distribute themselves along the dimension, adopting distinctive policy positions. The former is dominated by centripetal forces in which electoral competition drives candidates toward one another, while the latter is dominated by centrifugal forces that drive candidates away from one another in order to differentiate themselves.

Cox shows how the number of competing candidates is a key parameter in determining whether centripetal or centrifugal incentives dominate. Cox cuts the cases according to whether the system permits cumulation of votes or not (see the column labeled c in Display 7.3). He then shows that when cumulation is not allowed (c = no), "if the number of candidates competing for election is small enough relative to the number of votes per voter [v in Display 7.3], then centripetal forces will dominate (in the sense that equilibria will be centrist); but if the number of candidates is large enough, then centrifugal forces become strong enough to create a certain amount of dispersal in equilibrium. When cumulation is allowed (c = yes), then "centrifugal forces will always dominate."[16]

---

[16] "Centripetal and Centrifugal Incentives of Electoral Systems," 912. Cox makes "small enough" and "large enough" precise.

In principle, the reader could take a copy of Cox's paper (in which more carefully and precisely stated propositions may be found) and a governmental handbook describing a specific electoral system and, on the basis of these two sources of information, make forecasts about how candidates will actually distribute themselves politically in election contests. Cox illustrates this for the case of Japan, a country whose electoral system (at the time Cox wrote) was described by SNTV:

> Most of the 511 members of the Japanese House of Representatives are elected in districts of magnitude 3, 4, or 5 in which each voter has a single nontransferable vote. . . . In all of Japan's multimember districts [the number of candidates is large relative to the number of votes per voter]. This means that there is never a median voter or central clustering result predicted for Japan. Instead, the dispersion result applies and predicts that, if there is an equilibrium, then candidates will not be bunched together anywhere along the left-right spectrum; and some candidates will adopt [extreme positions].[17]

Social scientists are not rocket scientists—that's already been conceded. But we are growing increasingly sophisticated about how various procedures of social choice actually work. In this section I have done no more than to illustrate a small fraction of the rich class of pluralitylike electoral systems and how they may be analyzed. Electoral systems can be boiled down to a relatively small number of parameters and equilibrium analysis conducted on them. Depending upon the resources given a voter (particularly, the number of votes), how those resources may be deployed (particularly, whether they can be cumulated and whether they may be only partially used), and the nature of the task (particularly, the number of legislators to be elected), it is possible to determine whether candidates have incentives to cluster centrally or disperse

[17] "Centripetal and Centrifugal Incentives of Electoral Systems," 915.

themselves. This, in turn, tells us something about the kinds of legislatures these electoral systems produce.

We should remember, however, that not all electoral systems are horse races among individual candidates. A large class of systems operates at a more highly aggregated level— one in which parties, rather than individual candidates, are the strategic players. Legislative representation in these systems is determined by the proportion of the popular vote each party receives. We shall look at these systems before comparing them to the horse-race variety. Even before doing that, however, we will look at one last interesting pluralitylike system that would seem to defy Cox's classification scheme.

A Most Unusual Plurality System: The Single Transferable Voter (STV)

The single-transferable-vote system, sometimes called the *Hare system* after one of its early students, differs from other multimember plurality systems in that each voter essentially reports his or her entire preference ordering over the candidates. Riker describes it as follows:

> The rule for the *single transferable vote method* is: For districts with S seats and m candidates ($m \geq S$), the voters, V in number, mark ballots for first choice, second choice, . . . , and m^{th} choice. A quota, q, is calculated thus:
>
> $$q = V/(S + 1) + 1$$
>
> and q is rounded down to the largest integer contained in it. If a candidate receives at least q first-place votes, he or she wins, and any surplus votes (i.e., the number of first-place votes in excess of q) are transferred to nonwinning candidates in proportion to the appearance of these candidates in next place on all ballots of the initial winner. Another candidate who then has q first-place [plus] reassigned votes wins, and his or her surplus is transferred to the next nonwinning candidate on his or her supporters' ballots (again in proportion to their appearance in next place) and so on

until all seats are filled. If at any point in the process (including the beginning) no candidate has q first-place and reassigned votes, the candidate with the fewest first-place and reassigned votes is eliminated and all the ballots for her or him are transferred to candidates in the second (or next) place on those ballots; and this is repeated until some candidate has q votes.[18]

To make all this concrete, suppose there were 100 voters ($V = 100$) in a district charged with electing 3 representatives ($S = 3$). The quota—known as the Droop quota (Mr. Droop was a friend of Mr. Hare)—is $q = 100/(3 + 1) + 1 = 26$. That is, any candidate receiving 26 votes can be assured that no more than two other candidates can get as many as she.[19] If, in fact, a candidate got in excess of 26 first-preference votes, and all the remaining candidates did not, then the preference orderings of the excess voters are consulted for the second preference listed and those votes are distributed to them. If this pushes some other candidate over the 26-vote quota, then he or she is deemed elected. This continues until all three candidates have been elected or until fewer than three have been elected and no remaining candidate has the quota. In this case, the process starts eliminating candidates, starting with the one with the fewest total votes. All of that candidate's votes are distributed to the candidates named second on each ballot. This continues until all seats are filled.

The STV method is used to elect the parliament in Ireland (called the *Dail*) and the city council of Cambridge, Massachu-

---

[18] Riker, *Liberalism Against Populism*, p. 49. Duncan Black refers to STV as a system of *proportional representation* because it tends to approximate the representativeness that many PR systems display. See his famous *Theory of Committees and Elections* (Cambridge, U.K.: Cambridge University Press, 1958). But it is decidedly a plurality system in that election is dependent on getting more (first-preference plus transfer) votes than other candidates.

[19] If *three* other candidates got at least 26 votes, then they would jointly have 78 votes, which would mean that, together with the candidate who already has 26 votes, 104 votes had been cast. But this cannot be, since only 100 votes can be cast. Therefore, it also cannot be that more than three candidates receive 26 or more votes each.

setts. In Ireland there are 41 districts from which 166 members of parliament are elected; typical district magnitudes are 3, 4, and 5. The City of Cambridge elects a city council (nine members) from one at-large district. In both locations, there is much local lore about strategic behavior, as candidates campaign not only among their own supporters but also among opponents' supporters. The purpose for a candidate is both to energize his own supporters and to try to get listed high up in the preference orderings of voters supporting other candidates, the latter in order to benefit from potential "reassigned" votes. Cambridge has refused to computerize its operations, so it takes nearly two weeks following an election to allow tens of thousands of paper ballots to be counted and recounted; many a local political junkie socializes at election headquarters during this period, cheering as one candidate or another surpasses the Droop quota and claims a council seat.[20]

CASE 7.1
OSCAR NOMINATIONS

The Academy of Motion Picture Arts and Sciences organizes the nomination process for Academy Awards. Each section of the academy is eligible to participate in the nomination processes for its particular award. According to the *New York Times* reporter Tom O'Neill, here's how it works (with my occasional kibitzing in brackets):

> In the best-director category, for example, there are about 300 Academy of Motion Picture Arts and Sciences members who de-

---

[20] For those interested in learning more about this system, they should consult Gideon Doron, "The Hare Voting System Is Inconsistent," *Political Studies* 27 (1979): 283–86; and Gideon Doron and Richard Kronick, "Single Transferable Vote: An Example of a Perverse Social Choice Function," *American Journal of Political Science* 21 (1977): 303–11.

cide the nominees by listing their favorites from 1 to 5. When the ballots are received by PricewaterhouseCoopers, they are put into piles based upon who is listed as the No. 1 choice, said Greg Garrison, one of the eight accountants who spend a week determing the nomination lineup. "We divide the number of ballots [V = 300] by six [S + 1] to determine how many No. 1 votes are needed to establish a nominee," he said. So a director with 50 or more No. 1 votes is automatically a nominee. "Let's say only two directors have that many," he continued. "We take all of their ballots and set them aside. Then we conduct a second pass-through. We start with the smallest stacks of ballots, discard the No. 1 choice and redistribute them according to who's listed in second place. We work through all the stacks that way, from smallest to largest, redistributing ballots until we have five stacks with more than 50 of the same names in each one."*

As a reader can see, this is very close to STV as described in the last few pages. The only apparent difference is that "excess" votes of those who qualify as nominees aren't redistributed.

* Tom O'Neill, "Oscar Watch: Winner Takes All," New York Times, January 9, 2005, Arts & Leisure section.

We conclude by noting that a version of this method is used to elect members of the parliament in Australia. In that country, however, districts have a magnitude of only one, so the method is given a different name just to confuse everyone (naturally); it is known there as the *alternate vote*. With S = 1, the quota formula above becomes $q = V/2 + 1$. With 100 voters, a candidate needs 51 first-preference plus reassigned votes to be declared the winner.[21]

[21] STV is also used to elect members of the Faculty Council of Harvard University. (It is something of a historical irony that it was recommended to the university by Kenneth Arrow while he was a member of the faculty!) It runs smoothly, virtually without controversy, and certainly with no strategic behavior, because so few faculty members offer themselves as candidates.

Proportional Representation

I will be analytically less precise about PR systems because, quite frankly, not much work has been done on them. The purpose of a proportional system is to produce a legislature that mirrors, in some fashion, the larger society. If, for example, the main cleavages in society are ethnic (as in many of the democracies in Africa and the Middle East), or religious (Northern Ireland), or linguistic (Belgium), then a PR system will tend to reproduce them inside the elected legislature. Under most such systems, no stratum, unless especially small or poorly organized (or just plain stupid) is highly underrepresented.

One would think that the design of a PR system is straightforward. Let each citizen cast a single vote for his or her favorite party (or any other, for that matter). Add up the votes for each party. Give each party a proportion of legislative seats exactly equal to its proportion of the total popular vote. Voilà!

Not so fast! First of all, the legislature's size is typically fixed in advance. For most "reasonably" sized legislatures, it is typically not possible to translate electoral proportions evenly into seat proportions. Suppose the Beer Lovers Party (an actual party in Poland) captured 1 percent of the popular vote. How many seats should it receive in the 450-seat *Sejm* (the Polish House of Representatives)? It cannot be given the 4.5 seats to which it is entitled according to its electoral proportion. Most PR schemes—and there are actually quite a large number of them—differ primarily on how they handle the problem of allocating these "fractional seats."

A second issue involves exactly who should get elected to the legislature in the first place. If the Polish Beer Lovers Party receives one percent of the popular vote, as in the previous paragraph, should it get *any representation at all*? If the answer is in the affirmative, then at what point does the answer change to negative—0.5 percent? 0.25 percent? 0.10 percent? Where do you draw the line? PR systems differ quite dramatically on this matter. In practice most require that a party exceed a specific minimum popular vote proportion before it is entitled to *any* parliamentary representation. This parameter, known as the *threshold*, varies dramatically from country to country. Poland (in its first few democratic elections) and Israel (throughout its democratic history) have had very low thresholds. For the 450-seat *Sejm* in the 1990s, a Polish party needed to obtain 1/450th, or 0.22 percent, of the popular vote to be awarded a seat. For the 120-seat *Knesset*, an Israeli party (until recently) needed 1/120th, or 0.83 percent, to win a seat. Germany, on the other hand, has a very high threshold; a party must obtain 5 percent of the vote before it qualifies for seats in the *Bundestag*. Thus, in the 1987 elections, the Green Party won 8.7 percent of the popular vote and was awarded 42 seats in the 497-seat *Bundestag* (8.45 percent of the seats); in the 1991 election their popular vote percentage fell just a hair below 5 percent *and they lost their entire legislative representation.* Clearly, high thresholds make for more disproportionality.[22]

Representation versus Governance: PR v. Plurality

There are few results to report on equilibrium properties of various PR systems, so I turn in this concluding section to a brief comparison of the two broad families of electoral systems I have been discussing. In all our discussion I have been vague

[22] For a full discussion of this and related issues, the reader may wish to consult Rein Taagepera and Matthew Soberg Shugart, *Seats and Votes: The Effects and Determinants of Electoral Systems* (New Haven: Yale University Press, 1989). For an interesting discussion on PR, consult the debate between Cox and Gallagher in the pages of the leading journal on electoral systems: Michael Gallagher, "Proportionality, Disproportionality, and Electoral Systems," *Electoral Studies* 10 (1991): 33–51; and Gary W. Cox, "Comment on Gallagher's `Proportionality, Disproportionality, and Electoral Systems,'" *Electoral Studies* 10 (1991): 348–52. For recent information on PR systems, see Josep M. Colomer, ed. *The Handbook of Electoral System Choice* (London: Palgrave-Macmillan, 2004).

about the actual number of candidates who compete for legislative seats. Indeed, I have not ventured a conjecture about
whether many or few candidates compete and, more significantly, whether or not the electoral system has anything to do
with this.

In fact, there is a long literature on this very subject, the
most famous proposition of which is known as *Duverger's Law*,
named after the famous French political scientist who dared
to call it an empirical regularity. Duverger's Law comes in two
parts. The first, for which there is both strong argument and
evidence, states that first-past-the-post, single-member-dis-
trict systems are strongly associated with two-party (or two-
candidate) competition. The idea here is that third parties and
third candidates (or both) will ordinarily be loath to enter the
race because they have so little chance of winning; in turn,
they have so little chance of winning because neither voters,
nor campaign consultants, nor campaign contributors are
likely to waste their votes, time, and money, respectively, on
hopeless candidacies.[23] The second part of Duverger's Law, for
which there is ample empirical support but less compelling
analytical argument, states that PR systems are associated
with multiparty competition.

As an analytical claim, it seems to me that the kernel of
truth here is that districts in which there are, by design, a
very small number of winners—only one in first-past-the-
post; exactly k in k-past-the-post—discourage independent political entry and encourage cooperation, coordination, coalition, and merger-like political activity *before* elections. In
districts where there are many possible winners, as in most
PR systems (especially those with a very low threshold) and
even in those k-past-the-post systems where k is quite large,
independent political entry is encouraged and various forms of
cooperation, coordination, coalition, and mergerlike political

[23] See Case 6.5.

activity are either discouraged altogether or deferred until after elections. First-past-the-post systems typically, and other "small" *k*-past-the-post systems often, resolve many conflicts *before* legislative politics commences. PR and "large" *k*-past-the-post systems, on the other hand, defer this kind of conflict resolution until the legislature convenes. Thus, parliamentary political conflict tends to be more muted and centrist in legislatures elected by FPP; indeed, there is typically a single majority party that can get on with the business of implementing its agenda. Legislatures elected by PR *reflect* rather than *resolve* political conflict in advance, depending upon post-election parliamentary politics—coalition government, for example—to discover the means for resolution.

It should not be surprising, then, that a number of democratic regimes seek to obtain the best of both worlds by implementing a "mixed" method. Accordingly, a certain proportion of legislators is elected from districts according to plurality rule, with the remaining legislators elected by PR based on the national vote proportions received by parties. In 1993, both Italy and New Zealand underwent changes in electoral law. Like ships not quite passing in the night, New Zealand deserted plurality for an approximation of the mixed method, while Italy deserted PR for the mixed method.[24] The mixed method appears to enhance governance by keeping the number of parties relatively small, on the one hand, while maintaining a modicum of representativeness, on the other.

Experimental Corner
Voting Rules and Jury Verdicts

Choices over voting methods don't affect only electoral politics. Indeed, one of the most consequential decisions on a

---

[24] In 2006 Italy returned to full PR.

voting method that any society can make concerns voting rules for *juries*, which are responsible for determining guilt and innocence in criminal proceedings in dozens of countries. For example, for criminal trials in the United States, generally the jury must unanimously agree to convict, otherwise the defendant is set free. This very high standard of agreement is regarded by most as an important procedural safeguard, reducing the possibility of the conviction and incarceration of innocent individuals accused of serious crimes. So imagine the surprise provoked by two game theorists, Timothy Feddersen and Wolfgang Pesendorfer (hereafter, FP), when they claimed in a 1998 article that unanimity rule may actually lead to *more* false convictions of innocent defendants than less stringent alternatives like simple majority rule.[a]

How could this be? First, some background. The prevailing formal models of jury decision making before FP involved each juror independently assessing the evidence and reaching a conclusion. But due to psychological, cognitive, or some other differences across jurors, it is possible that some might conclude that the defendant was innocent, and others that the defendant was guilty. Assuming that jurors vote *sincerely* (see Chapter 6), based on their best guess given the evidence, unanimity rule would then be far less likely than a less demanding procedure to produce a false conviction, because it requires that each and every individual—no matter their differences—be truly persuaded of the defendant's guilt.

FP turned this logic on its head, however, asking whether it might be optimal for jurors to vote *sophisticatedly*. Consider the following scenario: You are a single juror

---

[a] Timothy Feddersen and Wolfgang Pesendorfer, "The Inferiority of Unanimous Jury Verdicts under Strategic Voting," *American Political Science Review* 92 (1998): 23–35.

on a twelve-person jury operating under unanimity rule, which is about to take an anonymous ballot. Your best guess is that the defendant is innocent, but you are completely unsure what the other jurors think. Two arrangements are worth considering. First, in the unanimity-rule situation it is possible, if unlikely, that all eleven other jurors are voting to convict and so if you vote sincerely, you will be freeing an individual who in all likelihood is guilty (or at least all of your fellow jurors seem to think so!). However, if fewer than eleven jurors are convinced of the defendant's guilt, then misrepresenting your instincts and voting guilty will have no impact on the outcome (since at least one other individual also votes innocent). That is, voting to convict is, in the language of game theory, a *dominant strategy*. In this sense, there may be subtle pressures on jury members to vote for conviction—even when they believe the defendant is innocent—to avoid freeing a guilty party. When these pressures exist across all twelve jury members, the likelihood of false conviction rises markedly.

In a *majority-rule* situation, however, these pressures would be far weaker, as long as the juror's perceptions of guilt and innocence are fairly good on average, because any one vote is less likely to be determinative of the final outcome. Put another way, the harm from a single member incorrectly pegging a defendant as innocent is much less in the majority rule case than under unanimity rule.

This discussion suggests two fundamental questions about jury behavior—Do jurors vote sophisticatedly? Is unanimity rule associated with more improper convictions of innocent defendants?—which Serena Guarnaschelli, Richard McKelvey, and Thomas Palfrey put to the test in a series of experiments.[b] Here's the setup: Each member of

[b] Serena Guarnaschelli, Richard McKelvey, and Thomas Palfrey, "An Experimental Study of Jury Decision Rules," *American Political Science Review* 94 (2000): 407–23.

their experimental juries was asked (while blindfolded) to choose a ball from a jar, which either has predominantly red balls or predominantly blue balls. They were told to keep the color of their ball a secret from the other jurors and then to cast a vote about whether the jar they drew from was either one of the "mostly red" jars or one of the "mostly blue" jars. If the group voted correctly, then everyone shared a large prize. This experiment was run with two voting rules, however. For *unanimity rule*, the jurors were told that correctly identifying the red jar required that all members vote for red, and if a single member voted for blue, then the group's vote would be blue. The *majority rule* was undertaken as usual, however, with ties going to an overall vote for blue. Thus, the experiment was meant to recreate the circumstances of FP's original article, with a series of individuals each possessing a private signal about the true state of the world and using group decision making under two different rules to cast their collective ballot. The red jar and red balls stand in for "guilty" here, while "blue" stands for innocent; the experimental subjects were given no inkling that they were contributing to research that cuts to the core of our judicial system.

The first major result of the experiment is that jurors most assuredly do vote sophisticatedly under unanimity rule. In a small jury of three individuals operating under majority rule, only about 6 percent of individuals voted contrary to their signal if they drew a blue ball, while in the case of unanimity rule, 36 percent did so. (It is worth noting in passing that relatively few—but nonetheless between 3 percent and 10 percent—voted against their signal if they drew a red ball.) Why this sharp divergence? Recall the logic of FP's argument. Voting blue is a precarious act under *unanimity rule*. If the true state of the world is a "mostly red" jar, then you've lost your chances at winning the prize. A logical question is whether the high rate of so-

phisticated voting observed in the experiment under unanimity might be tamped down if the jury were larger. In
fact, exactly the *opposite* occurred. More than 47 percent of
those drawing a blue ball voted for the "mostly red" jar, a
result that is in fact consistent with the theory articulated
by FP. Why? More voters, in a sense, gives you more cover
to vote contrary to your signal. If everyone else has drawn a
red ball, than you're most likely wrong, even though you
drew a blue ball, and your incorrect vote would be decisive.
If the true state of the world is a "mostly blue" jar, then in
all likelihood several others will have drawn blue and will
vote accordingly, so no harm is caused by voting red . . . unless, of course, others think similarly.

While the premise of FP's approach to jury voting (jurors are sophisticated voters) was confirmed, their conclusion (unanimity rule leads to more false convictions) was
not. For six-person juries drawing from the "mostly blue"
jar, almost 30 percent falsely voted for a red jar under majority rule, while only 3 percent voted for a red jar using
unanimity rule—exactly the opposite of what FP's logic
would lead you to expect. (The rates of false conviction were
roughly the same, at about 18 percent, for three-person juries.) Why did this happen? The authors hypothesize that
certain voting rules are not very resistant to inaccurate or
erroneous voting, especially unanimity rule which requires
that all individuals vote one way. Recall from above that
3 percent to 10 percent of voters voted against their signal
if they drew a red ball, and in fact that 10 percent was for
six-person juries using unanimity rule. The effect of just
every tenth individual receiving a red ball voting for blue—
a choice that is difficult to defend on rational grounds—was
more than enough to counteract the sophisticated voting
that was predicated to lead to false convictions. In other
words, unanimity rule led to fewer false "convictions,"
mostly because erroneously cast ballots by red ball holders

prevented juries otherwise dead set on conviction from securing that end.

So can we safely draw from this experiment the conclusion that unanimity rule is after all an effective bulwark
against falsely convicting the innocent? Probably not. It's
hard to believe that voters on a real jury, knowing that a
human being's fate lies in the balance, would vote as casually as in a laboratory experiment involving balls in a jar.
Moreover, voter error hardly seems like a sound basis on
which to rest as important an issue as the credibility of jury
verdicts. At the same time, it remains an open question
whether or not jury members in actual criminal trials—outside the arid confines of the lab—truly vote sophisticatedly.
These experiments certainly suggest that this is a possibility, however, and this is clearly a topic that merits much
further research.

PROBLEMS AND DISCUSSION QUESTIONS

1. A small society of nine people holds the following preferences: $w \mid zxy$ (3 people); $xzy \mid w$ (4 people) and $y \mid zwx$ (2 people), where all outcomes to the left of the vertical line are
"approval-worthy." Which outcome will win if the society employs simple plurality voting? What about if it employs plurality runoff, approval, or Borda count voting? Would the society
select a clear winner if it used the Condorcet procedure?

2. The election of 1844 featured two major-party candidates
(the Democrats nominated James K. Polk and the Whigs,
Henry Clay), with a final electoral vote count of 170 for Polk
and 105 for Clay. Polk was a strong supporter of the entry of
new slave states into the union, while Clay (himself a slave
owner) opposed the addition of new slave states. James Birney

entered the race as a committed abolitionist for the Liberty Party and managed to secure 2.3 percent of the popular vote overall. Here are the results for the State of New York (with 36 electoral votes) in the election of 1844: Polk, 48.8 percent of the popular vote; Clay, 47.85 percent; and Birney, 3.25 percent. In the following analysis, assume that any Birney voters strictly preferred Clay to Polk.[a]

a. Suppose that New York's electoral votes were allocated according to sequential runoff. Who would then have won the election? Explain why.

b. Suppose that New York's electoral votes were allocated according to approval voting. Suggest a scenario in which Clay wins the U.S. presidential election. How plausible do you think your scenario is?

c. Social choice theorists have suggested that "independence of entry of clones" (IEC) might be a useful criterion for judging voting rules. IEC states that the addition of a candidate identical (or very similar) to one of the current candidates should not cause the winner of the election to change. Does plurality rule satisfy IEC? What about approval voting? Do you think this is a reasonable criterion for a voting rule to satisfy?

3a. Suppose that candidates a and b are in a lopsided race, so 58 percent of the population feels that $b > a$, and 42 percent that $a > b$. Candidate a, who is to the left of b, contemplates paying the conservative spoiler candidate c to enter the race to siphon off the approximately 17 percent of the electorate with the preference ranking $c > b > a$. Would this be a sound investment under either plurality rule or sequential runoff? Assume sincere voting.

---

[a] This example and many others are contained in William Poundstone, *Gaming the Vote: Why Elections Aren't Fair* (and *What We Can Do About It*) (New York: Farrar, Straus and Giroux, 2008).

b. Now consider a different three-way race where opinion polls report the following: 40 percent feel $a > b > c$; 31 percent prefer $c > b > a$; and 29 percent $b > a > c$. Who will be the winner if an election were held today under SR? Suppose that by campaigning hard, a is able to steal 3 percent of c's voters. Who would win the election now? Which of the properties employed in May's Theorem has been violated in this example?

c. Based on your answers to the first two parts of this question, does sequential runoff have desirable normative properties? What do you think about sequential runoff as a voting system on practical grounds?

*4. This question asks you to again consider equilibria in plurality systems, and specifically Cox's (1990) claim that if the number of candidates (let's call it m) is less than two times the number of votes per voter, then a centrist tendency is predominant. Assume that preferences are single-peaked and voters are honest. What is a stable equilibrium for a first-past-the-post system when $m = 2$? What voting model does this result reiterate? Is that same value an equilibrium when $m = 3$ or 4?

Now suppose the same setup except now each voter has two votes ($v = 2$) which are not cumulable ($c = $ no) (this is one form of a Limited Vote system). If $m = 3$, what is a stable equilibrium? Is that same value an equilibrium when $m = 4$ or 5?

5. Here are the first- and second-ranked preferences for several groups of voters in a thirteen-member voting body that uses STV with the Droop quota: $b > d$ (4 members); $b > e$ (3 members); $c > e$ (2); $e > c$ (2); $d > b$ (1); and $a > d$ (1). The group wishes to select three outcomes from a, b, c, d, e. Which three do they select?

6. Duverger's first hypothesis is that FPP, single-member district systems should be conducive to two-party or two-

candidate competition. Do you suppose that this hypothesis is more accurate at the *national* level or at the level of *electoral districts*? Does the observed outcome occur because FPP deters candidate *entry* or because it changes *voters' behavior*? In answering this second question, consider the importance of campaign contributions, organization, and endorsements, as well as voters, in producing a winning electoral campaign.

7. The world's democracies may be broadly divided into those that choose their legislatures by proportional representation (like much of Europe) and those that elect legislators from local districts according to plurality rule (like the British House of Commons or the U.S. House of Representatives). What differences are likely to be observed between FPP, single-member district systems and proportional representation systems? You might consider the kinds of politicians each approach attracts, the kinds of party systems each approach encourages, the kinds of legislatures associated with each approach, or the kinds of public policies legislatures of each type are more likely to produce. In light of the answers you have given, which system do you feel better embodies democratic ideals?

8. Presidents, legislators, judges, and voters often justify their political choices with an appeal to "the public interest." Mark Twain cast a skeptical eye on this concept, however, writing "no public interest is anything other or nobler than a massed accumulation of private interests." Having now read Part II on the peculiarities associated with transforming rational individual preferences into a group choice, what do you think of the notion of "the public interest"? What effects do preference cycles, chaos, all sorts of strategic behavior and manipulation, and alternative methods for aggregating individual preferences have on the idea of a "public interest"?

Summary of Part II

Nominally, in the previous five chapters I have written about group choice—ways to think about it, and ways to analyze it. Having said that, the second thing to be said is that I have barely scratched the surface. There are large and fascinating literatures on every facet of group choice, and there is much I have not touched upon here. I have focused on group choice as achieved through *voting*, and within that sphere focused primarily on *majority rule*. Little ink has been devoted to super-majorities (e.g., two-thirds voting), simple yes-no voting (in which a single alternative is posed and the group votes thumbs up or thumbs down), or bicameralism (in which majorities in two bodies must come to some common agreement). Then, of course, there is participatory democracy (New England town meetings), and recent suggestions of an electronic town hall democracy (in which each of us sits at our computer console voting on the great issues of the day). Any or all of these topics would make for great group discussions, short essays, or longer term papers.

Arrow's Theorem, with which we began our discussion, applies to many of these forms of group choice (indeed, just how it applies would make an interesting research topic). And in fact, the material in Part II has conveyed an important general message that is applicable to the broad range of group choice: *Group decision making may depend upon individual preferences and may reflect individual preferences, but it depends upon and reflects much more besides.* First, as I have mentioned throughout these chapters, individual preferences do not announce themselves. They are not transparent or self-evident. Rather, they depend upon the disposition of each individual to reveal preferences sincerely or strategically. Second, even if the disposition to report preferences honestly or not were of no consequence, the fact remains that there are many procedures by which to reveal preferences and combine them into social outcomes—procedures that produce profoundly different social outcomes.

To these considerations I must add one more: Collectivities are unlike individuals in the sense that their "preferences" rarely add up in a coherent fashion. For nearly any method of group decision making that we would find minimally acceptable on grounds of fairness, the group outcome often violates the central notion of coherence (transitivity). In important ways, the actual outcome of group choice is *arbitrary*. So much depends upon the frictions of institutional minutiae—the order of voting, who gets to make motions, and who gets to decide when enough motions have been made.

All of this, in turn, causes a certain amount of philosophical distress. As much as we would like to anthropomorphize the group by endowing it with a will, an interest, a preference, group choices can hardly be conceptualized in this fashion. They simply lack the coherence of individual choices, and depend much on idiosyncracy and ephemera.

We might even become dubious about the idea of a *public interest*. A public has no identifiable interest if its preferences are either incoherent or overly idiosyncratic. An electorate's decision, a legislature's policy, a (multimember) court's opinion—all these things are decidedly outcomes. But the materials of the previous five chapters might give us pause before imbuing these decisions with anything more normatively consequential. Like Rousseau's *general will*, the public interest is a normative ideal that cannot be given concreteness in most real settings. In real settings, there are usually too many majorities, too many methods of deciding, too much strategizing, too much incoherence. The models of Part II, then, provide the means for *analyzing* politics and, at the same time, short-circuit the tendency to *judge* politics. At the very least, they force us to come to terms with our weakness for anthropomorphizing groups and institutions. We must understand, when we judge a political outcome, that it is often the result of split-second coordination by some temporary majority that exhibited coherence for a nanosecond before "morphing" into some new political entity—hardly a firm foundation on which to build a philosophy of public interest.

This is actually something quite constructive. In raising questions about the *general will* and in casting doubt about such a thing as the *public interest*, the materials of Part II have laid a revisionist foundation. They have caused us to suspend momentarily, at the very least, ways of thinking about politics that many of us had probably taken for granted. Groups cannot be legitimately personified—they may make decisions, but those decisions hardly constitute mandates or other reflections of a collective consciousness. The philosophical vacuum left by Arrow's Theorem and these other materials only suggests that there is plenty of work left to do.

The materials of Part II are constructive in another, perhaps more important, sense. They provide tools of analysis for understanding, explaining, and perhaps predicting politics. The theorems and formulations I have presented are tools of discovery and inquiry. They will help us to think systematically about political institutions, the task of Part IV. But first, I turn to "politics writ large": the politics of collective action and mass political behavior.

Part III

COOPERATION, COLLECTIVE ACTION, AND PUBLIC GOODS

8

Cooperation

In this and the next two chapters I focus quite intently on what people do as members of groups. Clearly, they vote, at least some of the time. But I want to extend the conversation beyond this procedural feature of group life and look at what people actually do in a substantive sense. This chapter focuses on the activity of cooperating, a microlevel phenomenon in which individuals have to decide whether to be naughty or nice to their friends, colleagues, roommates, spouses, coworkers, coconspirators, allies, partners, or fellow club members. In Chapter 9 the problem is examined in a somewhat larger context: If cooperation is a form of group activity "in the small," then collective action is its analog "in the large." Finally, Chapter 10 each of these considerations is linked to the social production of what economists call *public goods*. In assembling these chapters, I have sought to find a middle ground between the extremes of the "isolated individualism" of psychology and the "groupthink" of sociology. Along with economics, the study of politics is the study of individual rationality and social interdependence.

A WORLD WITH NO COOPERATION: WHAT WOULD IT BE LIKE?

In nineteenth- and early twentieth-century America, much was made of the virtue of "rugged individualism." People were thought to be virtuous if they were self-reliant—if they developed the requisite coping skills and other forms of "human capital" to enable them to survive and prosper in a world full of opportunities, to be sure, but full of pitfalls and hazards as well. This ideology assumed mythic proportions, personified in the famous Horatio Alger stories about a young lad who succeeded in a cruel world by dint of individual effort and cunning.

The ideology of rugged individualism, however, was qualified by an abiding faith in two forms of community. First, it was not really individuals, per se, who were to be rugged and self-reliant, but *families*. Responsibility for, and cooperation within, families (sometimes of a rather extended sort) were values held dear in an earlier era, putting to shame the purported "family values" of contemporary political debate. Second, the idea of *neighborliness* apparently sat comfortably alongside that of self-reliance. Groups of neighbors engaged collectively in activities ranging from helping one another at harvest time to barn-building parties to volunteer fire departments to taking the law into their own hands (posses and vigilantism).

In contrast, the modern urban landscape, with its combination of social isolation (despite physical proximity), alienation, and individual surliness, is often portrayed as a world devoid of the cooperative spirit of that earlier era. (Try flagging a motorist down to help you with your disabled vehicle during the evening rush hour in New York or Los Angeles.) It is, however, only a pale approximation of the quintessential world of no cooperation—the fictive "state of nature" invented by the seventeenth-century English philosopher Thomas Hobbes. Hobbes described the life of the individual human before the advent of civil society as one that was "solitary, poor, nasty, brutish, and short." In this world, individuals had to scrape and scratch for survival not only against the natural elements—hunting and gathering food, providing for shelter and clothing, and so on—but also against other humans. Individuals, that is, had to make provision not only for the hazards that nature furnished but also for the predation and thievery that other humans inflicted upon them. These were not happy campers!

As Hobbes and many commentators after him observed, human effort devoted to protection against assault from others was necessary, to be sure, but was also quite wasteful in either of two circumstances. If humans would restrain themselves from preying on others (*moral principles*) on the one hand, or if social mechanisms of some sort could be put into place to provide the restraints (*civil society*) on the other, then individual energy devoted to protection would become unnecessary, and that effort could instead be redirected toward productive activities.

Much energy has been devoted down through the ages to creating systems of values, both philosophical and religious, which, if internalized, would release human resources from otherwise wasteful protection activities. But philosophers like Hobbes have not been optimistic about this prospect. For one thing, systems of values have, throughout human history, often come into conflict with one another and have probably killed more people than they have saved. Nearly all crusades, holy wars, and ideologically inspired conquests have had, at root, a philosophical or religious foundation; they have rarely produced anything resembling civility, much less utopia. For another thing, humans are hardwired with various wants and needs that cannot always, because of scarcity, be simultaneously provided to all. Scarcity thus breeds conflict. While reli-

gious principles and moral dicta may have a partially re-
straining effect—the music that soothes the savage breast, so
to speak—the history of humankind suggests they are insufficient to the task.

Most, therefore, have placed their bets on the creation of a
civil society (in which individuals are restrained from taking
advantage of their fellow "citizens") as the way to liberate
human energy for productive uses. A command—for example,
"Thou shalt not steal or otherwise prey on your neighbors"—
backed by a capacity to detect violations and to punish violators is what we are talking about here. Hobbes named the
entity with this capacity to command, detect, and punish
Leviathan, and saw it as humankind's solution to its "problem
of order."

There is no doubt that various aspects of civil society have
come to provide order to the lives of many people, and much of
this book is devoted to studying the institutions of civil society
for precisely this reason. But before I jump into an analysis of
institutions (reserved for Part IV), let me first examine the
possibility that a false dichotomy has been posed. It was suggested above that problems of protection from predation—
what we called the "problem of order"—can be solved either by
causing individuals to internalize pacific attitudes and intentions, in the form of altruism, religion, or other moral principles, or by endowing Leviathan with the power to root out
predatory behavior and otherwise regulate social life for
peaceful ends. Might there not, however, be a third alternative? The remainder of this chapter will provide an affirmative
answer to this question. Cooperation may emerge and be
maintained, even though people have not internalized pacific
or otherwise touchy-feely attitudes, and even though there is
not the heavy sword of Leviathan hanging over them. This is
no conjurer's trick; it is ruthless self-interest at work.

THE SIMPLEST CASE:
TWO-PERSON COOPERATION

Individual behavior typically involves bearing some costs in order to secure some benefits. The student studies hard in school in order to secure a good job after graduation. The suburban homeowner devotes weekend time and energy to her garden in the spring in order to enjoy its beauties in the summer. The consumer exchanges some of his hard-earned cash for a new Audi or a tube of toothpaste. In each of these situations, a rational individual weighs benefits against costs. The former are enjoyed exclusively by her; the latter are borne exclusively by her. It is an individual optimization problem for which the kind of decision theory briefly surveyed in Part I (and covered in any standard economics course) is relevant.

What about group situations in which a *collection* of individuals is pursuing some objective? Individual group members must bear the burdens—club dues, effort, investments of time, perhaps—but the benefits are often not exclusively private. (Indeed, some of the so-called private situations in the previous paragraph may have consequences beyond the individual taking the action; the homeowner's beautiful summer garden provides pleasure for her neighbors, for example.)

The classic illustration of a group interaction of this sort is provided by another British philosopher, David Hume. Hume tells the story of two farmers whose respective fields abut a common marshland. If the marsh were drained, common benefits would be generated—for instance, the destruction of a mosquito habitat. Farmer *A*'s individual effort in draining the marsh, itself a burden, would produce this benefit not only for himself, but also for Farmer *B*. Each farmer is certainly desirous of the benefit, but is loath to pay the price—especially if he can get the other guy to do all the heavy lifting!

In this circumstance the key is what game theorists refer

to as *strategic interdependenc*e. We can analyze the situation systematically as follows. Suppose each of Hume's farmers valued the drained marsh at 2 utiles.[1] If either were to take the project on by himself, the cost to him (in terms of the things he would have to forgo in order to take on the bother of the job) would be 3 utiles. Thus, if there were only one farmer available to take on the task, then it certainly would not be worth his while. Suppose, however, that if each farmer worked "cooperatively" with the other, then it would cost each only 1 utile.[2] In this case each farmer would enjoy 2 utiles' worth of drained marsh at a cost of but a single utile—a pretty good deal. Still, though, the best deal of all would be for the marsh to be drained entirely by the other farmer. This can be seen in Display 8.1.[3]

If both choose to drain the marsh (top left cell), then each gets 2 utiles of benefit at 1 utile of cost for a net payoff of 1. If neither chooses to drain (bottom right cell), then with nothing ventured there is nothing gained: the payoff is 0. If one farmer does all the work (either of the off-diagonal cells), then he gets 2 utiles of benefit for 3 utiles of cost—a net payoff of –1—while the nonworking farmer *also* gets the 2 utiles of benefit but at no cost—a net payoff of 2. How would a ruggedly individual (read: rational) farmer choose?

---

[1] A *utile* is a made-up unit of value or utility. All that matters for our purpose is that more utiles means more value to a person. If it makes it easier, you may think of the units as thousands of dollars, so that each farmer values the drained marsh at $2000.

[2] That is, there are increasing returns to marsh-draining effort. One person, working alone, would end up expending 3 utiles of energy, whereas two working together would jointly expend only 2 utiles.

[3] Some readers may recognize this payoff matrix. In game theory it is known as the *Prisoners' Dilemma*. Two petty criminals are arrested for a burglary. If both keep quiet, the district attorney has to release them (payoff of 1 utile). If both squeal they get time in the slammer, but with a plea-bargained reduction (payoff of 0 utiles). But if one squeals and the other keeps quiet, then the squealer is given a reward and the book is thrown at the "squealee" (payoffs of 2 and –1, respectively). This story yields the same payoff matrix as Display 8.1, so our analysis will be the same.

DISPLAY 8.1
HUME'S MARSH-DRAINING GAME*

	Farmer B's *Choice*	
	Drain marsh **(Cooperate)**	**Do not drain marsh** **(Do not cooperate)**
Farmer A's *Choice*		
Drain marsh **(Cooperate)**	1, 1	–1, 2
Do not drain marsh **(Do not cooperate)**	2, –1	0, 0

* The first number in each cell is the net payoff in utiles to Farmer *A*; the second number is the payoff in utiles to Farmer *B*.

Suppose you are Farmer *A* (recall that your payoffs are the left-most number in each cell). If Farmer *B* chooses to drain (so we're looking at the left-most column of Display 8.1), then you get 1 utile if you drain and 2 utiles if you do not. If Farmer *B* chooses not to drain (right column of Display 8.1), then you get –1 utile if you drain and 0 utiles if you do not. *No matter what Farmer* B *does, Farmer* A *always gets a higher payoff if he chooses not to drain.* The reasoning is precisely the same if you are Farmer *B*: *No matter what Farmer* A *does, Farmer* B *always gets a higher payoff if he chooses not to drain.*

From the perspective of either farmer, there is a double reason to choose not to drain. First, you do better by not draining no matter what your counterpart chooses to do. But second, and perhaps more psychologically compelling (since you never trusted your neighbor very much anyhow), precisely because the same payoff profile holds for your counterpart he is likely not to drain, making it clearly in your interest not to do so either. That is, the other guy's incentives reinforce your own inclination not to drain, and vice versa, ad infinitum. Each farmer has a "dominant" strategy to be uncooperative, not because either is mean-spirited, but rather because neither has an incentive to cooperate and neither wants to be taken advantage of. This is the *paradox of cooperation*: Neither farmer lifts a finger, the mosquitos flourish so each farmer gets a 0 payoff, yet each could have gotten a payoff of 1 if only the two had cooperated. The result is that ruggedly individualistic rational behavior has produced a state of affairs *less preferred by both farmers than an available alternative*. This is the rational individual/irrational society conundrum in another form. Another example, also drawn from Hume, is perhaps a more poignant illustration of the tragedy arising from the failure to cooperate. Hume writes of two corn farmers:

> Your corn is ripe today: mine will be so tomorrow. 'Tis profitable for us both that I shou'd labour with you today, and that you shou'd aid me tomorrow. I have no kindness for you, and know that you have as little for me. I will not, therefore, take any pains on your account; and should I labour with you on my account, I know I shou'd be disappointed, and that I shou'd in vain depend upon your gratitude. Here then I leave you to labour alone: You treat me in the same manner. The seasons change; and both of us lose our harvest for want of mutual confidence and security.[4]

This is not the end of the story, though Hume's example should be taken seriously because it stands as a metaphor for a host of social situations having a similar incentive profile. A quick glimpse of this prospect is found in Case 8.1.

---

[4] See David Hme, *A Treatise of Human Nature*, ed. L. A. Selby-Bigge and P. H. Nidditch (Oxford: Clarendon Press, 1975 [1737]). I thank Dr. Mark Yellin for bringing this to my attention.

Case 8.1
The Paradox of Cooperation: Nuclear Disarmament in the Cold War and Congressional Pork-barreling

Examples of the Humean marsh-draining, corn-growing farmers abound in politics. As we have seen, the cooperation game can be characterized as "I would, if you would, but I can't trust you, so I won't." When self-interest outweighs trust, the outcome is less satisfactory than it might be for both parties. The Cold War between the former Soviet Union and the United States provides an excellent example of the two-player cooperation game. Both countries kept enormous arsenals of nuclear weapons pointed at each others' major cities and defense sites. Both countries incurred substantial economic and psychological costs maintaining these arsenals. Since neither country was able to generate a clear advantage in its nuclear threat, and since use of these weapons was suicidal, an outcome superior to this "standoff" was for both countries to get rid of their weapons. If they had, then neither side would suffer strategic harm, yet both would save the maintenance costs they currently incurred. As the nearby payoff matrix displays, this desirable outcome could not be achieved. If both disarm, each receives a payoff of 10; if each maintains its weapons, the payoff is 0; if one disarms and the other doesn't, then the now superior player gets a payoff of 100 and the now inferior player gets a payoff of –100.

		SOVIET UNION	
		Maintain	**Disarm**
UNITED	**Maintain**	0, 0	100, –100
STATES	**Disarm**	–100, 100	10, 10

Given their incentives, both countries preferred to maintain their forces rather than disarm regardless of the other's actions. Each side considered unilateral disarmament equivalent to surrender. The specter of this event, indicated by the –100 payoff above, prevented the mutually preferred outcome of bilateral disarmament. The dynamics of the cooperation game kept the nuclear weapons in place despite intentions and preferences to the contrary.*

Though substantively quite different, the politics of pork-barreling in the U.S. Congress is theoretically another instance of the paradox of cooperation. The term "pork-barrel politics" refers to the appropriation of federal funds for inefficient projects that benefit individual congressional districts but offer little benefit to the nation as a whole. The incentive to engage in pork-barrel politics is the opportunity it affords for legislators to claim credit at election time for prominent, federally subsidized projects in their districts. Pork-barrel politics often centers on agricultural subsidies, defense contracts, and transportation projects. A $180-million-a-year wool and mohair subsidy, the $31-billion NASA space station, the mass-transit system in downtown Buffalo, and the "Big Dig" harbor tunnel connecting the city of Boston to its airport have all been accused of being "pork." Pork-barrel politics has come under close scrutiny recently as budget pressures force politicians to reexamine their budget expenditures.

---

* Interestingly, disarmament has occurred over the last two decades, but it has not been unilateral and it has not been all or nothing. It has proceeded, in a sense, in baby steps: "You get rid of some of your arsenal and we'll get rid of some of ours." The result has been a reduction in nuclear weapon stockpiles but not their elimination.

The phenomenon of pork-barrel politics can be understood as arising from the paradox of cooperation. Since a pork-barrel project benefits only the district or geographic area that receives it, with the costs to all taxpayers in the country far outweighing this benefit, all legislators would be better off if there were no pork-barreling at all. But each legislator nonetheless has a strong incentive to continue trying to get projects for his or her own district. Thus, everyone knows that despite everyone being better off in a pork-free world, everyone will continue to push for projects for his or her own districts. That is, the "cooperative dividend" of no pork-barrel projects—in which a district loses its own project but more than makes up for this by not having to shell out its share of cash to finance projects everywhere else—is not stable, because politicians continue to have an incentive to use whatever influence they can muster to continue targeting projects for their states or districts.†

† For an analysis of contemporary pork barreling, known as *earmarking*, see Kenneth A. Shepsle, Robert P. Van Houweling, Samuel J. Abrams, and Peter C. Hanson, "The Senate Electoral Cycle and Bicameral Appropriations Politics," *American Journal of Political Science* 53 (2009): 343–59.

COMPLICATING THE SIMPLE CASE: TWO-PERSON COOPERATION WITH REPEAT PLAY

In Hume's example, the occasion for cooperation between the two farmers involves jointly working to drain a marsh. The opportunity for a net benefit for each exists *only* if both farmers put their backs into it, so to speak. That is, there is a *cooperation dividend* to be had for this two-person society, if only its members can structure relationships appropriately to capture it. But the relationship, as portrayed in Display 8.1, is not appropriate for capturing the dividend. Were this the entirety of the relationship between Farmer *A* and Farmer *B*, the sad fact of the matter is that the cooperation dividend would remain uncaptured and life for each farmer would be slightly more impoverished than it might otherwise have been.

Hume's example, then, is best thought of as a self-contained situation in which there is the prospect of a cooperation dividend in this one circumstance. It is a one-shot deal. Most societies, however, including the one consisting of Hume's two farmers, are more enduring. They do not usually materialize for that one opportunity of securing a cooperation dividend; nor do they immediately disintegrate thereafter. Rather, this week it's the marsh that needs draining, next week it's the common fence between the farmers' fields that needs patching, the week after there is the two-man job of replacing a roof on one farmer's barn, and the week after that it's the other farmer's pond that needs to be sealed. In short, societies consist of a series of repeated (or even continuous) encounters, not one-shot plays of a game (as suggested in the second Hume example of farmers who have a sequence of opportunities to help with one another's harvest).

This fact of repetition changes things dramatically, but only if some other conditions are satisfied. To see this, imagine that the strategic interaction portrayed in Display 8.1 is played not once, but twice—*exactly* twice—and both farmers know it. Suppose, for example, there are two marshes that need draining. If this is the case, then each farmer will know that the second play of the strategic interaction will be the last—it will be a one-shot affair. So, in that last interaction each farmer will, for all the reasons given a moment ago, play his noncooperative strategy. But then, backing up to the play before that (the first play), the farmers will realize that, effectively, *that* one is the last play, since the second play will be determined no matter what happens in the first play. So once again, each will rationally play his "do not cooperate" strategy. More generally, even if a strategic interaction like Hume's marsh-draining game is played repeatedly, if the number of repeat plays is finite and commonly known to the members of the society, then each encounter will be played out as though it were a one-shot affair. Repetition in this instance is no more than a string of one-shot games, and the cooperative dividend in each case is lost.[5]

The idea of a known finite number of repetitions, however, seems almost as artificial as the one-shot example with which we began. Societies are ongoing and continuous. Farmers *A* and *B* may not live forever, but they don't know when their microsociety will come to an end. Thus, they don't know when the last play for a cooperation dividend will arise. Consequently, they might as well proceed as though their society is unending. It is this form of repeat play that allows for the capture of cooperation dividends . . . sometimes.

If each farmer assumes the string of opportunities for cooperation will be very long, then each may be willing, on the first occasion, to take a chance. The worst that could happen is that he will be exploited that one time, learn his lesson, and simply refuse to cooperate on subsequent occasions. Given the symmetry of the situation, *both* farmers may take a chance in that first encounter, resulting in an outcome in the top left cell of Display 8.1 and a payoff of 1 utile. On the next occasion, each farmer will remember that the previous encounter had

[5] This paragraph gives the *theoretical* answer to the question of what will happen when a commonly known finite number of repetitions of the game in Display 8.1. occurs. If that finite number is small, then the logic conveyed in the paragraph is, in my opinion, quite compelling. If, on the other hand, the number is very large, even if it is still finite and still is commonly known by all members of society, the logic becomes less compelling. There is a strong incentive, it seems to me, for the members of society to seek out some means for pretending that their own rationality has been disabled, thereby allowing, at least for a while, for some of the cooperation dividends to be captured. This is a very complicated question in game theory.

elicited cooperation from the other, thereby encouraging each to try it again. In short, a little positive reinforcement may well set them on a "cooperation path" for quite some time. It is the "shadow of the future"—the prospect of cooperation dividends not just now but stretching out over the longer haul—that make cooperative moves look very attractive.

In his famous work on this subject, Robert Axelrod[6] calls the behavioral strategy of "being nice" the first time and then, on each succeeding occasion, doing what the other guy did the time before the *tit-for-tat* strategy. The first time, cooperate. The next time, cooperate if your colleague cooperated the last time. But don't cooperate if he didn't the last time, and don't cooperate again until he changes his wicked ways. That is, cooperate *conditionally* after the first play of the game.

It is but the tiniest of steps from the observation of each farmer playing his tit-for-tat strategy in the repeat play of Hume's marsh-draining game (or, as we called it in note 3, the Prisoners' Dilemma) to the claim that a *norm of reciprocity* exists in this society. The farmers have not internalized a religious principle (like the Golden Rule), although their behavior seems to exhibit it. Nor is there a sword-wielding Leviathan making the two cooperate. Instead, each of two ruggedly individualistic, rational egoists has, by virtue of being embedded in an ongoing social relationship, found it in his interest to cooperate with his counterpart.

Before breaking out the champagne, let us hasten to note that there is an "evil twin" to the norm of reciprocal cooperation. If the relationship had gotten off to a bad start—with one or more of the farmers not being "nice" at the outset—then tit-for-tat would echo this misfortune. At each play each farmer will "punish" the other for failing to cooperate the time before.

[6] Robert Alexrod, *The Evolution of Cooperation* (New York: Basic Books, 1984). An earlier and highly influential analysis is Michael Taylor, *Anarchy and Cooperation* (New York: Wiley, 1976).

This social interaction would look more like a blood feud or a civil war than a love fest.[7] And surely the world is full of ethnic, tribal, racial, and interpersonal hostilities that look like tit-for-tat gone mad.

The happier point of our exercise, however, is to demonstrate that the dividends of cooperation may be captured as a sensible and rational response by individuals to the circumstances in which they find themselves. Religious and philosophical dogma, not to speak of external enforcers, may well reinforce this sort of thing. But we believe that these latter alternatives would have a much harder time if they could not rely on the self-interest of the cooperators. What we have shown is that there are circumstances in which this self-interest exists.

Alternative Mechanisms Inducing Cooperation

I. Internalized Values

As strongly as I believe that rational responses to ongoing relationships are responsible for quite a lot of the cooperative dividends most of us realize in everyday life, they clearly aren't the only thing going. Let us look briefly at some alternatives.

People do, in fact, internalize values that dispose them to cooperate, if only to cause them to be "nice" at a first encounter so that reciprocal norms might develop. But this does not account for why one set of moral or religious principles rather than another is internalized. Moreover, we observe

[7] This situation is nicely analyzed in Avinash Dixit and Barry Nalebuff, *Thinking Strategically* (New York: Norton, 1991), Chapter 9. For the interested reader, this volume is perhaps the most accessible, and certainly the most delightful, book on game theory available.

that, with unfortunate frequency as I noted earlier, these principles often fail, as the best of Christians or Muslims or Jews manage to slaughter one another in the name of their favorite religion. But I can comment, in a superficial sort of way, about the mechanism by which such internalized principles might operate.

To do so, let us return to Display 8.1 but rename it the Prisoners' Dilemma (the reader should reread note 3). Suppose the two prisoners are Mafia soldiers who have sworn *omertà* (conspiracy of silence) in dealing with anyone outside the family.[8] The payoff matrix in the display does not seem to capture this internalized value very well. Failing to cooperate in this situation—namely, squealing on the other guy—is not looked upon kindly by the family. Indeed, the squealer, if discovered by the family, typically will be found lying in a dark alley with a slit throat and a canary stuffed in his mouth. I think the payoffs of Display 8.1 are wrong! They should be those given in Display 8.2.

I have transformed Display 8.1 into Display 8.2 by changing one payoff in each of the off-diagonal cells. Thus, if one of the Mafia soldiers implicates his partner, but the other does not, then his payoff is now $-\beta$—a very large and nasty negative number. A game-theoretic analysis of this situation suggests that there are two possible outcomes for this game. Either both will squeal and receive 0 utiles each, or neither will squeal and receive 1 utile apiece. Each of these is an "equilibrium point" in the sense that in each of these outcomes neither player has an incentive to change his strategy if he believes the other guy isn't going to change his. For example, if mafiosos *A* and *B* are both planning to squeal (the lower right cell), then mafioso *A* hardly has an incentive to clam up (not

---

[8] Clearly, the larger society would be better served if the two prisoners were *not* able to capture the dividends of cooperation. But that is not our concern here; we want to remain neutral for the time being about whether the cooperation we're investigating is good or bad in some broader sense.

DISPLAY 8.2
THE MAFIOSO (NON) DILEMMA*

	Mafioso B's Choice	
	Don't squeal (Cooperate)	**Squeal (Do not cooperate)**
Mafioso A's Choice		
Don't squeal (Cooperate)	1, 1	−1, −β
Squeal (Do not cooperate)	−β, −1	0, 0

* The first number in each cell is the net payoff in utiles to mafioso *A*; the second number is the payoff in utiles to mafioso *B*. The symbol β, which stands for "bad," is a very large number!

---

squeal), since this would change his payoff from 0 utiles to −1 utile; and likewise for mafioso *B*. Alternatively, if both are cooperating by keeping quiet (upper left cell), then neither would be so foolish as to squeal, changing his fortunes from 1 utile to −β utiles.

But the game theoretics, in my view, do not give sufficient psychological weight to that big negative payoff of −β. I suspect that neither of the soldiers would take a chance on being the only one to squeal (no matter how good the Federal Witness Protection Program is). *Omertà* frequently wins out, the Mafia soldiers cooperate, and many a prospective conviction eludes an ambitious district attorney. Internalized values, then, can produce cooperation, even in one-shot games. But they do so by *changing* the game.

II. External Enforcement

In the previous discussion of internalized values, noncooperative choices were "punished." Something (your conscience) or someone (the Don) transforms the payoff of the original game for the circumstance in which you behave inappropriately. When it is very explicitly someone else fiddling with the payoff matrix, then it is probably more appropriate to think of this as a case of external enforcement, the subject of this section.[9]

The idea of *third-party enforcement* of agreements reached by two contracting (or cooperating) individuals is the principal mechanism upon which the entirety of neoclassical economics rests. In economic contexts it is normally assumed that contracting individuals are assured that their contracts will be enforced by a judge, court, or sheriff and, moreover, that these agreements are enforced costlessly and in an error-free fashion. Third-party enforcement, in this instance, is precisely the kind of assurance that is required in order to consummate many trades (that is, to capture the dividends of cooperation).

Imagine a seller whose product is sufficiently complicated that a prospective buyer could not tell, by just looking at it or kicking the tires, whether the product were any good or whether it would last very long. Although there are risk takers (and suckers) in any crowd, it will be difficult for this seller to consummate a sale, even with a buyer who might otherwise be interested in the product if it lives up to expectations. Yet there is a cooperation dividend to be shared between buyer and seller if the seller can convince the buyer that the product is as she represents it. To facilitate this, suppose the seller announces, "I guarantee it. If the product does not meet your satisfaction within one week, I will return your money in its entirety. Should the product fail to perform for a full year as represented, I will give you a prorated return of your money." The problem is, What is this guarantee worth? The seller may disappear (as happens with fly-by-night opera-

---

[9] In a sense, though, there may not be a clear distinction between these two mechanisms all the time. In the presence of external enforcement, individuals will often take this fact on board and act as though they had internalized some value. In effect, they have anticipated the external sanction that would be forthcoming and have avoided it in advance by displaying proper behavior.

tions) or she may claim that the guarantee does not cover what the buyer complains about. ("In the fine print we said only the *left* widget wouldn't fail, not the *right* widget.") But if the incentives for the seller to renege are strong, then the buyer will probably anticipate that the guarantee is "not worth the paper it's written on." Thus, guarantees, by themselves, may not do the trick.

If, however, a guarantee were enforceable because there existed a third party prepared to make the guarantor deliver on her promise, then a buyer might well be prepared to make the purchase. Both the buyer and the seller would be pleased by the existence of this enforcement institution. Coercing her to deliver on her promise makes the seller's promise *credible*. It is the credibility of her promise that induces the buyer to buy, after all. So, the institution of thirdparty enforcement allows cooperation (Buyer: "I'll buy your product." Seller: "I'll guarantee its quality."). The absence of this exogenous enforcement institution makes both buyer and seller worse off.[10]

In the Mafioso Dilemma, for example, imagine the payoffs are as they originally were in Display 8.1. Mafioso *A* says to mafioso *B*, "I won't squeal." Mafioso *B* says to mafioso *A*, "Neither will I." These promises are credible because there is a third-party enforcer, Don Corleone, who imposes sanctions on those who break their promises. The presence of Don Corleone effectively transforms Display 8.1 into Display 8.2. What is especially interesting in this instance is that as long as mafioso *A* and mafioso *B believe* they are playing the game in Display 8.2, the Don never has to display his might. Indeed, to those ignorant of the Don's existence, the two prisoners might be thought simply to be honest men who keep their promises! Al-

---

[10] A buyer may still buy under these circumstances, but because the seller cannot credibly commit to honor her guarantee, the buyer will require a break on the price. This difference between the price a buyer would pay under a fully enforceable guarantee and one that is not enforceable is, in effect, the insurance premium the buyer requires.

ternatively, it may be thought that there is "honor among thieves" (a moral principle).

By introducing a third-party enforcer, much like Hobbes did with his invention of Leviathan, we have effectively *coerced* people to behave in a manner that yields them a cooperation dividend. But our analysis would be woefully incomplete if we failed to inquire further into the nature of this enforcer. To be precise, I need to take up three matters: costly enforcement, imperfect enforcement, and the incentives of the enforcer.

COSTLY ENFORCEMENT. When your food processor breaks down, and the merchant from whom you purchased it tells you that it is not his responsibility but rather that of the manufacturer, how much bother are you prepared to undertake to redress your grievance? You might assume a low-cost burden, like writing a letter of complaint to the manufacturer. But you most likely would not hire a lawyer to take the manufacturer to small claims court. The fact of the matter is that enforcement is not costless, and "small" departures from cooperative agreements (so that the guarantor is forced to honor her guarantee only if the guaranteed party bears a substantial cost) are likely to go unpunished, at least most of the time. Sometimes institutions arise to handle these problems. An enterprising lawyer might enter a "class action" suit on behalf of all those victimized. Each victim will have suffered a small cost, perhaps, but if there is a large enough number of victims, the total amount at stake could be rather large—large enough to interest a lawyer whose take is a proportion of the settlement![11] Nevertheless, before invoking Hobbes's Leviathan as a

---

[11] In fact, precisely this happened in the 1980s in regard to a food processor manufactured by the Cuisinart Corporation. A class action suit was lodged against the company and, in a settlement, the company compensated every purchaser of its food processor. The author was a beneficiary! My recollection is that each beneficiary was sent a catalog of Cuisinart products from which a choice might be made. My heavy frying pan is still in use nearly three decades later.

solution to the problem of capturing cooperation dividends, one ought to take into account the probable costs of implementing enforcement. They may not be worth the candle.

IMPERFECT ENFORCEMENT. Even if the costs are small enough to permit enforcement to operate, it may not do so perfectly. It may not be that much bother, for example, to take a local merchant or landlord to small claims court for cheating you. But there is no guarantee that the judge will come to the "correct" judgment. Enforcement is always bound to be imperfect because human judgments are fallible on the one hand, and because the landlord may be the judge's brother-in-law on the other. The point is that, despite what first-year law students are told about the majesty of the law, litigation is no less subject to human error and corruption than anything else that human beings undertake. Judges, police officers, parole officers, official investigators, and other "players" in the justice system are often called upon to make judgments under less-than-ideal circumstances. Mistakes will be made.

ENFORCER INCENTIVES. As long as the normal execution of enforcement is not too expensive, and as long as mistakes are neither too frequent nor too egregious, then these possibilities will not much diminish the value of third-party enforcement. Put more constructively, in many circumstances neither costliness nor imperfections will be so out of line as to undercut the value of outside enforcement. The incentives-of-enforcers problem, however, is not so easy to duck. Mind you, most economists do precisely this: They *assume*, by fiat, that enforcement involves an honest discovery procedure in which fault is determined and compensation ordered. This, in turn, provides incentives for people not to defect from cooperative agreements in the first place. But it does raise the issue of what institutional features provide the incentives for enforcement agents to do this. Why shouldn't the town traffic officer, for example, let his brother-in-law off for speeding but nail the town's "radical lawyer" who has been such a nuisance to the police department? Who would doubt that the rabbi, the third-party enforcer in the little Polish villages that the Nobel laureate Isaac Bashevis Singer wrote about, would make sure that his own son got small advantages in village life? What is to prevent a future black government in South Africa from stifling dissent within the white community? In short, while many communities—ranging from small-town America to villages in eastern Europe to the national community in South Africa— rely on institutions of third-party enforcement, all are vulnerable to difficulties arising from inappropriate incentives. The traffic officer above responds not only to his official responsibilities but also wants to keep his wife out of his hair and his buddies in the department off his case. We all look after our own.

That third-party enforcers may march to their own drummers is especially troubling when it is offered, as it was by Hobbes, as a solution to disorder in the state of nature. Third-party enforcement is often offered as a rationale for the very existence of the *state*. The state is seen as the community's mechanism, first and foremost, for allowing its citizens to avoid wasting their resources on their own protection and, more generally, for permitting cooperation to occur. The state, with its monopoly of force, empowers state officials not only to provide the assurances that permit cooperation to take place among citizens but also to use that force for their own purposes.[12] But, as the saying goes, "Who will guard the guardians?" Until one can be satisfied that the incentive problem for third-party enforcers is resolved, one should not embrace this solution.

---

[12] The incentives-of-enforcers problem is demonstrated vividly by the case of New York City's parking meters. According to *Road and Track* (June 1994, p. 15), half of all of the city's parking-meter change collectors were charged with stealing over $1 million from their collections.

PRELIMINARY CONCLUSION

At the end of this chapter I offer only the most preliminary of conclusions, because the discussion continues in the next two. I have set out the problem of cooperation and examined various manifestations of cooperation in the simplest of societies—the world of two persons. We have seen that this world is not always a happy one, inasmuch as there may be no effective means for capturing prospective dividends of cooperation. Internalized value systems and third-party enforcers offer some promise but are not without their dangers. Repetition of social interactions may allow for cooperation to develop, because the prospects of ongoing, long-term relationships may be too valuable to jeopardize by cheating at any one opportunity. But repetition has its darker side, with jealousy, feuding, and revenge as by-products. Cooperation is a complicated business, and it is no surprise that humankind has only slowly lifted itself out of the state of nature, and done so only imperfectly at best.

The next chapter expands the discussion. A society of two, as I have considered it in the current chapter, is pretty artificial and should be thought of only as a building block or module for a larger society. It is this larger society to which we turn next, and the topics of *n*-person cooperation and collective action.

EXPERIMENTAL CORNER

Altruism and Trust in the Prisoners' Dilemma

The social circumstances modeled in the Prisoners' Dilemma (PD) have proven extraordinarily adaptable to a variety of political situations—everything from the decision of political opponents to engage in negative attack ads to international environmental agreements. However, this adaptability to real-life situations is only part of the game's appeal. The PD also touches on core themes in the *emotional life* of social beings, and humans, after all, are social animals. Perhaps most important among these are the questions of *altruism* and *trust* that this ubiquitous game raises. Thus, a great number of experimental social scientists have attempted to assess the extent to which these social virtues contribute to cooperative play, some with results that might surprise you.

First, some background: The Prisoners' Dilemma was among the first games to be tested in laboratory experiments by social scientists and, owing to the widespread application of the game, was considered an important test of the theory of equilibrium behavior. Recall that the sole equilibrium in the usual one-shot PD is for both players to defect, leaving everyone worse off than if both had somehow managed to cooperate. Is this prediction supported by behavior in the lab setting? In a 1960 test, Minas et al.[a] found that among their experimental subjects, 38 percent of players cooperated in any given play of the game, while 62 percent defected, leading to mutual cooperation in only about 16 percent of plays. Results with a similar flavor—although adjusted up or down depending on a variety of factors, including payoffs, number of rounds, participant communication, and gender and nationality of participants—were replicated in laboratories across the world. The obvious conclusion from these experiments is that rates of cooperation in one-shot and finitely repeated PD games are consistently higher than zero (contrary to predictions of equilibrium

[a] Sayer Minas, et al., "Some Descriptive Aspects of Two-Person Non-Zero-Sum Games," *Journal of Conflict Resolution* 4 (1960): 193–97.

analysis) but consistently much lower than 1; the obvious question is, why? Why would a player cooperate with an opponent—especially a nameless, faceless opponent—in a one-shot Prisoners' Dilemma?

Of course, there are in principle a variety of personal, cultural, and situational factors involved, but systematic thinking about cooperation in the ensuing years increasingly focused on two distinct social values that the PD combines to exquisite effect: *altruism* and *trust*. Why altruism? Suppose in the one-shot version of the PD that a player feels with near certainty that his partner will cooperate. If he decides to respond in kind by cooperating, one interpretation of his behavior is that he has in some sense internalized the desires of the other player and takes into account the harm he would have caused that individual by playing defect, even though it would leave him personally better off. One immediate question this raises is how an altruistic player might balance his own payoffs relatives to others'. But a related and more cutting question concerns the player's level of certainty that his partner will cooperate in the first place, which raises the issue of *trust*. A player might be quite altruistic and therefore absolutely unwilling to stick his partner with the sucker's payoff. But unless you're a saint, at some point altruism will fall victim to a lack of trust, and even the kindest player won't be willing to sacrifice his own well-being for a partner who might—but probably won't—meet him halfway.

Unfortunately, because the PD combines these two issues in such an interesting way, experimental tests of this game are the wrong way to ascertain the relative importance of these factors in the interactions of humans who know one another only imperfectly. If we observe in one round of the Prsioners' Dilemma that one player has defected on her cooperating partner, should we conclude that

that player is a heartless competitor or that she simply felt insecure about her partner's trustworthiness? We could never answer such a question in this context without peering inside her brain, and while magnetic resonance imaging may someday make this a possibility, in the meantime experimentalists have innovated two new games to test separately for the presence of these attributes: trust and altruism. They have now become classics in the experimental literature of games.

In order to ascertain the extent of altruistic behavior, game theorists set to work innovating a model of social interaction that generates an opportunity for altruistic behavior with no corresponding need for trust from the partner. The solution, an elegant little social interaction called the Dictator Game, works as follows: Player A is given a small budget and told that she can give as much as she would like to Player B and the rest she can keep for herself. Player B does nothing but get handed an envelope with the amount A deigned to share (A is the dictator, after all!). Forsythe et al.[b] were among the first to test this model systematically in the lab and found that when Player A was given $10 to allocate, on average she gave $2.33 to B. Moreover, only 21 percent of those in the Player A role gave $0; on the other hand, 21 percent split the pot evenly, giving $5. The rest fell somewhere between $1 and $4. A variety of other tests of the Dictator Game with different experimental conditions, including raising the stakes considerably and varying the level of participant anonymity vis-à-vis the experimenter and the other player, have confirmed that, on average, dictators give between 15 percent and 30 percent of the pot to their partner, but a hard core of selfish types

[b] Robert Forsythe et al., "Fairness in Simple Bargaining Experiments," *Games and Economic Behavior* 6 (1994): 347–69.

(giving nothing) and generous types (giving lots) exist across societies.[c]

These experiments confirm that altruism is prevalent although far from complete in many societies. But what form does this altruism take? Clearly, very few are willing to sacrifice everything for a fellow participant. At the same time the reasoning behind giving 20 percent versus 40 percent is not entirely clear either. Andreoni and Miller[d] attempted to untangle varieties of altruism in the following way. As in the usual dictator experiment, one subject gets a budget to allocate; however, he is told that whatever money he gives to the other participant will be multiplied by a factor p. For Andreoni and Miller's experiments, p varied between one-third and three depending on the pair. What does this do for us? Well, a subject whose altruism is based on notions of fairness would be likely to increase his allocation to his partner if he knows she has a low p, and decrease it if she has a high p. Alternatively, a subject who is concerned with maxmizing collective welfare would likely keep almost everything if p is less than 1 and give away almost everything if p is greater than 1. Of course, some people are just plain selfish no matter what. Andreoni and Miller in fact found that for different subjects, different forms of altruism were practiced, and that a healthy majority of subjects behaved consistently across rounds. About 40 percent of sub-

[c] Henrich et al., in a superb comparison of these types of games across fifteen different societies worldwide (some industrial, some agricultural, and some foraging; some sedentary and some nomadic), note that only among their American college student participants was allocating 0 percent the most common outcome; among the Orma, a tribe in Kenya, the most common offer was 50 percent. See Joseph Henrich et al., "In Search of Homo Economicus: Behavioral Experiments in 15 Small-Scale Societies," *American Economic Review* 91 (2001): 73–78.

[d] James Andreoni and John Miller, "Giving According to GARP: An Experimental Test of Consistency of Preferences for Altruism," *Econometrica* 70 (2002): 737–53.

jects could be squarely placed in the "just plain selfish" category, usually taking everything or just about everything for themselves. Another 25 percent or so corresponded more to the fairness model, carefully calculating an even distribution of payouts to ensure rough parity in winnings between the dictator and his partner. Another 11 percent seemed to be maximizing overall social welfare, and the final 24 percent acted idiosyncratically from round to round. Of course, this is just a small sliver of an interesting and diverse literature, but I hope it has illustrated that altruism is present, but not omnipresent, in social interactions.

So getting back to our other question, how might a participant in a Prisoners' Dilemma decide whether or not his partner can be *trusted* to play nice? Another literature in experimental social science has emerged to measure the extent of trust among anonymous players, using another simple game. Player *A* is granted a sum of money and told that he can keep it all or invest some portion with Player *B*. Any money that is given to Player *B* will grow by some percentage *i* (like an interest rate). Then *B* can decide unilaterally how much she will return to *A*. The measure of trust here is the proportion of *A*'s funds he gives to *B*. In a world of perfect utility maximizers, you might think that *A* would give nothing to *B*, knowing full well that if given the chance, *B* will run off with all of *A*'s money. In a series of international experiments, Croson and Buchan[e] found that an average of 67 percent of the initial allocation was invested,[f] while experiments conducted in the United States have generally found lower rates of trust, hovering nearer to 50 percent of wealth invested on average.

[e] Rachel Croson and Nancy Buchan, "Gender and Culture: International Experimental Evidence from Trust Games," *American Economic Review Papers and Proceedings* 89 (1999): 386–91.
[f] Interestingly, they also found no significant differences between men and women in level of trust, but significant differences in trustworthiness. Women on average returned more of the investment than men.

How do these two strands of research help us understand the Prisoners' Dilemma? Well, it turns out that a great many people we interact with are fairly giving, at least when it comes to one-on-one interactions with relative strangers. Of course, a fair number are not quite so generous, so we certainly don't expect to see cooperation exclusively in experimental tests of the Prisoners' Dilemma. This manifestation of altruism explains half of our puzzle—why we might see individuals cooperate, even though they could make more by defecting on their gullible partners. But how do folks reach the point where they believe their partner will cooperate in the first place? Well, for whatever reason, it appears that trust is quite widespread, even trust in anonymous strangers in laboratory settings. Thus, a good number of individuals enter these experiments fully believing that their partner will cooperate, and some, due to their altruistic natures, even reciprocate in kind, leading to higher rates of cooperation in the Prisoners' Dilemma than predicted by pure theory alone (although still only a measly 16 percent!).

PROBLEMS AND DISCUSSION QUESTIONS

1. Explain how the insights of Hume's marsh-draining game might be used to understand the following situations: (1) two politicians competing for the same office must decide whether or not to use negative "attack ads"; (2) two opposing interest groups consider whether or not to contribute to a senator's re-election campaign; and (3) the major industrialized countries decide on the extent to which they will reduce greenhouse gas emissions.

2. This chapter proposed repeat play as a plausible solution to cooperative dilemmas. Explain the intuition behind this proposed solution and then give some features of a cooperation game (e.g., particular payoffs, number of repetitions, value of present versus future payoffs) that you think might be conducive to cooperation. Is cooperation always achieved in such repeated settings, in theory or in practice?

*3. An alternative vision of the problem of social cooperation is provided by the Stag Hunt game, in which two hunters can cooperate in hunting a large deer or can each individually bag a small hare. As Rousseau noted, the crux of the problem is that if two hunters have partnered to hunt a deer, one partner might be tempted to abandon the hunt to grab a passing hare for himself, leaving his companion in the lurch. The payoffs are as follows:[a]

| | Hunter B: | |
	Stag	Hare
Hunter A: Stag	3, 3	0, 1
Hare	1, 0	1, 1

What is the most-preferred outcome, and is there another outcome in which neither player has an incentive to alter his strategy (assuming the other player's strategy stays fixed)? Does either player end up doing better playing either Stag or Hare *no matter what his partner chooses to do*, as in the marsh-draining game? How certain must A be that B will be playing Stag to do the same? Explain how this game illustrates the role of *trust* in cooperation.

4. Hume's marsh-draining game involved a problem of *cooperation*, whereas the following game is generally thought to in-

---

[a] *A*'s payoff is the left number in each cell; *B*'s is the right number.

volve a problem of *coordination*. The setup is that two friends have a disagreement about whether to go to the movies or play basketball, though neither wants to be on his own, even doing his preferred activity:

	Friend *B*:	
Friend *A*:	Basketball	Movies
Basketball	3, 1	0, 0
Movies	0, 0	1, 3

Does either player end up doing better with either Basketball or Movies *no matter what his friend chooses to do*, as in the marsh-draining game? What are the outcomes in which neither player has an incentive to alter his strategy (assuming the other player's strategy stays fixed)? Explain why this game illustrates the problem of *coordination*.

*5. An alternative to punishing defection, commonly employed by criminal gangs in the United States, is rewarding cooperation, for example, by looking after an individual's family while he is in prison. Suppose, using the payoffs given in Display 8.1, that a bonus of β_{CD} is given to a criminal who cooperates but whose partner defects, while a payoff of β_{CC} is given to a criminal who cooperates and whose partner also cooperates. Rewrite the payoff matrix, suitably updated for the new payoff regime. For what values of β_{CD} and β_{CC} is cooperation an equilibrium? For what values is it the *only* equilibrium?

6. This chapter has discussed several solutions to the cooperative dilemma which variously find their forms in the institutions of state, civil society, and religion. Discuss how each of these social institutions has evolved features to facilitate cooperation, with reference to external enforcement, internal enforcement, and repeated interaction.

9

Collective Action

To many readers of this book, the decade of the 1960s seems a long time ago—ancient history. Besides the Beatles, bell-bottom pants, granny glasses, afro hair styles, droopy moustaches, and love beads, this decade is perhaps remembered most vividly (through that haze of imperfect memory, for those of us old enough, or from documentary-film collages for younger folks) as a period of intense group protest and collective action. Early in the decade, first at the University of California at Berkeley and then throughout the country, students protested against the seemingly arbitrary and capricious authority of university officials. The Free Speech Movement and the Movement to Save People's Park were two major protests aimed at carving out both personal and physical space within which to "do one's own thing." ("Movement" was the collective noun of choice at the time.)

This was not the silliness many elders portrayed it as; it was serious politics with a serious political agenda. Indeed, as the decade wore on, mass action moved beyond the college campuses and the agenda of protest became more explicitly political:

- protest on behalf of civil rights, culminating in a march on Washington that involved hundreds of thousands of participants, and ultimately producing landmark civil and voting rights legislation;

- protest against the war in Vietnam, culminating in a march on the Pentagon (also involving hundreds of thousands of people, as brilliantly described in Norman Mailer's *Armies of the Night*), and ultimately causing an incumbent president to decline to seek reelection;
- protest against environmental degradation, culminating in a mass rally in Washington on Earth Day, and ultimately in landmark environmental-protection regulations and the creation of a cabinet-level agency devoted to the environment.

The seeds of mass protest were cultivated with loving care during this period, producing offshoots of mass protest in the seventies, eighties, nineties, and into the twenty-first century, concerning women's rights, gay and lesbian discrimination, and continuing environmental causes (global warming, ozone depletion, destruction of rain forests, strip mining, nuclear energy, toxic waste disposal, and endangered species, to name a few). Perhaps the most salient of these today involves both sides of the abortion issue—the pro-choice and the pro-life movements.

Having become used to reading about mass action on our campuses and in the streets of our cities, we may have taken it as customary and failed to appreciate that it is, in fact, a puzzling phenomenon. Mass action involves huge numbers of individuals deciding to participate. Yet what possible difference could any one person make to a final outcome by attending one of these rallies? His or her individual contribution is bound to be minute, while the cost of taking this action is far from trivial. Participation involves time, possibly expense, and perhaps risk to life and limb. Putting these together, it would appear that the instrumental benefit is small and the potential cost large. Participation sounds crazy, doesn't it? I will explore this question in the next few pages.[1]

I will also examine other manifestations of collective action to understand why it occurs. Why do individuals in a community seem to follow conventions—like everyone driving on the right side of the road (except the English and Japanese, who drive on the left)? How are large numbers of people able to co-ordinate their behaviors—as when the members of a large symphony orchestra all manage to play together? How do we make sure that people do their fair share in collective under-takings—like cleaning up the common room in the dormitory or the TV room in the frat house? In short, much of what we do in life we do in groups, so much so that we often com-mit the fallacy of false personification and talk as though these groups had a life of their own. In fact, for much of this century, the study of politics was typically cast as the study of groups.

THE GROUP BASIS OF POLITICS

It is no accident that much political discourse is conducted in terms of groups. In any large society it is simply impossible to think in highly disaggregated terms. Instead, we think about an issue in terms of the categories of people taking an interest in it, and a conflict in terms of the groups that line up on one side or the other of the divide. Farmers lobby both for price supports for their crops and for high tariffs to keep crops from other nations out of their domestic market; consumers, of course, are on the other side of these issues. Labor unions

[1] An exceptionally subtle treatment of instrumental behavior and collective action is found in Richard Tuck, *Free Riding* (Cambridge, Mass.: Harvard University Press, 2008). Tuck, a political philosopher, treats these topics in terms of both philosophy and the history of ideas.

push for mandated wage increases and improvements in fringe benefits, which employer groups oppose. Minority groups urge passage of civil rights legislation, while those whose competitive advantage is eroded by it are in opposition. Economic producer organizations seek various protections from market competition, again at the expense of consumers. Professional groups want licensing authority, while those who use professional services want this authority regulated and market power of professionals restrained. Associations of colleges and universities seek large student aid allocations and research budgets from governments, only to be opposed by those who want those limited budget allocations devoted to their own activities. The list is endless.

In a pluralistic political system these groups are known as "lobbies," "interest groups," or more pejoratively as "pressure groups." At the highest level of aggregation these groups are actually collections of groups—so-called *peak associations* ranging from the AFL-CIO (whose members are unions), to the National Association of Manufacturers and the Business Roundtable (whose members are corporations), to the Farm Bureau Federation (whose members are local farm bureaus). At less august levels groups simply represent aggregations of individuals sharing a common interest—the Possum Hollow Rod and Gun Club, the Harvard-MIT Apple User Group, the Boston Policemen's Benevolent Society, the Massachusetts Federation of High School Basketball Coaches, or the New England Political Science Association.

The very ubiquitousness of groups in pluralistic political systems explains why, for most of the first half of the twentieth century, the study of politics *was* the study of groups. Political outcomes were seen as the result of struggles among groups. Indeed, in its most famous representation, Arthur Bentley wrote almost like a physicist about the "parallelogram of forces" that constituted group interactions and infighting.[2] He thought of the status quo in any policy domain as a point on a page. Change occurs as this point gets pushed around by various forces impinging on it. Bentley treated each group in this political fray as a vector consisting of a "direction" and a "magnitude." Direction indicated what changes in the status quo a group wanted; magnitude measured the group's political strength. One group might "push" the status quo—that point on the page—far to the east; another to the southwest, but a shorter distance (reflecting its weaker political clout); still a third due north with yet another magnitude. The net effect of this pushing and shoving—the resultant of the various group forces applied to the existing status quo—is a new policy status quo. Politics, in this view, becomes physics, each group is a "force vector," and the political outcome of a struggle is simply the mechanical resultant of the various forces at play.

The pull and tug of group infighting was, to nineteenth-century observers like Alexis de Tocqueville, the definitive feature of American political life. Indeed, they admired the voluntaristic political pluralism that was absent in less liberal societies.[3] In either its pluralistic or less liberal form, however, the group-based formulation of politics took groups as fundamental and assumed their existence. The essential axiom was this: *Common interest, however defined and however arrived at, leads naturally to organizations coherently motivated to pursue that common interest; politics is all about how these coherently motivated organizations support and oppose one another.*

---

[2] Arthur Bentley, *The Process of Government* (Evanston, Ill.: Principia Press, 1908). Its famous midcentury companions were V. O. Key, *Politics, Parties, and Pressure Groups*, 3rd ed. (New York: Crowell, 1952), and David B. Truman, *The Governmental Process* (New York: Knopf, 1951).

[3] Even in these less liberal societies, conflicts were often portrayed in group terms as struggles between large social aggregates: bourgeosie versus proletariat; aristocracy versus merchant class; various racial, religious, linguistic, or regional groups in opposition to one another; and so on.

CASE 9.1
WHO IS REPRESENTED?

The pluralists believe that groups form naturally out of shared interests. If this belief is correct, groups should form roughly in proportion to people's interests. We should find a greater number of organizations around interests shared by a greater number of people. The evidence for this pluralist hypothesis is quite weak. Kay Schlozman and John Tierney examined interest groups that represent people's occupations and economic roles.* Using census data and listings of interest groups, they compared how many people in the United States have particular economic roles and how many organizations represent those roles in Washington. For example, they found that (in the mid-1980s) 4 percent of the population was looking for work, but only a handful of organizations actually represented the unemployed in Washington.†

There is a considerable disparity in Washington representation across categories of individuals in the population, as the table below suggests. Schlozman and Tierney note, for example, that there are at least a dozen groups representing senior citizens, but none for the middle-aged. Ducks Unlimited is an organization dedicated to the preservation of ducks and their habitats; turkeys, on the other hand, have no one working on their behalf. The pluralist's inability to explain why groups form around some interests and not others led some scholars to investigate the dynamics of

---

* *Organized Interests and American Democracy* (New York: Harper & Row, 1986), pp. 69–71.
† Of course, the number of organizations is at best only a rough measure of the extent to which various categories of citizen are represented in the interest group world of Washington.

collective action. Mancur Olson's work, discussed later in this chapter, is the best-known challenge to the pluralists.

Economic Role of Individual	% of U.S. Adults	% of Orgs.	Type of Org. in Washington, D.C.	Ratio of Orgs./ Adults
Managerial/ Administrative	7	71.0	Business association	10.10
Professional/ Technical	9	17.0	Professional association	1.90
Student/ Teacher	4	4.0	Educational organization	1.00
Farm Workers	2	1.5	Agricultural organization	0.75
Unable to Work	2	0.6	Handicapped organization	0.30
Other Non- Farm Workers	41	4.0	Union	0.10
At Home	19	1.8	Women's organization	0.09
Retired	12	0.8	Senior citizens organization	0.07
Looking for Work	4	0.1	Unemployment organization	0.03

COOPERATION ACCOUNTS

Collective Action as Multiperson Cooperation

Groups of individuals pursuing some common interest or shared objective—maintenance of a hunting and fishing habitat, creation of a network for sharing computer software, lobbying for favorable legislation, playing a Beethoven symphony, or whatever—consist of individuals who bear some cost or make some contribution on behalf of the joint goal. Each member of the Possum Hollow Rod and Gun Club, for example, pays annual dues and devotes one weekend a year to cleaning up the rivers and forests of the club-owned game preserve.

We can think of this in an analytical fashion, somewhat removed from any of these specific examples, as an instance of two-person cooperation writ large. Accordingly, each of a very large number of individuals has, in the simplest situation, two options in his or her behavioral repertoire: "contribute" or "don't contribute" to the group enterprise.[4] If the number of contributors is sufficiently large, then a group goal is obtained. However, just as in Hume's marsh-draining game of the previous chapter, there is a twist. If the group goal is obtained, then *every member of the group enjoys its benefits, whether or not he or she contributed to its achievement.* As long as the marsh is drained, neither farmer is bothered by mosquitoes, a benefit completely detached from contribution levels. In the next chapter I refer to a goal like this as a *public good*, since once it is provided it becomes available to all, whether or not they participated in its provision.[5]

Although this may seem like a simple extension of the two-person cooperation problem of the previous chapter, there are several complications on which we must dwell. First, we need to designate whether the situation is *dichotomous*, in which case the group goal is either attained or it is not, or *continuous*, in which case the outcome varies quantitatively with the number of contributors (or the amount of contribution). It is

[4] A more complicated version of this situation, one not pursued here, enriches each person's behavioral repertoire. Instead of a twofold choice, there is some continuously variable input, like effort or money, that the individual may choose to contribute.

[5] Surely there are situations in which individuals may actually be denied the benefits of a group if they do not contribute to its production. If the benefit is highly valued, then this capacity to deny it makes it easier for the group to elicit contributions. If you want to ride on the Massachusetts Turnpike, for example, you must make a contribution, called a toll. If you want to fish on the Possum Hollow River, then you must pay your club dues. If you want to hear the Boston Symphony Orchestra play a Beethoven symphony, then you must purchase a ticket. These activities are not quite public goods, and I defer further consideration of them to the next chapter. In the present discussion I take up the polar case of a group good or goal, once produced, being available to all.

almost always possible to transform a dichotomous situation into a continuous one, though it is often easier to think in terms of a dichotomous outcome. For example, consider alliance behavior during wartime (or team behavior during the Super Bowl). Allies, depending upon the number of individual contributions (relative to contributions obtained by the other side), may either win the war or lose it (dichotomous outcome); but surely one can think of the "victory" as varying from total success to one barely better than a draw (or, even worse, a Pyrrhic victory), and "defeat" ranging from a scant last-minute loss to total humiliation. In the remainder of this chapter, to keep things sufficiently straightforward, I will stick with the dichotomous circumstance: The group goal is either achieved or not.

Second, in a multiperson situation, we need to specify how many contributors are *necessary* to attain the group goal. Put differently, we need to specify the relationship between each of the individual contribute/don't contribute choices and the final outcome (what economists call the *production function*). At one extreme, unanimous participation is required: unless every person in the group contributes, the group goal is not achieved. This is a particularly interesting situation to analyze. Suppose each individual in the group evaluated the group goal at some level, say B utiles (where B stands for "benefit"); assume that $B > 0$.[6] Suppose further that the utility value of contributing to the group project is $-C$ utiles (C stands for "cost"), where $C > 0$, too. If $C > B$, then no one will contribute, no matter how many others do. It's just not worth the candle, since the benefit net of costs, $B - C$, is negative. On

---

[6] I could complicate the story by individualizing evaluations, so that Mr. i values the group goal at $B(i)$ utiles, while Ms. j values it at $B(j)$, where $B(i) \neq B(j)$. But this enrichment does not change the thrust of this story, so I will not employ it here. Conflict of interest among group members—that is, differential evaluation of group goals—will be explored below.

the other hand, if $B > C$, then every member of the group will contribute. Why?

Actually, there are two possible outcomes when $B > C$, but we argue that only the one in which everyone contributes makes sense. Suppose everyone has chosen not to contribute, and, of course, the goal is not attained. Would any group member be so unwise as to reconsider her choice? Hardly, for if, say, Ms. *j*, decided to contribute, then her payoff would be $-C$ (the cost she bears) and there would still be no compensating benefit (since the latter is produced only if everyone contributes). So, it is possible for a group to be stuck in an "equilibrium trap" in which no one is contributing, even though everyone would be better off if everyone contributed.

But this outcome is not very likely. Everyone will realize that everyone else benefits from achieving the group goal, and *that the only way for this to happen is if everyone contributes.* So, Ms. *j*, like every other group member, makes the following calculation:

> If I don't contribute, then I get a payoff of 0. If I contribute, and so does everyone else, then I get a payoff of $B-C > 0$. If I contribute, but someone else does not, then I get $-C$. Everyone else makes the same calculation. Everyone will realize that everyone in the group appreciates his or her own essential status to achieving the group goal on the one hand, and that there is nothing to be gained by not contributing (aside from avoiding putting oneself at risk) on the other hand.

That is, individuals will often manage to coordinate on contributing, because there is a net benefit to doing so relative to the equilibrium-trap outcome, because every person's participation is absolutely essential, and because everyone knows this and knows that everyone else knows this. In short, there are a number of reinforcing factors causing individuals to see contribution as the sensible thing to do in this circumstance and to believe that everyone else will see it as the sensible thing, too. The "everyone contribute" event is what Thomas Schelling has called a *focal point*.[7]

Suppose, now, that a unanimous contribution rate is no longer necessary. Indeed, of the n persons in our group, suppose that only k contributors are necessary for the group objective to be obtained (where k is a number greater than zero but less than n). Ms. j's calculation is considerably different in this case, as may be seen in Display 9.1. If fewer than $k-1$ of her colleagues are contributing, or more than $k-1$, then it doesn't pay for Ms. j to contribute. In either of these cases she garners a higher payoff by not contributing (0 instead of $-C$ and B instead of $B - C$, respectively). Only if *exactly* $k-1$ others are contributing is Ms. j's contribution essential, in which case she would obtain $B - C > 0$ instead of 0 by contributing. Ms. j does not have a clearcut course of action, because she does not know in advance whether less than $k-1$, more than $k-1$, or exactly $k-1$ of her colleagues are going to contribute.

Ms. J's CHOICE	NUMBER OF OTHER GROUP MEMBERS CONTRIBUTING		
	less than $k-1$	exactly $k-1$	k or more
Contribute	$-C$	$B - C$	$B - C$
Do not contribute	0	0	B

DISPLAY 9.1

This development suggests that there are two rational, or equilibrium, outcomes possible. Either no one contributes or exactly k do. In either of these cases, no group member will have reason to reconsider his or her action. If no one is contributing, then Ms. j (or any other member, for that matter)

---

[7] This idea was first developed in his famous book, *The Strategy of Conflict* (Cambridge, Mass.: Harvard University Press, 1960).

would be foolish to decide to contribute. On the other hand, if exactly k people are contributing, then those not contributing have no need to contribute (and would be ill-advised to do so, since they enjoy the group benefit even though they haven't contributed), while the k that are contributing know that each and every one of them is absolutely essential.

Thus, for the group objective to be accomplished, it is clear that something of a "knife-edge" condition must hold for sufficient contribution to occur. Exactly k individuals will need to believe that they, and only they, are likely to contribute. I claim that this poses a much more complicated problem for group members than the case where unanimity was required. Indeed, the "tipping point," k, is a crucial determinant of whether or not this group is able to get its act together.

Let's take a concrete example. Suppose $n = 100$. I have already analyzed the case of $k = 100$, the requirement of unanimous contribution, and concluded that unanimous contribution is a likely occurrence. What if k were a relatively large number but less than 100, say, $k = 95$. Most group members, Ms. j included, are bound to think that if they are going to achieve the group goal, then an awful lot of them are going to have to contribute. The group cannot stand too many defectors without losing the goal altogether. It seems to me that the likelihood between the outcome of no one contributing and k of them contributing will be a tendency for k (or possibly even more than k) to end up contributing. What about $k = 85$? Again, there will be considerable psychological pressure on people to contribute, although not so much as when k equals 95 or 100. As k gets smaller, the pressure is reduced.

Consider the case of $k = 25$. In this instance, there are bound to be an awful lot of group members who calculate that their contribution is just not needed. It's not (necessarily) that they are mean-spirited but rather that they feel liberated to make alternative uses of their effort without risking the achievement of the group goal. Instead of going out with twenty-four other members of the Possum Hollow Rod and Gun Club to clean up litter along the Possum Hollow River, for example, Ms. j may conclude that that particular Saturday afternoon is best devoted to taking her children shopping for spring clothes. Cooperation is especially hard to elicit from members of a group when it is patently evident that the members' cooperation is probably inessential; this evidence mounts as k becomes small relative to n.

When k gets very small, nearly everyone in the group will bail out, devoting their energies to nongroup activities. The "rational" forecast is that the group objective will simply not be accomplished. Yet other factors may come into play in these circumstances, factors not incorporated into the analysis given in Display 9.1. In every group there are always some people who "do the right thing" no matter what. For one thing, they may secure utiles directly from the participation itself (it feels good to tramp up and down the Possum Hollow River on a beautiful spring afternoon). For another, as noted in the previous chapter on two-person cooperation, they may have internalized a value system that encourages contribution to group life. Surely, as the psychological/strategic pressures to which I've alluded above decline, people will drop out of participation—but perhaps not all, and if it takes only a few to secure the group goal, then it may well be achieved.

The general conclusion of this analysis is that the combination of strategic and psychological pressures that encourage contribution rise as k gets large relative to n. Holding n fixed (as I did in the development above), the likelihood that there will be sufficient contribution *declines* as k declines—certainly a nonobvious conclusion, inasmuch as it would appear that as k declines it gets "easier" to secure the group goal; as a qualification, however, I suggested that for very small k there may be an uptick in the likelihood of group success, since there is often a "dependable few" who will contribute for nonstrategic reasons.

These general tendencies, I claim, get more pronounced as n gets large, as C gets large, or as $B - C$ gets large, holding k fixed. As n gets large, the general conclusion reported in the previous paragraph holds—it is practically equivalent to holding n fixed and letting k get smaller. But not quite. As n gets large it seems to us that the psychological identification with the group, an identification that may well affect the benefit utiles one enjoys upon achieving a group goal, becomes more tenuous. It's hard to feel part of a group of ten million others. Sure, all the residents of Greater New York City have an obligation to keep its streets and parks litter-free, but it is hard to appeal to in-group feeling in urging folks to come out on a beautiful Saturday afternoon to clean up the shores of the Hudson River.

As C gets large, holding n, k, and $B - C$ fixed, there will be a tendency for the group to fail to secure its objective. The "no one contributes" equilibrium seems specially compelling in the case of large C, even if $B - C$ remains fixed, because the psychological risk of contributing (paying the cost of $-C$) but the group falling short of the k contributors is inhibiting.

Finally, as $B - C$ gets large, holding everything else fixed, the importance of the group goal grows, and people are prepared to take psychological risks in these circumstances. For any size group n, and decisive contribution level k, the prospect of the group obtaining enough contributors grows as $B - C$ grows.[8]

[8] As a first cut this analysis is plausible. But it is not satisfactory as a fully strategic analysis. For example, I claimed in the text that as $B - C$ grows, the prospects for group provision grow for every group size, n, and decisive contribution level, k. Surely it is correct to believe that, for any specific group member, the pressure to contribute grows as the net benefit of group provision $(B - C)$ gets large. On the other hand, that same individual will just as surely appreciate that the pressure will also be growing on all her group colleagues. Thus, the large net benefit tugs her toward contributing, but the certain knowledge that others will also feel this way may allow her to rationalize letting them do all the heavy lifting. Weighing the relative force of these countervailing effects is the sort of consideration that is part of a deeper game-theoretic treatment.

Multiperson Cooperation and Coordination

In a sense I have just taken up the easiest kind of multiperson cooperation, since there is only one thing the group seeks— what we have been calling the group "goal" or "objective"— and everyone in the group shares an interest in achieving it. Into this analytical stew I now want to add a tablespoon of nonuniqueness and a pinch of conflict of interest.

NONUNIQUENESS Let us suppose that there are many things a group might like but that the group members are indifferent among those many things as long as they obtain one of them. A social club, for example, might enjoy an evening at the ballet or a night at the opera. They are indifferent as to which, so long as they do it together. Suppose then that a typical group member, Ms. j again, has two choices: go to the opera or go to the ballet. If every group member makes the same choice, then they each realize a benefit of B utiles. (Everyone's attendance is required for those utiles because the group qualifies for a group ticket price and gets premium seating.) Failure to coincide on a common choice yields a positive payoff smaller than B, say b utiles (where $b < B$), though with an exception. If everyone else coordinates on a common choice, but Ms. j does not, then her payoff is 0. The situation facing Ms. j is given in Display 9.2.

	DISPLAY 9.2		
	CHOICES OF OTHERS		
MS. J'S CHOICE	**Everyone else chooses opera**	**Everyone else chooses ballet**	**No consensus**
Opera	B	0	b
Ballet	0	B	b

The last column of the display is irrelevant for Ms. *j*; her payoff is the same no matter what she does, since there is already division among her prospective companions. So, for analytical purposes, it is only necessary to look at the two-by-two part of the display consisting of the first two columns and rows. Game-theoretic analysis tells us the obvious—that there are two "rational" or "equilibrium" outcomes to this group activity. Thus, about the only thing game theory can tell us is that the group should coordinate. It doesn't tell us how, nor what Ms. *j* should do. To be more precise, it tells us no more than that each person should "flip a coin."

In this situation, then, the nonuniqueness of desirable goals for the group means that it will be problematic for the group actually to achieve one of them. If there were only two people, for example, each of whom flipped a coin, then there would be a fifty-fifty chance that they would coordinate choices—one chance in four that both would go to the opera, one chance in four that both would go to the ballet, and two chances in four that they would go their separate ways. For three people, the chances of all coordinating drop to one in four, and for four people, to one in eight. Generally, for an n-person group, the chances that all will choose ballet or all will choose opera is $(\frac{1}{2})^{n-1}$, a number that rapidly approaches zero as n gets large. (If $n = 10$, for example, the probability of successful coordination is .00195.) Thus, it is difficult for groups to obtain the dividends of cooperation when there are alternative directions in which its members may head, absent some sort of coordination mechanism.

Although I will not develop the analysis at length, it would appear that repeat play of this kind of group interaction may have the same sort of salutary effect it had in the two-person world. People would probably coordinate on which side of the road to drive, even in the absence of a traffic cop, just by virtue of doing it over and over again. If an alien plopped down in the middle of Beacon Street in Boston, I expect it would learn to stay to the right quite quickly (and there would be all manner of Boston drivers to let it know if it did otherwise). Similarly, I could imagine our social group, after some trial and error, implicitly coordinating—for example, going to the opera in even-numbered months and to the ballet in odd-numbered ones.[9]

	CHOICES OF OTHERS		
Ms. J's CHOICE	Everyone else chooses opera	Everyone else chooses ballet	No con- sensus
Opera	$B_1, B_2, \ldots, B_n$	0	b
Ballet	0	$\beta_1, \beta_2, \ldots, \beta_n$	b

DISPLAY 9.3

CONFLICT OF INTEREST Now let's consider the situation, probably the typical one, in which there are several different goals a group might pursue *and* members of the group value the different goals differently. This situation is portrayed in Display 9.3. Ms. j, the typical group member, gets B_j utiles if everyone

---

[9] I have said nothing about *communication*, and the curious reader may have begun to wonder why the members of this allegedly *social* group seemed incapable of talking to one another! Communication surely is an option, but it adds an additional layer of complexity that I'd just as soon not tackle. For one thing, communication may be costly. For another, it may be asymmetric (some people having the power to transmit, others to receive, still others to do both, and finally some poor sods who can do neither). For yet another, it opens up all kinds of strategic possibilities (one person leaving a voice-mail message for everyone else that he's going to the opera and will not be able to receive any incoming calls from this point on—a fait accompli). A rigorous treatment of strategic communication may be found in Jeffrey Banks, *Signaling Games in Political Science* (Chur, Switzerland: Harwood, 1991).

in the group coordinates on going to the opera and β_j utiles if they all go to the ballet. These two payoffs need not be the same and, depending on their relative magnitudes, Ms. *j* will have very distinct preferences as to which venue she would prefer her colleagues to coordinate on, even if both B_j and β_j are bigger than *b*. Of course, if *every* group member ranks the same alternative highest, then there will be no problem, but then there will be no conflict of interest. However, in the interesting case where there *is* conflict of interest—where $B_j > \beta_j$ but $B_k < \beta_k$ for group members *j* and *k*, respectively—cooperation among group members is exacerbated as members not only have to overcome the normal difficulties of coordination associated with nonuniqueness (as discussed just previously) but also must overcome inherent intragroup differences of opinion about where to go.

It is conceivable that, in some specific situations, the conflict of interest is resolvable in a relatively painless way. If, for instance, five of the six members of a group strongly prefer opera to ballet, then it doesn't take much figuring by the one ballet lover that, if the group is to obtain *either* of its goals, it's going to end up at the opera. But what about the situation in which a fifteen-person group is hopelessly divided into five intense opera lovers, five intense ballet lovers, three mildly opera-oriented members, and two mildly ballet-oriented members. This situation is sufficiently complicated that it requires some sort of *institutional* solution, as indeed are most situations that involve both nonuniqueness and conflict of interest. I am not saying that groups, even large groups, don't manage to overcome these difficulties in interesting, often idiosyncratic, ways. Repeat play, for example, might help here as it has in other situations I have examined. But the reality is that, rather than depending upon the problem to resolve itself in some fashion, a group will typically institutionalize a solution. This, I believe, is the important insight of Mancur Olson in his seminal book, *The Logic of Collective Action*.[10]

OLSON'S *LOGIC OF COLLECTIVE ACTION*

Olson, writing in 1965, essentially took on the political science establishment. He noted that the pluralist assumption of the time, that common interests among individuals are automatically transformed into group organization and collective action, was problematic. Individuals are tempted to "free-ride" on the efforts of others, have difficulty coordinating on multiple objectives (nonuniqueness), and may even have differences of opinion about which common interest to pursue (conflict of interest). In short, the group basis of politics is a foundation of Jell-O: One cannot merely assume that groups arise and are maintained; rather, formation and maintenance are the central *problems* of group life and politics generally.

Olson is at his most persuasive when talking about large groups and mass collective action. In these situations, like many of the demonstrations and rallies of the 1960s, n is very large and k is relatively small. This is another way of saying that no one individual is very significant, much less essential, to the achievement of a group goal. In these circumstances, the world of politics is a bit like Hume's marsh-draining game writ large, where each individual has a dominant strategy of not contributing.

Olson claims that this difficulty is severest in large groups, for three reasons. First, large groups tend to be anonymous. Each household in a city is a taxpaying unit and may share

[10] (Cambridge, Mass.: Harvard University Press, 1965). For an excellent and highly accessible game-theoretic treatment of collective action, the reader is encouraged to consult Avinash Dixit, Susan Skeath and David H. Reiley Jr., *Games of Strategy*, 3rd ed. (New York: Norton, 2009), Chapter 12.

the group objective to lower property taxes, but beyond that it is difficult to forge a group identity on such a basis. Second, in the anonymity of the large-group context, it is especially plausible to claim that no one individual's contribution makes much difference. Should the head of a household kill the better part of a morning writing a letter to his city council member in support of lower property taxes? Will it make much difference? If hardly anyone else writes, then the council member is unlikely to pay much heed to this one letter; on the other hand, if the council member is inundated with letters, would one more have a significant additional effect? Finally, there is the problem of enforcement. In a large group, are other group members going to punish a slacker? By definition, they cannot prevent the slacker from receiving the benefits of collective action, should those benefits materialize. (Every property owner's taxes will be lowered if anyone's are.) But more to the point, in a large, anonymous group it is often hard to know who has and who has not contributed, and, because there is only the most limited sort of group identity, it is hard for contributors to identify, much less take action against, slackers. As a consequence, many large groups that share common interests fail to mobilize at all—they remain *latent*.

This same problem plagues small groups, too, as Hume's marsh-draining game in Display 8.1 reveals. But Olson argues, much as I have in this text, that small groups manage to overcome the problem of collective action more frequently and to a greater extent. Small groups are more personal; therefore, their members are more vulnerable to interpersonal persuasion. In small groups, individual contributions may make a more noticeable difference (k is large relative to n) so that individuals feel that their contributions are more essential. Contributors in small groups, moreover, often know who they are and who the slackers are. Thus, punishment, ranging from subtle judgmental pressure to social ostracism, is easier to effectuate. Finally, small groups often engage in repeat play and therefore can employ tit-for-tat strategies to induce contributions.

In contrast to large groups that often remain latent, Olson calls these small groups *privileged* because of their advantage in overcoming the free-riding, coordination, and conflict-of-interest problems of collective action. It is for these perhaps ironic and counterintuitive reasons that small groups often prevail over, or enjoy privileges relative to, larger groups: producers over consumers, owners of capital over owners of labor, a party's elites over its mass members.

Olson elaborates on this asymmetry between large and small in suggesting that it applies *within* groups as well. If group members are unequal in important ways, these inequalities may actually help the group achieve its goals. But in doing so, it often leads to inequality at the level of contribution, with the *larger* or *more powerful* members being exploited by their smaller, weaker colleagues. Because a large, powerful group member is likely to "make a difference" in many situations, he or she will be under intense pressure to contribute. The enterprise may succeed even if one of the weaker members opts not to contribute, but it is more apt to fail if one of the powerful members does not contribute. Could the United States free-ride on its NATO allies, or the former Soviet Union on the former Warsaw Pact? There is evidence, in fact, that both the United States and the Soviet Union paid more than their "fair share" to support their respective alliances, and that many of their smaller partners paid much less than their fair share.

CASE 9.2
THE LARGE AND THE SMALL

In the case of NATO and the Warsaw Pact, the large participants, the United States and the Soviet Union, respectively, subsidized the other members of their alliances.* Their large size and their belief in the necessity of the alliance structure handicapped them in negotiating with their allies over a more equitable division of alliance costs.

David Marsh's research on corporations in Great Britain belonging to the Confederation of British Industry (CBI) suggests a similar exploitation of the large by the small.† Large firms are more dependent on the group and small firms are more likely to free-ride. The managing director of one large firm said, "If the CBI didn't exist we would need to create it. We need someone to stand up and talk for industry" (p. 264). An executive at a small firm said, "Whether we were members of the CBI or not we would derive some benefit from the part it plays for industry. You get that type of benefit whether you are a member or not" (p. 264). In support of Olson's theory, smaller group members often free ride on the efforts of larger members whose participation is more critical to the group's existence.

* Mancur Olson and Richard Zeckhauser, "An Economic Theory of Alliances," *Review of Economics and Statistics* 48 (1966): 266–79.
† "On Joining Interest Groups: An Empirical Consideration of the Work of Mancur Olson, Jr.," *British Journal of Political Science* 6(1976): 257–71.

Olson's By-Product Theory and Large-Scale Collective Action

The politically powerful conclusions of Olson's argument are, first, that groups are difficult to create and maintain, and second, that smaller groups seem less afflicted by these difficulties than larger groups. In rejecting the group basis of politics that much of twentieth-century political science took as its foundation, Olson provides a cogent explanation for the power of *small* numbers, even in political democracies that nominally count noses and reward size.

Let us not, however, cast a blind eye to the reality of large-scale collective action. The free speech movement, the civil rights movement, and other mass-action activities do, in fact, arise, and sometimes change the course of history. Olson would not want to deny these powerful facts; he does, however, claim that they require explanation. The existence of groups cannot merely be assumed. Olson's explanation for this large-scale collective action is known as the by-product theory.

Olson argues that large groups are able to elicit contributions from members by providing them more than just the successful achievement of group objectives. Remember that individuals enjoy successfully achieved group goals, whether they contribute or not. So, the prospect of the goal itself is often not sufficiently compelling to induce contribution. But what if members are given other things, *conditional on whether they contribute*? That is, what if one of the *reasons* members join groups is for the private things that they get only by making their contributions? If this is the case—if the motivational force for contribution is the private goodies in addition to the collective goals—then the goals achieved are, in a manner of speaking, achieved as *by-products*. The contributions to large groups are forthcoming because of the benefits that contributors, and only contributors, enjoy. These benefits operate as *selective* incentives to contribute.

Why, for example, would minimum-wage earners contribute time and money to lobby the state legislature to raise the minimum wage? If the wage is raised, then all benefit, whether they contribute or not; and no single contribution makes much difference anyhow. The problem for a large group with a common interest is that it cannot deny successes to noncontributors. Suppose, however, that only contributors (who contributed by joining the group and paying annual dues) received such selective benefits as low-cost term life insurance, a group rate for membership in a health club, special airfares to Florida in the winter, drug and alcohol counseling services, and a Wednesday night bowling league. These selective incentives might be sufficient to induce contribution. Over and above these tangible benefits that might be denied to noncontributors, any individual member may assert further that what he or she really values is the solidarity that being part of the group allows—another selective incentive.

In sum, the by-product theory suggests that a group that provides *only* collective group goals may have a hard time. Especially if the group is large and anonymous, it simply may not be possible for the goal itself to elicit enough contribution from prospective members to permit the goal to be achieved. The group, in effect, remains latent. So, groups search for things separate from the main group mission that *can* be withheld from those who do not contribute:

- worker groups, nominally organized to raise wages and improve working conditions, offer Wednesday night bowling;
- those organizing donation campaigns for National Public Radio give donors coffee mugs and sweatshirts identifying them as contributors to public radio;
- trade associations, officially organized to lobby Congress for policies beneficial to their entire industry, offer members (contributing companies in the industry, in this case) specialized access to trade statistics and other industry-relevant data;
- environmental groups, campaigning for public action in behalf of the environment, offer contributors discounts

in the purchase of camping equipment, inexpensive fares to exotic environmentally unique destinations, and reduced prices on books about the environment.

This list could be multiplied endlessly, which only gives further testimony to the plausibility and persuasiveness of Olson's by-product theory. Most mass associations and organizations do precisely these sorts of things to attract and retain members. And yet, the by-product theory seems incomplete in several respects. To some, the by-product theory does not take ample account of the role played by *leaders*. To others, it strikes a rather cynical chord in its failure to incorporate genuinely nonmaterialistic motivations. Don't some people join groups and make contributions because they believe in the group's cause and require nothing more than the good feeling that they have made a contribution to it? In the next two sections I take up each of these in turn.

Political Entrepreneurs

It is very unusual in the academic world for a book review to become an important part of the literature on a subject. But this is precisely what happened to Richard Wagner's review of Olson's book.[11] Wagner noticed that Olson's arguments about groups and politics in general, and his by-product theory in particular, had very little to say about the internal workings of groups. In Wagner's experience, however, groups often come into being and then are maintained in good working order not only because of selective incentives but also because of the extraordinary efforts of specific individuals—leaders, in ordinary language, or *political entrepreneurs* in Wagner's more colorful expression.

Wagner was motivated to raise the issue of group leaders

---

[11] Richard Wagner, "Pressure Groups and Political Entrepreneurs," *Papers on Non-Market Decision Making I* (1966): 161–70.

because, in his view, Olson's theory was too pessimistic. In the real world, labor unions, consumer associations, senior-citizen groups, environmental organizations, and so on all exist, some persisting and prospering over long periods. Likewise, mass activities like those described at the beginning of the chapter seem to get jump-started somehow in the real world. Wagner suggests that a special kind of by-product theory is called for. Specifically, he argues that certain selective benefits may accrue to *those who organize and maintain otherwise latent groups*.

Senator Robert Wagner (no relation) in the 1930s and Congressman Claude Pepper in the 1970s each had *private reasons*—electoral incentives—to try to organize laborers and the elderly, respectively. Wagner, a Democrat from New York, had a large constituency of working men and women who would reward him by reelecting him—a private, conditional payment—if he bore the cost of organizing (or at least of facilitating the organization of) workers. And this he did. The law that bears his name, the Wagner Act of 1935, made it much easier for unions to organize in the industrial north.[12] Likewise, Claude Pepper, a Democratic congressman with a large number of elderly constituents in his South Miami district, saw it as serving his own electoral interests to provide the initial investment of effort for the organization of the elderly as a political force.

In general, a political entrepreneur is someone who sees a prospective cooperation dividend that is currently not being enjoyed. This is another way of saying that there is a latent group that, if it were to become manifest, would enjoy the fruits of collective action. For a price, whether in votes (as in

---

[12] The Wagner Act made it possible for unions to organize by legalizing the so-called closed shop. If a worker took a job in a closed shop or plant, he or she was *required* to join the union there. "Do not contribute" was no longer an option, so workers in closed shops could not free-ride on the efforts made by others to improve wages and working conditions.

the cases of Wagner and Pepper) or a percentage of the dividend, or the nonmaterial glory and other perks enjoyed by leaders, the entrepreneur bears the costs of organizing, expends effort to monitor individuals for slacker behavior, and sometimes even imposes punishment on slackers (such as expelling them from the group and denying them any of its selective benefits).

To illustrate this phenomenon, there is the (no doubt apocryphal) story about a proper British lady who visited China in the late nineteenth century. She was shocked and appalled upon noticing teams of men pulling barges along the Yangtze River, overseen by whip-wielding masters. She remarked to her guide that such an uncivilized state of affairs would never be tolerated in modern societies like those in the West. The guide, anxious to please in any event but concerned in the present circumstance that his employer had come to a wildly erroneous conclusion, hastily responded, "Madam, I think you misunderstand. The man carrying the whip is *employed* by those pulling the barge. He noticed that it is generally difficult, if you are pulling your weight along a tow path, to detect whether any of your team members are pulling theirs or, instead, whether they are free-riding on your labors. He convinced the workers that his entrepreneurial services were required and that they should hire him. For an agreed-upon compensation he monitors each team member's effort level, whipping those who shirk in their responsibilities. Notice, madam, that he rarely ever uses the whip. His mere presence is sufficient to get the group to accomplish the task."

Thus, political entrepreneurs may be thought of as complements to Olsonian selective incentives in motivating groups to accomplish collective objectives. Both are helpful, and sometimes both are needed to initiate and maintain collective action. In this respect, groups that manage, perhaps on their own, to get themselves organized at a low level of activity often take the next step of *creating* leaders and leadership institutions in order to increase the activity level and resulting cooperation dividends. Wagner, in other words, took Olson's by-product theory and suggested an alternative explanation, one that made room for institutional solutions to the problem of collective action.

Political Ideology and Belief Systems

I noted just before the previous section, as I noted in our earlier discussion of multiperson cooperation, that some people contribute to collective undertakings without either selective incentives or leaders staring over their shoulders. Some, that is, have internalized a value system that makes contributing to group life a priority, whether or not it is accompanied by material incentives or overseers. This value system is often referred to as an *ideology* or *belief system*.

Rational-choice explanations of group phenomena—of which my analysis of multiperson cooperation, Olson's by-product theory, and Wagner's theory of political entrepreneurs are standard instances—tend to give short shrift to ideological explanations, principally because they ignore the question of where a particular ideology originates. That is, why would an ideology or belief system that disposes one toward cooperative/contributory behavior survive in a population and be sufficiently numerous to overcome all the problems of multiperson cooperation that I have discussed? These are important issues, so important that an ideological explanation, in my view, is bound to fall short unless it can satisfactorily account for them.

Nevertheless, I should point out (and will do so more extensively in the next section) that behavior may be thought of in either of two ways. Most rational analysis takes behavior to be *instrumental*—to be motivated by and directed toward some purpose or objective. But behavior may also be *experiential*. People do things, on this account, because they like doing them—they feel good inside, they feel free of guilt, they take pleasure in the activity for its own sake. We maintain that this second view of behavior is entirely compatible with rational accounts. Instrumental behavior may be thought of as *investment activity*, whereas experiential behavior may be thought of as *consumption activity*. I still will not have answered the question of where such beliefs and values originate nor why they survive. But economists do not tell us where consumer tastes originate either, and yet they make central use of those tastes in constructing their theory of price. The key thing to appreciate here is that we can still make precise statements about how dispositions toward both investment and consumption affect the prospects of collective action. I shall do this in more detail when discussing voting, our next topic.

But before leaving this section, let me briefly note one other aspect of experientially oriented behavior: It is the behavior itself that generates utility, rather than the consequences produced by the behavior. To take a specific illustration of collective action, many people certainly attended the 1963 March on Washington because they cared about civil rights. But it is unlikely that many deluded themselves into thinking their individual participation made a large difference to the fate of the civil rights legislation in support of which the march was organized. Rather, they attended because they wanted to be a part of a social movement, to hear Martin Luther King Jr. speak, and to identify with the hundreds of thousands of others who felt the same way. Also—and this should not be minimized—they participated because they anticipated that the march would be fun, an adventure of sorts.

So, experiential behavior is consumption-oriented activity predicated on the belief that the activity in question is fulfilling apart from (or in addition to) its consequences. Individuals, complicated beings that we are, are bound to be animated both by the consumption value of a particular behavior that I just described *and* its instrumental value, the rational (investment) explanation that has been used throughout this book. To insist on only one of these complementary forms of rationality and to exclude the other is to provide only a partial explanation. This is no more apparent than in the activity of voting, the centerpiece of democratic politics.

CASE 9.3
WHAT DOES THE EVIDENCE SAY?

What does the evidence say about these different explanations of collective action: Olson's by-product theory, Wagner's theory of political entrepreneurs, and the rationality of ideology and experiential behavior? In various studies group members have been surveyed to determine why they become members. The survey results indicate that people join for a combination of reasons. In support of Olson's theory, members of economic groups are more likely to join for selective, material benefits than for collective benefits. Economic groups include unions, farm groups, and business associations. Members of these groups often disagree with the political goals of the group, suggesting that the latter are not the chief reason for joining.*

In opposition to the by-product theory, some studies have found that members of noneconomic groups are motivated primarily by collective benefits. Individuals often join noneconomic groups such as Common Cause or the Sierra Club primarily because they agree with the group's political goals.† Overall, the evidence indicates that the motivation for membership in interest groups is a combination of selective and collective benefits, differing slightly for economic

* Terry Moe, *The Organization of Interests* (Chicago: University of Chicago Press, 1980).
† John Mark Hansen, "The Political Economy of Group Membership," *American Political Science Review* 79 (1985): 79–96.

and noneconomic groups. Members of economic groups join primarily for the selective benefits (instrumental behavior), while members of noneconomic groups join primarily for the collective benefits (experiential behavior).

Whether they join for the selective or the collective benefits, members appear to be behaving rationally. A study of members in thirty-five national organizations in the United States found that "members are attracted to, or seek out, those inducements that are most closely related to their central interests in an organization."‡ The study is important because it shows that ideology can be incorporated into a rational choice account of political behavior. Individuals committed to saving endangered species, an instance of a collective benefit, may "shop around" among different groups in order to find the one they believe will best serve their objectives.

Wagner's theory of political entrepreneurs is also supported by social science research. Two studies have found that outside support is often vital to forming and maintaining a group. In addition to Hansen, cited above, Walker found that most political action is supported by large, wealthy institutions, such as charitable foundations.§ Thus, the collective action problem for some interest groups is overcome by political entrepreneurs in the form of patron institutions. But what about these latter institutions—how do they solve *their* collective action problem? Robert H. Salisbury points out that these institutions are, in Olson's terms, privileged groups small enough to overcome the collective action obstacles they face.** If we expand the concept of political entrepreneur to include patron institutions, Wagner's argument holds up quite well.

‡ David Knoke, "Incentives in Collective Action Organizations," *American Sociological Review* 53 (1988): 311–29.
§ Jack L. Walker, Jr., *Mobilizing Interest Groups in America* (Ann Arbor: University of Michigan Press, 1991).
** *Interests and Institutions* (Pittsburgh: University of Pittsburgh Press, 1992).

THEORIES OF VOTING AND COLLECTIVE ACTION

The kind of collective action with which nearly all citizens of democracies are most familiar is that of choosing leaders. Indeed, Americans elect more officials at all levels of government than any other democracy in the world. Rarely a year goes by for the typical American eligible to participate in elections without there being a race for the House or Senate, a presidential election, a state legislative or gubernatorial race, or even a contest for the proverbial town dog catcher. Involvement in the electoral process, whether attending campaign rallies, contributing money to a favorite candidate or distributing her literature door to door, helping to "get out the vote," or voting itself, is collective action par excellence. Participation in election activity, then, like any other group activity, cannot be assumed, but rather must be explained. Why participate? That is the question. A strictly instrumental analysis is the appropriate starting point but, as we shall see, does not provide the last word. In one of the most famous articles on voting in the political science literature, William Riker and Peter Ordeshook supply the following analysis.[13]

Suppose there are two candidates for a public office, Jackson and Kendall. A typical citizen eligible to vote in this election, Ms. j again, must decide whether to vote and, if so, for whom to vote. The act of voting costs Ms. j C utiles, reflecting the time and energy, and perhaps the financial expense, of informing herself and actually going to the polls. Suppose, without loss of generality, that Ms. j prefers the election of Jackson to that of Kendall. That is, $u(J) > u(K)$, where u is Ms. j's utility function and J and K stand for the election of Jackson and Kendall, respectively. Put equivalently, if Jackson should win

---

[13] William H. Riker and Peter C. Ordeshook, "A Theory of the Calculus of Voting," *American Political Science Review* 62 (1968): 25–42.

rather than Kendall, then Ms. j gets a benefit $B = u(J) - u(K)$ > 0. If Ms. j were the only voter, then the answer to the question of participation is straightforward. If the benefit of picking the winner, B, exceeds the costs of doing so, C, then she should do so, picking Jackson; if, on the other hand, $C > B$, then she shouldn't bother (allowing the choice to be made randomly instead), since the utility difference between the candidates is not worth the cost Ms. j would bear to make the choice. But of course Ms. j is not the only voter, so she must take the intentions and capabilities of others into account.

Ms. j, we shall suppose, lives in a district in which there are n eligible voters in total, each of whom has a preference between the two candidates, bears costs if he or she exercises the franchise, and hence must go through essentially the same kind of analysis as Ms. j. The task must seem daunting, even for moderately sized n, if one must try to scope out, for each and every other eligible voter, who is going to vote and for which candidate. In fact, however, the task simplifies quite naturally. There are really only five circumstances that Ms. j (or any other voter) needs to consider. These involve how the other $n-1$ voters (excluding Ms. j) behave in the aggregate, and may be partitioned into five "states of the world" (labeled S_1 through S_5). *These "states" are the outcomes that would transpire if Ms.* j *abstained.*

S_1: Jackson loses to Kendall by more than one vote.
S_2: Jackson loses to Kendall by exactly one vote.
S_3: Jackson and Kendall tie.
S_4: Jackson beats Kendall by exactly one vote.
S_5: Jackson beats Kendall by more than one vote.

If Ms. j believes S_1 prevails, then her vote will have no effect on the final result, no matter how she casts it, since Kendall wins in any case. If she believes that S_2 is the prevailing state, then she knows that she can cast a vote for Jackson that produces a dead heat. With S_3 she can break what would otherwise be a tie. In state S_4 her vote for Kendall would produce a tie (though why she would ever want to do this is beyond us, since she prefers Jackson). Finally, if S_5 is the prevailing state, then, like in S_1, her vote, however she casts it, will have no effect since Jackson wins regardless. Display 9.4 gives the complete picture.

Each cell of the display gives the utility payoff to Ms. *j*, which depends both on the state of the world (what everyone else is doing) and her own choice. Notice that if Ms. *j* votes, then her utility for the outcome, whatever it is, is always reduced by *C*, the utility cost of her participation. Of course, if she abstains, then she does not pay this cost. The only term in this display requiring further explanation is *L*, which enters once in each row. *L* stands for "lottery," and reflects the fact that the election ends in a tie. In this case, we assume that some random device is used to determine the winner; the lottery is a fifty-fifty chance of either Jackson or Kendall. The expected utility theorem (see Chapter 2) implies that $u(L) = 1/2\,u(J) + 1/2u(K)$.

A glance at Display 9.4 reveals that Ms. *j* should *never* vote for Kendall, since in each state of the world the payoff to her in the "vote for Jackson" row is at least as big as its counter-

DISPLAY 9.4					
MS. *J*'S CHOICE	STATE OF THE WORLD				
	S_1	S_2	S_3	S_4	S_5
Vote for Jackson	$u(K)-C$	$u(L)-C$	$u(J)-C$	$u(J)-C$	$u(J)-C$
Vote for Kendall	$u(K)-C$	$u(K)-C$	$u(K)-C$	$u(L)-C$	$u(J)-C$
Abstain	$u(K)$	$u(K)$	$u(L)$	$u(J)$	$u(J)$

part in the "vote for Kendall" row.[14] Undoubtedly the reader is thinking, "I didn't need a fancy analysis to tell me that!" Indeed, it should be obvious that when there are only two candidates, you either vote for your preferred candidate or don't bother voting at all. There's never anything to be gained by voting for your less-preferred candidate.

The analysis will have something to tell us that's not so obvious when we ask the fundamental question: Does the payoff from voting for Jackson exceed the payoff from abstention? This requires us to compare the first and third rows of the display. Unlike the comparison of rows 1 and 2, however, in some states (columns) "vote for Jackson" gives the larger payoff while in others "abstain" is more attractive. In order to sort this out, we must incorporate into the analysis Ms. j's beliefs about the likelihoods of the various states. Then we must use some simple algebra to figure out what Ms. j should do.

To simplify things, let us set $u(J) = 1$ and $u(K) = 0$.[15] Moreover, let us represent Ms. j's beliefs by probability numbers. In particular, Ms. j believes S_1 occurs with probability p_1, S_2 with probability p_2, S_3 with probability p_3, S_4 with probability p_4, and S_5 with probability p_5 (where each probability number is 0 or larger and together they sum to 1). This information is contained in Display 9.5, which is simply Display 9.4 with the "vote for Kendall" row deleted and the above revisions

---

[14] In the first and fifth states, the payoffs are identical. In the third state, since $u(J) > u(K)$, the statement in the text holds. The only places in which there may be some confusion is when L is involved. In the second state, a fifty-fifty chance of getting your preferred candidate is surely better than the certainty of getting your *worst* choice. In the fourth state, the certainty of getting your *best* candidate is surely better than a lottery in which your chances of getting him are only fifty-fifty. So, the conclusion holds that Ms. j does at least as well voting for Jackson as she does voting for Kendall.

[15] In our discussion of utility functions in Chapter 2, we mentioned that it is often convenient to "normalize" the analysis, without doing any logical damage, by setting the utility of the most-preferred alternative to unity and that of the least-preferred to 0.

DISPLAY 9.5				
MS. *J*'S CHOICE	STATE OF THE WORLD (PROBABILITY)			
S_1 (p_1)	S_2 (p_2)	S_3 (p_3)	S_4 (p_4)	S_5 (p_5)
Vote for Jackson $-C$	$\frac{1}{2}-C$	$1-C$	$1-C$	$1-C$
Abstain 0	0	$\frac{1}{2}$	1	1

incorporated—$u(J)$ set to 1, $u(K)$ set to 0, and $u(L)$ set to 1/2.[16]

We apply the expected utility theorem from Chapter 2 directly to this display as follows:

$$EU \text{ (vote for Jackson)} = p_1 (-C) + p_2 (1/2-C) + p_3 (1-C) + p_4 (1-C) + p_5 (1-C)$$
$$= 1/2\, p_2 + p_3 + p_4 + p_5 - C$$
$$EU \text{ (abstain)} = p_1 (0) + p_2 (0) + p_3 (1/2) + p_4 + p_5$$
$$= 1/2\, p_3 + p_4 + p_5$$

Ms. *j* should vote for Jackson rather than abstaining if and only if EU (Jackson) > EU (abstain). With a little more algebra, this means that Ms. *j* should vote for Jackson if and only if $p_2 + p_3 > 2C$. In words, she should vote if the sum of the probabilities that she either makes a tie (voting for Jackson in S_2) or breaks a tie (voting for Jackson in S_3) exceeds twice the cost of voting.

This is certainly not obvious, and is a good deal more complicated than the reader might have thought at the outset. What does this implication for Ms. *j*'s participation mean?

---

[16] The lottery giving a fifty-fifty chance of Jackson or Kendall is, given the normalization, a fifty-fifty chance of getting a utility of 1 or of 0. Thus, the expected utility of this lottery is equal to 1/2.

This deduction is actually quite rich in implications. First, it says that the costlier it is to participate, the less likely Ms. j will be to do so. This follows because the inequality of $p_2 + p_3 > 2C$ is more difficult to satisfy as C gets large. Indeed, if C is sufficiently large (specifically if $C \geq 1/2$), she should never participate (since probability numbers could not satisfy the inequality). Second, it says that Ms. j should be most disposed to participate if she believes the election is going to be close. This follows because $p_2 + p_3$—the likelihood of "making or breaking a tie"—is a serviceable definition of a close election; the larger those probabilities get, the more likely it is that the inequality will be satisfied.

In sum, the Riker-Ordeshook calculus of voting provides a rationale for participation based, first, on the cost of participating and, second, on the likelihood a prospective participator will make a difference. But there is a third, most disturbing, implication of this analysis. Suppose C were very small relative to $u(\text{Jackson}) - u(\text{Kendall}) = 1$; say, $C = 1/1000$. This is not an unreasonable supposition in important elections like presidential contests, since it asserts that the cost of voting to the average citizen is quite small relative to the difference it makes to them whether, say, Democrat or Republican wins. So the inequality $p_2 + p_3 > 2C$ now says that Ms. j should vote if and only if her probability of making or breaking a tie ($p_2 + p_3$) were larger than $2/1000$. What is the likelihood of making or breaking a tie in a mass election in the United States, where there are approximately 125,000,000 prospective voters? It is infinitesimal, and certainly much smaller than $2/1000$. So it is very unlikely that a sensible person, like Ms. j, will believe that $p_2 + p_3$ exceeds $2/1000$. Thus, when all is said and done, most sensible persons, according to this analysis, will conclude that they should not vote.

One interpretation of this strictly instrumental analysis of Riker and Ordeshook is that instrumental calculations are simply insufficient to induce participation in large-scale elections of the sort that occur in most modern democracies. The fact that in the real world of mass elections there is considerable participation proves embarrassing. Noting this, Riker and Ordeshook salvage their own analysis by conceding that there is more to a calculus of voting than computing the *consequences* of voting versus abstaining. They suggest, though not in the words I use, that there is an *experiential* as well as an *instrumental* basis for voting—that voting has consumption as well as investment value.

For one thing, individuals in democratic societies possess a belief system or ideology in which great stock is placed in participation. Abstention is frowned upon—by one's neighbors, by one's spouse, even by one's children.[17]

For another thing, punishments are often inflicted on nonparticipators. In some societies, a fine is imposed. In others there are "watchdogs": the neighbor who goes door to door or leans over her fence, imploring her neighbors to vote; the shop steward who makes it clear to the men on the shop floor that they had better make time at lunch hour to vote; the party activists who, late in the day, check with pollwatchers to see who has not yet voted.

Finally, it must be said that individuals participate in electoral activities not only to avoid feelings of guilt or to dodge the "punishments" inflicted by others but also because it can be fun. A voter may find satisfaction in standing in line at the polls chatting with neighbors. One enjoys the next-day conversations at the office, or over coffee with neighbors, not only about the election but about one's own participation in it.

Riker and Ordeshook account for this experiential source of utility by altering the payoffs in Displays 9.4 and 9.5. In the participation rows—"vote for Jackson" and "vote for Kendall"—

---

[17] The author remembers all too keenly how painful it was to face his children afer returning home from work on the evening of an election and confessing that he "just didn't have the time to vote." That experience, seared in his memory, has factored into all subsequent participation decisions for him!

but not in the "abstain" row, an additional consumption payoff is added. That is, while there surely are costs associated with participation (measured by the $-C$), there are also benefits, like those just discussed above. These benefits may be sufficiently large to induce some who would not otherwise participate on purely instrumental grounds.[18]

There is now a large literature on rational theories of voting.[19] Since my primary interest in voting here is to display it as an instance of collective action, I will not pursue the subject in further detail—except to note one feature that the perceptive reader may have already discerned. In my treatment of collective action, I have mainly considered a single group in isolation faced with prospective dividends from cooperation. Indeed, I went further by focusing on a generic individual in isolation, seeking to determine the conditions under which that individual would choose to contribute to a group enterprise. The example of voting, however, suggests that many collective action situations *pit groups against each other*. Ms. *j* may well be a Jackson supporter, and the question for her is whether to contribute, along with other Jackson supporters, to the Jackson cause. But somewhere out there is lurking a Mr. *k*, a Kendall supporter, with a similar problem. Yet, their respective problems are *interdependent* and should not be treated in isolation.

That is to say, many collective action problems are not only

---

[18] I will not burden the reader further with an analytical demonstration. Interested readers may consult the original analysis by Riker and Ordeshook. For a broad discussion of the issue, including a critique of the Riker and Ordeshook approach, the reader is encouraged to examine Brian Barry, *Sociologists, Economists, and Democracy* (Chicago: University of Chicago Press, 1970).

[19] The ambitious reader is directed to two companion volumes: James M. Enelow and Melvin J. Hinich, *The Spatial Theory of Voting: An Introduction* (New York: Cambridge University Press, 1984), and James M. Enelow and Melvin J. Hinich, eds., *Advances in the Spatial Theory of Voting* (New York: Cambridge University Press, 1990). Also see Samuel Merrill III and Bernard Grofman, *A Unified Theory of Voting* (New York: Cambridge University Press, 1999).

problems of individuals sharing a common objective and seeking to overcome incentives that discourage contribution. They also involve strategic interactions among competing groups. The fate of groups in securing their respective objectives often depend not only upon own-group success in encouraging participation but also upon other-group success in collective action. In short, life is complicated, and this analysis has only scratched the surface. In order to treat this more complicated manifestation of collective action, I would have to take up issues of strategy in considerable detail, entering the domain of game theory. Of course, I cannot do everything in a single textbook, but I encourage the student to pursue this matter independently.[20]

PROBLEMS AND DISCUSSION QUESTIONS

1. One vision of the thrust-and-parry of democratic politics is that it is essentially about the interaction of interest groups. So, if we wish to understand the outcome of some policy debate, we should focus primarily on the political groups with an *interest* in the issue at hand, and their *power* vis-à-vis one another. Can we take the existence of organized interest groups for granted in attempting to understand politics? Why or why not? What variables might we consider in attempting to quantify the power of political interest groups? For example, what role does the size of a group (latent or active), the structure of interests within the group, or the quality of its organization and leadership play in determining its strength?

---

[20] Excellent starting points are two books to which I have referred readers before: Avinash Dixit and Barry Nalebuff, *Thinking Strategically* and Avinash Dixit, Susan Skeath, and David H. Reiley, Jr., *Games of Strategy*.

2. Four friends live together in a college apartment and must work together to clean the common areas before their parents arrive for Parents' Weekend. For simplicity, suppose that this outcome is dichotomous (the apartment is either fully cleaned or it isn't) and has all the features of the collective action problem described in Display 9.1 and the surrounding text. Assume $B > C$ for each individual.

- What are the possible equilibrium outcomes when all four friends must contribute to clean the apartment? Which do you think is likely?

- What are the possible equilibrium outcomes when only two of the four friends must contribute to clean the apartment (i.e., $k = 2$)? Can you predict which outcome will occur without further information?

- How might your prediction change when $k = 2$ if B increases, or C decreases? What about if B is different for different members of the group?

3. Most industries (e.g., steel, sugar, or automobiles) organize one or more trade associations to lobby Congress on matters of regulatory, trade, and tax policy, among many others. For each of the following situations, describe the likelihood of successful organization for lobbying on policies favorable to that industry, the fruits of which are enjoyed by all individuals in the industry whether they contributed or not. If there is a clear answer, explain the thinking behind that prediction.

- One industry has a large number of small firms producing while another has only a few very large firms.

- Both industries have a medium number of firms, but in one, successful lobbying will require nearly universal support of the lobbying effort, while in another, successful lobbying will require only about 50 percent of firms to contribute.

- All firms within an industry agree on policy priorities, while in a second industry there is considerable disagreement over targets for lobbying efforts.

- One industry contains firms of relatively equal size, while another industry contains a few very large firms (whose contributions to lobbying are proportionally efficacious) and a large number of small firms.

4. AARP is a political organization that represents the interests of people over fifty, through lobbying, negotiation of special discounts for members, and research on issues of interest to its members. Members pay small yearly dues and in exchange are eligible for the above-mentioned discounts as well as AARP-affiliated insurance plans. In fact, AARP's insurance recommendations ended up being highly profitable for AARP co-founder Leonard Davis, who left the organization in 1979 over discontent with the nonprofit organization's links to the insurer Colonial Penn.[a] Today, AARP has roughly 40 million members, is one of the most powerful congressional lobby groups in Washington, and is a major player in all legislation of interest to senior citizens. Their lobbying activity is backed up by impressive registration and get-out-the-vote efforts every election cycle, although AARP itself is nonpartisan.

Based on this vignette, how has AARP been so successful in organizing senior citizens, securing massive membership and high rates of political engagement? Use the ideas presented in this chapter to make your case.

[a] "Leonard Davis; Helped Start AARP and Geronotology Programs at USC," *Los Angeles Times*, January 23, 2001.

5. What is the paradox of participation? Explain why voting can be considered a collective action problem, and why voting behavior based strictly on the utility of possible outcomes raises this paradox.

Now consider a further wrinkle: every district has at least some voters, but participation is much higher in some places than in others, and at some times more than at others. What might account for this variation in participation rates? Does the Riker-Ordeshook analysis suggest any possible implications, or are other explanations more compelling? In answering this question it might be useful to consider "motor-voter" laws, election day registration, mail-in ballots, and other programs designed to reduce C, as well experiential benefits of voting.

*6. This question is based on a model discussed in McCarty and Meirowitz (2007), which is in turn based on Palfrey and Rosenthal (1984).[b] Suppose that there are n individuals who desire a collective good that yields benefit B to all n individuals. Provision of the good requires only one individual ($k = 1$) to expend C to provide it ($B > C$).

- Show that there n possible sets of pure strategy equilibria (each player i plays "contribute" or "don't" with probability 1).[c]

- Now suppose that all players are playing an identical *mixed strategy*; that is, they probabilistically choose

---

[b] Nolan McCarty and Adam Meirowitz, *Political Game Theory: An Introduction* (Cambridge, U.K.: Cambridge University Press, 2007), and Thomas Palfrey and Howard Rosenthal, "Participation and the Provision of Discrete Public Goods: A Strategic Analysis," *Journal of Public Economics* 23 (1983): 171–93.

[c] Recall the definition of equilibrium that we have been using thus far: Taking all other players' strategies as fixed, each player has no incentive to alter his strategy. Thus, an equilibrium is a point of stability, in which no one wishes to change his or her "play."

whether to play C or D. Call p the probability that any one player plays C. First, show that for any player i, if he doesn't contribute, the probability that the good is supplied by someone else is $1 - (1 - p)^{n-1}$. Second, equate the expected utility for i of contributing with the expected utility of not contributing. Note that when these expected utilities are equal, i is happy to play C with probability p, just like the others. Third, solve the expression you just found for p. Fourth, show that p is decreasing in C, increasing in B, and decreasing in n.

7. Aristotle wrote in *Politics* (Book II, Chapter 3):

> For that which is common to the greatest number has the least care bestowed upon it. Every one thinks chiefly of his own, hardly at all of the common interest; and only when he is himself concerned as an individual. For besides other considerations, everybody is more inclined to neglect the duty which he expects another to fulfill; as in families many attendants are often less useful than a few.

In other words "everybody's business is nobody's business." How does this phenomenon affect groups with political interests, and why is it especially problematic for what Olson calls "large, latent groups"?

8. Chapter 2 articulated a relatively "thin" vision of rationality, defined in terms of an ability to discern among possible outcomes, and then purposive action to secure those preferred outcomes. From this perspective, is voting irrational (or paradoxical)? Does the idea of *experiential* benefits provide a satisfying rational choice explanation of voting? Does the paradox of voting call into question the enterprise of explaining political behavior with a rational actor model? Give arguments pro and con for this final question.

10

Public Goods, Externalities, and the Commons

The social dilemmas that arise from properties of goods, and the manner in which they are produced or consumed, bear a close relationship to the establishment and maintenance of co-operation and collective action. This may sound like economics but, in fact, it's politics through and through. Markets are best thought of as human constructions, not as elements of some natural order. They require that political understandings and institutions come into being and persist. Surely, politics can break markets, as economists are wont to remind us in their critiques of overly zealous regulation; but politics makes markets, too.

DEFINING TERMS

Most goods exchanged in economic markets are called *private* because the "owner" has full control over their use. If you buy a tube of toothpaste it belongs to you in the sense that its use is entirely under your control.[1] Specifically, you can exclude others from enjoying its use. This is an especially important

---

[1] Of course, there are (politically imposed) limits to your discretion. In most societies there are laws against squeezing toothpaste into someone else's iPod without their permission, for example.

form of control inasmuch as toothpaste gets "used up"; if the purchaser could not exclude others, then it would hardly be worth it for her to make the purchase in the first place. Consequently, private goods are defined by two properties: *excludability* (the owner may exclude others from enjoying the good) and *solitary supply* (use depletes the availability of the good).[2]

Goods lacking in both of these properties are called *public goods*. They are *nonexcludable*—anyone can enjoy them whether she has paid for that privilege or not—and are *jointly supplied* (nonrivalrous)—one person's use does not diminish the supply available to others. Classic examples of public goods include national defense and lighthouse services.

Consider the former. If defense services are extended over a broad territory, then anyone living in that territory is a beneficiary. Suppose, for example, that a feudal lord's castle, cannon, and knights in fourteenth-century England effectively protect a territory extending, say, twenty miles in any direction from the castle. The significance of this is that bands of robbers are discouraged from practicing their trade within the lord's jurisdiction.[3] Thus, anyone living within the boundary enjoys relative peace—and that enjoyment is not contingent on whether the person pays general feudal dues to the lord, pays specific user charges for protection, or is an ally of the lord. Just by being a resident of the castle's territory, one may "consume" the lord's protective services.

What, really, is this protective service? In effect, it is deterrence. The lord's might discourages predators, and this discouragement cannot be parceled out very effectively to some in the territory and denied to others. Thus, the entire territory

[2] Alternatively, these goods are sometimes called *rivalrous*.
[3] This does not mean there is *no* robbing and thievery. Robber bands may hide out in, say, Sherwood Forest and make raids on the lord's territory. The presence of the lord's defense forces, however, by raising the costs of thieving, discourages the frequency and intensity of the activity. Citizens, consequently, may not be spared entirely but are spared more so than if the lord's defense forces did not exist at all.

enjoys it. In this instance, we say that defense is a public good because it is nonexcludable (it is available to everyone if it is provided to anyone) and jointly supplied (one person's enjoyment of this deterrence does not diminish its availability for enjoyment by others in the territory).

In between the ideal types of private and public goods are mixtures of the two. Some goods are jointly supplied, but excludable. A Madonna concert comes to mind in which a high wall, a limited number of entry points, and turnstiles serve to exclude those without tickets, even though, within limits, Madonna's music is jointly supplied.[4] Other goods are nonexcludable but not jointly supplied. What is ideal about a Cape Cod beach in August is enjoyment of the sun and surf without feeling like you are crowded together with others like sardines. The ideal beach, then, shares with private goods the attribute of solitary (or at least limited) supply—beyond some level of density its enjoyment by an additional family diminishes its pleasure for other families. (This density threshold is often surpassed on Cape Cod in August!) But it does not possess the other private-good attribute of excludability. To the contrary, nonexcludability, at least as regards public beaches, means that on the hottest days of summer you are cheek-by-jowl with loads of others. All these distinctions are illustrated in Display 10.1. I shall focus mostly on the extreme cases of an ideal-type public good and an ideal-type private good.

---

[4] The limits have to do with the degree to which jointness of supply is compromised by crowding. If greater crowding, beyond some limit, actually affects the quality of the good, then we cannot claim that the good is jointly supplied. We shall pursue this prospect in the next illustration.

DISPLAY 10.1

PUBLIC AND PRIVATE GOODS

		Excludability	
		Yes	**No**
Jointness of Supply	**Yes**	Madonna concert	**Public goods:** defense, lighthouse services
	No	**Private goods:** toothpaste, BMW 320i	Crowded Cape Cod beach

---

PUBLIC GOODS AND POLITICS

Politics rears its ugly head because, like cooperation (which is often undersupplied) and collective action (which is often underachieved), the provision of public goods is subject to socially destructive incentives. Because a public good is nonexcludable, it may be enjoyed without paying a price for it. But a producer will be loath to provide a good if he cannot elicit payment for it. And even if there were some imperfect method by which a potential producer could extract a return from providing a public good, the amount supplied would likely be very much less than it would be if payment could be extracted directly. As a result, everyone is worse off.

Peasant farmers in a feudal world may well be willing to pay something for the lord's protection (certainly as much as they would have to pay, in terms of time, energy, and lost opportunities, to guard against predators themselves); but if the lord has no way of eliciting this payment from beneficiaries of his protection, then he will be less disposed to provide it, or very much of it at least, in the first instance. It was something like this that supported the enforcement of feudal arrangements in many parts of the world; accordingly, peasant families were coerced into contributing hours of labor in the lord's fields, a younger son to the lord's army, and a proportion of their crops to the lord's granary in exchange for being kept safe. Because protection is a public good, its supply by means of ordinary market exchange is problematic, necessitating the substitution of politics—the enforcement of coercive feudal institutions—for economic exchange. Political institutions, like feudalism, arise to fill the economic vacuum.

Sometimes the political arrangement is at one remove. The classic example of lighthouses illustrates this. The services of a lighthouse constitute a quintessential public good. If a lighthouse is erected on high ground near a shipping hazard, the warning it emits is available to every ship that passes (nonexcludability) and its use by one ship does not deny it to others (jointness of supply). No ship will willingly pay for lighthouse services, since nonpayment cannot lead to a refusal of service to nonpayers—if the service is provided at all. But if a private individual or firm cannot be compensated sufficiently to earn a normal return, it will not be inclined to invest in the provision of lighthouse services. For this reason, lighthouses turn up in introductory economics texts as the classic instance of a public goods problem—in which a public good is undersupplied owing to socially perverse incentives.

In a superb piece of economic detective work, the Nobel laureate Ronald Coase revealed that generations of undergraduates had been misled by the lighthouse example.[5] In England, at least, lighthouses were quite commonly provided along its western coastline by private enterpreneurs. But how could such entrepreneurs obtain a return on their investment? The ingenious answer Coase provided is that lighthouses typically were positioned near harbors, allowing ships to enter without crashing onto dangerous shoals. The lighthouse was primarily needed by precisely those ships coming into port.

---

[5] Coase's essay first appeared in 1974 and has been reprinted in R. H. Coase, *The Firm, the Market, and the Law* (Chicago: University of Chicago Press, 1988), pp. 187–215.

Ships not intending to put ashore would typically travel somewhat farther out to sea, thus not especially requiring the services of a lighthouse. Consequently, there was a way to discriminate between most users and nonusers. Was there a method for converting this capacity to discriminate into a capacity to extract payment? If a monopolist controlled the waterfront of the harbor, then he could price lighthouse services jointly with docking privileges in a manner that captured a return for the former. Lighthouse services, then, were part of a *tie-in sale*; if a ship owner wanted to use wharf and warehousing facilities of the port, he would be required to pay for the lighthouse services he consumed as well.

The monopoly position of the entrepreneur is crucial here. If the lighthouse provider was only one of many owners of wharfs and warehouses, he could not charge extra because of competition for customers. Other wharf and warehouse owners could charge a price for their services lower than the tie-in sale price. So, in order for a lighthouse to be provided, an entrepreneur must enjoy the *political protection* of his monopoly position.[6]

Consider one last illustration, this one of more contemporary vintage. In the 1970s the entire industrialized world was held hostage by a cartel known as OPEC—the Organization of Petroleum Exporting Countries. This organization, led by the oil ministers of the member states, conspired to jack up the price of petroleum by restricting the amount that would be available for export. The logic according to which they oper-

---

[6] Having just read a chapter on multiperson cooperation, the astute reader might wonder whether there are alternatives to granting an entrepreneur monopoly rights. That is, even if there were several wharves and warehouses in port, their owners might arrange to jointly finance a lighthouse and cover its costs through charges on their port services. This is an interesting possibility that the reader might like to think through. Note, however, that this type of cooperation is, in a modern context, regarded as collusion in restraint of trade and thus a violation of the law, because it essentially entails price-fixing. A waiver from antitrust prohibitions, like protection of monopoly power, is a *political* necessity.

ated was quite straightforward and well-known. From the simple law of supply and demand, for a given level of world demand for oil, if the supply were restricted, then its price would rise. Suppose the competitive price for and quantity of a barrel of oil—the ones that would emerge from competition among oil producers in the absence of a cartel—are P_c and Q_c, respectively, with total revenue, $R_c = P_c \times Q_c$. If the cartel could successfully restrict quantity to Q_{opec}, an amount less than Q_c, then the price would rise to P_{opec}, an amount higher than P_c. The new total revenue is $R_{opec} = P_{opec} \times Q_{opec}$. Under conditions prevailing in the 1970s, it was possible to find a Q_{opec} and its associated P_{opec} that produced a larger total revenue, that is, $R_{opec} > R_c$. Thus, if the oil producers could agree on a system of quantity-restricting production quotas—one for each exporter —that added up to Q_{opec}, and could hang together by honoring these quotas, they would thereby reduce the amount of oil available on the world market and have a bigger revenue pie to slice up among themselves.

The higher price that prevails because of this restriction on oil supply is a public good for OPEC (and a public bad for everyone else). Let's see how this works. I said that a public good is, first of all, nonexcludable, and this is certainly true of a prevailing price. Every oil exporter gets the prevailing price—certainly those in the cartel, but even those that are not members. Second, a public good is jointly supplied, and this, too, is true of the prevailing price. One supplier selling its product at that price does not deny that same price for some other supplier.

The joint actions that sustain this price require each supplier to stick to its production quota (so that the total amount of oil for sale adds up to the optimal Q_{opec}, thus generating the optimal revenue, R_{opec}). But providing this particular public good, like the provision of public goods generally, is problematic. Each supplier will be tempted to cheat on the cartel by producing more than its quota. If the little bit extra is sufficiently small so as not to affect the prevailing price, then a cheater can sell more than its quota at the cartel-supported higher price than it would if it honored the quota. But if each member of OPEC cheats on the cartel, then there will be more oil on the market, the price will decline, revenues will drop, and each member will have incentives to begin a further round of cheating. In the end, like so many instances of collective action that we have already examined, everything unravels and the cartel fails.

Indeed, this is what ultimately happened to OPEC in the 1970s. But it took quite a while for the cartel to break apart; in the meantime, OPEC did very well while the rest of the world suffered immense economic hardship. Why did the cartel last as long as it did? The answer, like our answers to the provision of defense and lighthouses, is that a *political* understanding sustained OPEC's operation. In this case, one petroleum exporter, Saudi Arabia, was dramatically larger than any of the other members of OPEC. Saudi Arabia vigilantly enforced the cartel agreement by using various carrots and sticks to induce compliance by its smaller cartel partners with previously set production quotas. Saudi Arabia (which was intent upon being the dominant state in the Arab world and, not uncoincidentally, also had the most to gain from cartel pricing, given its oil resources) took on the burdens of political leadership to hold the cartel together.[7]

We thus see that public goods will go underproduced, if produced at all, because individuals have private incentives at odds with those required to support their production. Individuals have private incentives to enjoy the benefits of defense and lighthouses without paying for them. Potential producers appreciate this prospect and, consequently, are discouraged

---

[7] A sophisticated strategic analysis of OPEC, with Saudi Arabia conceived of as a dominant member seeking to preserve its reputation, is found in James E. Alt, Randall Calvert, and Brian Humes, "Reputation and Hegemonic Stability," *American Political Science Review* 82 (1988): 445–66.

from producing them *unless they can find some means by which to elicit contributions*. Potential cartel partners often forgo cartel formation because they can anticipate that their various partners will cheat on the cartel, in effect seeking to enjoy cartel benefits without paying for them. Again, the public good—in this case a higher price for cartel products—will be produced only if members can assure one another that the behavior required to sustain the higher price will be forthcoming. In all these cases the solution, like the solution to the problems of cooperation and collective action reviewed in the two preceding chapters, is political. Perhaps the most common solution of all—the quintessential political solution—is the *public supply* of public goods. This solution requires a section all its own.

PUBLIC SUPPLY

I have argued that the provision of public goods is poorly handled by ordinary market means. They are undersupplied relative to the levels that the members of society would prefer. Absent some sort of political intervention, there is, as we have just seen, too little protection from predators and too few lighthouses. Politically enforced feudal arrangements and monopoly rights in ports, respectively, are solutions to these problems (though not perfect solutions). An alternative is to turn to the state for public goods provision. Let the government build lighthouses and raise armies.

In many parts of the world, lighthouses, the protective services of the police and army, judicial services, public utilities like water, sewage, and power, and provision for public health, roads, and other infrastructure are commonly provided by government. Telephone and television are also often provided publicly in many countries. The argument is that, because they are public goods (or at least "publiclike"), private market actors will not provide them (at least not in sufficient quantities) because they cannot be assured of adequate compensation. The state, on the other hand, may use its authority to *require* payment, either out of general revenue raised by taxation or from user charges of various sorts.[8]

However, there is a paradox associated with the public provision of public goods. Public provision does not just happen. Political pressure must be mobilized to encourage the institutions of government to make this provision a matter of public policy. Bills must be passed, appropriations enacted, and government agencies created. In short, political actors must be persuaded to act. But if the provision of a public good distributes a benefit widely, and if the enjoyment of that benefit is unrelated to whether a contribution has been made toward mobilizing politicians to act, then we may reasonably ask: Why would any individual or interest group lobby the government for public goods? Why wouldn't they, instead, free-ride on the efforts of others, thereby freeing up their own resources either to lobby for some other private benefits or to deploy in the private sector for private gain? That is, if many public services are like public goods, then their supply depends upon individuals and groups successfully engaging in collective action to get the government to provide them. Since magic wands are not available, the "public supply" solution to the provision of public goods becomes a problem in collective action.

---

[8] The reader should notice that public goods, as we have defined them, and publicly provided goods may not be the same. The latter *may* be public goods, like lighthouses and national defense; but the state provides lots of other goodies—like mail delivery, for example—that are sufficiently like other private goods that they undoubtedly could be provided reasonably well in the marketplace. (Indeed, courier services, overnight mail delivery, and package delivery are provided privately in direct competition with the U.S. Postal Service.) Publicly provided goods and services—the activities in which governments engage—reflect the political advantages possessed by interests in the political process that are sufficient to induce the public sector to do their bidding. Some of these things are public goods, but not all of them.

At this point, the reader may wish to return to Chapter 9 to review various conventional solutions. However, there is a less conventional answer. First, we must distinguish between the *consumption* of a public good and its *production*.[9] When designating a good as public or private, we are really talking about consumption properties—whether you can exclude others from consuming the good or not and whether consumption diminishes the availability of the good. I have not remarked at all about production. In fact, in nearly every instance public goods are produced with substantial private input.

When the U.S. government began constructing the massive interstate highway system in 1956, it was not intended for the government to get into the concrete business, the paint business, the sign- or guardrail-making business, or even the highway construction business. The government would use its taxing and borrowing powers to raise money on the one hand, and its substantive political authority to make choices about highway routes and road attributes on the other. But it would then request proposals for building highways from private contractors subject to these specifications. Successful contractors—actors from the market economy—would then make the concrete, pour it according to design, paint the yellow lines in the middle, assemble guardrails, signage, overpasses, and so on.

The highway system, surely public in consumption, is in fact mostly *private* in production. Various aspects of the production process can be divvied up among contractors. The contract to provide concrete, for example, is excludable (the winning contractor gets the contract and can bar losing bidders from sharing in the associated profit) and is solitarily supplied (giving the contract to *A* eliminates its availability to

---

[9] This distinction is made persuasively by Peter Aranson and Peter Ordeshook, "Public Interest, Private Interest, and the Democratic Polity," in Roger Benjamin and Stephen Elkin, eds., *The Democratic State* (Lawrence: University of Kansas Press, 1985).

B, C, D, . . .). According to the criteria in Display 10.1, highway construction fits squarely in the private-good category.

So, who do you suppose lobbies for a highway system? On
the consumption side, as we have seen, there are collective-
action problems. By conventional means they may be overcome
to some extent. Thus, the American Automobile Association
and the American Truckers Association, representing different
segments of the consuming public, undoubtedly brought their
political muscle to bear on legislators and executive branch officials on behalf of a highway program. Similarly, there are
likely to have been political entrepreneurs taking up the
cause—for example, legislators representing districts containing large transshipment centers (Chicago, Denver). But those
most likely to gain *directly and immediately* (and less likely to
have been as plagued by collective-action problems as groups
on the consumption side) are those who would actually *produce* the public good. Concrete producers, highway contractors, makers of heavy equipment, manufacturers of guardrails
and steel supports for overpasses, owners of rights-of-way, and
many others all stood to make enormous sums of money from
this multibillion-dollar project. In short, the politics of public
supply is as much about the production of public goods as it is
about their consumption.

The lesson here is that the politics of public supply cannot
be adequately understood as a collective-action phenomenon
among those wishing to *consume* public goods. Consumers of
public goods like good highways, clean air, lighthouses, and
security from national defense certainly play a role in providing political pressure. They are, however, limited by the
collective-action obstacles with which the reader is now familiar. In fact, their interests often never materialize into group
action; they remain latent.

On the other hand, for every reference to consumers of national defense, to take one of the most important public goods,
there are thousands of references to the "military-industrial

complex," those who profit directly from the production of national defense. They are Olson's "privileged groups" who have
the ability to surmount their own collective-action problems
and the incentive to do so (profits). They are found in the committee rooms and hallways of the Capitol, testifying, lobbying,
and spreading campaign dollars around to any legislator who
will take up their cause. Weapon systems constitute an excellent illustration of this phenomenon. In 2009, President
Barack Obama sought to eliminate the production of a number of F-22 fighter planes (at a saving of many billions of dollars). Some legislators, like Senator (and former presidential
candidate) John McCain, supported the president, arguing
that these weapons were no longer necessary for the national
defense. But most legislators fought the president tooth and
nail. The reason: Businesses in more than forty states and
three hundred congressional districts had subcontracts for the
production of these planes. These businesses, along with labor
unions representing workers and state and local officials concerned with the business climate in their localities, constituted a lobbying force their legislators in the House and
Senate found extremely difficult to ignore. In trying to understand the public supply of public goods, then, the astute observer will look at the supply side as well as the demand side
of the "market."

Before concluding this discussion let me note several complaints lodged against public supply. The major concern with
public supply as a solution to the problem of providing public
goods is that public-sector actors may not have "good" incentives. In this version of the "who will guard the guardians"
problem, the question is not whether government is capable of
supplying public goods but rather how well it does the job.

A classic instance of this involves the production of scientific knowledge. Many kinds of knowledge constitute public
goods to the extent that they cannot be patented or copy-
righted. Once it is known, for example, that $e = mc^2$, individu-

als cannot be excluded from this knowledge on the one hand, and one person knowing it does not diminish its availability on the other. Scientific knowledge belongs in the public goods cell of Display 10.1.

The production of scientific knowledge is undertaken very substantially by the private sector—in places like California's Silicon Valley, Boston's Route 128, and North Carolina's Research Triangle. But this kind of research tends to be very applied, tied to specific product development, conducted secretly, and often patentable (thereby preventing those who do not "own" it from making use of it). Thus, applied scientific research, to the degree that property rights may be assigned to its products, is essentially a private good. However, basic or fundamental research—research that often does not have immediate application—is not patentable and thus cannot be owned; it therefore tends to be underproduced by the private sector for all the public-goods reasons mentioned earlier.

Consequently, the U.S. government, through various agencies like the National Science Foundation, the National Institutes of Health, the National Aeronautics and Space Administration, the Department of Energy, and the Department of Defense, sponsor basic scientific research—a clear instance of the public provision of a public good. Some of this research is actually done in government laboratories. But much is contracted out to university scientists. Consider now the incentives facing, first, the legislators who provide the financial resources for and oversee the execution of this public good and, second, the bureaucrats who actually administer the programs.

As it happens, the universities that are best positioned to compete for basic research grants are not randomly distributed throughout the territorial United States. While many locations have the capability, there are discernible concentrations of excellence: the Bay Area, Los Angeles, and Seattle on the West Coast; Chicago and Minneapolis in the Midwest;

Chapel Hill–Durham–Raleigh, Miami, and Atlanta in the
South; and Washington, New York, and Boston on the East
Coast—to name some of the most prominent. If the National
Science Foundation (NSF), for example, were to support research proposals strictly on the basis of merit, a disproportionate amount of its budget would be spent in these pockets
of excellence.[10] Institutions in a great majority of the legislative districts of the nation would do rather poorly in the competition. And this, in turn, would not kindly dispose their
representatives toward NSF. In short, while legislators may
generally approve of producing public goods like scientific
knowledge, they are much more focused on getting federal dollars for citizens and institutions in *their* districts. A government agency that flouted this concern of large numbers of
legislators would undoubtedly not fare well in the annual appropriations process.

The administrators at NSF are not stupid. They can forecast the profound budgetary problems their agency would encounter if it did not attend to the conditions of representative
government. So, they arrange for alternatives to the merit-
based allocation of their budget. Instead of earmarking their
entire budget for basic research—which would end up being
spent chiefly in a small number of pockets of research
excellence—they invent new categories and new programs in
which less-well-endowed parts of the country are competitive.
Research in science education (as opposed to pure science), for
example, may be quite competently conducted in many places
around the country, places that do not require advanced research laboratories and cutting-edge scientists.

Constituency-oriented legislators and survival-oriented bureaucrats and administrators, not philosopher kings, support,

---

[10] If, instead, we were discussing the production of art and culture as financed
by grants from the National Endowment for the Arts, merit-based concentration would be even more extreme, with New York and Los Angeles securing the lion's share of support.

finance, and administer public programs that produce public goods. Their incentives dispose them to move away from what would be optimal if only the most effective production of public goods were motivating them. Public provision, then, is watered down by these competing, indeed distracting, objectives. Thus, while public provision may seem the best way to go in correcting for the underproduction of public goods, it is not without its shortcomings.

A second incentive distortion associated with public provision involves *time horizons*. Many scientific projects are years in the making. The initial phases are often relatively inexpensive and invisible, as ideas are examined, developed, and tested in small ways. Only after these initial hurdles are cleared are greater sums spent on large-scale testing and development. It is the latter, however, that involve new laboratory facilities, expensive high-tech equipment, or advanced testing sites—the sorts of things to which the local legislator can point with pride (and snip the ribbon at the dedication ceremony heavily covered by the local media). The political pressures associated with public provision, as a result, involve truncating the longer incubation and percolation process ideally associated with scientific research into a much shorter time horizon.[11]

To sum up, the production of public goods is a problem for communities because of the very nature of these products. Private incentives are typically insufficient to encourage sufficient production voluntarily. Some sort of political fix is required, examples of which include grants of monopoly privilege, waivers of antitrust laws, public subsidy of private production, and outright public provision. None of these is ideal because each entails the grant of extraordinary privilege or authority to some individual—the lord of the manor, the firm

---

[11] This argument is elaborated in Linda Cohen and Roger Noll, *The Technology Pork Barrel* (Washington: Brookings Institution, 1991).

granted a monopoly, a public-sector bureaucrat—whose incentives may not be aligned properly to the social objectives being sought. The lord of the manor wants prestige and glory, not public defense; the firm wants profits, not the optimal national highway system; the bureaucrat wants turf and budget authority, not scientific discoveries. Though perhaps an overly cynical view, the public good is the incidental by-product of, not the motivation for, their behavior.

It is, therefore, not surprising that different communities at different times experiment with alternative (imperfect) solutions. In the past few decades, for example, we have witnessed a tidal wave of change in which public sectors that formerly provided public goods directly are abandoning these activities. Under the rubric of *privatization*, both developing political economies and already developed ones are selling off state-owned assets to the private sector, hoping that, imperfect as they may be, private-sector incentives will be better aligned to social objectives than under the former arrangement of direct public provision. This may also entail technological enhancements that mitigate some of the "publicness" of the good.[12]

One of President Obama's early initiatives was a "cap-and-trade" program to control the air pollution that contributes to global warming. The idea is to set a pollution target, issue "pollution permits" (either giving them away initially or auctioning them off), and then allow permit holders either to use them (enabling them to employ production technologies that have pollution as a by-product up to the limit allowed by the pollution permit) or to trade them (sell them) for others to use.

[12] For example, electronic lighthouses emit an electronic signal, rather than a light, which is received only by those ships that *purchase* the special signal detector. Cable television, likewise, requires a cable box and hookup that permits exclusion (thereby privatizing a public good). A public water supply may be metered at each household, thereby permitting user charges; so, too, may a firm's effluent (via sewer or smokestack), thus allowing for the pricing of its use of the environment as a dumping site.

The objective is to limit pollution, as well as to allow the "right" to pollute to gravitate, via a market for permits, to those most needing to use polluting technologies. (For a good source of information on these developments, see the blog of environmental economist Robert Stavins, "An Economic View of the Environment," at http://belfercenter.ksg.harvard.edu /analysis/stavin, and, in particular, his May 29, 2009, entry, "The Wonderful Politics of Cap-and-Trade.")

We also observe the related phenomenon of *deregulation* in which heavy-handed bureaucratic oversight, command, and control are being relaxed or relinquished altogether. The imperfectness of any solution to the production of public goods stimulates this experimentation; but politico-economic change of this magnitude is, as we have emphasized, political through and through, with winners and losers determined at the end of the day in political arenas.

CASE 10.1
PUBLIC GOODS, PROPERTY RIGHTS, AND THE RADIO SPECTRUM

An interesting example of a public good is the radio spectrum. As a public good, the radio spectrum is nonexcludable and jointly supplied. In other words, anyone is physically able to broadcast on the radio spectrum, and my broadcast doesn't prevent you from broadcasting. The problem is that my broadcast interferes with your broadcast if both are simultaneous and on the same (or a closely neighboring) frequency. To make radio transmission coherent, there must be some means for allocating the radio spectrum.

Frequencies on the radio spectrum in the United States are allocated by the Federal Communications Commission (FCC). Different frequency bands have different uses, including television, radio, cellular telephones, and radar. Individuals and organizations are given exclusive rights to particular frequencies. Broadcasting on a frequency for which you do not have rights is illegal. (The movie *Pirate Radio* (2009) depicted one such station.) By allocating property rights to the radio spectrum, the public good is made excludable and the crowding that might otherwise result from joint supply is prevented.

The example of the radio spectrum demonstrates that there are numerous approaches to allocating property rights. Historically, the FCC has distributed licenses at no charge, either through application or lottery. The Clinton administration, seeing an opportunity to bring some revenue into the federal coffers, explored the possibility of auctioning radio licenses for new personal communications technologies.* At one point the administration predicted revenues of $4.4 billion over four years. What is common to all of the arguments about plans like this one is their fundamental political nature. Who will benefit from the plan? Who will be hurt? Is the plan fair? What are the values that determine how we manage our public resources? Although discussions of topics like auctions, revenue sources, and externalities often appear purely economic and technical in their nature, it is important to remain conscious of the political issues that lie beneath the surface.

* Edmund L. Andrews, "Radio Rights: A Move to Auction Licenses that Sell," *New York Times* (March 21, 1993), p. E6.

EXTERNALITIES

An *externality* is a special kind of public good. It is typically the unintended by-product of voluntary activity that is imposed on others. Thus, an externality is jointly supplied and, because it cannot be easily avoided, nonexcludable (although here we might more accurately say it is *unavoidable*). Some externalities are valued—the scent and appearance of the roses planted in a neighbor's garden; the freedom from infection others obtain when we innoculate our children against communicable diseases; the protection provided to both partners when one uses a condom in sex—so we call them *positive* externalities. In each case someone *else* benefits, perhaps unintendedly, from an individual's action. Other externalities are loathed—the effects from the burning of high-sulfur coal in a manufacturer's boiler; litter in public parks; the loud music of boom boxes in Harvard Square—thus we call them *negative* externalities. Since externalities are special instances of public goods ("bads"), we may deduce that the positive ones are undersupplied and the negative ones oversupplied, relative to what would be optimal for the community as a whole. Neither the neighbor planting her roses nor the factory burning coal takes our preferences into account. If, as we are often advised, we "stop to smell the roses," we discover that there are too few roses and too many other things to smell.

The phenomenon of externalities is nicely illustrated by an experiment the author regularly runs in an undergraduate class at Harvard University.[13] An even number of students is selected, half of whom are designated as "buyers" and half as "sellers" in a make-believe market. Each buyer is given a schedule informing him how much the experimenter will pay

[13] The experiment is described in great detail by its designer in Charles Plott, "Externalities and Corrective Policies in Experimental Markets," *The Economic Journal* 93 (1983): 106–27.

him at the end of the session for each unit of the product purchased during the experiment. For example, the experimenter may pay 30 points for the first unit, 28 points for the second unit, 25 for the third, and so on. A buyer, then, makes a profit if his first purchase in the market is for less that 30 points, the second purchase is for less than 28 points, the third for less than 25, and so on. Each buyer wants to earn as many points (as much profit) as possible, since these points will be added to the score of his midterm examination. Similarly, each seller is given a schedule informing her of the cost of producing each unit. For example, the first unit may cost 12 points, the second 15 points, and so on. A seller makes a profit if she sells each unit for more than its cost (the first unit for more than 12 points, the second for more than 15, and so on). She, too, wants to earn as many points as possible—for the same reason.

The buyers and sellers sit across a table from one another. When the market opens, bargaining begins with buyers shouting out "bids" and sellers shouting out "asks" in what is known as a *double oral auction*. When a buyer and seller come to an agreement on a price p, the sale of a unit is registered. If the buyer with the schedule given in the preceding paragraph is buying his first unit, then his profit is $30 - p$; if the seller is selling her second unit (having already sold one earlier), then her profit is $p - 15$. (If p lies between 15 and 30, then both make a profit.) The market remains open until no one can agree on a price for consummating any further sales. Since the experimenters have fixed the schedules so that the "ceiling" on acceptable prices for a buyer gets lower and lower with each purchase, and the "floor" on acceptable prices for a seller gets higher and higher with each sale, there will always come a time when it is no longer possible for a buyer and seller both to make a profit.[14] The market closes at this point.

---

[14] The seller's floor ultimately becomes higher than the buyer's ceiling.

As described, this experimental market is a model of the trucking, bargaining, and haggling that goes on in a bazaar or city market. It is well understood according to the law of supply and demand, and experimental results validate this law quite impressively. But we are not interested in that, since this experimental market setting has a twist. Every time a sale is consummated, *everyone* in the market, both the buyer and seller participating in the particular sale as well as all those buyers and sellers not participating, is charged 1 point each. In effect, the consummation of a sale generates a negative externality, harming participant and nonparticipant alike. The particular buyer and seller can take this "damage" on *themselves* into account. Factoring in the externality, the buyer in the previous paragraph will figure his profit at $30 - p - 1$ (so that p will have to be less than 29, or "no sale"), while the seller will figure her profit at $p - 15 - 1$ (so that p will have to be greater than 16). The effect of the externality is to narrow the bargaining range for this buyer-seller pair.[15] But neither buyer nor seller has an incentive to take into account the impact of the externality on *others*.

And they don't. Even though the experimenter provides each participant with a table informing them of the impact *on the entire market* of each sale they consummate (1 point of "damage" on every buyer and seller per unit sold), the subjects never take this information on board. The only things they care about are their profit thresholds (ceiling and floor for buyer and seller, respectively), the negotiated price p, and the impact of the externality on each of them. Each participant is intent on maxing out on points, thereby raising his or her midterm examination grade (and, presumably, increasing the chances of getting into law school). Nevertheless, on other occasions these very same students are heard denouncing pol-

---

[15] With no exernality, the bargaining range for p is 15 to 30. With the exernality, this range becomes 16 to 29.

luters of the atmosphere, destroyers of the ozone layer, litterbugs, and producers of secondhand smoke! The fact is that it is easier to see the scoundrel in others than in ourselves.

Public policy economists, at least since Adam Smith, have worried quite a lot about how externalities, both positive and negative, might be taken into account by those who produce them. I cannot review all these solutions here, but will mention a few in passing. Probably the most popular and widely used solutions are *taxes* and *subsidies*, the former to discourage negative externalities and the latter to encourage positive externalities. In the experiment above, suppose the experimenter informed the market participants that there would be a sales tax, t, charged against the seller each time a sale was consummated. The seller two paragraphs back would now earn a profit of $p - 15 - 1 - t$, effectively raising the minimum price she must now secure to show a positive profit.[16] From Econ 101 it is well known that the effect of raising a price is that fewer sales will be consummated (at higher prices), and hence fewer externalities generated. We don't want to eliminate sales altogether (unless the externality were so horrid as to overwhelm the benefits from having this market in the first place). But there is an "optimal" tax, one that internalizes the full effect of externalities. The tax, in this case, implicitly forces the buyers and sellers in a market to take account of the external consequences of their actions, something they were not willing to do unless coerced in this manner.

The argument is exactly analogous when positive externalities are involved. In place of a tax, a subsidy is given to one or the other of the market participants in order to encourage more sales (and more externalities) than would otherwise transpire.

---

[16] The reader should not think that I am being unfair here in placing the tax only on the seller, since some of it will be passed on to the buyer in negotiating a final purchase price.

Experimentally, taxes and subsidies work as this theoretical argument suggests. And, in the real world, taxes on the sulfur content of coal, on gasoline, and on solid-waste effluents cause their users to internalize the negative social effects of the pollution their activities are producing. Subsidies for innoculating against communicable diseases (available at less than cost), securing a higher education (tuition never covers costs), taking public transport (fares never cover costs), carpooling (designated commuter lanes), using solar power (tax breaks), and moving to the frontier (free or cheap land), in precisely the same fashion, reduce the costs of engaging in these activities, thereby increasing their levels (and the positive externalities associated with them).

There are two major shortcomings associated with this strategy for dealing with externalities. The first is that of setting the appropriate level for taxes and subsidies. In the experiment described above, each sale generated one point's worth of "damage" for every market participant. If there were, say, six buyers and six sellers, then twelve points of externality would be generated per unit sold. As we have already seen, two of these twelve points are taken account of—namely, the one point of "damage" falling on each party to the exchange. It's the ten points falling on those *not* party to the exchange that are ignored by the parties to the deal. Thus, by setting the sales tax at ten points per transaction, the contracting parties are forced to act as though they are considering the external effects of their actions. The equilibrium number of sales in this market now is socially optimal.[17]

The matter of setting the optimal tax rate is quite straight-

---

[17] The reader should note that in taking account of the external effects of transactions, this solution does not eliminate externalities altogether. Rather, the damage done by the externality is *balanced* against the benefit that accrues from allowing buyers and sellers to capture gains from exchange. In general, we typically do not, as a matter of public policy, want to drive negative externalities to zero because this would mean passing up profitable exchanges.

forward when demand conditions, supply conditions, and externality effects are known with quantitative precision, as in our experimental world. In the real world, however, matters are not so straightforward, since we rarely know everything we need to know (that is, the things provided by the experimental design). The consequence is that tax or subsidy rates are often little better than educated guesses. They may improve the situation, but they may also make matters worse.[18]

The second, more serious drawback to the tax-or-subsidy solution to externality problems involves the matter of exactly what activities should be taxed or subsidized. If one were to survey the activities that are taxed or subsidized in any place at almost any time, it would be impossible to claim that control of externalities had much bearing on these policies. Surely *some* goods are taxed or subsidized to deter negative or encourage positive externalities, and I have given examples of these in the preceding discussion. But many goods are taxed or subsidized because *political machinery* for taxing and subsidizing exists in the first place and comes under the influence of those who benefit from its policies, quite independent of any consideration of externalities. On the other side of the coin, so many other goods are not taxed or subsidized, even though a control-of-externalities case could be made, for much the same reason—political influence. "Optimal" taxes and other ideas from welfare economics theory, even if they might work in principle, get steamrolled in the rough and tumble of politics.

A classic instance is found in America's experience with air

---

[18] Although I will not trouble the reader with details, in the running example from the experiment, a tax of ten points per sale will still permit some sales to be consummated, though a smaller number than in the absence of the tax. If we had not been sure about the damage done by externalities, and (incorrectly) guessed that instead of one unit per person the damage was two units per person, the tax (now twenty units per sale) would have completely shut the market down. No sales would have occurred. Thus, mistaken guesses about the right tax or subsidy rate may make matters worse than no tax or subsidy at all.

pollution. In the 1970s much pollution was created by stationary sources, like power plants, burning high-sulfur coal. When coal with high sulfur content is burned, sulfur compounds spewing out of smokestacks combine with water in the atmosphere to produce "acid rain," which damages crops, forests, wildlife habitats, and fresh water sources, not to mention human lungs. Much of this dirty coal was (and still is) mined in Pennsylvania, Kentucky, and West Virginia. A clean alternative exists in low-sulfur coal, mined in the western United States. This was a clear circumstance for the imposition of a tax. If coal were taxed in proportion to its sulfur content, then stationary sources would find it in their interest to switch at least some of their energy demand from eastern to western coal: the higher the tax rate, the more the substitution of clean for dirty coal.

Enter politics. The West Virginia coal industry had during this period a very powerful protector—West Virginia senator and the majority leader of the U.S. Senate, Robert Byrd. The Senate is an institution in which well-positioned individuals (especially committee and subcommittee chairs and party leaders) can exercise significant veto power. It is relatively difficult to get a bill through the Senate, and it is considerably easier to *prevent* a bill from passing. And this Byrd did. Despite a powerful environmental lobby, and an administration sympathetic to its preferences, Byrd managed to thwart sulfur-content taxes by acceding to a much milder policy of requiring the installation of pollution scrubbers on smokestacks.[19]

There are countless stories of this sort in which a powerful politician uses his or her position to block either the imposition of taxes on key supporters or the reduction of their subsidies. Only under the direst of fiscal circumstances (like the

---

[19] The entire story is told in Bruce Ackerman and William Hassler, *Clean Air/Dirty Coal* (New Haven: Yale University Press, 1981).

large federal deficits in the United States during the late 1980s), when the insatiable revenue requirements of government cause it to raise taxes and scale back subsidies wherever it can, is this protection insufficient. Tax-or-subsidy solutions to externality problems are only occasionally effective, because politics constrains their proficiency when the shoe pinches the wrong toes.

Two other categories of solution to externality problems merit brief consideration. We have just seen that Senator Byrd was able to replace what would have been an onerous tax on his dirty-coal constituency with a more tolerable *regulatory regime*. Regulation is a more hands-on approach to the control of externalities. It typically entails the creation of a governmental bureaucracy—an agency, bureau, or commission—charged with setting standards, prices, fees, or practices in consumption or production activities that generate externalities. Statutory authority usually spells out the purposes to which this bureaucratic control should be put and the discretion the bureaucratic entity has in pursuing those purposes. Through administrative procedures, or the civil and criminal court system, the agency has an ability to enforce its commands. Thus, a governmental entity such as the Environmental Protection Agency, with authority granted to it by a law such as the Clean Air Act, can specify the kind of smokestack scrubber required of a stationary-source polluter.

Alternatively, externalities can be contolled by a *respecification of property rights*. Part of the quandary underlying externality problems is poorly specified rights of ownership and use. Since nobody "owns" the air, anyone can use it as a repository for dumping things (like sulfur-based particulates). To take an example a little closer to home, since no one owns or has responsibility for the common room in the dormitory, it is forever a mess. In some situations, however, it is conceivable that one could respecify property rights so that damage done by externalities can be held in check. I pursue this alternative in more detail in the next section, where I discuss "commons problems." Here, however, I remind the reader of an interesting property-rights solution to air pollution (noted earlier).

Partially in reaction to the poor performance of other methods for controlling externalities, some economists have suggested that there may be a way to allow the atmosphere to be "owned." By "owned" it is meant that someone has the right to use the atmosphere as he or she sees fit on the one hand, and may sell or trade that right instead of using it if that is preferred. This is accomplished by distributing marketable pollution permits, each one entitling the holder to pollute the atmosphere in some standardized quantity. This is the "cap and trade" policy described earlier. A factory in Los Angeles, for example, might hold a 10-dirt permit ("dirt" being a fictitious unit of pollution). If its production process generated only 5 dirts of pollution, then it could sell the remaining 5 dirts on its permit to some other user for cash, for the promise of an 8-dirt permit five years from now, or for something else of value. The Environmental Protection Agency, for example would set the overall quantity of permits available at any one time, after which a market in permits would arise.

Pollution is suddenly *costly* to its producer, because he or she must now devote dirts to it that have alternative uses (like selling or trading them). The Los Angeles factory may now determine whether it is worth its while to retrofit its production process so that less pollution is generated; if the cost of retrofitting is exceeded by the sale of the pollution permits it currently owns or would otherwise have to purchase in the market, this move makes sense. The result, then, of this market for pollution permits is that polluters now have incentives to reduce their pollution and that pollution rights will flow to those that value them the most. These latter polluters are those for whom it is cheaper to buy pollution permits than it is to reduce their emissions.

The key, of course, and the place where politics is central, is the determination of the aggregate amount of pollution to be permitted on the one hand, and the initial distribution of pollution permits on the other. The first is a straightforward political judgment call of the sort that our political institutions are charged with making all the time. The second is political dynamite, since so much is at stake. But as long as the market works smoothly once an initial distribution is made, the permits ultimately will flow to their highest-valued uses. Even the judgment call on the aggregate amount of pollution to permit in the first place has a certain self-correcting quality to it. If Friends of the Earth or the Audubon Society feels that the political authorities have set the aggregate pollution level too high for, say, the Los Angeles metropolitan area, then these environmental groups can jump into the dirt market there and buy up pollution permits. These they can either permanently retire or resell in some other area of the country with an ambient air quality that can absorb additional emissions.

This section on externalities can be summed up by noting that none of the solutions I have reviewed—taxes and subsidies, regulatory regimes, redefined property rights—are without problems. In each case there are practical or logistical complications that must be overcome. Even putting these difficulties to one side, however, there is always the problem of politics. Once the machinery to tax and subsidize, to regulate, or to redefine ownership is put in place, it may be used or abused. It is absolutely essential to be aware that the problem of externalities is transformed into a problem of providing appropriate incentives to those in charge of the externality-control apparatus. It is the same "who will guard the guardians" problem that we have encountered elsewhere in this volume, a problem I shall examine very closely in Part IV in our treatment of institutions.

THE PROBLEM OF THE COMMONS

Sitting just outside the office in which these words are being written is the Cambridge Common, a lovely urban public place most famous for the fact that it was there that General George Washington mustered the twelve hundred volunteers of what became the Continental Army in 1776. Publicly owned parks and land reserves are today the object of great passion by those who place significant value on "green space." In an earlier time in Europe (and still today in various parts of the world), commons were valued for more practical reasons—notably as places to graze cattle and to forage.[20] Today, examples of commons include not only green space and sites for grazing and foraging but also bodies of water utilized for commercial fishing, irrigation systems, urban water supplies, and, indeed, even the earth's atmosphere.[21]

A commons is, by definition, owned by everyone (in common), and therefore is the responsibility of no one. Consider a field owned by a village and used by its residents' herds as a grazing commons. Each villager gets to graze his or her cattle "for free." If a villager is contemplating adding a head to his herd, he will take into account his costs of doing so, but this calculation will *not* include the cost of grazing. If the commons is large, and the village demands on it minimal, this will not pose serious problems. But even if demands on the commons grow, no villager has an incentive to restrict his use of this "free" resource, resulting in what Garrett Hardin called "the

---

[20] Several hundred years ago in England and elsewhere, there were political movements that succeeded in enclosing common lands, that is, dividing them into parcels and distributing or selling them to individuals as private property. The modern counterpart of this practice is the sale of state-owned assets (privatization) in both socialist and capitalist economies.

[21] The most insightful discussion of "common pool problems," of which these are examples, is Elinor Ostrom, *Governing the Commons* (New York: Cambridge University Press, 1990). Ostrom was awarded the Nobel Prize in Economic Sciences in 2009 for this work.

tragedy of the commons."[22] The commons will be overgrazed and ultimately destroyed, inasmuch as its capacity to regenerate itself will have been disabled.

Overgrazing the commons is a metaphor for a host of problems, large and small, in which lack of restraint in using the commons leads to social catastrophe:

- The portion of the North Atlantic off the coast of New England is a common habitat for lobsters. Overgrazing in this instance takes the form of too many lobstermen harvesting too many lobsters (especially small lobsters that haven't reproduced).
- The acquifer under Cape Cod is a commons constituting the source of fresh water for that beautiful strip of land. Overgrazing this commons occurs because of residential and commercial development. With more people on the Cape, pollutants seep into the acquifer, affecting its purity. Perhaps more profoundly, with more people drawing more fresh water from the acquifer, salt water penetration from Massachusetts Bay and the Atlantic Ocean intensifies. Ultimately, rain- and spring-fed renewal will be insufficient, and the acquifer will be destroyed.
- The earth's atmosphere is a commons into which pollutants are dumped. It is replenished by oxygen created as a by-product of photosynthesis. The destruction of vast forests for development simultaneously increases the production of pollution and reduces the atmosphere's capacity to replenish itself.

The problem of the commons, like the problems associated with cooperation, the production of public goods, and the control of externalities, is a problem of private and social incen-

---

[22] Garrett Hardin, "The Tragedy of the Commons," *Science* 162 (1968): 1243–48. This now classic paper is must reading for the interested student.

tives in conflict. A commons is a free lunch to its common own-ers. Indeed, each possessor of rights to the commons has a very strong incentive to use those rights. Let us return to the village with a common grazing field. A hundred villagers are each grazing two cows on the commons, a number that the commons can support and still regenerate itself. Each villager considers adding one cow to his herd, concluding that this would be profitable, especially in light of the free grazing priv-ileges. If any one villager were to proceed, the commons would be damaged only marginally, indeed hardly at all, since the herd size will only have increased from 200 to 201. But if all the villagers proceed, there will be a 50 percent increase in grazing, an amount exceeding the carrying capacity of the commons. So, if all proceed, each will be worse off, since they will have destroyed their field. But if any one villager pro-ceeds, he will be better off and all the others will hardly be af-fected at all. Thus, individual incentives and social necessity clash. Indeed, overgrazing the commons is, in many respects, the large-number analog of the Prisoners' Dilemma and Hume's marsh-draining game that I discussed in Chapter 8.

As the reader is now undoubtedly aware, preservation of the commons is a public good. I will not rehearse again all of the standard methods for its provision, leaving this to the reader as the proverbial homework assignment. I will, how-ever, comment briefly on two aspects of this knotty problem.

First, it is well known that commons problems arise be-cause of imperfectly specified property rights. If a single indi-vidual rather than an entire community owned the commons, or if she and her fellow villagers each owned well-defined plots within the commons, then she would have all the incentives associated with ownership of a private good to preserve the value of this asset. An individual would no more overgraze her commons, or overharvest her forest, or overfish her pond than she would abuse any other physical asset she owned. The en-closure movement in England in an earlier era and contemporary experiments with marketable permits in rights to pollute are instances of redefining property rights, reallocating ownership from the community to specific individuals.

Second, as I have emphasized throughout this chapter, political arrangements affect both the solutions selected to deal with commons problems and the likelihood of success. In her pathbreaking study of common pool problems, *Governing the Commons*, Elinor Ostrom makes very clear that humankind has been incredibly inventive over millennia in coping with—and, indeed, sometimes avoiding—the tragedy of the commons. These coping strategies are much like the constitutions (both written and informal) by which communities govern themselves. They involve mechanisms by which collective decisions about the use of the commons are made, monitored, enforced, and changed in an orderly manner. Ostrom provides instances of both successful and unsuccessful "commons constitutions," emphasizing that the successful ones are those with design features possessing:

- clearly defined boundaries;
- congruence between rules for using the commons and local needs and conditions;
- individual rights to formulate and revise the rules for operating the commons;
- monitoring arrangements in which the monitors are ultimately responsible to the community;
- graduated punishments for violation of rules;
- low-cost arenas for resolving disputes; and
- relative freedom of users of the commons from external governmental authorities.[23]

In short, Ostrom has found that the management of a commons is a political problem. If rights over this commons cannot be parceled up into private bundles—the property-rights

---

[23] Ostrom, *Governing the Commons*, pp. 88–102.

solution—then, to encourage the cooperation required to pre-serve the commons and to discourage the practice of over-utilization, the group of users must enter into a political agreement—a form of self-enforcing self-restraint.

CASE 10.2
FISHING AND THE
TRAGEDY OF THE COMMONS

Fishing provides an excellent subject for inquiring into the tragedy of the commons. As we have seen, the tragedy of the commons is a problem when individuals share a common, depletable resource. In their efforts to maximize their individual gains, users often overuse the resource to the detriment of all. Oceans, lakes, and rivers have largely been viewed by fishermen as a commons. The result is over-use: two-thirds of all assessed fish stocks in 1994 were either overexploited or fully to heavily exploited, according to the United Nations Food and Agricultural Association.* Overuse remains a problem today.

Governments have responded to the problem with a variety of approaches. Their responses provide evidence for Ostrom's theory that a commons can be managed through the allocation of property rights or the evolution of self-enforcing restraints. Several nations, including Iceland and New Zealand, have addressed the problem of overfishing by allocating property rights. Their system of individual transferable quotas (ITQs) divides up the catch within national waters among commercial fishermen. Quota owners can either keep or sell their fishing rights. The government sets the total quota to maintain and conserve the resource over time.

* Mark Trumball, "Fisheries Crisis Stretches across the Globe," *Christian Science Monitor* (July 6, 1994), p. 8.

There is considerable debate over the use of ITQs. Many organizations and governmental authorities are seeking alternative mechanisms. In New England, the government, the fishermen, and the fisheries worked to address the sharp decline in fish catches over the course of the 20th century.† The importance of politics is apparent in the case of New England fishing. Government programs and interest group politics accelerated the overutilization of the commons. In 1977, the United States banned foreign trawlers from fishing within 200 miles of the U.S. coastline, partly to prevent overfishing of New England waters. But a federal loan program at the end of the 1970s and the beginning of the 1980s led to a boom in domestic boat construction. Fishermen organized to lobby against catch quotas and fishing limits. In 1982 the New England Fishery Management Council gave in to the pressure from fishermen and dropped the quotas and limits. The result was a rapid increase in overuse, and fish catches declined by over a third in four years. The decline led many fishermen to see the connection between their individual behavior and their collective fate. The vice president of the Atlantic Offshore Fish Association in Newport, Rhode Island, remarked, "I used to be strongly opposed to any kind of limited entry in fisheries. But I've come to feel we have to have some way of rationally allocating fishery resources just as we do other resources."

What happens when fishery resources can't be "rationally allocated"? In other words, what happens when the resource is not conducive to assignment of property rights? Ostrom predicts that users will enter into a political agreement involving self-enforcing self-restraint. We find support for this prediction in the case of "straddling stocks," fish that migrate between national and international wa-

---

† Lawrence Ingrassia, "Overfishing Threatens to Wipe Out Species and Crush Industry," *Wall Street Journal* (July 16, 1991), p. 1.

ters. Straddling stocks account for about one-fifth of the fish caught around the world each year. Their migration between national and international waters prevents countries from declaring ownership of the stocks and assigning property rights through fishing quotas. Countries have been forced to work cooperatively on the problem. The United Nations has been used as a forum for creating agreement and addressing issues of monitoring and enforcement, just as Ostrom's theory would predict.

The importance of enforcement can be seen in a "natural experiment" created by the fall of the Soviet Union.‡ Ninety percent of the world's sturgeon stocks are in the Caspian Sea, which is bordered by Iran and the former Soviet Union. For decades, the harvest of caviar from spawning sturgeon was tightly regulated by the Soviet government. Quotas for the annual sturgeon catch were established by the Ministry of Fisheries in Moscow and enforced by armed inspectors who kept the lid on poachers and illegal dealers. In 1992, the birth of four new independent states and two new autonomous regions along the spawning grounds of the sturgeon, together with the breakdown of the chain of command out of the Kremlin, led to a marked decline in the enforcement of these quotas. The result was a rapid increase in sturgeon fishing. The director of the Fisheries Research Institute in Astrakkan, at the mouth of the Volga River, said, "Central authority has disappeared. People are living by the law today: Catch whatever you can and don't care about tomorrow. If things are allowed to go on like this, within three to five years sturgeon stocks will be completely depleted."

The importance of reaching an agreement on how to use the sturgeon resource was emphasized by Moscow's chief fisheries inspector: "Either we agree on rules for catching

‡ Michael Dobbs, "A Warning by the Sturgeon General," *Washington Post National Weekly Edition* (June 8–14, 1992), p. 1.

sturgeon or we simply destroy the fish altogether. If we can reach agreement with the United States on limiting production of nuclear missiles, surely we can reach an agreement with other [former Soviet] republics on catching sturgeon." The reader may want to ruminate on this last remark. Knowing what you now know about cooperation, collective action, and problems of commons, is it really as easy to cut a deal on sturgeon among various new states and autonomous regions as it is for two superpowers to sign a bilateral agreement?

Conclusion

The problems we have confronted in this chapter are, in many respects, those we met in the previous two chapters. Too little cooperation, too little collective action, too few public goods, too many negative and too few positive externalities, and too much use of common resources are all social dilemmas in which individual incentives are in conflict with socially desirable outcomes. These are summarized in Display 10.2.

The problem of cooperation, as exemplified by the marsh-draining game of Chapter 8, is one that pits the joint benefits of cooperation against the individual motives to defect (since "do not cooperate" is the individually advantageous option whether the other guy cooperates or not). The problem of collective action is the problem of cooperation writ large, where defection takes the form of free-riding on the effort of others. This, in turn, is directly analogous to "not contributing" to the provision of a public good; to defect, in this interpretation, is to withhold payment for a public good, since, if it is provided, noncontributors cannot be prevented from enjoying it. Likewise, paying no attention to the (positive or negative) external effects of your actions is a bit like not controlling your production of public "bads" or ignoring your production of public

---

DISPLAY 10.2

**COOPERATION, COLLECTIVE ACTION, PUBLIC GOODS
SUPPLY, EXTERNALITY CONTROL, COMMONS
GOVERNANCE: COMPARISONS**

Problem	Behavior to Be Controlled	Illustrative Solution
Cooperation	Defection	Repeat play
Collective Action	Free-riding	By-products, political entrepreneur
Public Good Supply	Noncontribution	Public provision
Externality Control	Inattention to external effects	Tax/subsidy scheme
Commons Governance	Overutilization	Property rights regime, governance structure

---

goods; each is a by-product of your actions for which you shun responsibility. Finally, overutilizing a common resource is "antisocial" in the sense that this action fails to take account of the damage your actions wreak on others.

For each of these social dilemmas, numerous solutions are advocated (a representative one of which is listed in the last column of Display 10.2), and a variety of human experience with all of them. Rarely are the solutions, even those that work tolerably well, ideal. (If any solution were, then we wouldn't be spending so much time writing about them.) One thing is clear, and bears repeating one last time. Solutions are *political*, both in their advocacy and in their implementation. To understand why they work or why they fail, the observer must come to terms with the political ambitions and motives of the actors involved, and with the institutional contexts in which these ambitions and motives get played out. In the concluding section of this text, I turn to an analysis of political institutions.

EXPERIMENTAL CORNER

Punishing Free-Riders

Public goods, as we have seen, are underproduced because individual incentives to contribute to their production are weak. Especially in large anonymous groups, individuals are strongly tempted to free-ride on the contributions of others, since they can enjoy whatever public good is produced while avoiding any of its costs. Indeed, if the group is large enough and anonymous enough, their failure to contribute will often go unnoticed. Of course, they risk being punished for their antisocial behavior, but then punishment itself is costly for others so it is unlikely to be much of a detriment to free-riding. But what if, despite its cost, people *did* punish "irresponsible" behavior?

In a wonderful experiment, Fehr and Gachter demonstrate that "free riding generally causes very strong negative emotions among cooperators and that there is a widespread willingness to punish the free riders . . . even if punishment is costly and does not provide any material benefits for the punisher."[a] Moreover, they show that the punishment increases in severity the more the free riding deviates from cooperative levels, so that the opportunity and inclination to punish will have the effect of diminishing free riding.[b]

Their public goods experiment has a no-punishment and a punishment treatment. In the former, theory tells us that there should be widespread free-riding, possibly undermin-

---

[a] Ernst Fehr and Simon Gachter, "Cooperation and Punishment in Public Goods Experiments," *American Economic Review* 90 (2000): 980–94. Quotation is on p. 980.

[b] A closely related experiment that inspired Fehr and Gachter deals with the problem of the commons described in the text. See Elinor Ostrom, James Walker, and Roy Gardner, "Covenants with and without the Sword: Self-Governance Is Possible," *American Political Science Review* 86 (1992): 404–17.

ing the provision of any of the public good. In the punishment treatment, if punishing is costly, then again we should expect massive free-riding. The possibility of punishment, so the argument goes, is irrelevant because no potential free-rider will expect anyone to engage in this costly behavior. Thus, the theoretical expectation is that the mix of cooperation and free-riding should be the same in each treatment. Surprisingly (from a theoretical perspective, at least), they are not!

Fehr and Gachter's experiment, described below, is quite subtle. They note that in repeated interactions it might be argued that engaging in costly punishment *now* may have material payoffs *later*—that is, that someone could rationally develop a reputation for being willing to punish so as to induce cooperation over the long run. I noted in Chapter 8 that the prospect of punishment in indefinite repeat play of the Prisoners' Dilemma game can induce a positive level of cooperation through reputation-building. Fehr and Gachter, therefore, are careful to remove this material incentive in their experimental design. They do this by having a *stranger* treatment and a *partner* treatment. In the former, each subject plays a public goods game several times with different, randomly selected, subjects; in the latter, he or she plays several times with the same set of subjects.

The experimental design thus has four treatments—the stranger treatment with and without punishment opportunities and the partner treatment with and without punishment. In the partner treatments, it is a certainty that a subject will be matched with the same other players. In the stranger treatments, the probability is less than 5 percent that an individual will be matched with someone with whom he or she was matched in an earlier round.

In each round of the no-punishment treatment of the game, a player is provided with y tokens and makes a choice of how many tokens, g_i for the ith player, to invest in a public project, where $0 \le g_i \le y$. These choices are made simultaneously by the players, and the payoff for Ms. i is $\pi_i = y - g_i + a \Sigma_j g_j$, where $0 < a < 1$. That is, in each period, Ms. i pays in g_i token from her endowment of y tokens but gets back a proportion a of the total contributions made. In this circumstance it is easy to see that Ms. i's dominant strategy is to set $g_i = 0$, thereby free-riding on the contributions of others. Why? Because with $a < 1$ for each unit of contribution she makes, she gets only a units in return from her own investments.

If punishment is available, then the game is the same as in the preceding paragraph, with the following twist. At the end of a round the experimenter announces individual contributions. Subject j can punish subject i by assigning her *punishment points*, p_j^i. For each punishment point assigned to i, her payoff, π_i, is reduced by 10 percent (but not below zero). The *cost of punishment*, $c(p_j^i)$, is strictly increasing in p_j^i. So, the *revised* payoff for Ms i is $\pi_i^R = \pi_i [1 - (1/10) \Sigma_{j \ne i} p_j^i] - c(\Sigma_{i \ne j} p_i^j)$—that is, her original payoff reduced by 10 percent of however many punishment points she receives and also by the cost of her assigning punishment points to others.

The experimental sessions are run in a computer laboratory. Subjects anonymously interact with each other, knowing that it will be the same set of people over multiple sessions in the partners treatment and randomly selected individuals each session in the strangers treatment. Subjects were randomly assigned to the four treatment categories. The experimenters looked at different parameter settings for initial endowment (y), return from total contributions (a), and the cost of punishing ($c(p_j^i)$). All of these details may be found in the original article.

What transpired? The results are quite dramatic. Even in the strangers treatment, where an individual's reputation could not be developed because his or her cosubjects changed each session, contributions to the public project rose dramatically when the opportunity for punishment existed. Given an initial endowment of twenty tokens, the mean contribution level in the no-punishment treatment is 3.7, a fairly paltry amount. In the punishment treatment, in contrast, the mean contribution level was 11.5, more than triple the no-punishment level. Even in the last period, where everyone knew there could be no future benefit from punishing now, the no-punishment mean was 1.9 tokens and the punishment mean was 12.3. This result quite forcefully rejects the hypothesis that there should be no difference (in the strangers treatment) between a punishment and no-punishment condition. (The existence of punishment opportunities in the partners setting also produces much higher contribution levels than in the no-punishment treatment.) Interestingly, comparing the partners and strangers settings under punishment, in both cases contributions are high and remain high, but in the partners setting the contribution level approaches *full cooperation*, with an average contribution of 17.0.

Fehr and Gachter were quite careful to remove, as much as possible, the possibility of any material gain from punishing. Especially in the strangers condition, where punishing someone this time would not affect a subject's prospects in the next round, costly punishment nevertheless occurred. They conclude that even highly rational people have a consequential *emotional life* in which there is a strong propensity to punish others for inappropriate behavior, even if the punisher must bear a cost to do so. Thus, as they note, we observe drivers expressing their rage when someone butts into line, striking workers conveying strong disapproval of strike-breaking "scabs," students shunning fellow dorm residents for not cleaning up after themselves in common rooms, and so on.

At least two puzzles generated by these experiments are worth pondering. First, why do people come, possibly hard-wired, with the emotional responses leading them to punish as described above? Might an evolutionary story of some sort help explain this? The second puzzle is why people don't *free-ride on punishing*—that is, let someone else punish a transgressor? If Ms. i is offended by Mr. j's inappropriate behavior, why doesn't she avoid punishment costs by letting k, l, and m do the punishing? The answer to both puzzles may reside in the neurobiological prospect that we take emotional pleasure in expressing our disapproval of those we believe violate expectations of cooperation—that part of our *identity* is tied up in acting on these emotional impulses.

PROBLEMS AND DISCUSSION QUESTIONS

1. Write out an empty 2x2 chart like that in Display 10.1, and then for each square develop an original illustrative example of the type of good, explaining why your example is either excludable (or not) or jointly supplied (or not). Then, explain what "problems" arise from nonexcludability and from jointness of supply (or lack thereof!).

2. The website YouTube.com hosted approximately 75 billion videos in 2009, charging both uploaders and viewers nothing for the service and placing no restrictions on the quantity of content that it would host (although it does enforce some limits on inappropriate content). YouTube expends hundreds of millions of dollars on bandwidth, as well as infrastructure

and maintenance costs, and earns money primarily by hosting ads on its pages. To date, the company has not turned a profit.[a]

Identify what type of good YouTube is offering based on the categories outlined in Display 10.1, explaining carefully how you reached your conclusion. Is it possible to supply profitably the type of good you have identified? Are there alternative modes of delivery that YouTube could adopt to deliver the same service more profitably?

*3. Five civic-minded patrons of a public library contemplate donations of time to its annual fundraiser. Each individual i bases his or her decision of how much time to donate, x_i, on the following utility function:

$$U_i(x_i) = q^{.25} - .25x_i$$

where $q = \sum_{j=1}^{5} x_j$ (the total amount of time given by all library patrons) and $.25x_i$ is the cost of losing x_i of one's leisure time.

    a. What is the socially optimal amount of time donated? Determine this by summing the utility functions of five individuals, and finding the q that maximizes this function.

    b. Now consider the case of an individual who assumes that everyone else will contribute no time. How much time will this individual donate, and is it at the socially optimal level?

    c. Now assume that each individual assumes that the other four members will donate .8 units of time. Does this individual donate more or less time than before? Why is this?

[a] Malcolm Gladwell, "Priced to Sell," *The New Yorker*, July 6, 2009.

d. Why is a socially suboptimal amount of time donated in parts b and c? Consider the balance between internalized costs and internalized benefits.

e. [Bonus] Repeat the same exercise for the case of ten individuals. What proportion of the socially optimal amount is donated in an equilibrium now? What does this suggest about the difficulties of supplying quasi-public goods as the number of people increases?

4. Perhaps the default solution for the provision of public goods is public supply—by the state. Does public supply happen automatically where markets fail to provide public goods? Explain your reasoning. If not, outline some of the ways in which public supply is secured. What are some of the problems that recur in the state supply of public goods?

*5. A factory located in a small village produces a good with increasing marginal costs, given by equation $MC(q) = 12 + q$, so, for example, the first unit costs 13 to produce, the second 14, and so on. This firm can produce at most 15 units and cannot produce fractional amounts (e.g., 1.5 units). The market price for that good is currently at $p = \$20$, and the firm's level of production does not affect this price. Assume that the factory owner maximizes profit, and her utility is measured in dollar terms. Profit is calculated by summing up the differences between the price and the marginal cost of each unit produced, so the first unit earns a profit of 7, the second of 6, and so on.

Unfortunately, it turns out that the factory is quite noisy and interferes with the practice of a neighboring doctor. In fact, for every extra unit produced by the factory the doctor loses $2 worth of profits. Just as for the factory owner, assume the doctor's welfare depends only on his profits, which are $50 - 2q$.

- How many units of the good will the factory produce if it ignores the externality imposed on the doctor in its profit maximization? What will be the aggregate social utility (sum the factory's and doctor's total profits)?

- Identify the level of production that is socially most preferred, that is, maximizes aggregate social utility.

- Propose a government taxation scheme that will lead to the socially preferred outcome.

6. Taxes/subsidies, regulation, and respecification of property rights are three canonical solutions to the problem of externalities. Explain the thinking behind each of these solutions and discuss any difficulties with the implementation of such a solution. Then, provide an example, real or of your own devising, of each of these solutions applied to situations where externalities arise.

7. One interesting example of a positive externality is so-called network effects: each additional user of some good or service increases the value of that good or service to all other users. The New York Stock Exchange, telephones when they were first introduced, and Facebook are often cited as examples. Using one of these examples, or one of your own, explain why network effects fit the definition of an externality. Do networks then suffer from the problem of underprovision, as with other positive externalities? at what stage in their development? What are some possible solutions to overcoming these problems?

Part IV

INSTITUTIONS

11

Institutions: General Remarks

I spent a good deal of time in Part III on the circumstances and conditions in which political actors (who may be no more than ordinary citizens) engage in cooperation and collective action in order to solve problems related to public goods, externalities, and the overutilization of commons. We would not expect a political community to devote much effort to the solution of intermittent and relatively unimportant problems. Most likely these problems would be dealt with in an ad hoc fashion—sometimes successfully, other times not. A small town in Mississippi, for example, would be unlikely to devote much energy or many resources to the public good of snow removal, even though once every other decade the town is shut down by a freak snowstorm. A political community is much less likely to treat recurring, consequential problems in an ad hoc manner. Instead, it develops routines—standard ways of doing things by organizations endowed with resources and authority. Thus, the city of Cambridge, Massachusetts, has a Department of Public Works with authority and an annual budget for snow removal. In a word, responses to regularly recurring problems are often *institutionalized*. Collective action comes to pass in the political community because standard procedures are established that provide political actors with appropriate incentives to take the action necessary to provide a public good or control an externality.

In the next several chapters I focus on institutions as

repositories of authority and resources to solve such problems. I emphasize *official* institutions—executives, legislatures, bureaucracies, courts—though I hasten to add that institutions like these are not encountered only in the public sphere. Despite the fact that political scientists tend mostly to study these public institutions, the form of analysis that is elaborated below is applicable to a wide array of private-sector organizations—families, firms, houses of worship, universities, charitable organizations, unions, and so on. Each of these is a "political community" in its own right and institutionalizes procedures to deal with recurring, important problems it faces. The institutionalization of politics arises not only in Washington, D.C., but also around the dinner table, in the board room, in the College of Arts and Sciences, and in the union hall. Politics is omnipresent in human society, and its more routine aspects are dealt with by institutions.

The institutionalization of aspects of political life, reserved, as I noted, mainly for recurrent, significant problems, has important consequences. Political performance is now no longer exclusively a function of the "quality" of political actors. Cooperation in a political community, for example, does not now depend only on the good fortune of that community to have cooperatively inclined political agents in place. Collective action, for another, is not held hostage to altruistic inclinations or the charitable dispositions of its citizens. Rather, even if "men are not angels," as Madison once observed, the *methods* for doing political business may have a salutary effect. This was noted in the eighteenth century by the philosopher David Hume. He observed that people

> ought not to trust the future government of a state entirely to chance, but ought to provide a system of laws [by which he means institutions] to regulate the administration of public affairs to the latest posterity. . . . [W]ise regulations in any commonwealth are the most valuable legacy that can be left to future ages. In the

smallest court or office, the stated forms and methods [institutions again], by which business must be conducted, are found to be a considerable check on the natural depravity of mankind.

He goes on to comment that it may be commonly observed in the history of governments that "one part of the same [government] may be wisely conducted, and another weakly, by the very same men, merely on account of the difference of the forms and institutions, by which these parts are regulated."[1] The take-home message of Part IV of this book, emphasized by Hume and emphasized again here, is that institutions, not just individual preferences, matter for collective results.

A FRAMEWORK FOR STUDYING INSTITUTIONS

Before turning to specific institutions in subsequent chapters, it will be useful to think about these matters a bit more generally. While I want to convey loosely what I mean when I talk about institutions, I do not want to get hung up on definitions. (Students should put their highlighters away!) The framework I elaborate consists of four components: division of labor and regular procedure; specialization of labor; jurisdictions; and delegation and monitoring.

Division of Labor and Regular Procedure

The tasks confronting actors in an institutional setting often lend themselves to preliminary structuring. For example, anyone who has ever attended a meeting of a club knows that its proceedings are divided into a number of categories—officer

---

[1] David Hume, *Essays* (Indianapolis: Liberty Fund, 1985), Essay III. My thanks to Richard Tuck for bringing this passage to my attention.

reports, old business, new business, and so on. A school board seeking community input may begin its sessions with a "citizens speak" slot, in which any resident may raise a school-related issue. The presiding officer then assigns the topic to the agenda of a subsequent board meeting. The U.S. House of Representatives has a well-structured division of labor, which is reflected in the various categories of its "calendar." Time is allotted for representatives to make remarks on subjects near and dear to their constituents, for committees to meet and make reports, for debates and votes to take place, for legislation to be received from the Senate, and for messages to be delivered by the president.

There is nothing very surprising in all this. Actors meeting regularly in an institutional context evolve procedures by which the various bits of business are divided into manageable units and then sequenced into a specific order. They do so, most obviously, to bring order to their deliberations. Economists would remark that this aspect of the division of labor is an *efficiency-enhancing* aspect of an institution. Without some procedural regularity, the proceedings would be more chaotic than they need to be. Dividing up the business and proceeding according to an institutional script economizes on the costs of doing business (or what economists call *transaction costs*).

There are, however, additional purposes served by this division of labor. Procedures governing a division of labor not only regularize a group's official affairs but also allow its individual members to plan their own participation. This is because a set of procedures and a division of labor define a strategic context in which individuals may think about whether to participate at all, in what parts of the sequence to participate, and, finally, precisely how to participate. Moreover, they may condition these choices on what will already have transpired, as well as on what they know is coming up. A member's preferences about what new undertaking the organization should pursue, for example, may well depend on how the organization resolves some current undertaking. Thus, it is necessary to dispatch "old business" before considering new departures. An organization that allows deliberation and decision on "new business" *before* this old business is resolved would prevent its individual members from conditioning their behavior on the latter's resolution. Members would then have to make judgments with insufficient information, raising the prospect that the issue would have to be revisited (wasting members' time) once the relevant information is available. In this sense, procedures embodying a division of labor are *strategy enhancing*.

Another purpose served by the division of labor and regular procedure is the *empowerment* of the organization's members. Reliable and publicly known procedures provide a check against arbitrary and capricious behavior by institutional leaders. Leaders, as we will see at several points in the next few chapters, have considerable discretion that they can direct toward their own ends. Partly this is a reward to leaders—a *selective incentive*, in Mancur Olson's language—for shouldering organizational burdens. This reward, however, becomes a blank check if leaders are not held responsible for observing a modicum of regularity in the ways they proceed. Official procedures provide this regularity.

Finally, I should note that a particular divison of labor or set of procedures is not carved in stone. There are, in the constitutions, bylaws, or standing rules and orders of most institutions, mechanisms by which to change the way the institution's business is conducted. Two categories of departure from regular procedure arise, depending upon whether the change is permanent or temporary. Standard operating procedures may be *amended*, so that some particular piece of business, and all subsequent business of a similar sort, is conducted in a different manner. Or procedures may be tem-

porarily *suspended* to handle a specific matter, after which the
original procedure is reinstated. The former represents a permanent change in the institutional status quo, assumed to
apply to future proceedings unless subsequently amended.
The latter is a "short-circuiting" device by which some specific
piece of business is conducted in a different manner, but the
rules governing future business of the same sort revert to the
earlier institutional status quo. Each of these techniques has
been employed by the two houses of Congress and is illustrated by a specific example.

Until the mid-1970s, a motion to close debate and bring a
matter to a vote in the U.S. Senate, called *cloture*, required
the support of "two-thirds of those present and voting." This
rule empowered a minority of 34 senators (sometimes fewer if
fewer than 100 senators were "present and voting") to *filibuster*, thereby preventing the Senate from bringing a motion
to a vote. The standing rules of the Senate were amended at
that time—mainly to break the stranglehold of southern senators preventing the Senate from voting on civil rights bills—so
that cloture could be voted by 60 senators.[2] This rule change
became part of the standing rules governing future Senate
business.

In contrast, the House of Representatives often operates in
suspension-of-the-rules mode in order to avoid procedural com-

---

[2] The Senate has always prided itself on being "the world's greatest delibera-
tive body," and some defenders of the earlier rule on cloture believed that it
facilitated debate and deliberation by preventing the body from taking a
vote until an extraordinary majority felt there was nothing further to deliberate on or debate. Detractors, on the other hand, felt that the old cloture
rule was simply a procedural device behind which a disciplined minority
could extract concessions from the majority, if not defeat the majority's objectives altogether. During the civil rights revolution, detractors had the votes
to pull off the procedural coup described in the text (though southerners actually filibustered during the debate on whether to change the cloture rule!).
The House limited debate in its formal rules more than a century earlier,
coming to the conclusion that no large group of politicians could be expected
to keep quiet long enough to take a vote unless forced to by institutional procedures.

plexities that would make it difficult for the House to complete its business. The rules of the House are contained in a rather thick volume, and the precedents and interpretations about how to apply these rules now comprise a library shelf full of thick volumes. If the House actually had to follow its rules to the letter each time it took up even the most trivial of matters, it would give gridlock an altogether new meaning, making the operation of the present House look sleek and efficient by comparison. In order to keep the rules intact—for there actually are circumstances in which it is important for all the hoops to be jumped through—yet facilitate the expeditious prosecution of the people's business, it is always in order for a member of Congress to move to suspend the rules and proceed directly to a vote on the matter at hand without further delay. A combined motion both to suspend the rules and to pass the bill before the House is approved if supported by two-thirds of those present and voting; ordinary procedures to pass the bill would only require a simple majority. So an extraordinary majority may expedite business by temporarily bypassing standard operating procedures, but this maneuver is successful only for relatively uncontroversial legislation. Moreover, and in contrast to amending the rules, the suspension is only temporary, with procedure reverting to its standard form in subsequent deliberations.

Specialization of Labor

In an institution, each actor is not a perfect copy of any other actor. Instead, actors tend to have different talents, interests, and preferences. Many institutions reflect this fact and make good use of it, by *specializing labor*. Some professors, therefore, spend disproportionate amounts of time in the classroom; others spend large amounts of time in the lab or library. Some legislators specialize in particular policy areas, others specialize in different areas of policy, while still others remain generalists.[3] By specializing labor in the sense of allowing different members to do different things, in light of their different interests and talents, an institution is able to capitalize on the rich endowment of "human capital" contained in its membership.

Not all institutions embrace specialization. Perhaps the most prominent American national institution lacking a specialization of labor is the Supreme Court. All justices hear all oral arguments, attend conferences with their colleagues, write draft opinions, engage in deliberation and bargaining, and ultimately sign a majority opinion or draft a concurring or dissenting opinion. Unlike legislators, who typically serve on a small number of committees handling specialized areas of public policy, and thus who devote the lion's share of their energies to these special domains, justices are generalists par excellence.[4, 5]

It is not unusual for an institution to evolve from a relatively unspecialized form to a more specialized form. In the

---

[3] A wag (probably a member of the House of Representatives) once asked: "What do a U.S. Senator and the mouth of the North Platte River have in common? Both are a mile wide and an inch deep." Senators, because of their larger, more heterogeneous constituencies, normally cannot afford to specialize in terms of policy as much as representatives can. They remain generalists rather than specialists (or, as the wag would have it, superficially informed about nearly everything).

[4] This is a slight (but only slight) overstatement. Justices tend to develop reputations, owing to past training and personal interest, as experts in specific areas of law. This expertise is reflected in the fact that specific justices tend to pay extraordinary attention to specific areas—some focusing on capital punishment cases, others on regulation, still others on individual liberties. But each justice devotes time to every case that comes before the Court and is not prepared to defer even to expert colleagues. To our knowledge, satisfactory explanations for the lack of specialization in the Supreme Court have never been provided. Nevertheless, for a fascinating description of how the Supreme Court operates as a relatively unspecialized political institution, see H. W. Perry, *Deciding to Decide* (Cambridge: Harvard University Press, 1991).

[5] This lack of specialization on the Court may reflect a deeper prohibition against "trading across issues." The administration of justice, it may be believed, is compromised if it is the result of logrolling. I thank a reader, Jay Hamilton, for this interpretation.

marketplace, for example, production often begins as an arti-
sanal activity or a household industry in which a producer
makes the entire product and is paid according to the number
(and quality) of units produced.[6] This is known as the *piece-
rate* method of compensation, in contrast to the *wage system*,
in which compensation is in accord with a specific activity and
the amount of time spent on it. The latter system is often associated with mass production, in which each worker devotes
himself or herself to a specific part of the production process
in an assembly-line arrangement. Accordingly, in mass production labor becomes specialized, allowing for the acquisition
of expertise that makes the production process more efficient.

The same evolutionary pattern is observed in the history of
the U.S. Congress, as well as in most of the state legislatures.
They began as relatively unspecialized assemblies with each
legislator (essentially like a contemporary Supreme Court justice) participating equally in every step of the legislative
process in all realms of policy. This was certainly true for the
U.S. Congress in the first decade or so after the adoption of
the Constitution. By the time of the War of 1812, if not earlier,
Congress began employing a system of specialists (the standing committee system), as members with different interests
and talents wished to play disproportionate roles in some
areas of policymaking while ceding influence in other areas in
which they were less interested.[7]

The great advantage of the specialization of labor is that
an institution benefits from the acquisition of expertise by its

---

[6] The image ordinarily conjured up is of some nineteenth-century cottage industry, like weaving, in which the artisan is paid for each finished article of
clothing produced. Late-twentieth-century high-tech analogs include the famous story of Steve Jobs and Steve Wozniak assembling the first machine of
what was to become Apple Computer in Jobs's family's garage.

[7] The story of the evolution of the standing committee system in the House
and Senate in the early part of the nineteenth century is told in Gerald
Gamm and Kenneth Shepsle, "Emergence of Legislative Institutions: Standing Committees in the House and Senate, 1810–1825," *Legislative Studies
Quarterly* 14 (1989): 39–66.

members. By divvying up activities, giving disproportionate influence in different areas to different members of the institution, incentives are created for members to "learn their area," developing specialized knowledge and accumulating relevant current information. This expertise has the prospect of making the institution more effective in whatever activities it pursues.

Jurisdictions

The incentive for those with special interests or talents actually to specialize in those activities is facilitated by parceling activities into jurisdictions. Each jurisdiction is a bundle of activities, and members of the institution assigned to a specific jurisdiction become jurisdictional specialists. Universities, firms, and legislatures are institutions that manifest this organizational feature most clearly.

In universities, for instance, the world of knowledge is divided into disciplines, each of which is assigned to the jurisdiction of a department. The students of that department specialize in mastering the knowledge of that discipline, while the professors specialize in creating new knowledge in that field and teaching it to others.

In exactly the same manner, corporations partition their activities; indeed, there are alternative ways to bundle activities. For example, firms may be organized in a functional manner, with separate divisions devoted to separate functions—finance, advertising, production, distribution, marketing, research and development, and so on. Or firms may be organized according to product line, with each division's jurisdiction consisting of all the activities associated with developing, producing, and bringing to market a specific product. In either case, members of this institution are assigned a jurisdictional niche in which their activities are specialized.

Legislatures, too, are organized into specialized jurisdictions. The world of policy is partitioned into policy jurisdictions that become the responsibility of committees. The members of the Committee on Armed Services, for example, become specialists in all aspects of military affairs, the subject matter defining their committee's jurisdiction. Committee members tend to have disproportionate influence in their respective jurisdictions, not only because they have become the most knowledgeable members of the legislature in that area of policy, but also because they are given the opportunity to exercise various forms of agenda power—a subject I will develop further in the next chapter.

An interesting consequence of the division and specialization of labor, institutionalized into jurisdictional arrangements, is that members of an institution often become so highly specialized that they know little about their institution outside their own bailiwick. A Harvard political scientist typically knows more about what is happening in the Department of Political Science at Stanford than she knows about developments in Harvard's Department of Chemistry. Likewise, a congressman serving on the House Agriculture Committee keeps abreast of political developments in his own committee and perhaps those of the Senate Agriculture Committee, while knowing little (and caring less) about the goings-on in the House Committee on International Relations (except on matters of agricultural trade).

In discussing these abstract features of institutions, I am claiming that organizations arrange their procedures and structures in specific ways, the most notable characteristics of which are jurisdictional division and specialization. Some of the push to do things in these ways comes from the outside environment:

- Firms that organize themselves in ways that entail unnecessary costs or other inefficiencies find it difficult to survive in the competitive struggle.
- Legislatures that fail to take advantage of specialization

find themselves outmaneuvered at every turn by the executive branch.
- Universities that fail to foster the specialized disciplinary development of their faculty lose both professors and students to those universities that do.

External pressures, however, are not the only conditioning factors. Institutions—self-governing ones, at least—are to some degree creatures of their members and thus are subject to internal pressures as well. Even if Stanford did not exist, Harvard would still be disposed to encourage the disciplinary development of its faculty, because that's the way its faculty wants things to be. Members of Congress want an organizational arrangement in which they can gravitate to, and have disproportionate influence in, those areas of policy that are most central to their own interests and those of their constituency. The institutional profile that results, therefore, balances requirements of the external environment against the desires of internal institutional actors.

Delegation and Monitoring

Dividing up institutional activities among jurisdictions, thus encouraging participants to specialize, has its advantages. But it has costs, too. If the research and development division of a firm could do whatever it wanted in its jurisdiction, then there is no guarantee that it would put its specialized talents to work for the best interests of the entire firm. If the political science department of a university could pursue whatever activities its faculty members desired, then some central missions of the university (advising undergraduates, for example) might go wanting. If the Armed Services Committee of the House of Representatives had no restraints, its members would undoubtedly shower their own districts with military facilities and contracts. In short, the delegation of authority and resources to specialist subunits exploits the advantages of the division and specialization of labor but risks jeopardizing collective objectives of the group as a whole.

The *monitoring* of subunit activities, thus, goes hand in hand with delegation. Firms, for example, institute financial controls to make sure that subunits devote resources to activities approved of by central management. The dean of faculty, partly through resource allocation and partly through the control of hiring and firing, influences the missions his or her faculty pursues. A political majority of the full legislature, controlling the assignment of members to committees, the assignment of policy areas to a committee's jurisdiction, and the final disposition of any legislation the committee approves, keeps committees from pursuing a private agenda at the expense of the larger institution.

In sum, the division and specialization of labor, underwritten by the creation of jurisdiction-specific subunits, allows an institution to decentralize its operations. This, in turn, facilitates the delegation of authority and resources to specialists who, because they have disproportionate influence over events in their respective bailiwicks, also have incentives to develop their expertise further. The very act of delegating, however, generates a problem of control in which specialists may have opportunities to pursue private objectives at odds with the public purposes of the institution (what organization theorists refer to as the *moral hazard problem*). It is probably impossible to solve this problem entirely, but institutions normally institute mechanisms both to monitor subunit performance and to control behavior wildly at odds with institutional objectives.[8]

---

[8] I have made much of the phenomenon in which a parent body delegates authority and resources to its subunits because this organizational format is so pervasive in the real world. Presumably it reflects a gain in the capacity of an organization to achieve its goals, relative to what it would otherwise achieve in a more centralized format. Delegation and decentralization, it should be noted, are instances of a more general *principal-agent* relationship. I do not have time to go into this in detail. Suffice it to say that when-

CONCLUSION

This brief introduction to the world of institutions has been intended to emphasize that, while institutional arrangements come in different sizes and shapes, there is a common set of considerations by which they may be analyzed and understood. Without giving a formal definition, I have suggested that an institution consists of a division of activities, a partitioning of individuals, and the matching of activities with individuals so that a subgroup of individuals has jurisdiction over a specific subset of activities. An institution also consists of mechanisms of monitoring, control, and other incentives that connect the jurisdiction-specific activities of subgroups to the overall mission. I have pointed to the divisional structure of firms, the departmental structure of universities, and the committee structure of legislatures as quintessential illustrations of these kinds of institutional arrangements. Indeed, it is appropriate to think of an institution as a *governance structure*, permitting individual ambition and organizational purpose to be blended. Finally, I have emphasized that institutions are not static—that they change in response to their external environment and internal pressures—so that they are rarely born whole in the first instance and they rarely stay undisturbed over long stretches of time. They go with the flow.

---

ever a delegator (the principal) selects a delegatee (the agent) whom he or she entrusts with authority and/or resources to accomplish some purpose for the delegator, there is a problem of control. Thus, the problem that a constituency has in controlling its representatives is a principal-agent problem, as are the problems followers have in controlling their leaders, faculties have in controlling their departments, assemblies have in controlling their committees, executives have in controlling their staff, and so on—the list is endless. In each instance some form of monitoring accompanies the delegation of authority.

12

Legislatures

There is a rather ambitious agenda for the next chapters—namely, to squeeze into a very few pages analyses of specific political institutions, each of which has preoccupied generations of scholars who have filled library shelves with their studies. I certainly do not intend to replicate or even compete with the work of these scholars. Rather, I intend to put the analytical developments of the previous parts of the book on display in specific institutional contexts. In the case of legislatures, the subject of this chapter, the spatial analysis of the operating properties of majority rule developed in Part II[1] is combined with the analysis of cooperation and collective action developed in Part III,[2] while keeping in mind the framework for studying institutions developed in the previous chapter.

COOPERATION AMONG LEGISLATORS

A popularly elected legislative assembly—the Boston city council, the Massachusetts legislature, the U.S. Congress, the French National Assembly, or the European Parliament—

---

[1] The reader may wish to return to "Spatial Models of Legislatures" in Chapter 5 for a quick review.

[2] Chapters 8 and 9.

consists of politicians who harbor a variety of political objectives. Since they got where they are by winning an election, and many hope to stay where they are or possibly advance their political careers, these politicians are intimately aware of whom they must please to do so:

- Because campaigns are expensive propositions, most politicians are eager to please those who can supply resources for the next campaign—financial "fat cats," political action committees, important endorsers, small contributors, party officials, volunteer activists.
- The most recent campaign—one that the politician won —provided her with information about just why the victory was secured. It is sometimes quite difficult to sort out the myriad of factors, but at the very least the politician has a good sense of what categories of voters supported her and may be prepared to support her again if her performance is adequate.
- Many politicians aim to please not only campaign contributors and voters; they also have an agenda of their own. Whether for virtuous reasons or evil ones, for private gain or public good, politicians ordinarily come to the legislature with goals of personal importance.

We may think of all the people to whom the legislator is accountable (including to himself or herself) as the legislator's *constituents*. Different legislators will give different weight to personal priorities and the things desired by campaign contributors and past supporters. Some regard themselves as perfect agents of others; they have been elected to do the bidding of those who sent them to the legislature, and thus act as *delegates*. Other legislators conceive of themselves as having been selected by their fellow citizens to do what the legislator thinks is "right," and thus act as *trustees*. Most legislators are mixes of the two ideal types.

A legislative assembly therefore consists of a motley crew

of legislators, each motivated by a combination of desires—
wanting to please those who control his or her political future
and wanting to achieve personal goals. Broadly speaking,
their instrumental objectives involve trying to secure things
for their constituents, however they might define the latter.
The first premise, then, is that legislators come to the legislature with political purposes that motivate them to want to
pursue specific public policies (*instrumental behavior*).

The second premise is that in a representative democracy
the specific public policies that representatives want to pursue
are heterogeneous (*preference heterogeneity*). We mean this in
two respects. First, owing to their different constituencies, legislators will give priority to different realms of public policy. A
Cape Cod congressman will be interested in shipping, fishing,
coastal preservation, harbor development, tourism, and ship-
building. A Philadelphia congresswoman may not care much
at all about any of those issues, focusing her attention instead
on welfare reform, civil rights policy, aid to inner-city school
systems, and job retraining programs. Montana's sole member
of Congress is probably not interested in coastal preservation,
nor in inner-city schools, but rather in issues of ranching,
agriculture, mining, and public land use. An assembly contains a mélange of legislative priorities.

Legislative assemblies are also heterogeneous in the opinions their members hold on any given issue. While some may
care passionately about the issue in question, and others not a
whit, there is bound to be conflict, both at the broad philosophical or ideological level and at the practical level, on how
to proceed. Thus, while interest in environmental protection
ranges from high priority among those who count many Sierra
Club members among their constituents to low priority among
those who have other fish to fry, once environmental protection is on the agenda there is a broad range of preferences
over specific environmental initiatives. Some want pollution
discharges carefully monitored and regulated by a relatively

powerful environmental watchdog agency. Others believe that more decentralized and less intrusive means, such as marketable pollution permits, are the way to go. Still others think the entire issue is overblown, that any proposed cure is worse than the disease, and that the republic would best be served by leaving well enough alone. This preference heterogeneity is modeled in Chapter 5 in terms of a spatial model in which the distribution of individual preference curves reflected a range of ideal policies.

To the two premises of instrumental behavior by legislators and preference heterogeneity among them, I add a third premise. Diversity in priorities and preferences among legislators is sufficiently abundant that the view of no group of legislators predominates (*diversity*). Legislative consensus must be built—this is what legislative politics is all about. Each legislator clamors to get her priority issue the attention she believes it deserves, or to make sure that her position on a given issue prevails. But neither effort is likely to succeed on its own merits. Support must be assembled, compromises made, deals consummated, and promises and threats utilized. In a word, legislators intent upon achieving their objectives must *cooperate*.

Cooperation, as we learned in Part III, may be assembled separately on each occasion. But one-shot efforts at cooperating often run into insurmountable difficulties. Cooperating parties are often suspicious, for one thing, and thus guard against being taken advantage of. At the very same time, they contemplate the pros and cons of taking advantage of others. Finally, they loathe having to waste resources on securing compliance each and every time. A more promising possibility arises, it would seem, when cooperation can be spread across recurrences of the same issue over time or across lots of different issues at any specific point in time. I'll scratch your back on this issue at this time; you scratch mine on that issue at some other time. But still, there is the problem of one party securing another's cooperation at one point in time, only to renege on reciprocating as promised at some other time. Problems of compliance do not go away, even if cooperation is spread across issues and time.

Cooperation, especially on recurring matters, is facilitated by *institutionalization*. Indeed, we shall claim that many institutional practices in legislatures reflect the requirements of facilitating cooperation in an environment of preference heterogeneity, diversity, and instrumental behavior. This leads to legislative effort being divided and specialized, legislative procedures regularized, legislative subjects partitioned into jurisdictions, specific forms of agenda power and other distinctive advantages delegated, and the interactions fostered by these arrangements monitored to assure compliance with cooperative objectives. All of these features arise as part of a cooperative *governance structure*.

Underlying Problems

Before we can understand why legislative assemblies select particular ways to institutionalize their practices, we need a finer appreciation of the underlying problems with which legislators must grapple. We have encountered many of these previously in this text in rather abstract form. Here we give them more concreteness.

Majority Cycles

Preference heterogeneity and diversity mean, first and foremost, that no particular view on public policy predominates in the legislature. Were this not true—if, that is, a large proportion of the members were more or less in agreement on how to proceed—then the problem confronting a legislature would merely be one of providing expedited procedures to enable this consensual group to vote its program through and implement it. But because there is typically preference heterogeneity and diversity, no specific program of policy distinguishes itself as an obvious course on which to proceed. Worse still, as Part II made clear, if issues are multidimensional in nature (and surely they are much of the time), then heterogeneity and diversity mean there is no equilibrium to majority voting. Any status quo can be beaten, any policy alternative beating the status quo can be beaten, any policy that beats the policy that beats the status quo can also be beaten, and so on without end.

Procedures are required to cut through all this instability. But procedures that give asymmetric advantages to some at the expense of others would not be tolerated if they extended across all issues. Putting such concentrated power to one side, the best a legislator can hope for is that whatever procedural practices are instituted to bring orderliness to legislative decision making allow him or her to have some say in those issue areas he or she cares about most. Our Philadelphia legislator, for example, would probably be content to trade away her influence on mining or fishing issues to the Montana and Cape Cod legislators, respectively, in exchange for having a disproportionate say on aid to inner-city school districts.

Matching Influence and Interest

Legislatures are highly egalitarian institutions. Each legislator has one vote on any issue coming before the body. Unlike a consumer, who has a cash *budget* that she may allocate in any way she wishes over categories of consumer goods, a legislator is not given a vote budget in quite the same sense. Instead, his budget of votes is "earmarked"—one vote for each motion before the assembly. He is a bit like a consumer who is given a series of $1 bills, each designated for a different consumer good category; he cannot aggregate the votes in his possession and cast them all, or some large fraction of them, for a motion on a subject near and dear to his heart (or those of his constituents). This is a source of frustration, since, as we have noted, the premise of instrumental behavior means that legislators would, if they could, concentrate whatever resources they commanded on those subjects of highest priority to them.

In principle, this frustration could be alleviated by a system of vote trading. Votes cannot literally be traded, but promises about casting them in particular ways can. Our Philadelphia legislator can promise her Montana colleague to vote as the latter wishes on an upcoming mining bill if the latter, in turn, supports the Philadelphian's preference on an upcoming jobs bill. There are two problems (at least) with this idea, however. First, can you imagine the negotiating and bookkeeping complexities of a system of vote trading in any but the smallest of assemblies? It's one thing to think through an isolated bilateral exchange of votes. The sheer cost of organizing and sustaining a "market" in votes involving 435 traders across a myriad of issues boggles the mind. Second, vote-trading agreements, like other deals among politicians, are not enforceable contracts. If the Philadelphia legislator casts her vote for the Montanan's mining bill, but the Montanan then reneges on his promise to vote for her jobs bill, what can she do? She can certainly refuse to do business with him in the future, but she can't sue in a court for nonperformance of a contractual obligation. For both of these reasons, a market in votes entails very high costs of transacting, and thus is a very costly way to match legislator influence with legislator interests.

It is sometimes thought that party leaders act as liaisons in vote-trading transactions, matching up legislators interested in making exchanges, and generally facilitating the making of deals. The problem with this view, indeed with nearly any highly centralized manner for organizing exchange, is the almost superhuman burden on a leader to know who is willing to trade what at what price. Again, in small societies this is conceivable. And some legislative leaders, like Lyndon Johnson in the U.S. Senate in the 1950s and Robert Byrd in that same body in the 1970s and 1980s, developed enormous reputations for their cunning and insight concerning what buttons to push on which members. But even here it is unlikely that all the deals that could have been consummated were, in fact, struck. Leaders will have a role to play in the solution I suggest below, but that role is not primarily as an intermediary in a market for votes.

Information

The refrain of many urban legislators in the last few decades, like our Philadelphia congresswoman above, is "more jobs at a living wage." This is a response both to the disappearance of many jobs from most American cities (they gravitate to lower-wage regions of the country or out of the country altogether to lower-wage regions of the world) and, of those that remain, the often unattractive wages, benefits, and career prospects attached to them. Many legislative solutions to this serious problem have been proposed. Some urge a higher minimum wage; some mandate better fringe benefits—health care coverage, day care subsidies, pension benefits, parental leave policies, and so on; some underwrite training programs to improve the productivity of workers; some advocate all these things and more. What works? These are very complicated matters; even those legislators for whom the problems are most pressing are often quite unsure how to answer this question.

If legislators voted directly for social outcomes, then this wouldn't be a problem at all. The Philadelphia legislator could simply offer a bill "mandating" more jobs at a better wage in urban areas and, if it passed, then—abracadabra!—the mandated effects would become a reality. Alas, legislators do not vote for outcomes directly, but rather for *instruments* (or policies) whose effects produce outcomes. Thus, in order to vote intelligently, legislators must know the connection between the instruments they vote for and the effects they desire. In short, they must have information and knowledge about how the world works.

Few legislators—indeed, few people in general—know how the world works in very many policy domains in all but the most superficial of ways. Nearly everyone in the legislature would benefit from the production of valuable information—at the very least, information that would allow legislators to eliminate policy instruments that make very little difference in solving social problems, or even make matters worse. Producing such information, however, is not a trivial matter. Simply to digest the knowledge that is being produced outside the legislature by knowledge-industry specialists (academics, scientists, interest groups) is a taxing task. In short, policy-relevant information is a *public good* and we know, from Part III, that public goods are undersupplied. Clearly, institutional arrangements that provide incentives to some legislators to produce, evaluate, and disseminate this knowledge for others will permit public resources to be utilized more effectively.

Compliance

The legislature is not the only game in town. The promulgation of public policies is a joint undertaking in which courts, executives, bureaucrats, and others participate alongside legislators. If the legislature develops no means to monitor what happens after a bill becomes law, then it risks public policies implemented in ways other than those stipulated in the law. Cooperation, that is, does not end with the successful passage of a law. If legislators wish to have an impact on the world around them, especially on those matters to which their constituents give priority, then it is necessary to attend to policy *implementation* as well as policy *formulation*. But it is just not practical for all 435 representatives and all 100 senators to march down to this or that agency at the other end of Pennsylvania Avenue to ensure appropriate implementation by the executive bureaucracy. Compliance will not "just happen" and, like the production and dissemination of reliable information at the policy formulation stage, the need for oversight of the executive bureaucracy is an extension of the cooperation that produced legislation in the first place. It, too, must be institutionalized.

We have suggested that legislative politics, reflecting the diversity and heterogeneity of the preferences of representatives, requires various forms of cooperation that generally are hard to manufacture. The fact that majorities cycle in their preferences means that to break the policy indeterminacy, it is necessary to institute procedural regularities that bring closure to legislative subjects. To do this, however, is to risk giving advantages to some at the expense of others, unless asymmetric advantages can be held in check, on the one hand, and subdivided and distributed widely, on the other. Related to this, representatives are not uniformly interested in all subjects that come before the legislature, since there is normally heterogeneity among their respective constituencies. Yet they are endowed with one vote each on every subject that comes to a vote. This imbalance between interests and influence provides a setting in which there are prospective gains from exchange in order to improve the match between the two. Finally, part and parcel of the cooperation that is required to get anything accomplished in a legislative assembly is the generation of information and the monitoring of results in the wider political system. To produce these public goods, incentives must be properly arranged.

Legislative institutions emerge and evolve in response to these problems. They also respond to other problems, like wartime emergencies or environmental crises; but those described in the preceding paragraphs are the most enduring ones to which institutional solutions are matched. Institutional solutions, moreover, are not static, one-time-only responses, both because the problems change from time to time and because the solutions arrived at are not always the best ones. Learning and adaptation to changes in the policy environment surely occur in institutional life. Finally, I would be remiss if I did not mention that institutions incorporate conflict. Legislatures are not only forums in which teams of kindred spirits try to solve common problems. They are also battlefields on which the deployment of public authority is determined (and indeed, at its most ideological, on *whether* public authority should be deployed at all).

LEGISLATIVE STRUCTURE AND PROCEDURE

With the stage thus set, I can now apply our framework for analyzing institutional politics to legislatures. Throughout I assume the legislature consists of n legislators (where $n = 435$ for the U.S. House, $n = 100$ for the U.S. Senate, $n = 650$ for the British House of Commons, and so on). I maintain as working premises that legislators are instrumental in seeking policies that will please various of their constituents, that legislator preferences over policy options are heterogeneous, and that no legislator preference is sufficiently numerous in the legislature as to be decisive. Finally, I assume that legislative policy may be represented by a spatial formulation, with each dimension reflecting an aspect of public policy salient to at least some legislators. With these features as background, I argue that legislators choose a division and specialization of labor, regular procedure, a jurisdictional arrangement, and delegation and monitoring technologies in order to facilitate cooperation and other gains from exchange. After making my case for these claims, I will go on to analyze additional layers of institutional detail that constitute the operating features of real legislatures.

Jurisdictional Division and Specialization of Labor

All of the elements of my model of an institutionalized legislature fit together almost seamlessly. So it is somewhat arbitrary where to start the discussion. Perhaps it is best to begin with the policy space. The dimensions of this space constitute the parameters of public policy, which the legislature may set and reset through legislation. By voting larger appropriations for the military than in the past, for example, the legislature moves a parameter of defense policy from a less hawkish to a more hawkish setting. By granting broadly interventionist statutory authority to the Environmental Protection Agency, the legislature moves a parameter for regulatory policy from a more restrained to a more activist setting. There are many such dimensions of public policy on which the legislature works its will. Legislators, we have assumed, have policy preferences on these various dimensions (though any one legislator may care passionately about only a small subset of them). Some prefer hawkish defense policies, while others are more dovish; some want a proactive environmental protection policy, while others want less public intervention; and so on.

Suppose, for the sake of argument, we can describe public policies in terms of some specific set of m policy dimensions, $D = \{d_1, d_2, \ldots, d_m\}$. Now let's group these m dimensions into a set of jurisdictions. A *jurisdictional arrangement*, J, is a collection of these groups—$J = \{J_1, J_2, \ldots, J_t\}$. That is, there are t jurisdictions, each of which contains some relatively small number of dimensions of public policy. We assume that each policy dimension in D is in exactly one of the jurisdictions in

J, so that the jurisdictional arrangement partitions D into a collection of mutually exclusive and collectively exhaustive groupings. For example, if there are five policy dimensions, $D = \{d_1, d_2, d_3, d_4, d_5\}$, then one of the possible jurisdictional arrangements puts the first two dimensions in a jurisdiction, the third dimension in a second jurisdiction, and the last two dimensions in a third jurisdiction—$J = \{J_1, J_2, J_3\}$, where $J_1 = \{d_1, d_2\}$, $J_2 = \{d_3\}$, and $J_3 = \{d_4, d_5\}$.

Now let's do the same thing to the members of the legislature, $N = \{1, 2, \ldots n\}$, grouping these n members into *committees* exactly equal in number to the number of jurisdictions. Call $C = \{C_1, C_2, \ldots C_t\}$ a *committee system*, where each member of N is on exactly one committee.[3] Finally, we connect C to J, assigning each committee one of the t policy jurisdictions. Thus, J_1, consisting, say, of the various policy dimensions associated with agriculture, might be assigned to C_1, thus identifying the legislators in that group as members of the Agriculture Committee.

In this manner we have characterized a jurisdictional division and specialization of labor in a legislative setting. The policymaking business of the legislature is divided up into jurisdictional responsibilities. Legislative labor is specialized by dividing up the membership into committees, each of which is assigned one of the specialized jurisdictions.

Camouflaged beneath all this notation are two crucial political processes. The first involves the assignment of issues to committees. In many, perhaps most, instances, the subject matter of issues fall squarely into one or another committee jurisdiction. However, new issues arise that often fit neatly into no jurisdiction. Some, like the emerging issue of energy supplies during the 1970s, are so multifaceted that bits and

---

[3] Actually it is quite all right, and factually accurate in the case of the U.S. Congress and most of the state legislatures, to allow members to serve on more than one committee. What is normally forbidden is to give a member *no* committee assignment.

pieces of them are spread across many committee jurisdictions. Thus, the Commerce Committee of the U.S. House of Representatives had jurisdiction over the regulation of energy prices, the Armed Services Committee dealt with military implications, the Ways and Means Committee dealt with tax-related energy aspects, the Science and Technology Committee claimed jurisdiction over energy research, the Agriculture Committee dealt with grain-to-energy conversion matters, and several other committees picked off still other pieces of this hydra-headed issue. Other issues, like that of regulating tobacco products, fall in the gray area claimed by several different committees—in this case the Commerce Committee, with its traditional claim over health-related issues, fought with the Agriculture Committee, whose traditional domain includes crops like tobacco, for jurisdiction over this issue. Turf battles between committees of the U.S. Congress are notorious.[4] These battles, often extending over many years, involve committee chairs, the Parliamentarian's Office, the political leadership of the chamber, and, from time to time, selected committees appointed to realign committee jurisdictions. All in all, jurisdictional conflict is the raw stuff of politics, since, as we shall see, committees with jurisdiction over issues have significant leverage over their resolution.

The second political process submerged beneath our abstract description of legislative institutions is the committee assignment process—the assignment of members to committees. The process determining who gets on what committees is significant because it designates which members will have extraordinary influence over the issues falling into the jurisdiction of each committee. In most legislatures, this process is conducted within the political parties. Each party has a cer-

---

[4] An outstanding description and analysis of these battles is found in David C. King, "The Nature of Congressional Committee Jurisdictions," *American Political Science Review* 88 (1994): 48–63. See also his *Turf Wars* (Ann Arbor: University of Michigan Press, 1996).

tain number of vacancies per committee with which to work; these are assigned to new and returning members (the latter of whom typically retain the committee assignment they held in the just-completed legislative session). It is a highly charged political process, especially for the newcomers, having major ramifications for policy making in that legislative session.[5]

Delegation of Jurisdictional Authority

In order to give operational significance to the division and specialization of labor described above, it is necessary to assign committees specific forms of authority in their respective jurisdictions. If committees had no authority, or if whatever they did had little impact on the policies ultimately selected in the legislature or the outcomes in the larger political system, then about the only thing a committee member could do would be to list her membership on her résumé, along with memberships in other clubs and honorary societies.[6] Committees in the U.S. Congress, however, have considerable authority, some of which I described briefly in Chapter 5.

It needs to be said at the outset that committee jurisdictions and authority, like nearly all other aspects of structure and procedure, are created by the parent legislature.[7] In the U.S. Congress, the House and Senate give these things to, *and*

[5] For an extensive discussion of the committee assignment process in the U.S. House, see Kenneth A. Shepsle, *The Giant Jigsaw Puzzle: Democratic Committee Assignments in the Modern House* (Chicago: University of Chicago Press, 1978). An extremely comprehensive and up-to-date study is Scott A. Frisch and Sean Q. Kelly, *Committee Assignment Politics in the U.S. House of Representatives* (Norman: University of Oklahoma Press, 2006).

[6] Many parliamentary democracies have committee systems in which the committees actually have very little to do. The business of government in various policy jurisdictions is dominated by cabinet ministers and senior civil servants. Committees, for the most part, are window dressing.

[7] In the United States, for example, the Constitution does designate certain requirements for the two houses of Congress. But it also permits each house to set its own rules, thereby giving the parent bodies tremendous discretion to revise structural and procedural features as they wish.

may take them away from, their subunits. In this view, committees may be thought of as *agents* of the parent body to whom jurisdiction-specific authority is provisionally delegated. Of what does this delegation consist? I describe committee authority in terms of gatekeeping power, proposal power, interchamber bargaining power, and oversight authority.

In all of the dimensions of public policy falling within a committee's jurisdiction, there is always some status quo policy in place. It may be that the issue is new, in which case "currently doing nothing" is the prevailing policy. On other issues there are well-established laws keeping a bevy of bureaucrats and other government officials busy at implementation and administration. At any time on any of these dimensions, a committee may choose to "open the gates" by proposing new legislation to change the status quo ante. Although a slight exaggeration, it is fair to say that in many legislatures committees have, in their jurisdiction, exclusive *gatekeeping authority*. That is, it is practically impossible for the full legislature to consider changes in the status quo in a committee's jurisdiction unless the committee consents to open the gates. This makes a committee an agenda monopolist in its jurisdiction.

A committee's agenda monopoly should be thought of as provisional. It is a standing decision by the parent legislature. At any time, however, the parent legislature can revise that standing decision. This is the parent legislature's "club behind the door." A committee, in exercising agenda power, is always at risk of inducing the parent legislature to revise its agenda authority. A second mechanism by which the parent legislature can discipline a committee is the *discharge petition*. This is a temporary procedure in which the legislature, upon a majority of its members signing a petition, removes a particular bill from the committee and brings it directly to the floor.

Closely related to gatekeeping is a committee's *proposal power*. Normally, any member of the legislature can submit a bill calling for changes in the status quo in some policy area.

Almost automatically, this bill is assigned to the committee of jurisdiction and, very nearly always, there it languishes. In a typical year in the House of Representatives, nearly fifteen thousand bills are submitted. Fewer than a thousand are taken up by that committee and assigned to the appropriate committee of jurisdiction. In effect, while any member is entitled to make proposals, the *real* proposal power inheres in committee majorities. So, committees get to decide not only whether to open the gates but also what proposal emerges through those gates. Committees, then, are lords of their jurisdictional domains, setting the table, so to speak, for their parent chamber.[8]

Finally, a committee has responsibilities for bargaining with the other chamber and for conducting oversight, or what we call *after-the-fact authority*. Because many legislatures are bicameral—the U.S. Congress, for instance, has a House and a Senate—once one chamber passes a bill, it must be transmitted for consideration to the other chamber. If the other chamber passes a bill different from the one passed in the first chamber, and the first chamber refuses to accept the changes made, then the two chambers ordinarily call a *conference* in which representatives from each chamber (called *conferees*) meet to hammer out a compromise. In the wide majority of cases, conferees are drawn from the committees that had original jurisdiction over the bill. For example, in a sample of Congresses in the 1980s, of the 1,388 House members who served as conferees for various bills during this period, only seven were not on the committee of original jurisdiction; similarly, in the Senate on only seven of 1,180 occasions were conferees not

[8] This clearly gives committee members extraordinary power in their respective jurisdictions, allowing them to push policy into line with their own preferences—but only up to a point. If the abuse of their agenda power becomes excessive, the parent body, as noted above, has structural and procedural remedies available to counteract this—like stacking the committee with more compliant members, deposing a particularly obstreperous committee chair, or removing policies from a committee's jurisdiction.

drawn from the "right" committee.[9] The committee's effective
authority to represent its chamber in conference committee
proceedings constitutes after-the-fact power that complements
its before-the-fact gatekeeping and proposal powers.[10]

A second manifestation of after-the-fact committee authority consists of the committee's primacy in *legislative oversight*
of policy implementation by the executive bureaucracy. I will
have more to say about this in the next chapter. Suffice it to
say here that even after a bill becomes a law it is not always
(indeed, it is rarely) self-implementing. Executive agents—
bureaucrats in the career civil service, commissioners in regulatory agencies, political appointees in the executive branch—
march to their own drummers. Unless legislative actors hold
their feet to the fire, they may not do precisely what the law
requires (especially as statutes are often vague and ambiguous). Given this possibility, the Legislative Reorganization Act
of 1946, a law that reformed and redefined how the House and
Senate have conducted their business through most of the late
twentieth century to the present day, instructed congressional
committees to be "continuously watchful" of the manner in
which legislation is implemented and administered. Committees of jurisdiction play this after-the-fact role by allocating
committee staff and resources to keep track of what the executive branch is doing and, from time to time, holding oversight
hearings in which particular policies and programs are given
intense scrutiny. Anticipating this surveillance, and knowing

---

[9] See Kenneth A. Shepsle and Barry R. Weingast, "The Institutional Foundations of Committee Power," *American Political Science Review* 81 (1987):
85–104. The evidence for the claim in the text is found in Table 1.

[10] Forty-nine of the fifty U.S. states have bicameral legislatures and thus have
mechanisms for the bicameral resolution of differences. Only Nebraska is
unicameral. Interestingly, to my knowledge there is only one city in the
United States with a bicameral legislature. Everett, Massachusetts, has a
seven-member Board of Aldermen and an eighteen-member Common Council, together comprising the City Council. Why more cities and towns do not
have bicameral arrangements is a puzzle, one deserving research and
thinking.

what grief a congressional committee can cause an executive branch agent found deviating from what legislators want, these officials are very keen to keep their congressional "masters" content. This, in turn, gives congressional committees an additional source of leverage over policy in their jurisdictions.

CASE 12.1
CAMPAIGN CONTRIBUTIONS*

I have argued that committees are powerful institutions in legislatures because of their gatekeeping power, proposal power, interchamber bargaining power, and oversight authority. The ways in which interest groups allocate their campaign contributions provides evidence of this committee influence.

Interest groups often contribute money to legislative campaigns in an attempt to influence legislative outcomes. Charles H. Keating Jr., the bank executive prosecuted for his role in the savings and loan crisis of the 1980s, was asked about the $1.4 million in campaign contributions he gave to five senators, all members of the Senate Banking Committee, who came to be known as "the Keating Five." Keating replied:

> One question, among the many raised in recent weeks, had to do with whether my financial support in any way influenced several political figures to take up my cause. I want to say in the most forceful way I can: I certainly hope so.†

---

* This chapter examines the effects of institutional arrangements on legislative behavior. Interest groups are often accused of biasing this behavior by "buying" legislators with campaign contributions. The two cases in this chapter examine the role of campaign contributions and interest group activities using the institutional approach to legislatures.

† Cited in James Ring Adams, *The Big Fix: Inside the S & L Scandal* (New York: Wiley, 1990), p. 254. Also see Dennis F. Thompson, *Ethics in Congress* (Washington, D.C.: Brookings Institution, 1995).

Assuming that interest groups are rational and that
their primary goal is influencing legislation that affects
them, we would expect groups to allocate their contributions to legislators with the most influence. So where do interest groups allocate their money? Based on the material
in this chapter, you shouldn't be surprised by the answer: to
legislators who sit on committees that have jurisdiction
over the groups. Banks give to the members of the banking
committees, food and tobacco producers to those sitting on
the agriculture committees, doctors and insurance companies to those serving on the health-related committees. The
power of committee chairs is also apparent from the allocation of campaign contributions. Of the legislators who sit on
the committees relevant to a particular interest group, committee chairs often receive a greater share of the campaign
contributions.‡

‡ See Larry Sabato, *PAC Power: Inside the World of Political Action Committees* (New York: Norton, 1984). Also see Kevin B. Grier and Michael C.
Munger, "The Impact of Legislator Attributes on Interest Group Campaign Contributions," *Journal of Labor Research* 7 (1986): 349–61.

Monitoring and Control

As should be apparent by now, committees are quite consequential players in their respective policy jurisdictions. If
unchecked, committees could easily take advantage of their
authority. Indeed, what prevents committees from exploiting
their before-the-fact agenda power and their after-the-fact
bargaining and oversight authority? To answer this question
we have to see what "taking advantage" means. And this requires us to think about which legislators become members of
which committees.

To make this clear, suppose a committee's jurisdiction were
one-dimensional. In the full legislature the policy that a legislative majority prefers in this jurisdiction is, from Black's

Theorem in Chapter 5, the most-preferred policy of the *median legislator*, x_m. The policy most preferred by the committee, on the other hand, is the most-preferred policy of the *median committee member*, x_c. Only by accident would these two ideal points be the same (but accidents can happen, as I remark on shortly). Thus, the committee wants to pull policy toward x_c, whereas the full legislature wants to pull policy toward x_m. It is this tension that pits legislature against committee, principal against agent, delegator against delegate.

Recalling our analysis in Chapter 5, the form this tension takes depends partly on the order along the policy dimension of committee median and legislative median in comparison to the status quo, x^0. If x^0 lies between the two medians, in which case committee and chamber want to move policy in opposite directions, the tension is caused by the committee's refusing to open the gates. (Of course, if they did stupidly open the gates, then any proposal they made to improve their lot would be voted down or, to make matters worse, amended in a direction *away* from the committee median.) If x_m lies between the committee median and the status quo, or if x_c lies between the chamber median and the status quo, then it is possible for both committee and chamber to improve their respective lots, depending on the way in which committee bills are handled in the full house (see the analysis in Chapter 5 for details). In either of these latter cases, however, the tension does not go away even under the best of circumstances, and it gets worse the greater the distance is between x_c and x_m.

There are basically two "ordinary" ways in which the parent chamber keeps committees in check, thereby reducing their frustration with potential committee abuses of authority: committee assignments and amendment control rules.[11]

---

[11] In addition, an "extraordinary" way, much like dropping a bomb, entails taking committee jurisdiction away or, the equivalent of capital punishment, disbanding the committee and dispersing its jurisdiction to other committees. A prominent example of this form of capital punishment involved the

Regarding committee assignments, the key issue is the degree to which a committee is representative of the entire chamber. *Representative* committees may be thought of as "little legislatures." Majorities there are likely to behave much in accord with majorities in the larger chamber from which they were drawn. *Outlier* committees, on the other hand, have a composition significantly different from the parent chamber. In these situations the distribution of preferences in the committee is very different from that of the full legislature. If a committee's jurisdiction consists of one policy dimension, for instance, the differences between these two types of committees is captured in the distance between the median committee ideal point, x_c, and the median legislator in the full legislature, x_m. Roughly speaking, representative committees are associated with small deviations between the two, whereas it is larger for outlier committees.

Why, one might ask, doesn't the legislature *ensure* committee responsiveness to preferences in the chamber by appointing only representative committees? That way, so the argument goes, the legislature would gain the benefit of a small jurisdictionally specialized group, one producing public goods like information and oversight of the executive, without having to risk abuse of the asymmetric authority it possesses.

The reason legislatures typically do *not* do this follows from our preference heterogeneity premise. Many committee jurisdictions consist of policy areas of interest to relatively

---

infamous House Un-American Activities Committee (HUAC), in 1969 renamed the House Internal Security Committee (HISC), 1938–75. This committee, regardless of its name, embarrassed much of the House during the postwar period by exaggerating fears that communists were infiltrating American public and private institutions. Publicity-seeking members of the committee held public hearing after public hearing, pillorying guilty (of which there were a few) and innocent (of which there were many) alike, with low regard for the civil liberties or the presumption of innocence of those appearing before it. By the early 1970s most members of the House had had enough, and the committee was dispatched to the junk pile of history.

small numbers of legislators. Congressmen and congress-women from coastal districts, for instance, and virtually no others, give priority to the jurisdiction of the Merchant Marine and Fisheries Committee. Fewer than a quarter of the House of Representatives would kill to get on the Agriculture Committee; ditto for the Banking and Housing Committee. These committees deal with problems and issues of great importance to rural districts and central city districts, respectively, whose representatives constitute relatively small proportions of the entire chamber. It is chiefly legislators from the Maryland and Virginia suburbs of Washington, D.C., who want a seat on the Post Office and Civil Service Committee, since so many of their constituents are employed by the federal government. Contrast these committees with the Appropriations Committee, the Ways and Means Committee, the Armed Services Committee, the Budget Committee. These latter committees deal with issues of general importance regarding taxing, spending, budgeting, and defense. Nearly every district and state is affected by their decisions; nearly every member of the House of Representatives or Senate would delight in serving on one or another of these committees.

Most of the legislature is not particularly concerned about what goes on in many of the specialized committees listed early in the preceding paragraph, and most are highly concerned with decisions coming out of the more generalist committees listed toward the end of the paragraph. Thus, one would expect an arrangement in which

- legislators were allowed freely to flow to the *specialist* committees to which they give priority, even though committees populated this way would look like outliers to an outside observer; but
- the composition of *generalist* committees would be more carefully monitored by the parent body, with greater effort expended to make these committees representative.

Evidence from the House of Representatives is consistent with this expectation: on average, the difference $|x_m - x_c|$ is larger for specialist committees than for generalist committees.[12] The committee assignment process, while generally responsive to requests for committee positions coming from the chamber's members, is especially responsive if the request is for a specialist committee whose jurisdiction is not a high priority to a large proportion of the membership. In these cases there does not appear to be much concern if a committee is not representative of the full chamber. Responsiveness, however, is constrained by concerns for representativeness if the request is for a generalist committee whose policies generate external effects on committee member and nonmember alike.[13]

There is a second, complementary tool by which the parent chamber monitors and controls its subunits. Whenever a committee brings a proposal to the floor, the legislative chamber must decide how it will deliberate on the proposal. In many legislatures there are predetermined standing rules governing the disposition of legislation. In the U.S. House, however, it is customary to craft a rule specific to the legislative proposal in question. This rule, which is called an *amendment control rule*, regulates the amount of time devoted to debate, how that time is divided between proponents and opponents, and, most

---

[12] There is still controversy among scholars concerning this issue, but it mainly involves the very thorny problems of measuring preferences of real legislators. The most committed of legislative jocks who want more on this subject, may find it for the period through the mid-1970s in Shepsle, *The Giant Jigsaw Puzzle*. A study covering most of the postwar period up through the early 1990s is Gary W. Cox and Mathew D. McCubbins, *Legislative Leviathan* (Berkeley: University of California Press, 1993). Also see their *Setting the Agenda* (New York: Cambridge University Press, 2005).

[13] I remarked earlier that it would be quite accidental if $x_m = x_c$ but quipped that accidents do happen. We now know why. Because generalist committees have such pervasive policy impacts on the welfare of a large number of different constituencies, the legislature explicitly stacks these committees so that the committee median is relatively close to the chamber median. This is what it means to make these committees "representative."

important, what amendments are in order, if any. Thus, while committees may have disproportionate agenda power, controlling whether the gates are opened in their respective jurisdictions and, if so, what proposals come through them, they do not *dictate* final outcomes in their jurisdictions. Their proposals may be modified by the parent chamber.

The parent chamber's capacity to "keep an eye on" committee activities tends to be the most exacting, as the reader might guess, in the case of specialist committees. Their proposals normally are governed by an *open rule* (see Chapter 5), allowing for virtually unrestricted amendment activity by the parent chamber. Thus, even if such committees are outliers, their products must pass muster in a full chamber armed with an ability to make wholesale changes. Generalist committees, on the other hand, often receive *restrictive rules* for their proposals, limiting the chamber's ability to amend. The extreme version of the latter is the *closed rule* (also discussed in Chapter 5), according to which *no* amendments are in order.

The reader undoubtedly will concede that it makes sense for the proposals of outlier committees to be subjected to close scrutiny and control. Precisely because they are unrepresentative of the parent chamber, their efforts will need close attention.[14] The reader will also concede that it makes sense for the proposals of representative committees to be subjected to much more relaxed scrutiny, precisely because they are representative of the parent body. What may remain puzzling is

---

[14] The careful reader might note that because their jurisdictions are of relevance to narrow constituencies, specialist committees really don't need to be monitored closely since their policy effects are confined. While this is true most of the time, it is not always true. In particular, whenever proposals entail the expenditure of revenues, they have implications for the activities of every other committee, since these expenditures draw from the same common revenue pool from which other committees hope to draw. Most of the House would not be pleased with an Agriculture Committee, for example, that proposed a level of price support for agricultural products that consumed a large proportion of the annual public budget.

why *some* protection from wholesale change in the larger legislature is (at least some of the time) afforded the proposals of
outlier-specialist committees while, on the other hand, the
chamber grants itself *some* ability to amend the proposals of
representative-generalist committees.

An answer to the first part of this puzzle is provided by
Keith Krehbiel in his masterly study *Information and Legislative Organization.*[15] Krehbiel argues that most legislative activity takes place in a context of great uncertainty about the
relationship between proposed legislative solutions and social
problems. Information about these cause-and-effect relationships helps to reduce this uncertainty. Thus, encouraging committee members to become expert specialists in the subject
matter of their jurisdictions and to disseminate this expertise
to their noncommittee colleagues enhances the legislature's
capacity to cut through the uncertainty that surrounds most
occasions for legislating. The promise of at least partial protection for their proposals is, in effect, the price the legislature
is prepared to pay in exchange for reliable information. This
will mean that the committee can, in fact, extract some advantage from their prelegislative and postlegislative authority (by
having their proposals protected from wholesale revision on
the floor), but it will also mean that the legislation that ultimately results is likely to have benefited from the expertise
which committee members have been encouraged to develop.
In short, the system of protection of legislative products is an
incentive system that encourages the development of legislative expertise.

The second part of the puzzle is why a chamber nearly always retains some ability to revise committee proposals, even
those of representative-generalist committees. At least part of
the answer lies in the fact that no committee can be represen-

[15] (Ann Arbor: University of Michigan Press, 1991).

tative in every respect. A committee, for example, may have slightly more westerners on it than are found in the full legislature, or be slightly more liberal than the rest of the chamber. The disparity between committee and chamber preferences may not be as large in generalist committees as in specialist committees, but it may not be zero either. And there is one way in which *any* committee is unrepresentative. The specific members of a committee represent specific geographic districts, and represent *none* of the districts of members not on the committee. On matters that involve distributing goodies—ranging from the classic pork barrel of dredging rivers and harbors, building post offices, and locating military installations, to the more subtle forms of pork-barreling like siting sexy scientific facilities, giving grants to favorite universities, or enriching particular contractors—members of a committee, if unmonitored and unchecked, will undoubtedly find ways to distribute the lion's share of their goodies to their own districts.[16] The chamber, by retaining rights to amend, deters at least the more egregious instances of this kind of opportunistic behavior.[17]

[16] Evidence on this may be found in one of the classics of this literature, John Ferejohn, *Pork Barrel Politics* (Stanford, Calif.: Stanford University Press, 1974). For an alternative perspective, see Robert M. Stein and Kenneth N. Bickers, *Perpetuating the Pork Barrel* (New York: Cambridge University Press, 1995). For an excellent recent study, also see Diana Evans, *Greasing the Wheels* (New York: Cambridge University Press, 2004).

[17] Nevertheless, in the 1960s it was rumored that Charleston, South Carolina, was sinking under the weight of all the naval installations the chair of the House Armed Services Committee, Mendel Rivers, had managed to secure for his district. More recently, there has been concern that the same fate is being suffered by the state of West Virginia, whose powerful senior senator, Robert Byrd, the chair of the Senate Appropriations Committee and former majority leader, has managed to entice numerous government agencies to relocate to his state from Washington, D.C.

CASE 12.2
INTEREST GROUP INFLUENCE

In the 2008–10 electoral cycle, many millions of dollars in campaign contributions were given by interest groups and political action committees (PACs) to incumbent legislators and challengers. What does this money buy? A popular conception is that campaign contributions buy votes. In this view, legislators vote for whichever proposal favors the bulk of their contributors. Although the vote-buying hypothesis makes for good campaign rhetoric and newspaper editorials, it has little factual support. Empirical studies by political scientists show little evidence that contributions from large PACs influence legislative voting patterns.*

If contributions don't buy votes, then what do they buy? My claim is that campaign contributions influence legislative behavior in ways that are difficult for the public to observe and for political scientists to measure. The institutional structure of Congress provides opportunities for interest groups to influence legislation outside the public eye. Committee proposal power enables legislators, if they are on the relevant committee, to introduce legislation that favors contributing groups. Gatekeeping power enables committee members to block legislation that harms contributing groups. The fact that certain provisions are *excluded* from a bill is as much an indicator of PAC influence as the fact that certain provisions are *included*. The difference is that it is hard to measure what you don't see. Committee oversight powers enable members to intervene in bureaucratic decision making on behalf of contributing

---

* See the important early Janet M. Grenke, "PACs and the Congressional Supermarket: The Currency Is Complex," *American Journal of Political Science* 33 (1989): 1–24.

groups. In the case of Charles Keating Jr., described in Case 12.1, for example, five senators on the Senate Banking Committee used their oversight authority to induce bank regulators to ease up on their supervision of Keating's savings and loan (which ultimately failed).

The point here is that voting on the floor, the alleged object of campaign contributions according to the vote-buying hypothesis, is a highly visible, highly public act, one that could get a legislator in trouble with his or her broader electoral constituency. The committee system, on the other hand, provides loads of opportunities for legislators to deliver "services" to PAC contributors and other donors that are more subtle and disguised from broader public view. Thus, I suggest that the most appropriate places to look for traces of campaign contribution influence on the legislative process are in the ways committees deliberate, mark up proposals, and block legislation from the floor; existing, as they do, outside public view, these are the primary arenas for interest group influence.

LEADERSHIP AND COORDINATION

I have argued that the committee system reflects the desire, common in legislatures and most other organizations, to divide up business and specialize labor to cut through indeterminacy, to generate informed decision making, and to guarantee that the legislature has impact in the larger political system. An important by-product of this arrangement (indeed, some would say it is the *main* product) is that it permits legislators to bring their interests and their authority more into line, allowing members, subject to constraints on representation to flow to those committees whose jurisdictions reflect their priorities and interests. Thus, while legislatures are one-person, one-vote institutions, most legislators have a larger, more in-fluential voice in those policy areas of greatest concern to their constituents.

Committees, in effect, are legislatures writ small; they have the corresponding motive to divide business and special-ize labor. Thus, the roughly twenty standing committees of the U.S. House are, in turn, divided into about a hundred, even more specialized *subcommittees*. With so many of the Montana congressman's constituents involved in growing wheat, for example, he could best serve them—and best posi-tion himself to secure their votes in the next election—if he were not only a member of the Agriculture Committee but also on its Subcommittee on Feedgrains. These subcommittees serve their full committees in precisely the same manner the full committees serve the parent chamber. Thus, in their nar-row jurisdictions, they have gatekeeping, proposal, intercham-ber bargaining, and oversight powers. In order for a bill on wheat to be taken up by the full Agriculture Committee, it has first to clear the Feedgrains Subcommittee. All of the issues involving assignments, jurisdictions, amendment control, and monitoring that we discussed earlier regarding full commit-tees apply at the subcommittee level as well.

Taking this all in, the reader may already have arrived at the conclusion that institutions are not just collections of indi-viduals; they also consist of specific structural and procedural arrangements for the conduct of business. Obviously if these additional arrangements generated more bother than benefit, an organization might not adopt them at all. Families, for ex-ample, while specialized to a certain extent, do not display the fine-grained division and specialization of labor of, say, Micro-soft. That these features of institutional governance carry with them additional burdens for an organization should thus not be underestimated. Institutionalization is not pure profit.

In the case of legislatures, the burden of layers of institu-tional complexity is reflected in the need for coordination and leadership. One cannot turn twenty committees with a hundred subcommittees loose without some means of guaranteeing that their work is supervised by the parent chamber. The supervision, moreover, cannot merely involve one committee or one subcommittee at a time. Someone must coordinate across institutional subunits. Someone must lead. I discuss leadership more generally in Chapter 14, so I can be brief here.

At the committee level the mantle of leadership falls on the committee chair. He or she must orchestrate the proceedings of the committee's staff, investigatory resources, and subcommittee structure.[18] For many years the Congress followed a rigid *seniority rule* for the selection of these chairs. Accordingly, a person was elevated to the chair if he or she had the longest continuous service on the committee. The benefits of this rule are twofold. First, the chair will be occupied by someone knowledgeable in the committee's jurisdiction, familiar with interest group and executive branch players in the wider Washington community, and politically experienced. Second, the larger institution will be spared leadership contests that often reduce the legislative process to efforts in vote grubbing by contenders. There are costs, however. Senior individuals may well be knowledgeable, familiar, and experienced, as suggested above; but they also may be unenergetic, out of touch, even senile. Even when these liabilities do not appear, senior members may nevertheless be out of step with their committee and the parent chamber. From the time of the 1965 Voting Rights Act to what the press called the Republican Revolution of 1994 (when Republicans won majorities in the House and Senate for the first time in nearly half a century), old-fashioned southern conservatives have been a declining force within the Democratic Party; even so, those who remained benefited from a seniority system that elevated them to chair-

---

[18] Subcommittee chairs do essentially the same things in their narrower jurisdictions, so I won't provide a separate discussion of them.

manships. It was thus not at all unusual for a committee consisting chiefly of northern and "New South" Democrats to be
run by a southern dinosaur who had been around for thirty
years.

Different legislatures make the trade-off differently between seniority-rule automatic elevation, with its profile of
benefits and costs, and leadership election, the main alternative to seniority. The U.S. House operated according to a strict
seniority principle from about 1910 until the mid-1970s, when
most members felt the burdens of this arrangement were beginning to outweigh its advantages.[19] With Democrats controlling the House since 2006, committee chairs are now elected
by the majority-party members of the full legislature, though
there remains a presumption (which may be rebutted, of
course) that the most senior committee member assumes the
chair. Thus, the House added leadership selection to the other
control mechanisms employed by the parent body over its subunits.

If committee chairs are the principal vehicles through
which the activities of subcommittees are coordinated, then
party and other institutional leaders from the full legislature
are the ones to coordinate the activities of committee chairs.
The Speaker of the House, Majority Leader, and Minority
Leader, all elected either by the full house or their respective
party caucuses, are granted responsibilities and authority
aimed at making sensible use of the institution's resources.
They don't always have a completely free hand, just as com-

---

[19] In 1972 the Democratic Caucus approved caucus-wide election of committee
chairs, though it was assumed at the time that no incumbent, previously elevated to a chair because of seniority, would lose his or her chairmanship.
This, in fact occurred, though John McMillan (D-S.C.), chair of the District
of Columbia Committee and one of those crusty southerners referred to in
the text, attracted considerable opposition. After the 1974 election, however,
three committee chairs were defeated (and a fourth resigned to avoid defeat). When the Republicans captured the House in the 1994 election, they
abandoned both seniority and election, effectively allowing their leader to
appoint chairs.

mittee chairs do not, but they are delegated responsibility from the chambers and the parties to choreograph the proceedings; the electoral mechanism by which they hold on to their jobs is designed to make sure they are responsive to relevant institutional constituencies.

CONCLUSION

Much of the original work reported in Part II on the theory of majority rule was done by (political) economists. They thought they understood the political world once they grasped how abstract majority rule worked (or failed to work). Many years ago one remarked to the author in a private conversation, "Now that we know all about median voters and that sort of thing, we have a pretty good understanding of how the House of Representatives works." Starting with this chapter, we hope to convey the naïveté of that sentiment. It's one thing to think of a legislature as n politicians taking votes by majority rule. Indeed, it is just like thinking of a firm as personified by a boss single-mindedly pursuing profits. Each of these is an abstraction that may be useful for studying legislatures in the context of a larger political system or firms in the context of a larger industry. But once one shifts the magnifying glass from political system and industry to legislature and firm, these particular abstractions are no longer nearly as serviceable. Structure and procedure, an institution's lifeblood, become much more central to understanding life on the inside of an institution. The divisional structure of the firm, or the committee structure of a legislature, abstracted away in more general studies, take on a much greater descriptive and analytical salience. And once one opens his or her mind to these features, issues of authority and control become important. In short, the observations of some economists to the contrary notwithstanding, there's no getting away from politics.

The characterization of a legislature throughout this chapter, it is only fair to note, describes the practices of some of the world's legislatures—particularly the U.S. House and Senate, the legislatures of the U.S. states, and the national and regional legislatures in parts of Latin America. The British House of Commons and most of the continental European legislatures have a much less internally elaborated structure. They are more centrally organized, with a prime minister and his or her cabinet calling most of the shots. Because this arrangement is radically different from the American-style legislature, I will take it up separately in Chapter 16.

PROBLEMS AND DISCUSSION QUESTIONS

1. Look at the preferences over issues x and y in the seven-person legislature shown in Figure 12.1. The utility of legislator i is maximized at i's ideal point and decreases with distance from that point. Consider three common institutional features of legislatures: committees of members with proposal power, specific jurisdictions attached to committees, and rules of amendment once a committee has sent a bill to the full legislative body. Suggest one possible partitioning of legislatures into committees and structure of jurisdictions for those committees that would give rise to a stable, predictable equilibrium under a closed rule. What would the likely outcome be under an open rule, assuming that a germaneness rule is in effect (all proposed amendments must relate to the substance of the original bill)?

Would a change in the committee membership invalidate the equilibria you just found under the closed or open rule? Could

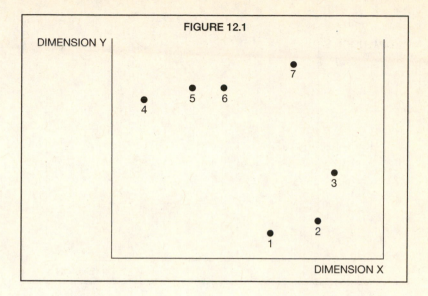

FIGURE 12.1

it invalidate the existence of *any* equilibrium? Answer the same questions for the jurisdictional setup and germaneness rules. How does this exercise illustrate the link between institutional rules and stable decision making?

*2. Figure 12.2 represents a stylized legislature with three blocs, 1, 2, and 3, whose preferences on a two-dimensional issues space are shown. Any two of the three legislative blocs constitute a majority for the purposes of passing legislation. A legislative committee that consists solely of members of group 3 has proposal power, but the legislature operates under an open rule. Suppose that the status quo is at point *q*. If the committee "opens the gates" and proposes a point like *p* to the whole house, could it achieve final passage of that bill? Would the committee be guaranteed final passage of a bill that it prefers to *q*? If not, what might another plausible outcome be? (Hint: Check the winsets of various point.)

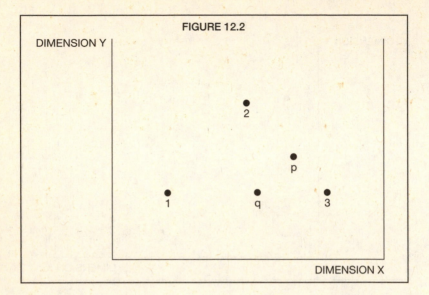

FIGURE 12.2

Now suppose that there is a rule which grants the members of the committee, 3, an after-the-fact veto, allowing it to reject any final bill passed and reinstate the status quo. If the committee "opens the gates," proposing p, would it be guaranteed final passage of a bill that it prefers to q? Comparing the two outcomes, what role does the institutionalization of committee power play in matching legislator interest with influence?

*3. A persistent feature of American political life is legislative gridlock, an inability to change the status quo (even during periods of unified party government) that is not consistent with the McKelvian vision of political chaos and instability. Keith Krehbiel[a] proposed a novel explanation for gridlock using a unidimensional spatial model combined with some institutional details. Assume a liberal president with ideal

[a] Keith Krehbiel, *Pivotal Politics: A Theory of U.S. Lawmaking* (Chicago: University of Chicago Press, 2008), Chapter 2.

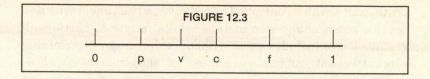

FIGURE 12.3

0   p   v   c   f   1

point p, and a moderate Congress controlled by the president's party in which both houses have median ideal points c. Congress can override a presidential veto if two-thirds of the members vote to do so: The ideal point of the pivotal member of Congress needed to override a veto lies at v. Finally, note that most bills can only escape the Senate with a vote for cloture (to close debate ending a filibuster). The ideal point of the sixtieth Senate vote needed to close debate is located at f. Suppose that these "pivot points" yield the spacing along the single policy dimension provided in Figure 12.3.

If the status quo lies between c and f, can the Congress secure implementation of any preferable law? What if it lies between v and c, or p and v, or to the right of f? How does this help us understand the circumstances that generate gridlock?

4. The House and Senate delegate aspects of policy making from the full chambers to a variety of committees and subcommittees, some of whose members are quite unrepresentative of the Congress as a whole. Why does the Congress delegate authority to these specialized committees? What are the costs associated with delegation, and what institutional tools has the Congress developed to ensure that committees "stay in line," acting in accord with the interests of the entire legislative body?

5. Reacting in part to a sharp decline in "party voting" during the 1960s and early '70s (i.e., the extent to which parties vote as unified blocs on important pieces of legislation), the Demo-

cratic party, which controlled the House at the time, instituted
several policy changes to increase the strength of party leadership. These included greater leadership role in determining
committee assignments, expanion of the system of whips
(tasked with vote counting and arm twisting of Democratic
caucus members) and Democratic leadership committees, and
increasing leadership control over committee referral and
amendment rules for bills.[b]

In what ways does cooperation among legislators suffer in
general from the cooperation and coordination problems discussed in Chapter 9? What role does party leadership play in
ameliorating these problems, and what did the decline in
"party voting" suggest about House leadership before the reforms? Why would representatives with little hope of rising to
the top of the leadership hierarchy go along with reforms
strengthening House leadership at the expense of committees
and committee chairs?

[b] A thorough discussion of these changes and their implications is provided in
David W. Rohde, *Parties and Leaders in the Postreform House* (Chicago: University of Chicago Press, 1991), Chapter 4.

13

Bureaucracy and Intergovernmental Relations

The term *bureaucrat*, a perfectly innocent word describing a government official or civil servant (and also sometimes used for clerks and managers in the private sector), has acquired disagreeable connotations of heartlessness and sluggishness. At the same time that we accept the pursuit of self-interest by the butcher, baker, and candlestick maker, we expect our public servants to be motivated by a higher calling and are merciless in our condemnation when they appear to let us down. We appreciate that the people we interact with in the marketplace are, like the rest of us, trying to make an honest living, and coping with mortgages, car payments, and college tuition for the kids. While we hold some professionals in the private sector to a stricter standard—priests, physicians, and therapists come to mind (perhaps professors, too)—we rarely insist on self-sacrifice to the exclusion of all else. Public servants, in contrast, are expected to be on call, ready to serve expeditiously and efficiently, and certainly not afflicted with any of the personal burdens or ambitions the rest of us carry around.

This idea in the popular consciousness, that government employees somehow are expected to shift moral and behavioral gears when they are transformed from private citizen to public servant, is unrealistic, to be sure, and unfair to those in public service who probably do not perform with significantly less devotion to their jobs than the rest of us. Nevertheless, this view persists, as do the high expectations that are shattered when civil servants fail to perform as demanded. Moreover, given its emphasis on *judging* performance, this view has provided a largely useless basis for *analyzing* bureaucratic behavior.

In this chapter I want to unleash our rational choice engine on this subject. In order to analyze bureaucratic behavior properly, it is necessary to embed it in the larger political system. I begin by examining one model of bureaucratic behavior carefully. It is probably the most famous such model, emphasizing the bureaucratic pursuit of resources controlled by elected politicians. After that I examine, though briefly, some alternative approaches to the bureaucrat-politician connection. Thus, this study of bureaucracy is really a way to investigate the relationship between policy formulators (primarily legislators) and policy implementers (primarily bureaucrats), or what we refer to as *intergovernmental relations*.

INTERGOVERNMENTAL RELATIONS, I: BUDGET-MAXIMIZING BUREAUCRATS AND A PASSIVE LEGISLATIVE SPONSOR

Motivational Considerations

The popular view of bureaucrats as failing to live up to the expectation that they will serve the public interest is judgmental and emotionally laden, not analytical. In a now classic treatment, the economist William Niskanen rejected this misbegotten view entirely.[1] Instead, he proposed that we consider a bureau or department of government as analogous to a division of a private firm, and conceive of the bureaucrat just as

---

[1] *Bureaucracy and Representative Government* (Chicago: Aldine, 1971).

we would the manager who runs that division. In particular, Niskanen stipulates for the purposes of modeling bureaucratic behavior that a bureau chief or department head be thought of as a maximizer of his or her budget (just as the private-sector counterpart is a maximizer of his or her division's profits).

There are quite a number of different motivational bases on which bureaucratic budget maximizing might be justified. A cynical (though some would say realistic) basis for budget maximizing is that the bureaucrat's own compensation is often tied to the size of his or her budget. Not only might bureaus with large budgets have higher-salaried executives with more elaborate fringe benefits, there may be enhanced opportunities for career advancement, travel, a poshly appointed office, possibly even a chauffeur-driven limousine.

A second, related motivation for large budgets is not material compensation but nonmaterial personal gratification. An individual quite understandably enjoys the prestige and respect that comes from running a major enterprise. You can't take these things to the bank or put them on your family's dinner table, but your sense of esteem and stature are surely buoyed by the conspicuous fact that your bureau or division has a large budget. That you are also boss to a large number of subordinates, made possible by a large bureau budget, is another aspect of this sort of ego gratification.

But personal salary, "on-the-job consumption," and power-tripping are not the only forces driving a bureaucrat toward gaining as large a budget as possible. Some bureaucrats, perhaps most, actually *care* about their missions. They initially choose to go into public safety, or the military, or health care, or social work, or education—as police officers, soldiers, hospital managers, social workers, and teachers, respectively—because they believe in the importance of helping people in their communities. As they rise through the ranks of a public bureaucracy into management responsibilities, they take this mission orientation with them. Thus, as chief of detectives in a big-city police department, as head of procurement in the Air Force, as director of nursing services in a public hospital, as supervisor of the social work division in a county welfare department, or as assistant superintendent of a town school system, individuals try to secure as large a budget as they can in order to succeed in the missions to which they have devoted their professional lives.

Whether from cynical, self-serving motives or for the noblest of public purposes, it is entirely plausible that individual bureaucrats seek to persuade others (typically legislators or taxpayers) to provide them with as many resources as possible. Indeed, it is sometimes difficult to distinguish the saint from the sinner, since each sincerely argues that he or she needs more in order to do more. This is one of the nice features of Niskanen's assumption of budget maximizing: It doesn't really matter *why* a bureaucrat is interested in a big budget; what does matter is *that* she wants more resources rather than less.

Niskanen's Model

Imagine, then, a government bureau whose chief is interested in eliciting as large a budget as his legislative overseers will appropriate. The legislature, we assume, is interested in the bureau's output—number of crimes solved, quality of weapons procured, number of patients served, number of juveniles counseled, number of high school students graduated. But, like almost any other good or service, this preference for bureau output increases at a decreasing rate (and may even turn down after it reaches some level). In pecuniary terms, the legislature (or more precisely, its median voter) is prepared to pay more for the first unit of output than the tenth, and decidedly more for the first than the hundred and tenth. Its *willingness-to-pay curve* (labeled B for "budget") is graphed in Figure 13.1. The quantity (Q) of the bureau's output is plotted

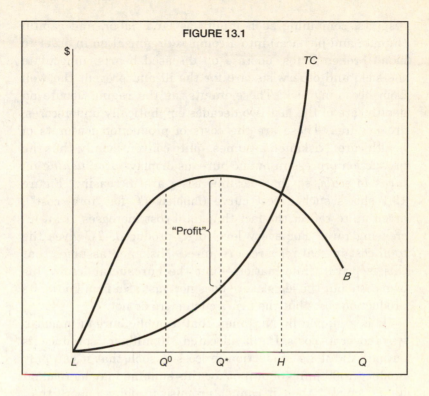

FIGURE 13.1

on the horizontal axis. The total budget in dollars that the legislature is prepared to pay for various values of Q is on the vertical axis. It is assumed that the bureaucrat knows this information about the legislature. Notice that the curve arcs down, reflecting the marginally diminishing nature of the legislature's preferences.[2]

A public bureaucracy, like a private firm, must institute a production process to enable units of output to be produced. A public hospital, for instance, looks just like a factory in many

[2] In Figure 13.1 I have graphed B as turning down for values of Q greater than Q^*. The argument in the text does not require this; it only requires that if B increases it does so at a decreasing rate (so that it has an arced-down shape).

respects, combining such inputs as land, labor, and capital (human and physical) into a complex organization in order to mend broken limbs, operate on diseased hearts, innoculate the sick, and otherwise care for the ill and prevent the well from becoming sick. These inputs, as the raging debate on health care of the last two decades emphatically underscores, are not free. These are the costs of production for units of health care. Niskanen assumes, quite conventionally, that the production process in public bureaus displays *diminishing returns to scale*, so that per-unit costs are increasing. Figure 13.1 shows such a cost curve (labeled *TC* for "total cost"), arced up to reflect the fact that total cost increases at an increasing rate.[3] For every level of *Q* produced, *TC* gives the total cost in real resources required. Niskanen assumes that this is private information—that the bureaucrat knows his own costs but the legislature does not, just as a firm knows its production costs but the firm's customers do not.

It is assumed by Niskanen that a public bureau must always cover its costs. If it is allocated $10 million to produce its output, and if its production process is such that it can only produce 1000 units of output for this sum (as may be read off its *TC* curve), then it cannot promise to deliver more than 1000 units. This means that the bureau can only agree to produce values of *Q* in the range in which the legislature's willingness-to-pay curve lies above the bureau's total cost curve. In Figure 13.1, this is indicated by the interval [*L*, *H*] (standing for "low" and "high" production, respectively). Thus, a budget-maximizing bureaucrat, constrained to cover production costs, will choose the value of *Q* that is associated with the highest point on the *B* curve in the range [*L*, *H*].[4]

---

[3] Algebraically, we may write the equations for these curves as: $B = aQ - bQ^2$ and $TC = cQ + dQ^2$, where a, b, c, and d are positive constants.

[4] In Figure 13.1, *L* is displayed there as zero; this is not necessary (as shown in Figure 13.2). In terms of the equations in the previous note, a budget maximizer will choose the quantity *Q* that maximizes $aQ - bQ^2$, subject to $B \geq TC$, or $aQ - bQ^2 \geq cQ + dQ^2$.

In Figure 13.1 the value of Q associated with the highest point on the B curve is labeled Q^*. Notice that it lies within $[L, H]$, and therefore satisfies the cost-covering constraint.[5] Notice also that this yields the bureau a "profit"—the difference between B and TC when Q^* units are produced. Since this profit depends upon the bureau's costs of production (TC)—something the legislature is ignorant about—legislators have no way of determining the bureau's "profit margin." However, because the bureau is a public entity there are no "owners" who can pocket this profit. Instead, the bureau has some "pin money" with which it can enable its managers to "consume on the job" (nice offices, posh furnishings, more staff to boss around, new desktop computers, resources to send managers to conferences in pleasant locations).[6]

In Figure 13.2 we have, owing to different parameter values for the willingness-to-pay (B) and production cost (TC) equations (see footnote 3), a very different situation. The unconstrained maximum of the willingness-to-pay function, Q^*, lies outside the $[L, H]$ interval. Given this bureau's production costs, it cannot secure the largest budget its legislative sponsor is prepared to provide *and* cover the costs required to produce Q^* units. Its costs are simply rising too steeply. The best a budget-maximizing bureau, which must cover its costs, can do is given by Q^{**} in that figure—it represents the production level associated with the largest budget consistent with cost-covering.[7] As is shown in that figure, Q^* is well enough defined; it simply lies outside the feasible set of production possibilities available to the cost-constrained bureau.

---

[5] The unconstrained maximum of B is derived by taking its first derivative and setting it to 0. This yields $a - 2bQ = 0$. Solving for Q gives $Q^* = a/2b$. So, the most the bureau will produce, given sponsor willingness-to-pay function B, is $a/2b$ units.

[6] If there were a way to pocket this, through bonuses, extra raises, or extra vacation time, then no doubt the bureaucrats would find a way. This is typically precluded in the public service of most countries by civil service law.

[7] This is the value of Q for which $B = TC$. Substituting for B and TC (as defined in footnote 3) and solving this equality for Q yields $Q^{**} = (a - c)/(b + d)$.

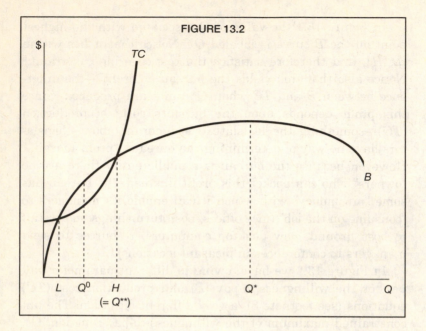

FIGURE 13.2

Niskanen compares the *demand-constrained* level, Q^*, and the *cost-constrained* level, Q^{**}, to what he defines as the *socially optimal* level, Q^0. This production level is the one that maximizes the difference between willingness to pay and total cost (and is shown on both Figure 13.1 and Figure 13.2). Thus, it is akin to the production level that would be chosen by a profit-maximizing firm. On the assumption that "society" and not the bureau keeps this profit, it represents the point of maximum net social satisfaction. Niskanen demonstrates, as the previous figures make clear, that the socially optimal level of bureaucratic production is *less* than either the demand-constrained level or the cost-constrained level—$Q^0 \leq Q^{**} \leq Q^*$. That is, bureaus with a propensity to seek budgets as large as possible also have a propensity to produce *too much*.

Niskanen concludes, therefore, that public bureaucracies are too big, their budgets too large, and their social output more than society wishes. Relative to the willingness of their representatives to pay for units of Q, society is burdened, according to Niskanen, with too many weapons; too many police, welfare, and health services; too much money spent on education, and so on. The government, driven by budget-maximizing bureaus and political overseers who (passively) reveal their willingness to pay, is simply too big.

Variations on Niskanen

Niskanen's model of bureau behavior, although attractive for a variety of reasons, is certainly not without controversy. Whether or not one "likes" the conclusions of a neoclassical economist intrinsically suspicious of government, Niskanen, to his credit, has laid all his assumptions out on the table in full view. It is thus up to the critic to point to specific features of the model that, if changed, would produce different conclusions—not merely to criticize the conclusions. In this way debate is focused on analytical or empirical features of a theoretical argument, not on matters of taste and personal ideology.

I will mention a few changes that might be considered, though I hardly have the space to elaborate on forty years of reaction to Niskanen's famous book. The first place to start is with the matter of motives. I have defended Niskanen's budget-maximization hypothesis from a variety of perspectives, that should, at the very least, suggest to the reader that it is not entirely off the mark. Nevertheless, there are alternatives, and they are likely to produce very different views of bureaucratic phenomena.

For example, suppose that bureaucrats cared not a whit for their bureau's mission but mainly about the perquisites of bureaucratic life they might enjoy—the so-called on-the-job consumption that could be financed out of bureau revenues. If they are able to camouflage their costs of production from the legislators or taxpayers who provide their budget (something Niskanen assumes), then instead of maximizing B, suppose they seek to maximize $B - TC$ (allowing them to spend the difference on making life on the job comfortable).[8] This will lead to a bureau output of Q^0, precisely the socially optimal level of production identified by Niskanen (but the "profit" is *not* returned to the treasury). In this instance, the bureau operates at the "right" level, but does so inefficiently—society, so to speak, has to bribe the bureau to operate there by allowing the bureau to keep its profits. Under this motivational scenario, then, bureaus are not too large—they do not produce "too much" output—but they are too expensive. This, in turn, suggests that the root of the problem resides in the secrecy that protects the bureau's costs of doing business, a theme to which I return shortly.

Alternatively, suppose that bureaucrats are interested neither in operating at full throttle (maximizing B) nor in securing maximal perquisites (maximizing $B - TC$). Instead, suppose they are interested in "the quiet life," engaging in what has been termed "minimal squawk behavior."[9] It is often alleged in popular discussions, for example, that the personnel composition of the public sector is a product of self-selection. People seek out appointment to the civil service for its security (twenty or thirty years of steady work, no heavy lifting, a secure pension with the promise of an early and comfortable retirement). They are not the competitive sort who wish to expose themselves to the dog-eat-dog rivalry of the private marketplace. Nor are they eager to rock any boat (especially bureau managers closing in on retirement). "Steady as she goes" is the watchword. Such people tend to be risk averse, in-

---

[8] In the literature on bureaucratic performance, $B - TC$ is known as *organizational slack*.

[9] See Clare Leaver, "Bureaucratic Minimal Squawk Behavior: Theory and Evidence from Regulatory Agencies," *American Economic Review* 99 (2009): 582–607.

terested mainly in a modest pace, incremental change, and a commitment to routines and standard operating procedures.[10] Although I have hardly put this description into analytical form, it seems likely that bureaucrats defined in this way will *underproduce* relative either to Niskanenian bureaucrats (Q^* or Q^{**}) or to the social optimum (Q^0).

The point here, and I won't dwell on it further, is that it is quite possible to generate the conclusion that bureaus overproduce relative to the social optimum, underproduce relative to the social optimum, or produce exactly at the social optimum (but do so inefficiently). Analyzing politics in this manner requires the analyst to think hard about which motivational hypothesis is the more appropriate in any particular application.[11]

INTERGOVERNMENTAL RELATIONS, II: BILATERAL BARGAINING

There is a second major variation on Niskanen's model of bureau behavior, one that leaves the budget-maximizing motivation in place but calls into question two other features of his formulation: the asymmetry in information between bureau and legislature and the passivity of the legislature. Recall that Niskanen assumes that the willingness-to-pay schedule of the legislature (as represented by its median member), graphed as B in figures 13.1 and 13.2, is commonly known. Thus, the legislature, the only customer of the bureau's prod-

---

[10] A good example is the Federal Trade Commission (FTC) of the 1950s and 1960s. Today it is a very activist regulatory commission. But then it was staffed by political cronies of the chairman of the congressional oversight committee (the so-called "Tennessee crowd") and, because it aimed mostly to keep its head down and not make waves, the FTC was called, among other sobriquets, "the gentle matron of Pennsylvania Avenue."

[11] Of course, it is likely that no single motivational hypothesis applies everywhere equally well.

uct, in essence tells the bureau how much it is willing to pay
for various production levels, Q. The chief critics of Niskanen
on this issue, Gary Miller and Terry Moe, suggest that this is
akin to a customer walking onto a used-car lot and telling the
salesman precisely how much she is maximally willing to
spend for each of the vehicles.[12] On the other hand, the bureau's production cost schedule, graphed as TC in figures 13.1
and 13.2, is assumed by Niskanen to be private information,
known by the bureau but not by the legislature. To continue
the parallel, the used-car customer has no knowledge of what
the salesman paid for the various models on his lot. In effect,
Niskanen's approach can be characterized as a model of a *monopoly bureau with private information and a passive sponsor*.

We have seen in the preceding section what happens in
this situation. Whatever the bureau's motivations, it can exploit knowledge of its customer's preferences, the privacy of
the details of its own production, and the passivity of its customer. But we have also seen, in the previous chapter, that
legislatures are able to anticipate implementation problems of
this sort. Surely it does not take long before legislators realize
that if they neither discover the bureau's production parameters, nor disguise their own willingness to pay for bureau output, nor counteract their own passivity,[13] then they will be
hoodwinked every time by the permanent bureaucracy.[14]

In a representative democracy it may be difficult for the
legislature to keep silent on its own willingness to pay. The
bureau, at any rate, can do some research in order to judge

---

[12] This and other related points are drawn from Gary J. Miller and Terry M.
Moe, "Bureaucrats, Legislators, and the Size of Government," *American Political Science Review*, 77 (1983): 297–323.

[13] This takes the form in Niskanen's model of the bureau being permitted by
its legislative sponsor to select, from the latter's willingness-to-pay schedule, a budget, B, and associated quantity, Q, of deliverable bureaucratic
product.

[14] Much like the parliamentary minister is manipulated by his wily senior
civil servants in the British television series, *Yes, Minister*.

the preferences of various legislators based on who their constituents are. But legislators can do research, too. Indeed, I suggested in the previous chapter that the collection, evaluation, and dissemination of information—in this case, information about the production costs of bureaucratic supply—are precisely the things in which specialized legislative committees engage. Committees hold hearings, request documentation on production, assign investigatory staff to various research tasks, and query bureau personnel on the veracity of their data and on whether they employ lowest-cost technologies (making it more difficult for the bureau to disguise on-the-job consumption). After the fact, the committees engage in oversight, making sure that what the legislature was told at the time authorization and appropriations were voted actually holds in practice. In short, the legislature can be much more proactive than Niskanen gives them credit for. And, in the real world, it is.

Miller and Moe, for example, suggest that instead of an instance of a monopoly bureau facing a passive legislative sponsor—Niskanen's formulation—the reality in American politics is much more that of *bilateral monopoly*: a single customer (the legislature as represented by one of its specialized committees) bargaining with a single supplier (the bureau), each of which has information (about willingness to pay and production costs, respectively) that may or may not be known to the other party. In effect, Miller and Moe are saying that Niskanen failed to model the legislature as an active player in the making of policy.

What happens in the circumstance in which the legislature is more than passive depends upon the precise way it institutionalizes interactions with the bureaucracy. Miller and Moe show (the reader must consult their article for the details) that it need not follow that the bureau is in the driver's seat. An authorization or appropriation or oversight committee able to discover, through the hearing process, the parameters of bureau production, or able to disguise its own willingness to pay, can force the bureau into revealing a menu of production possibilities from which the legislature can then choose. In effect, Miller and Moe turn Niskanen on his head; instead of the legislature revealing information from which the bureau chooses in order to maximize budget size (or slack or quiet life), Miller and Moe have the bureau forced into revealing the intimate details of its operation, allowing the legislators to make choices in pursuit of their own objectives. Whether, under this alternative scenario, government bureaus are too big—producing too many units of their product—or too small—producing too few—will depend on a much more complicated set of considerations than those suggested by Niskanen.

INTERGOVERNMENTAL RELATIONS, III: PRINCIPALS AND AGENTS

In both Niskanen's model of a budget-maximizing bureau with a passive legislative sponsor, and Miller and Moe's model of a budget-maximizing bureau with a proactive legislative sponsor, it is presumed that the structure of intergovernmental relations is fixed in advance—as though it were some sort of life form discovered by the Puritans when they arrived in the New World. The reality, however, is quite different. In the United States the executive bureaucracy, piece by piece, was *created* by legislative enactment. Acts of Congress created the executive departments, regulatory agencies, intelligence agencies, and auxiliary entities like the Office of Management and Budget and Federal Reserve System. An act of Congress reorganized the Joint Chiefs of Staff. An act of Congress combined a host of health agencies and bureaus into the National Institutes of Health. Acts of Congress directly or indirectly created the alphabet soup agencies of the New Deal and World War II; subsequent acts of Congress dismantled many of them.

So, while presidential signatures were required on these congressional enactments and affirming judicial rulings were needed to keep them alive, Congress can lay claim to paternity (and maternity), birthing, and wet-nursing responsibilities for the structure of the federal bureaucracy. Moreover, Congress passed various pieces of legislation regarding both personnel practices and administrative procedures, which serve to regulate entry into, and advancement through, the civil service on the one hand, and the official procedures by which civil servants conduct bureaucratic business on the other. Finally, as I emphasized in the previous chapter, Congress maintains a constant presence in the affairs of the bureaucracy through

- the drafting of laws revising and extending bureaucratic authority;
- the approval of appropriations for the various divisions of government; and
- the subsequent ("continuously watchful") oversight of the uses to which this authority and these resources are put.

It is difficult to square Niskanen's view of a dominant bureaucracy manipulating its passive legislative masters with this litany of facts. The bureaucracy is created by Congress and sustained by Congress. Although there are bound to be occasions in which a bureau chief pulls the wool over a legislator's eyes, and there are surely times in which a department's budget people use "blue smoke and mirrors" to misdirect congressional inspectors, it is unlikely, I believe, for these abuses to persist for very long—certainly not without the implicit approval of congressional players in the bureau's jurisdiction.

In fact, it is even something of a strain to square with these facts the much more balanced view of Miller and Moe in which legislature and bureau bargain more or less as equals. They restore a modicum of symmetry to intergovernmental relations, allowing for monopsony legislative consumer and monopoly bureaucratic producer to be in rough bargaining parity (especially concerning information about preferences and production capability). But in doing so, they suppress the very consequential *asymmetry* described in the previous two paragraphs—namely, the legislature's awesome power to create and sustain, or destroy, bureaucratic organization.

Notice what these two approaches postulate. The first, Niskanen's, asserts that it is the bureaucrat who is in the driver's seat; she is constrained by the legislature to be sure (she must cover costs and accommodate herself to the legislature's maximum willingness to pay), but she gets to choose Q from the menu of alternatives presented to her in the legislature's willingness-to-pay schedule. The second approach, Miller and Moe's, claims that there is much greater balance in the relationship between bureau and legislature, so that rather than one choosing subject to constraints, it is more akin to bilateral bargaining (as, say, when Amalgamated Coal bargains with the United Mine Workers over the price and quantity of labor). There is, however, an alternative to both the Niskanen and Miller-Moe formulations, one that emphasizes the *subordinate* role of the bureaucracy and the *superior* position of elected politicians.[15] To describe this it is necessary to digress briefly on a general consideration of *principals* and *agents*.

---

[15] Throughout, I will suppose that these elected politicians are *legislators*. There is, in fact, an entire literature, known as the "Congressional Dominance School," that explicitly stipulates that the bureaucracy is a creature of legislative preferences. I would want to qualify this, however, by emphasizing that other elected and appointed politicians—especially the president and judges—influence bureaucratic activity, too.

Principal-Agent Relationships

Most people hire a doctor, lawyer, or contractor to tend to their health, to draw up their wills and other legal papers, or to renovate their kitchen, respectively. In principle we could do these things ourselves, but in practice we find it more satisfactory to spend our time and energy on other things. This is just another way of saying that most of us reject self-sufficiency and accept the superiority of market exchange. In effect, we retain *agents* to act in our interest, agents whose specialized knowledge and skills make them more effective in doing our bidding than we could ourselves. In these relationships, each of us is a *principal*, and the problem we face is that of controlling our agents.

When we hire a kitchen contractor, agreeing to pay him a particular sum of money in exchange for renovation services (typically stipulated in pages and pages of detailed specifications), we face the problem that we don't know how good he is and often aren't able to detect the quality of workmanship at the time it is performed. Suppose he used aluminum wiring rather than copper wiring, something we unhappily discover after a fire. Suppose he said he would use copper piping but in fact used plastic piping (obtained cheaply from his brother-in-law and hidden out of sight in the walls), something detected only years later when the less reliable plastic pipe springs a leak. Suppose he claimed to know how to assemble and install the extra-fancy gourmet cooking surface we purchased, only to concede (after our kitchen had been torn apart) that it was more complicated than he had figured.

There are two broad categories of control mechanism enabling a principal to guard against opportunistic or incompetent agent behavior. The first is employed before the fact and depends upon the *reputation* an agent possesses. One guards against selecting an incompetent or corrupt agent (one who cannot or will not perform with the principal's interests at heart) by relying on various methods for authenticating the promises made by the agent. These include advice from people you trust (your neighbor who just had her kitchen remodeled); certification by various official boards (county medical society, bar society, association of kitchen contractors); letters of recommendation and other testimonials, credentials (law or medical degrees, specialized training programs); and interviews. Before-the-fact protection relies upon the assumption that an agent's reputation is a valuable asset that he or she does not want to see depreciated.

The second class of control mechanisms operates after the fact. Payment may be made contingent on completion of various tasks by specific dates, so that it may be withheld for nonperformance. Alternatively, financial incentives (for example, bonuses) for early or on-time completion may be part of the arrangement. The agent may be required to post a bond that is forfeited for lack of performance. An inspection process, after the work is completed, may lead to financial penalties or bonuses or possibly even legal action. Of course, the principal can always seek legal relief for breach of contract, either in the form of an injunction that the agent comply or of an order that the agent pay damages.

This brief discussion identifies principal-agent relationships as arising because there are genuine advantages for individuals to specialize in their activities and trade with one another (in-kind or for cash) rather than depend on self-sufficiency. But balanced against these conspicuous advantages (none of us would want to set her own broken arm or install his new dishwasher) is the obvious fact that an agent does not work out of the generosity of her spirit—she has bills to pay, a mortgage to service, and kids to educate, too. She works for herself as well as working for you, and this can lead to potential conflicts of interest. While control mechanisms exist, they are not perfect.

In a principal-agent relationship it is the principal who stipulates what he wants done, relying upon the agent's concern for her reputation, appropriate incentives, and other control mechanisms to secure compliance with his wishes. Analogously, it may be argued that legislative principals establish bureaucratic agents—in departments, bureaus, agencies, institutes, and commissions of the federal government—to implement the policies promulgated by Congress and the president. Like any principal with an ounce of intelligence, the legislature would surely not create an agent in the image of Niskanen, one that could exploit the legislature for the agent's own benefit. Indeed, the legislature would not even wish to establish a bureaucratic agent with equal standing in a bilateral bargaining situation in the image of Miller and Moe. The legislature wants a compliant agent and will do its best to "hardwire" control mechanisms in the enabling legislation that creates the bureaucratic entity in the first place.

This is precisely the argument made in a series of important papers by Mathew McCubbins, Roger Noll, and Barry Weingast, known collectively as McNollgast.[16] For them, a piece of legislation creating a new agency or assigning some new mission to an existing agency creates a principal-agent relationship between an *enacting coalition*, consisting of legislators in the two houses of Congress and the president (themselves agents for constituents), and a bureaucratic entity. The enacting coalition has coordinated around a policy objective, seeking not only its faithful implementation, but also an arrangement possessing durability (extending beyond when

---

[16] These three authors have now written a large number of papers. The two that will get the interested reader started are "Administrative Procedures as Instruments of Political Control," *Journal of Law, Economics, and Organization* 3 (1987): 243–79; and "Structure and Process, Politics and Policy: Administrative Arrangements and the Political Control of Agencies," *Virginia Law Review* 75 (1989): 431–83.

the members of the particular enacting coalition have de-
parted from the scene.)[17] But this is not as easy as it seems, as
the following little argument suggests.

Suppose the original enabling legislation that created the
Environmental Protection Agency (EPA) required that new
legislation be passed after ten years renewing its existence
and mandate. The issue facing the House, the Senate, and the
president in their consideration of renewal revolves around
how much authority to give this agency and how much money
to permit it to spend. The House, quite conservative on environmental issues, prefers limited authority and a limited
budget. The Senate wants the agency to have wide-ranging
authority but is prepared to give it only slightly more resources
than the House (because of its concern with the budget
deficit). The president is happy to split the difference between
House and Senate on the matter of authority but feels be-
holden to Sierra Club types in this election year and thus is
prepared to shower it with resources. Bureaucrats in the EPA,
for all the reasons we provided earlier in this chapter, want
more authority than even the Senate is prepared to condone
and more resources than even the president is willing to
grant. These preferences are displayed in Figure 13.3, where
H, S, and P represent the ideal points of the political principals, and B the ideal point of the bureaucratic agent. An
enacting coalition—relevant majorities in the House and Senate (including the support of relevant committees) and the
president—agrees on a policy, x, reflecting a compromise
among their various points of view—something close to what

---

[17] Why, the reader might wonder, would politicians care about what happened
after they retired from political life? The reason is that the constituencies
they represent, and who reward them in the here and now for "good deeds,"
have long time horizons. Since *they* care about the long term, they are prepared to reward politicians who attend to the long term. Thus, politicians
will do their bidding, thereby attempting to influence policy even after their
active political life.

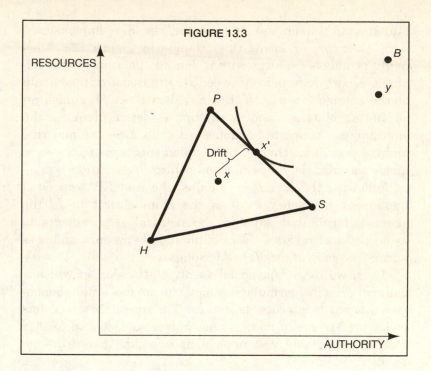

FIGURE 13.3

the president wants on the authority dimension and close to what the Senate wants on the resources dimension.

The bureacrats are not particularly pleased with *x*, since it gives them considerably less authority and many fewer dollars than they had hoped for. If they flout the wishes of the enacting coalition and implement a policy more to their liking—say, *y*—then they risk the unified wrath of the enacting coalition. For any policy outside the triangle connecting the ideal points of the House, Senate, and president, there is some other policy they *unanimously* prefer to it. Undoubtedly the politicians would react to the bureaucratic implementation of *y* with new legislation (and also presumably would find other political appointees and career bureaucrats at EPA to replace the current bureaucratic leadership). If, however, the EPA implemented some policy *on* or *inside* this triangle in Figure 13.3, they might be able to get away with it. For any point inside the triangle, departure from it makes either the House or the Senate or the president worse off. But new legislation to punish an out-of-control agency and its existing leadership requires the simultaneous support of a House majority, a Senate majority, and the president. Thus, if EPA implements some policy on or inside the triangle, they can avoid political retribution.

Following this strategic calculus, the best EPA can do is implement the policy x'. It is the point closest to B, the agency's ideal, that satisfies the political requirements to avoid political reversal.[18] The difference between x and x' is termed *bureaucratic drift* by McNollgast.

Thus, we have a principal-agent relationship in which a political principal formulates policy and creates an implementation agent to execute its details. The agent, however, has policy preferences of its own and, unless subjected to further controls, inevitably will implement a policy that drifts towards its ideal.

A variety of controls exist that might conceivably restrict the bureaucratic drift. Indeed, legislative scholars often point to congressional hearings in which bureaucrats may be publicly humiliated; annual appropriations decisions which may be used to punish "out-of-control" bureaus; and the use of watchdog agents, like the Government Accountability Office, to monitor and scrutinize the bureau's performance. But these all come after the fact and aren't really credible threats to the agency (since the bureau has nipped those threats in the bud, so to speak, by strategically implementing x' in the triangle rather than some more extreme policy more to its liking).

---

[18] If the bureau *must* observe the financial restraint of not spending more than has been appropriated (given by the component of x on the vertical dimension), then x' will simply slide down the side of the triangle to the point that is the same height as x.

The most powerful before-the-fact political weapon is the *appointment process*. The adroit control of the location of *B* by the president and Congress (especially the Senate), through their joint powers of nomination and confirmation, especially if they can arrange for appointees who more nearly share the political consensus on policy, is a self-enforcing mechanism for assuring realiable agent performance.

A second powerful before-the-fact weapon, one especially emphasized by McNollgast, is *procedural controls*. The general rules and regulations that direct the manner in which federal agencies conduct their affairs are contained in the Administrative Procedures Act. This act almost always constitutes the boilerplate that is part of the enabling legislation creating and renewing every federal agency. It is not uncommon, however, for the procedures for an agency required by the enabling legislation to be tailored to suit particular circumstances.

For example, a political consensus on environmental matters (policy *x* in Figure 13.3) might be somewhat more sympathetic to businesses that have to bear the cost of retrofitting their plants to help maintain environmental integrity than is preferred by bureaucratic leaders in the EPA (as well as various environmental groups). Politicians, who have to live with the prospect of bureaucratic drift all the time, anticipate that the bureaucrats in the EPA will want to be more aggressive than the political consensus warrants. To reduce the prospects of drift, the politicians can write into the enabling legislation that the EPA must proceed on a case-by-case basis rather than by promulgating general rules affecting a wide range of cases. By insisting on this procedure, the politicians anticipate that business interests are in a far better position (privileged groups, in Mancur Olson's terms) to mobilize their supporters to participate in the public part of agency decision making *a case at a time* than are the environmental groups to mobilize their members. Environmental groups, on the other hand, would be better served if the agency could make decisions that were fewer in number but of greater impact and magnitude, since they would find it easier to mobilize for a few big pushes than to expose their members to the incremental "torture" of case-by-case deliberations.

To sum up, the principal-agent perspective on bureaucratic behavior treats bureaus as agents of politicians, implementing policies formulated by an enacting political coalition. The problem for the politicians constituting this coalition is that bureaucratic agents have missions, interests, and objectives of their own that may conflict with those of the politicians. Indeed, clever agents will take into account that to sanction a bureau that does not do the precise bidding of an enacting coalition, the component members of that coalition must act *in unison*—this is the constitutional requirement in the separation-of-powers political order of the United States. As long as the agent makes sure that no alternative is preferred by all component members of the enacting coalition to whatever it does, it will be spared punishment. (It is a bit like a dog on a leash who wants to go in a slightly different direction than its master wishes. As long as the dog makes sure the leash is not taut, it can wander about as it pleases.) The McNollgast approach, however, emphasizes an asymmetric advantage for politicians (in contrast to Miller-Moe and diametrically opposite to Niskanen). The enacting coalition can *anticipate* bureaucratic drift and make provisions in the enabling legislation to reduce it, if not eliminate it altogether. Of especial importance in this regard are the exercise of prudence in the nomination and confirmation of political appointees to lead bureaus, and the stipulation of specific administrative procedures that make it difficult for the bureau to flout the will of the principals.

CASE 13.1
CONGRESSIONAL OVERSIGHT:
POLICE PATROLS, FIRE ALARMS,
AND FIRE EXTINGUISHERS

The rational choice approach to intergovernmental relations has demonstrated the importance of principal-agent relationships between Congress and the bureaucracy. Critical to any principal-agent relationship is *monitoring*—the process whereby the principal ensures that the agent is complying with the former's preferences rather than shirking by pursuing the agent's own preferences. In the regulatory arena we are quite familiar with monitoring devices. Many readers, for example, are aware of congressional hearings in which agencies are raked over the coals to justify their activities and their budgets.

Although these public incidents of explicit monitoring are the most obvious, they are only part of the picture. Congressional committees and subcommittees are "continuously watchful" (in the language of the Legislative Reorganization Act of 1946) in other ways as well. In a classic paper, McCubbins and Schwartz[*] distinguish between *police-patrol* and *fire-alarm* oversight. Police-patrol oversight, as the name suggests, involves centralized and direct surveillance—congressional committees and their staffs "cruise" their respective jurisdictions looking for bureaucratic malfeasors. Congress initiates inspections, supervision, and direct instruction and oversight for its bureaucratic agents. Fire-alarm oversight, on the other hand, is relatively decen-

---

[*] Mathew D. McCubbins and Thomas Schwartz, "Congressional Oversight Overlooked: Police Patrols versus Fire Alarms," *American Journal of Political Science* 28 (1984): 165–79.

tralized, reactive, and indirect. In this instance Congress establishes rules and procedures that enable private parties (the customers or victims of the agency in question) to monitor agency practices and bring inappropriate activities to congressional attention. The service recipients, that is, can pull the lever on a fire alarm whenever agencies misuse their authority. (A third form of oversight, not covered by McCubbins and Schwartz, might be termed *fire-extinguisher* oversight. Service recipients, in this case, bring agency malfeasance to the attention not of Congress but to the federal courts instead. Congressional rules, in effect, give various categories of service recipients legal standing to sue in court for agency abuses.)

Legislators often prefer putting fire-alarm and fire-extinguisher oversight in place because they are less costly and time-consuming for the legislature than police-patrol oversight. Since legislator time and expertise is often quite limited, having the public monitor agency activities shifts many of these costs away from Congress and takes advantage of a broader base of expertise. Fire-extinguisher oversight has become particularly common in recent years as the size of the legislative agenda has enlarged and the complexity of the issues on it has increased. Groups, including the handicapped, minorities, farmers, workers, and small-business owners, have all been given legal standing in the jurisdiction of one or another regulatory agency. Thus, it is fair to say that nowadays the norm is for Congress to legislate the requirement that agencies and courts react to complaints rather than to inspect for violations itself.

Principal-agent relationships are ubiquitous in politics, economics, and social life. Your senator, your professor, your auto mechanic, and the pilot of your airplane are all your agents. Which ones are monitored by police patrols? Which submit to fire-alarm or fire-extinguisher monitoring?

AGENCY SLIPPAGE

We can draw on all three of the approaches to bureaucratic politics presented in this chapter to point out various manifestations of tension between politicians and bureaucrats. In civics-book descriptions of political institutions, it is often supposed that official political decisions, as reflected in statutes passed by Congress, signed by the president, and validated by various courts, are the final word. The business of politicians is the formulation of public policy, and constitutional procedures specify how this is done. But policies formulated according to even the most rigorous constitutional provisions are *not* the final word. Policies are not self-implementing. Someone must exercise the authority and expend the resources warranted by a statute. This "someone" is the bureaucrat. However, if the policy actually implemented by a bureaucratic agent departs from the policy formulated by his or her political principals, there is *agency slippage* or *drift*. It is produced by a combination of agent discretion, agent preferences different from those of the enacting political coalition, and imperfect control mechanisms. The three approaches developed in the preceding pages of this chapter highlight the different ways this slippage manifests itself.

Budgetary Exploitation

From Niskanen we have seen that specialized bureaucratic agents are very knowledgeable about the intricate details of policy making in their jurisdiction, perhaps more so than even specialists on legislative committees. Even though the latter are themselves policy specialists, they have many other hats to wear and roles to fill; they cannot devote the time and energy necessary to absorb all the arcane minutiae associated with implementing a specific public policy. For bureaucratic agents, on the other hand, these details are the core of their very existence and a constant preoccupation. This produces an effective informational advantage for the bureaucrat; it also provides an opportunity. If the bureaucrat's preferences differ from those of the enacting coalition, then he or she may use this oportunity to pursue personal priorities. Niskanen's argument suggests that this may be accomplished by disingenuously attracting the resources and authority either to pursue a personal agenda of policy objectives, or to siphon off resources to devote to on-the-job consumption. This is made possible because, according to Niskanen, the politicians just cannot wrap their minds entirely around the bureaucratic production process—they cannot figure out the details of the relationship between costs and policy outputs. This enables the bureau to earn a "profit," displayed in Figure 13.1, which can be put to alternative uses. If this informational advantage is converted into opportunities for on-the-job consumption, we have a pure instance of bureaucratic budgetary exploitation.

Bureaucratic Drift

If, on the other hand, authority and resources are used to pursue other policy objectives, then we have an instance of bureaucratic drift, as described by McNollgast and depicted in Figure 13.3. This follows from the ability of the bureaucrat to exercise discretion in his or her pursuit of policy priorities that may not have been warranted in statutory authority. This policy drift, moreover, is protected from after-the-fact retribution as long as the bureaucrat is crafty enough to protect against unanimous opposition from the components of the enacting coalition. In effect, if the bureaucrat can keep this key senator or that house committee chair content, he or she may be home free.

Bureaucratic Capture

A third source of tension requires that I make some finer distinctions than heretofore. The bureaucratic drift that McNollgast describes is the difference between the compromise policy arived at politically (x in Figure 13.3) and the policy implemented bureaucratically (x'). In that figure, however, the careful reader may have noticed that both the Senate (with ideal point S) and the president (with ideal point P) *actually like* x' *better than* x. Only the House (with ideal point H) loses from the drift in this particular example. If we retreat from the myth that the Senate and House are unitary and possess ideal points, instead more appropriately assuming that there are 435 ideal points scattered about H and 100 ideal points scattered about S, then it is very likely that a number of representatives and senators sympathize more with the bureaucrat's preferences than they do with either the political preference arrived at in their legislative chamber (H and S, respectively, in Figure 13.3) or the policy compromise arrived at among House, Senate, and president (x). To push the argument one step further, taking on board some of the factors I considered in the previous chapter, it is likely that the committees with jurisdiction over this bureaucracy and policy area are populated precisely with legislators who are more likely to share the bureaucrat's preferences for larger bureaucratic output than the preferences of their political colleagues for more modest levels (i.e., an *outlier* committee). They are in a position to *protect* a drifting bureaucracy (through their gatekeeping and other agenda-control powers). Finally, behind these legislators are the interest groups and geographic constituencies whose well-being the legislators pursue; they, too, will be pleased by the drift. Indeed, the traditional political science literature makes frequent allusion to "cozy little triangles," involving legislators on key committees, bureaucrats, and interest groups, as the dynamos behind policy implementation.

They are also referred to as "policy whirlpools" and "unholy trinities," and the politics this arrangement sustains is called "interest group liberalism," reflecting effective *capture* of the bureaucracy by interests in the wider political world.[19] In this case the tension is not between politician and bureaucrat, but rather among the politicians, bureaucrats, and interest groups *inside* the policy whirlpool and those on the outside.

Coalitional Drift

At the very outset of this discussion I noted that politicians not only want the legislative deals they strike to be faithfully implemented, they want those deals to endure—they want "deals struck to stay stuck," as the inside-the-Beltway pundits put it. This is especially problematic in American political life with its shifting alignments and absence of permanent political cleavages. Today's coalition transforms itself overnight. Opponents today are partners tomorrow and the reverse. This makes dealmakers inside the legislature, and their interest-group backers in the hustings, insecure. A victory today, even one implemented in a favorable manner by the bureaucracy, may be undone tomorrow. What is to be done?

To some extent legislative structure leans against undoing the handiwork of an enacting coalition. If such a coalition votes handsome subsidies to grain farmers, say, it is very hard to reverse this policy without the gatekeeping and agenda-setting resources of members on the House and Senate Agriculture Committees; yet their members undoubtedly participated in the initial deal and are unlikely to turn against it. But even these structural units are unstable, old politicians departing and new ones enlisted. The problem, then, is that

---

[19] The classic in the traditional political science literature is Theodore J. Lowi, *The End of Liberalism*, 2nd edition (New York: Norton, 1979). In economics, the classic is George Stigler, "The Theory of Economic Regulation," *Bell Journal of Economics and Management Science* 2 (1971): 3–21.

the members of an enacting coalition whose product may not be very durable cannot expect the kind of support from interest groups and voters, in whose behalf they work, that they might have received if they had produced a more robust result.

In short, legislatively formulated and bureaucratically implemented output is subject to coalitional drift.[20] Today's enacting coalition may no longer be in power tomorrow. To prevent shifting coalitional patterns among politicians to endanger carefully fashioned policies, one thing the legislature might do is *insulate* the bureaucracy and its implementation activities from legislative interventions. If an enacting coalition makes it difficult for its *own* members to intervene in implementation, then it also makes it difficult for enemies of the policy to disrupt the flow of bureau output at a later date. This political insulation can be provided by giving implementing agencies long lives, their political heads long terms of office and wide-ranging administrative authority, other political appointees overlapping terms of office, and security to their sources of revenue—like many of the "independent" regulatory commissions, the Federal Reserve System, and, to some extent, the intelligence agencies. But it comes at a price. The civil servants and political appointees of bureaus insulated from political overseers are thereby empowered to pursue independent courses of action. Protection from coalitional drift comes at the price of an increased potential for bureaucratic drift. It is one of the great trade-offs in the field of intergovernmental relations.

---

[20] This idea, offered as a supplement to the McNollgast line of argument, is found in Murray J. Horn and Kenneth A. Shepsle, "Administrative Process and Organizational Form as Legislative Responses to Agency Costs," *Virginia Law Review* 75 (1989): 499-509. It is further elaborated in Kenneth A. Shepsle, "Bureaucratic Drift, Coalitional Drift, and Time Consistency," *Journal of Law, Economics, and Organization* 8 (1992): 111-18.

CASE 13.2
HOW TO TEST NISKANEN?

Most of this book has been theoretical, designed to give you the ideas, concepts, and theories that comprise the analytical, or rational choice, approach to politics. In the cases sprinkled throughout, I have endeavored to provide real-world examples and applications, both to display evidence for theoretical arguments and to demonstrate how to apply various ideas to political situations and events in everyday life. In the present case we look at how two political economists set out to distinguish among competing theories of intergovernmental relations. Barry Weingast and Mark Moran* employ statistical analysis of data drawn from regulatory policy making at the Federal Trade Commission to evaluate some of the competing claims of the theories I have reviewed in this chapter. Their study is a useful example of how to apply empirical analysis to rational choice theories; it contributes to our understanding of intergovernmental relations as they are practiced in the real world.

In 1979, Congress, through the auspices of relevant committees and subcommittees, actively intervened to restrain the Federal Trade Commission (FTC) and to curb what were seen as regulatory abuses. Policy initiatives were criticized, FTC activities were halted, and funds were cut off. Over the next year and a half, the FTC curtailed its controversial activities and brought itself into alignment with the preferences of the congressional principals who oversaw its performance.

A Niskanen-like view of the situation is that the FTC was a "runaway" agency that used its informational advan-

---

* Barry R. Weingast and Mark J. Moran, "Bureaucratic Discretion or Congressional Control? Regulatory Policymaking by the Federal Trade Commission," *Journal of Political Economy* 91 (1983): 765–800.

tage to underwrite activities well beyond its mandate. When Congress finally woke up to the fact that the FTC was living too high off the bureaucratic hog, it clamped down and brought it back into line. An alternative view consistent with McNollgastian coalitional drift is that Congress was in control of the FTC all along. According to this view, a change in the composition and preferences of the oversight committees is responsible for the intervention. Because the FTC was not sufficiently insulated from legislative intervention, and even though it may well have been doing the bidding of a previously empowered legislative coalition, a new coalition of legislators came to power in the late 1970s and was able to use its oversight tool kit of hearings, procedures, and budgetary authority to move the agency's output toward the new ideal policy they represented. In short, in the late 1970s the FTC's legislative principal changed—through electoral turnover, retirements, and committee reassignments. These new guys yanked on the leash, pulling the FTC into line with its preferences.

So which is it? Was the FTC a runaway Niskanian bureaucracy exercising policy discretion? Or was Congress always in control, but a change in congressional preferences required a wake-up call to the FTC from the new congressional principals? To test these two views, Weingast and Moran gathered evidence to evaluate whether preferences of the membership of relevant oversight committees did change in the late 1970s and whether the new committees did indeed influence subsequent FTC behavior. The data examined consisted of interest group ratings of legislators by the liberal interest group, Americans for Democratic Action (ADA), whose scores, ranging from 0 to 100, measure a legislator's general disposition toward liberal causes. The scores for members of the Senate consumer affairs subcommittees indicate that there was a significant conservative drift in these bodies between 1976 and 1979 after more than a decade of virtually no change at all. This was accompanied by (indeed, it reflected) a substantial turnover of membership on these panels—liberal members had left these panels in large numbers to be replaced by much more conservative senators. The preferences of the oversight groups, in short, displayed a shift from a proactivism in consumer matters to an antiactivism stance during this period. The evidence, then, is quite consistent with the Mc-Nollgast argument. Moreover, in looking at ADA scores over the two decades preceding this turning point, Weingast and Moran find that the oversight panels were much more liberal, according to ADA scores, than in the late 1970s, which suggests that the FTC was actually serving as a loyal agent to the politicians in control at the time.

The conclusion to be drawn from this evidence is that the FTC was hardly a "runaway" bureaucracy, exploiting its asymmetric informational advantage in accord with Niskanen's theory. Rather, it appears to have been an agent that failed to notice that its principal had changed in the late 1970s. Once this principal—the more conservative legislative coalition on the oversight panel in the Senate—yanked hard on the leash, the agent once more fell into line.

CONCLUSION

It used to be fashionable in political science to distinguish between "politics" and "administration." Indeed, schools of public administration and schools of government still exist in some of our most venerable universities alongside separate departments of politics or political science. Fortunately, political scientists no longer hold to the notion that policy making and policy implementation can be sealed off from one another.

In this chapter I have suggested several different ways to think analytically about the connections between politicians and bureaucrats. Three different, but related, connective arguments have been developed. The first, associated with Niskanen, suggested that the permanent bureaucracy exploits its informational advantages vis-à-vis elected politicians, leading to bureaucratic budgets too large, bureaucrats too numerous, and bureaucratic output too abundant. The second, associated with Miller and Moe, took exception to Niskanen's assumptions of political ignorance and passivity. More informed and proactive politicians yield a more balanced arrangement of bilateral bargaining with bureaucrats, they concluded, and this need not nurture the maladies identified by Niskanen. Finally, McNollgast reversed Niskanen's emphasis altogether, suggesting that any asymmetry that may exist favors the political class who, as principals, create their agents, participate in appointing their leaders, sustain them with authority and resources, monitor their activities, and ultimately pass judgment over their actions.

Needless to say, there are important insights and elements of truth in each of these approaches. This is not a horse race in which I (or you) need to declare one of these approaches the winner. Indeed, in combination they draw our attention to a variety of tensions that exist and trade-offs that must be made to accommodate the sometimes conflicting priorities and preferences of politicians and bureaucrats. All in all, the politics of policy and the politics of administration are inseparable and complicated. The theories summarized here help us to make sense of how representative policy formulation and expert policy implementation fit together.

Problems and Discussion Questions

1. The idea of *term limits* for elected legislators and for chairs of legislative committees has been hotly debated for a quarter of a century (while, of course, presidents have been term-limited since ratification of the Twenty-second Amendment in 1951). In light of the principal-agent framework discussed in this chapter, how might you attack the idea of term limits? How would you defend it? Do the same arguments make sense for bureaucrats?

2. Niskanen's model of legislative-bureaucratic relations makes three very strong assumptions that ascribe to the bureaucracy extraordinary power in securing an oversized budget[a]: 1) The bureau's cost schedule is private information, while the legislature's demand schedule is public knowledge; 2) the bureau is the only supplier; 3) in its bargaining with the legislature, the bureau drives the policy-making process by making a single take-it-or-leave-it proposal to the legislature. Which of these assumptions do you find unrealistic or overly strong? What solutions have legislatures and other principals adopted to limit bureaucratic power in bargaining over budgets?

*3. A Niskanian bureaucracy supplies some output Q at the following cost: $TC = 1.5Q^2$ where costs are measured in tens of millions of dollars. If the legislature's willingness-to-pay curve is $B = 8Q - 2Q^2$, what is the maximum budget that the bureau can secure? Be sure to consider both demand and cost constraints. Now the legislature institutes the following monitoring scheme: With probability p the bureaucracy is audited

---

[a] See Dennis Mueller, *Public Choice III* (New York: Cambridge University Press, 2003), p. 365.

(which would reveal that the optimal level of production from the legislature's point of view is $Q^0 = 1.2$). If the bureaucracy is caught producing more than Q^0 it is forced to pay a fine of $f(Q - Q^0) = f(Q - 1.2)$, which is measured in the same units as production costs. Write out an expression for the bureau's expected total costs when it produces less than or equal to Q^0, and for when it produces more than Q^0. If $p = .2$, and $f = 5$, how much will the bureau produce? What about if $p = .5$, and $f = 10$? Illustrate the intuition behind these answers.

4. Members of Congress and bureaucrats both act as agents for their principals (voters for the former, the Congress and president for the latter). However, while representatives must periodically face election, bureaucrats are appointed and face no reelection constraint. What is the source of preference divergence between principals and agents in each of these cases? Does the presence of elections provide effective control of legislators? Does the lack of elections prevent effective control of bureaucracies, or are there other mechanisms? Discuss the variety of before-the-fact (both institutional and reputational) and after-the-fact controls adopted by voters and Congress to limit agent drift.

5. The following game is a styled representation of the strategic interaction between a principal (who delegates some authority to an agent and can choose whether or not to audit that agent's effort in any period) and an agent (who chooses whether to "work" or "shirk"). An audit is costly to the principal, but he doesn't have to pay the agent if he detects shirking. The particular payoffs arise from the following values associated with the relevant activities. The principal earns 4 if his agent works, but doesn't earn anything if the agent shirks. He pays the agent 3 to work, but if he audits and catches the agent shirking he doesn't have to pay the agent anything. An audit costs one unit to conduct; thus, if the agent works and

the principal audits, the principal nets out 0. It costs the agent 2 to do his work, so he of course prefers to shirk and not be audited (earning his wage without doing anything!) but fears getting audited and earning 0.

	Principal:	
Agent:	Audit	Don't Audit
Work	1, 0	1, 1
Shirk	0, –1	3, –3

Does either individual have a strategy that is optimal no matter what the other individual plays (as in the Prisoner's Dilemma)? Are any of the four cells equilibria? What percentage of the time must the principal inspect to make the agent indifferent between working and shirking? What percentage of the time must the agent work to make the principal indifferent between auditing and not auditing?

6. What motivates bureaucrats? Discuss the various theories, and explain why answering this question is significant for understanding and controlling the bureaucracy. Does the empirical evidence validate any one theory over and above the others?

14

Leadership

In the discussion of legislatures and bureaucracy I have made implicit reference to their leaders—committee and subcommittee chairs, party and ideological leaders, senior civil servants and political appointees. But I have not, until now, pulled out our rational-choice magnifying glass to take a closer look at leadership. This I do ever so briefly in the present chapter. In doing so, however, I will resist the temptation to write separately about presidents, governors, mayors, prime ministers, committee chairs, cabinet officers, party leaders, and interest group leaders. Instead, I will take this opportunity to write about leadership more generally.

The general subject of leadership is widely studied in sociology, psychology, and organizational behavior, as well as in political science but, as far as I know, rarely thought about from the rational-choice perspective. I can, however, mobilize some of the bits of theory recounted in earlier chapters to see what light they shed on leadership phenomena. First I describe leaders as *agents* and then think about them as *agenda setters* and *entrepreneurs*. Since these treatments draw on materials already covered in some detail elsewhere in this text, I will assume that the reader has a passing familiarity with some of the underlying concepts.[1]

---

[1] I also draw on the survey of Morris P. Fiorina and Kenneth A. Shepsle, "Formal Theories of Leadership: Agents, Agenda Setters, and Entrepreneurs," in Bryan D. Jones, ed., *Leadership and Politics* (Lawrence: University Press of Kansas, 1989): 17–41. The interested reader should consult this essay for an elaborated version of the argument found in this chapter.

In addition to slicing up leadership in various theoretically interesting ways, I set a second task in this chapter. I want to explore in some detail the problem facing leaders in self-governing groups. In order to lead, the leader, naturally enough, needs to induce followers to follow. But doing this may be costly to the leader—after all, he needs the *support* of followers to retain his leadership position. This sets in motion an interesting strategic situation.

THE LEADER AS AGENT

In ordinary language, we normally conceive of the leader as someone in charge, the boss, the person who gives orders and instructions—the person on whose desk, as President Harry S Truman reminded us, the buck stops. The leader is thought to be *proactive*, whereas followers are *reactive*.[2] While there may be some truth to this conceptualization, it is only a partial truth, for it does not take into account the fact that leaders must secure the support, if not the cooperation, of their followers. This support is necessary not only to enable the leader to accomplish various group objectives but also to retain the leadership post itself. This is certainly true of self-governing groups—those that officially select their leaders. But even the authoritarian leader has to worry about followers who, under the right circumstances, might otherwise be tempted to move against him or her.

The leader as agent of his or her followers is no better illustrated than by the experience of Henry Clay. Clay was elected from Lexington, Kentucky, to the 10th Congress in 1810. When Congress convened in 1811, Clay, a freshman

---

[2] Some years ago there was a *New Yorker* cartoon showing a formation of geese, minus its leader at the apex, flying off, with the "lead" goose scrambling to get out in front.

member, was elected Speaker of the House of Representatives, a post he did not relinquish during the fifteen years he served in the House. Time and time again he was reelected to this position, and his very first acceptance speech on November 4, 1811, the statement of the quintessential agent, tells us why:

> Gentlemen. In coming to the station which you have done me the honor to assign me—an honor for which you will be pleased to accept my thanks—I obey rather your commands than my own inclinations. I am sensible to the imperfections which I bring along with me, and a consciousness of these would deter me from attempting a discharge of the duties of the chair, did I not rely confidently upon your generous support.
>
> Should the rare and delicate occasion present itself when your speaker should be called upon to check or control the wanderings or intemperance in debate, your justice will, I hope, ascribe to his interposition the motives only of public good and a regard to the dignity of the house. And in all instances, be assured, gentlemen, that I shall, with infinite pleasure, afford every facility in my power to the despatch of public business, in the most agreeable manner.[3]

In stating that he would "obey rather your commands than my own inclination," and "afford every facility in my power to the despatch of public business, in the most agreeable manner," Clay was adopting the classic role of leader as follower. He was acknowledging the fact that as a major political leader, he had ambition to remain leader at the very least and wholly comprehended that to do so meant to lead his followers by *serving* them. He understood that the compensation of leadership—namely, continued incumbency in the Speaker's position—was *performance based*. The reward structure of leadership ties ambition (to remain leader in the next period) to performance (in the current period).

[3] James Hopkins, ed., *The Papers of Henry Clay*, volume I (Lexington: University of Kentucky Press, 1959).

This is true even for those whose incumbency as leader is assured. The bureau chief whose position is guaranteed by civil service practices, for instance, nevertheless depends upon her underlings, whether it is to secure policy objectives of importance to her or merely to maintain the quiet life. As long as the leader has objectives that depend upon the contribution, cooperation, and morale of subordinates, the latter have some hold on her.

We saw in the previous chapter that a principal generally depends upon his or her agent. Indeed, he or she hires an agent in the first place because agents are often more skilled in accomplishing particular purposes than principals themselves are. Leaders are a specific sort of agent. They are relied upon by followers to coordinate their activities, to provide rewards and punishments for group objectives, to secure allies and defeat opponents, and generally to "grease the skids" for the things followers want. Leaders are normally chosen for the specialized skills they possess—to reason, persuade, bully, inspire, rally, intimidate, mediate, and so on. The problem for followers, a special instance of the problem facing principals more generally, is that the specialized skills that make a particular agent attractive as leader are also the skills by which that agent can exploit his or her followers for private gain. The "who will guard the guardians" question becomes "how will we control our agent?"

As in the general case developed in the previous chapter, leaders may be controlled by their followers through before-the-fact and after-the-fact mechanisms. Candidates for leadership positions, like agents more generally, have reputations. Even Henry Clay, who was but a freshman legislator when elected Speaker, was already well known in Washington as an avid "warhawk" (supporting war against Great Britain).[4] Rep-

---

[4] He had only recently completed a six-month term filling in as Senator from Kentucky, during which time he made a number of well-publicized speeches in favor of war and generally displayed his charismatic capabilities.

utation is, in effect, a summary of an individual's specialized skills as leader—it reflects not only her résumé of experiences and policy predispositions but also aspects of character, probity, and talent. Reputation is undoubtedly one of the central elements in the decision calculus of followers when they set about selecting a leader in the first place.

Reputation not only serves as a before-the-fact performance predictor, but also it is an asset highly valued by its owner. In a sense, a leader posts her reputation as a *bond* when she takes on a leadership responsibility. The reputation is put on the line, so to speak, and will either be enhanced or tarnished on the basis of her performance. By virtue of a leader caring about her reputation, whether to enable her to achieve some future leadership position, to maintain her current post, or merely to acquire "a place in history," followers have some control over her performance.

Thus, reputation is also an after-the-fact control mechanism, since it involves follower authority over the leader's future. Certainly whenever there are others waiting in the wings, an incumbent leader knows he or she is not indispensable. At the time of "contract renewal," he or she must be able to answer to the satisfaction of sufficient numbers of followers the age-old question, "What have you done for me lately?"

Thinking of leaders as agents puts an entirely different spin on the idea of leadership found in ordinary discourse. Leaders are dependent on followers for accolades, for cooperation, and ultimately for support. Leaders may be shrouded in authority, may act like the boss, may order and instruct, but all of these proactive leadership maneuvers are calculated to impress followers, thereby earning their subsequent support, not to bully them. What this suggests, therefore, is that we need to look beyond a leader's *capabilities*, which can sometimes be awesome, to his or her *intentions*, of which he or she is typically a prisoner. To the extent the latter depend upon follower support, the tables are turned—the master is servant and the servant master. We will need to keep these things in mind as we examine next some of the capabilities of leaders.

CASE 14.1
FDR AND WORLD WAR II

A leader is often placed in the difficult position of choosing between what his or her followers want and what he or she feels they need. This distinction was made especially clear by the eighteenth-century English philosopher Edmund Burke in his famous speech to the electors of Bristol. A member of Parliament at the time running for reelection, he made clear to his constituents that he would not go back to Westminster as a mere *delegate*—someone who simply represents and acts as an unreflective agent of constituency opinion. Rather, he regarded himself as a *trustee*—someone whose intelligence and expertise would be deployed in the service of what he considered to be the best interests of his constitutents. (Burke was defeated for reelection.) Henry Clay, on the other hand, cast his role as Speaker as more that of a delegate: "I obey rather your commands than my own inclination." (Clay was reelected to that post for fifteen years.) Should a leader continue to obey, or should he follow his own inclination? The answer depends to a large extent on how a leader interprets his mandate as an agent.

In the years leading up to World War II, Franklin Roosevelt was faced with a difficult dilemma. He followed the Nazi march through Europe with great alarm. Public opinion in the United States at the time was decidedly isolationist, but Roosevelt saw a need to begin providing aid to Great Britain and to prepare the country for war. He believed that delaying mobilization until Germany posed an immediate threat to the United States would be too late.

And yet, most Americans felt this was a "European problem," one in which the United States should not engage.

A delegate's course of action would have been to follow public opinion and wait. But Roosevelt saw himself, like Burke, as a trustee and began taking secret action early on to prepare the nation for war. He used his skills as an agenda setter and political entrepreneur to mobilize resources and generate popular support. His ability to take the lead—to get out ahead of public opinion—derived from the reputational capital he had accumulated during his years of grappling with the economic disaster caused by the Great Depression. Roosevelt's actions prior to World War II exemplify the interrelatedness of agent, agenda setter, and entrepreneur facets of leadership, as well as the importance of reputation in facilitating leadership maneuvering room. I examine these topics more explictly in the next several sections below.

The Leader as Agenda Setter

The alternative views of leaders that are surveyed in this chapter are by no means mutually exclusive. Indeed, implicitly at least, all of these views are compatible with the agent perspective I just finished reviewing. Once a leader is conceived as an agent for a coalition of followers, it is possible to turn to the more precise sorts of things he or she does in that capacity. In this section I do just that, envisioning the leader as the person in charge of the group's agenda.

A group, whether civil servants in a bureau, legislators on a committee, or members of a faculty, have a variety of things they may wish to achieve together with only finite resources. They can't do everything; choices must be made about where to devote their attention and other scarce resources. Of course, some of the activities of a group may be mandated by others. The Social Security Administration *must* churn out those checks every month. The Budget Committee *must* produce an annual budget resolution. The faculty of arts and sciences *must* determine and approve a list of degree candidates each year prior to graduation.[5] However, it is unusual for a group to have no discretion regarding its activities, so choices about how to exercise that discretion must be made. And this is precisely one of the things a leader does.

Consider a department in a university, say political science, and its chair. Many of the activities of that department are determined by others—university rules, the dean, the board of trustees. It must organize its curriculum for the coming academic year. It must have requirements for various degree programs in place. It must decide which graduate students to admit to its doctoral program. It must see to the administration of examinations, the grading of theses, and the determination of prizes and honors. But there is still room on the departmental plate for discretionary activities. Should the department focus its attention this year on revising the graduate program, or defer it to next year? Should the department fill the vacant assistant professor post for which it has authorization and, if so, should it search for someone whose specialty is rational-choice theory, congressional politics, or comparative judicial policy? Should the department promote an especially promising younger colleague to tenure, or put the promotion off for a year? Should the department begin negotiating with the Department of African American Studies over a joint undergraduate degree? The list is enormous, constrained only by the imagination of its faculty on ways to spend time and other resources.

---

[5] By "must" I do not mean these things are inviolable laws of nature, like gravity or the first law of thermodynamics. Rather, some things are so fundamental to a group that its very existence depends upon accomplishing them. Failure to do so risks having the group replaced or its jurisdiction altered.

Discretionary choices for a group about where to devote its energies are highly influenced by its leader. The department chair undoubtedly will be heavily lobbied on all the matters listed in the previous paragraph, and some of the decisions may not be hers alone to make. But her input will be important, mainly because in any group the buck must stop somewhere, authority to deploy group resources must reside somewhere, and deciding all such issues town-meeting style is exhausting and inefficient. Most members of a departmental faculty do not wish to spend most of their waking hours on departmental business—they have their own personal agendas to prosecute. Thus, even though not all of them will be pleased with every decision their agent makes on their behalf, the delegation of authority to the chair to set the department's discretionary agenda is often the efficient division of labor to institute. The members of the department content themselves with having had some say on who that agent would be in the first place (a before-the-fact control mechanism), how long she will survive in the job (an after-the-fact control mechanism), and whether she will enjoy an uncomfortable or exalted post-chair existence in the department (another after-the-fact control mechanism).

The chair, on the other hand, will weigh the effects of these various control mechanisms against her opportunity to steer the department's agenda in the direction of her own preferences. Suppose, for instance, she cares quite a bit about the graduate program but is not keen to promote her younger colleague at the present time. By announcing the appointment of a graduate review committee but not taking action on a tenure review, she accomplishes her ends but may have to endure the wrath of those with different preferences. Indeed, she may get "rolled"—one of her senior colleagues may, during a faculty meeting, argue that it is imperative that the department move on the tenure case, a view supported by many others in the department (even though the chair had tried to keep that off the agenda). Since a leader cannot afford to get rolled too frequently—if this occurs, it becomes increasingly difficult for an agent to convince her principals that she has their interests at heart—she will want to give careful consideration to the distribution of preferences among those she leads. Likewise, in deciding to exercise an after-the-fact control mechanism like rolling the chair, a follower must determine exactly how much damage this will inflict on a leader he otherwise thinks is satisfactory.[6] In short, care must be exercised to detect but not to cross any number of rather fuzzy lines. In the end the chair can extract some agenda advantages (an unavoidable form of agency slippage), but she must be prudent, not piggish. This problem is normally least serious at the *beginning* of a chair's term; at the end of a chair's term in office, especially one who would like to retire to her own work, agency slippage becomes more problematic (the so-called *end-game problem*).

I have developed the interaction over agenda setting between a chair and her colleagues in a university department, not only because it is interesting in its own right (at least to the author, whose life is substantially affected by this agency relationship), but also because it is an exemplar of the opportunities possessed by leaders of groups in general to trade off satisfying the preferences of their followers in order to secure some of their own objectives. Refining the group's agenda is one of the standard activities that a group delegates to a leader (or an agenda committee). In doing so, there is ordinarily an awareness in the group that a "pound of flesh" will be exacted by the leader-agent. Politically savvy choices, by the group in selecting the leader and by the leader in exercising her agenda authority, place limits on this "compensation." Should those limits be breached, revolt soon follows.

---

[6] He will also have to weigh the consequences of trying, but *failing*, to roll the chair. The age-old adage applies: "If you go after the king, you had better get him."

Before leaving the subject of leader as agenda setter, we should revisit some of the material of Part II of this volume, emphasizing the manipulation of agenda procedures at a more refined level. Not only does a leader have considerable sway over an institution's agenda "in the large," he or she also regulates the fine-grained deliberation over specific items on the agenda. This aspect of agenda setting is multifaceted.

The Speaker of the U.S. House of Representatives has a host of opportunities to influence, directly or indirectly, how member proposals will be treated by the full House. At the outset, when a bill is initially "dropped in the hopper" as a legislative proposal, the Speaker and his right-hand official, the Parliamentarian, determine which committee has jurisdiction over the proposal. As in our earlier discussion, the leader in this case may not have complete discretion. He cannot send a farm bill to the Merchant Marine Committee and he cannot transmit a bill reforming the criminal code to the Armed Services Committee. But many proposals do not match cleanly and naturally with the established jurisdictions of House committees, so the Speaker has some discretion. Indeed, since the mid-1970s, the Speaker has been given additional bill-assignment powers, known as *multiple referral*, permitting her to assign different parts of a bill to different committees, or to assign the same parts sequentially or simultaneously to several committees. We have already seen in Chapter 12 that committees, once assigned a bill, are in a position to exercise before-the-fact gatekeeping and proposal powers and after-the-fact negotiating and oversight powers. The Speaker is in a position to determine *which* panel(s) exercise(s) these powers.[7]

---

[7] The Speaker is often instrumental, moreover, on exactly who serves on which committee. Until 1910 in the House of Representatives, the Speaker made all committee assignments. Even after that date, up to the present, the Speaker's influence is felt in this absolutely crucial institutional process. In other legislatures, the Speaker or equivalent institutional officer remains the pivotal person in terms of committee assignments. And, of course, in other venues, the leader is often decisive in this respect. In most academic

Once the committee or committees assigned a bill have acted affirmatively, the whole bill or the various parts of it acted on by multiple panels are transmitted to another arm of the leader, the Rules Committee, which determines the specific rules under which the legislation will be considered by the full House. Here the leader influences when debate will be scheduled, for how long, what amendments will be in order, and in what order they will be considered. She also rules on all procedural points of order and points of information raised during the debate. We saw in Part II that, when a bill is multidimensional in nature, a modicum of preference diversity is all that is required to produce majority voting cycles. This means that the order of taking up amendments, and procedural rulings on what must seem to the outsider to be minor matters, will be decisive in determining what actually results at the end of the process.

Although I have used the leader of a legislature to illustrate points about fine-grained agenda control, I should emphasize that a crucial resource of all leaders is their procedural discretion. If every procedural issue were hardwired, then the leader would be impotent. But rarely is this the case. (To be so, the writers of rules would have had to anticipate just about every possible contingency that might arise in the history of that institution and to have bothered to write down in the rules exactly what must be done in each circumstance.) Thus, if a department interviews four candidates for an assistant professorship, the department chair often has the opportunity to suggest the voting method that will be used to choose among them. (Anyone opposing her suggestion will appear to have an ax to grind.) In claiming that she needs a final rank-

---

departments, for example, the chair composes committees. If, from our earlier example, the department chair did not want to promote a junior colleague to tenure, yet felt constrained from keeping the matter off the agenda entirely, she could influence the result by having the candidate reviewed by an artfully crafted committee that is likely to reflect her own doubts.

ordering (so that if the first choice were to decline the offer, she would know to whom to turn next), she could suggest that each voting faculty member write down a single name—and candidates would be ranked in terms of the total votes each got—or that each faculty voter submit a complete rank-ordering, from which a group rank-ordering would be derived (see Chapter 4). Indeed, as Chapter 7 makes clear, many different voting systems might be employed in this circumstance, any one of which the chair could defend by appealing to attractive criteria the voting system satisfied. If she has kept her ear to the ground, she will be able to make this "suggestion" in an informed strategic fashion. Such are the agenda-setting opportunities with which a leader is presented.

THE LEADER AS ENTREPRENEUR

The final conception of leader I consider here is that of the entrepreneur. Although compatible with agent and agenda-setter conceptions, it emphasizes something slightly different.[8] Entrepreneurs are leaders who, as often by self-appointment as by selection, perform necessary services to enable a group to accomplish some collective purpose. An entrepreneur, in fact, may not even be a member of the group in question. Indeed, the group in question may not even be a group in any manifest sense. Rather it may come into being, so to speak, because of the enterpreneur's activities. In this situation, an entrepreneur may be seen as an *agent who chooses (or creates) a principal*, rather than the more typical arrangement in which a principal hires an agent.

---

[8] The classics in the leadership literature emphasizing entrepreneurs are Richard Wagner, "Pressure Groups and Political Entrepreneurs," *Papers on Non-Market Decision Making* 1 (1966): 161–70; and Norman Frohlich, Joe Oppenheimer, and Oran Young, *Political Leadership and Collective Goods* (Princeton, N.J.: Princeton University Press, 1971).

I made mention in Chapter 9 of political entrepreneurs, suggesting them as one "solution" to the problem of collective action. I have little to add here, except to note that this conception of leadership emphasizes, perhaps more than the others we've discussed, the artistry of seizing opportunities. As entrepreneurs, leaders shop around for unrealized possibilities. These may be things the leader cares about. A young University of California graduate student, Mario Savio, became a folk hero in the 1960s when he coalesced Berkeley students into what became the Free Speech Movement. A young attorney named Ralph Nader took on General Motors in the 1960s in the first of many events that culminated in the consumer movement. In the 1950s a black minister named Martin Luther King Jr. led a boycott against the segregated public transportation system in Montgomery, Alabama, in an important early episode of what became the modern civil rights movement. At about the same time, the separate ideological and organizational acts of the entrepreneurs Malcolm X, Stokely Carmichael, and Huey Newton gave rise to the Black Power movement. In each case a political entrepreneur, committed ideologically to the cause for which he fought, seized leadership by his very acts of leadership. Sometimes this leadership involved mobilizing people who conceived of themselves as members of a group but had failed to achieve group objectives; other times it involved people who, by entrepreneurial acts of leadership, were forged into a group. The leader reaped not only ideological satisfaction but personal glory as well.

Implicitly, though, I have hinted that the entrepreneur need not care very much about the issue in which he or she plays a leadership role. Rarely will an entrepreneur be indifferent. But not so rarely, he or she may "entrepreneur" an issue for reasons other than achieving a satisfactory resolution of that issue. Sometimes the entrepreneur is a control freak who consumes utiles from the very act of leading. Other times, the entrepreneur derives payoffs from group members out of gratitude. Political leaders who act entrepreneurially occasionally fall into this latter category, pushing issues that they believe may have an electoral or campaign-finance payoff from grateful beneficiaries.[9] Finally, it should be noted that some entrepreneurs, especially young, politically motivated lawyers in Washington, D.C., or one of the state capitals, play the entrepreneurial game because they see it as a career investment, enabling them to build "can-do" reputations, networks of contacts, and opportunities for shoulder rubbing with potential mentors.

Political entrepreneurship is not for the weak-kneed or risk-averse. For every Mario Savio, Ralph Nader, and Martin Luther King, there are hundreds—perhaps thousands—of failed entrepreneurs. The market for political entrepreneurship, like the market for economic entrepreneurship, rewards creativity and insight, but many who think they have one or both are often sadly mistaken. Sometimes it is just dumb luck that elevates one entrepreneur to fame (or notoriety).

Agenda setting, agency, and entrepreneurship are but different facets of the same leadership phenomenon. What especially distinguishes them from one another is the degree to which they reflect greater or lesser structure in the context in which leadership is exercised. Although agenda setting has its capacity for displays of flair, it is a relatively highly structured activity within a tightly bounded institutional setting. Agency activities, though still exhibiting the characteristics of a structured relationship, are a bit broader. Entrepreneurship is broader still, emphasizing not only those actions that occur within a fixed structure but also the actions that create or

---

[9] The author, while interviewing congressional staff in the early 1980s, discovered that it was not uncommon for a legislative staff director to assign staffers to monitor committee hearings around Capitol Hill with the instruction, "Find something useful for the boss." Members of Congress, that is, often shop around for issues that they believe they can convert to some useful purpose for themselves.

transform structure. It is, in a sense, the richest conception of leadership but it is also the most vague. I return to the more rigorous form of analysis in the last part of this chapter, focusing on the strategic trade-offs facing a leader concerned with maintaining and enhancing her reputation.

REPUTATION AND LEADERSHIP

CASE 14.2
ONLY NIXON COULD GO TO CHINA

It is sometimes said in political circles that only Nixon could have gone to China. In the early 1970s the United States recognized the People's Republic of China (then referred to as Red China or Communist China), and President Richard Nixon visited the country, the first chief executive ever to have done so. Both actions were highly controversial at the time, given the severity of the Cold War, the strength of anticommunist sentiment, suspicions about Chinese motives during the end phase of the Vietnam War, and loyalty to our ally in Taiwan.

Why was it, then, that "only Nixon" could go to China? According to some, only a conservative with sterling anticommunist credentials could have gotten away with it. A liberal Democrat would have been seen as soft on communism and would not have been able to convince the public that his or her motives were aligned with the best interests of the nation rather than with some private ideological agenda. Is there any merit to this argument?

The discussion of reputation and leadership presented in this chapter can provide some help. Prior to his recognition of and trip to Communist China, Nixon had estab-

---

lished a reputation as a "red-baiter" of the highest order. The prospective cost to him in terms of his standing with the right wing of the Republican party was very high, indeed. He could therefore credibly claim that he was *not* prosecuting a private agenda. By bearing this cost he could persuasively claim that he was performing as an "agent of the nation," thereby persuading his principals (who not only controlled his political future but also would determine his "standing in history") that he was not shirking his official responsibilities. A more liberal president, acting in the same way, would have sent a much more ambiguous signal. His actions would therefore have been suspect, since it would have been difficult for the public to determine whether he was acting in behalf of a private agenda or with a broader view of the nation's welfare.

Similar interpretations may be offered for Lyndon Johnson's civil rights policies during the 1960s and Ronald Reagan's fiscal policies during the 1980s. Johnson, for many years a Texas politician with a local reputation for using race in unsavory ways, became one of the political pillars of the civil rights movement. His leadership in the U.S. Senate in the mid-1950s produced the first civil rights bill in nearly a century. His leadership as president was essential in passing the Civil Rights Act of 1964 and the Voting Rights Act of 1965. Nearly twenty years later, Ronald Reagan's presidency amassed the largest set of budget deficits in the history of the Republic (surpassed recently by the conservative George W. Bush). It is widely believed that only a conservative president with a strong reputation for fiscal prudence and a belief in smaller government could have gotten away with such policies. In each of these cases, as with Nixon, a strong reputation enables considerable counterintuitive flexibility. As they say, "only Nixon could have gone to China."

Every politician leader faces the problem of how most effectively
to sanction uncooperative behavior by followers. Sanctions may
be costly, but for the most successful leaders the mere threat of
such sanctions is usually sufficient. Since the strength of leadership can be an important determinant of how, and how well, a
political organization functions, students of political organization
need to understand the theoretical conditions for effective
leadership.

With these remarks, Randall Calvert introduces a provocative model about the trade-offs that confront the leader of a
political organization.[10] Although he focuses on *legislative*
leadership, the questions he worries about are generic, applying to bureaucratic leaders, university leaders, interest group
leaders—in short, leaders of any political organization.

The context is one in which a group of kindred spirits, seeking to accomplish group goals, creates a leadership structure
and appoints a particular incumbent to help them solve various collective action problems. As kindred spirits, members of
the group share much in common, but they are not perfect
copies of one another. Members of a university department,
for instance, may all want to appoint an assistant professor in,
say, American politics, but some favor a congressional specialist, others an expert on elections and voting behavior, still others an authority on the presidency. Similarly, the members of
the majority party in a legislature may share a preference for
health care legislation, but various factions among them push
for somewhat different versions (an unpleasantness that faced
President Barack Obama as he struggled with health care legislation in 2009–10).

Whatever is ultimately accomplished will, on net, make
the group members better off; however, some will be more
pleased with the result than others. And those less pleased

---

[10] "Reputation and Legislative Leadership," *Public Choice* 55 (1987): 81–120.
The passage quoted in the text appears on page 81.

may be tempted to defect from the group's effort, deserting it at a crucial vote, for instance. In order to keep this prospect from being totally debilitating, the leader must threaten, and sometimes actually employ, sanctions against renegades. For coordinating the group's activities, forging compromises among the heterogeneous preferences of group members, and holding enough of its members together to succeed in approving and implementing that compromise, the leader receives "compensation."[11]

Calvert assumes that in prosecuting the group's agenda of objectives, cajoling, exhorting, and sometimes punishing group members in the process, the leader must maintain a minimal level of group support. There are always leaders-in-waiting, ready to step in to take control if the incumbent leader should stumble. This means that sanctions by the leader against group members are *costly*, because they are administered against members whose support is desired by the leader. The leader must assiduously balance the benefits, in terms of group success, against the costs, in terms of threats to her leadership, of employing sanctions. As Calvert puts it, "any given punishment increases by a small amount the probability that the leader will face a full-scale rebellion, deposing him or impairing his ability to lead in the future. In this sense, the leader faces a kind of budget constraint on his ability to impose sanctions."

Calvert also assumes that the precise nature of the benefits to the leader (in terms both of achieving group goals and obtaining private "compensation"), and of her costs of employing sanctions and bearing the associated risks, is private information. The leader knows these benefits and costs, but followers have only the vaguest sense. By cultivating this un-

---

[11] This compensation comes in various forms, not the least of which is the opportunity for the leader to squeeze private advantage out of her agenda setting powers, something discussed earlier in this chapter.

certainty, the leader is able to make followers *believe* that punishment is possible more often than under conditions of complete information. And even in those cases where punishment is "too costly" (as objectively seen by a fully informed observer), the leader may nevertheless engage in sanctioning behavior in order to mislead followers into believing that her costs are lower than they actually are. In short, uncertainty about leadership benefits and costs allows the leader to bluff, deceive, and dissemble—the stuff of which *reputations* are made (and maintained).

In any given circumstance of leader-follower relations, the context is bound to be rich in history and details, making it hard to sort out the underlying factors at work. Calvert proposes a very simple formal model that permits attention to be focused on these underlying factors. In abstracting away from the substantive details of a specific situation, of course, much is lost. But doing so permits the investigator to capture the effects of factors that are present, in one manifestation or another, in all such circumstances. This is the advantage of a formal model.

Display 14.1 gives the formal structure of Calvert's setup. If the follower (Mr. t) supports the leader's proposal—say by voting for the committee chair's bill or supporting the department chair's job candidate—the leader earns "credit" toward reelection or reappointment, a (where $a > 1$), while follower t receives whatever payoff he associates with achieving the group's common objective (normalized to 0 without affecting the argument). If, on the other hand, the follower rebels, then the payoffs depend on what the leader does in response. If she acquiesces in the rebellion, allowing follower t to oppose her proposal, then she gets less than what she would have if the follower had obeyed (again normalized to 0) and the follower gets more (some positive level $b < 1$ rather than 0 if he did not rebel). Finally, if the follower's rebellion is punished, then the leaders bears a cost, $-x_t$ and the follower gets $b-1$, a number less than 0 (since *b* is less than 1). In this latter circumstance follower *t* does *not* know the value of $-x_t$; he does not know whether or not punishment in this case is costly to the leader or how much (since he does not know how solid her hold on office is). Rather, follower *t* has beliefs, namely that $-x_t$ is costly (equal to -1) with probability *w*, and costless (equal to 0) with probability $1-w$. Although follower *t* has only *probabilistic beliefs* about the costliness of punishment to the leader, the leader knows the value of $-x_t$ in advance—she is always fully informed of the consequences of her actions.

DISPLAY 14.1

Behavior	Payoff of Leader	Payoff of Follower *t*
Follower *t* obeys	*a*	0
Follower *t* rebels; Leader acquiesces	0	*b*
Follower *t* rebels; Leader punishes	$-x_t$	$b-1$

One more thing: followers are capable of learning. Their belief, *w*, that punishment is costly changes as they observe the leader in action. Thus, leaders not only have asymmetric information about the costliness of administering punishments, they also are able to influence subsequent beliefs of followers about this information. If, for instance, she is able to convince followers that punishments are mainly costless to her, then she is likely to induce more follower loyalty to her proposals (and thus not even have to use punishments). This might be accomplished by administering punishments early in her incumbency, even in those circumstances in which such acts are really costly to her. A department chair, for example, might deny a senior American scholar in her department an assignment he covets to the American politics recruitment committee, because he has announced a preference to appoint someone with a specialty different from the one the chair prefers. In fact, she will take a lot of heat for leaving him off the recruitment committee—something she knows in advance, but others in the department do not (at least not for certain). She does it anyhow to affect the beliefs of her colleagues about her freedom of action, conveying to them probabilistically at least that she doesn't regard this "heat" as of much consequence. Next time around, on some other issue in the department, fewer of her colleagues will be disposed to oppose because they believe it is more likely that she can "punish" them costlessly.

In short, she is on her way toward establishing a *reputation* for not tolerating rebellious behavior. It does not mean she will never encounter opposition, only that her colleagues will think hard before moving against her proposals. Of course, she too will think hard about the nature of the proposals she makes in the first place. Life will exist mainly and happily in the first row of Display 14.1 in which her colleagues enjoy the achievement of common objectives (if not always exactly to their liking), the chair is secure in her leadership, and punishments do not have to be meted out (looming only as a club behind the door).

Calvert models leader reputation-building by studying the "game" in Display 14.1 repeated exactly twice.[12] In effect, the leader faces the possible rebellion first of follower t_1 and then of follower t_2. What she does in the case in which follower t_1 rebels will affect what t_2 subsequently does, inasmuch as he will update his beliefs about how costly it is for the leader to punish rebellion. The actual cost to the leader of punishing rebellion on each occasion in which it occurs (equal to –1 with probability w and 0 with probability $1-w$) is known to the leader in advance of her choices.

---

[12] This keeps the math manageable while at the same time allowing the analyst to see what happens to the leader over time.

Calvert shows that there is actually a "best way" for each of the three players to play this game. Some of the details are obvious (but reassuring to see that his "toy model" has actually captured them). First, if $-x_t$ actually is 0 (costless punishment), then the leader should always punish rebellion. Second, if $-x_2 = -1$ (i.e., it is costly for the leader to punish the second follower), then she should never punish t_2; there would be no purpose served in doing so (since the game ends) and thus no point in bearing the cost of punishing.

Less obvious, and more interesting, is what the leader should do if $-x_1 = -1$. In providing insight on this issue, Calvert's model is far more than a toy for capturing the obvious. He shows that the leader's response to rebellion by t_1 when it is costly to punish depends in very specific ways on the beliefs followers hold about the leader's costs of punishment relative to the benefits they would secure from rebelling. It takes us too far afield to go into the details of Calvert's conclusion, except to say that Calvert identifies very precisely when t_1 should rebel, when a leader should punish that rebellion for certain, when a leader should "flip a coin" (or randomize in some other way) to determine whether to punish this particular transgression, and whether, conditional on all this, t_2 should rebel (for certain or with some probability).

The important conclusion of this analysis is that leaders, created to enable followers to achieve commonly held objectives despite their temptation to defect occasionally, need to establish a reputation for being willing to sanction uncooperative behavior. If such sanctioning were costless, leaders would be incredibly powerful, perhaps too powerful from the vantage point of followers. If, on the other hand, punishing followers for transgressions were too costly, then leaders would be so weak that they could not discourage such transgressions at all; group efforts would be plagued by defections, reneging on promises, and other forms of uncooperative behavior which the leadership institution was invented to control in the first place. But if leaders can maintain some uncertainty about the costliness to them of punishing transgressors, then (depending on many specific features of the situation detailed by Calvert's theoretical results) they may be in a position to build a reputation that causes potential rebels, at least some of the time, to have second thoughts about rebelling. We cannot improve on Calvert's concluding paragraph:

> Despite the apparent bare-bones nature of the model presented here, it serves to focus attention on a neglected aspect of political leadership. Since a successful leader cannot be constantly monitoring and punishing followers, it is necessary to establish in the followers a habit of obedience, a rule of thumb that the leader's wishes are to be followed. Habits and rules of thumb do not occur in a world of perfect and costless information. Thus the presence of uncertainty, and the artful manipulation of it, are crucial for successful leadership. Somewhat counterintuitively, this holds true regardless of whether the leader is a ruthless dictator or a benevolent provider of collective action.

CONCLUSION

Rather than writing separately about all the different kinds of political executives we find in the real world—presidents, premiers, CEOs, chairs, governors, mayors—I have instead described some interpretations of the institution of political leadership drawn from the analysis presented in earlier parts of this book. One message, I hope, comes through clearly: *An understanding of leadership depends upon an understanding of followership.* Leaders are often invented by followers. Even when they are not, they depend upon followers, both for the cooperation needed to secure group objectives and for the support enabling the leader to maintain her position. This is explicitly recognized in the agent perspective on leadership which we took to be the prevalent way of thinking about leaders. Accordingly, leaders must be empowered to accomplish for their followers what the followers are unable to accomplish without leaders, but not so empowered that they are able to pursue a private agenda without regard for follower preferences. Leaders must be proactive but, ultimately, under the control of their followers.

As to what leaders (and followers) actually do, I focused on agenda setting, general entrepreneurial activity, and reputation building as elements in a leader's behavioral repertoire. Throughout I have emphasized that leadership is a *solution* to a series of problems that groups face in trying to pursue common objectives. If these problems did not exist—that is, if we lived in a perfect world—then collective action could be pursued with ease. But the world is not perfect, so institutions like leadership must be devised as second-best solutions. And these solutions, in turn, possess problems of their own—hence the need for control mechanisms. Organizational life is a balancing act—between leaders and followers, between controlling agents and securing goals of principals, between exploiting the division and specialization of labor and giving advantages to specialized individuals. Our attention has been focused on those features of leadership in organizational life. For the nuance and subtlety that accompanies the interactions between real leaders and real followers in particular contexts, there is a rich vein of political biography for the interested reader to mine.

Problems and Discussion Questions

1. Benjamin Disraeli, the nineteenth-century British prime minister, held: "I must follow the people. Am I not their leader?" Discuss the two images of leadership implicitly com-

pared in this quotation: the leader as *trustee* and the leader as *delegate*. Are these visions of leadership necessarily in conflict?

2. This chapter has argued that the principal-agent framework developed in Chapter 13 can be productively applied to understanding the delegation of authority to leaders. Discuss the principal-agent problem in general, describe the ways in which it applies to the problem of choosing leaders, and then discuss a variety of before-the-fact and after-the-fact means of controlling leaders that ameliorate the principal-agent problem. In answering this final part, you may find it useful to contrast publicly elected officials (the president, members of Congress) and institutional leaders (the Speaker of the House, academic department chairs).

3. The Twenty-second Amendment to the U.S. Constitution, passed in 1951, limits any individual to only two terms as the president of the United States. In contrast, members of Congress do not face any limits on the number of terms in office they can serve, although fifteen state legislatures currently employ some form of term limits. Discuss the pros and cons of term limits, with special reference to agency slippage and the "endgame" problem. As applied to legislative leaders, in what ways do terms limits serve the intended purposes of leadership, and in what ways do they undermine those purposes? Explain your reasoning carefully.

4. Part II of this book argued that aggregating individual preferences into social choices can lead to incoherent, chaotic, or manipulable decisions; Part III argued that individual interests operating together can lead to suboptimal, inefficient, and even perverse outcomes. In what ways does the delegation of agenda-setting authority to leaders help to reduce these two problems, of social choice and group cooperation? Answer with

specific examples. What new problems are created when authority and discretion are vested in leaders?

*5. The following simplified treatment of electoral accountability is based on Ferejohn (1986).[a] Suppose that the median voter (V) has an ideal point at zero on some single-dimensional issue space, while any elected leader's (L) ideal point is normalized to one (for example, you might think that voters desire no corruption but politicians a lot—if they can get away with it). Assume that L's utility for any outcome $0 \leq p \leq 1$ is equal to p but he also secures a payoff of T for each term in office, which is measure on the same scale, so his total payoff in the first term is $p + T$. Also, payoffs in the second term are discounted by a factor of $\lambda < 1$ and L can be elected for only two terms, so if he is elected for a second term his payoff is $\lambda(p + T)$.

If L is reelected for a second term, what policy will he implement? Now assume voters use a "retrospective voting strategy" of the form: reelect if $p \leq r$ and vote out of office otherwise. Come up with two expressions for L's utilities, one if he is reelected and one if he is not, assuming for each case that L sets p as high as possible *consistent with the desired electoral outcome*. Then show that for voters, the optimal voting rule has $r = 1 - \lambda - \lambda T$ or 0 depending on the values of λ and T. How does voter utility in equilibrium change with λ and T?

*6. Why is uncertainty about the leader's costs of punishment a fundamental ingredient in Calvert's model of leadership reputation building? To answer this question, first show that if x_1 and x_2 are known in a two-period game, then t_1 and t_2 either

---

[a] See John Ferejohn, "Incumbent Performance and Electoral Control," *Public Choice* 50 (1986): 5–25.

always rebel and face no punishment, or never rebel. Then, explain the intuition behind why uncertainty and incentives to build a reputation can lead to punishment—even when it it is cheaper than nonpunishment—in the first period.

7. Chapter 12 argued that legislatures face several fundamental problems in generating legislation, including majority cycling, matching specific legislator interests to influence on those issues in the legislature at large, and imperfect information on both the policy and political impacts of legislation. These problems could be concisely summarized as a *vote aggregation* problem, a *cooperation* problem, and an *information* problem. Discuss the ways in which the House and Senate leadership, most obviously personified by the Speaker of the House and the Senate majority leader, help to solve each of these problems.

15

Courts and Judges

In the political science literature on rational choice approaches to political institutions, the "c" word and the "j" word are rarely uttered. Part of the explanation for this relative inattention to courts and judges is they are enigmatic. Elected politicians, though undoubtedly no less complex than judges, lend themselves to simple behavioral hypotheses—they want to be reelected; they pursue personal conceptions of "good public policy"; they aspire to positions of influence within their respective institutions. These simple behavioral hypotheses provide leverage on understanding the operating properties of legislative, executive, and electoral institutions. Judges, on the other hand, resent being included in the same category as elected politicians, preferring instead to be thought of as aloof from the daily fray of politics. They also remain aloof from the "trucking and bartering" of the private economy—they do not "market" their skills and services. Indeed, their compensation is ordinarily fixed in a manner quite independent of their performance. Consequently, we don't quite know what to make of judges or the legal institutions in which they operate.

Richard Posner, a federal appeals court judge as well as an eminent former professor and currently senior lecturer in law at the University of Chicago, writes with considerable authority on this puzzle:

> At the heart of economic analysis [or what in the present volume I have called "rational choice analysis"] of law is a mystery that is

also an embarrassment: how to explain judicial behavior in [rational] terms, when almost the whole thrust of the rules governing compensation and other terms and conditions of judicial employment is to divorce judicial action from incentives—to take away the carrots and sticks, the different benefits and costs associated with different behaviors, that determine human action in an economic model. . . . The economic analyst has a model of how criminals and contract parties, injurers and accident victims, parents and spouses—even legislators, and executive officials such as prosecutors—act, but falters when asked to produce a model of how judges act.[1]

As central players in important political institutions, judges *are* politicians; yet their links to "constituencies" are attenuated by the fact that, through lifetime tenure, they don't need to have their contracts renewed by those constituencies at regular intervals.[2] Not only is the reelection incentive absent; as Posner just noted, other "carrots and sticks" commonly found in employment relations (like performance-based levels of compensation) are missing. What, then, motivates judges? As Posner asks, "Are judges rational? Or have the elaborate efforts made to strip them of incentives placed their behavior beyond the reach of rational choice models?"

In addition to scrutinizing judges, in this chapter I will focus on the courts of which judges are a part. First, I provide an overview of exactly what courts are and what they do. Second, I will explore the role of courts in intergovernmental relations as they stand alongside legislatures and executives in a separation-of-powers system.

---

[1] Richard A. Posner, "What Do Judges and Justices Maximize? (The Same Thing Everybody Else Does)," *Supreme Court Economic Review* 3 (1993): 1–41. Quotation on page 2.

[2] Of course, in some states and localities judges *are* elected at regular intervals, thus making them much more like other elected politicians. However, judges on higher courts, in both state and federal systems, are typically appointed to lifetime posts.

COURTS: A BRIEF OVERVIEW.

In order to undertand what animates judicial behavior, I need to place the judge or justice[3] in context by briefly considering the role of the court system more generally. To do this I will blithely boil down hundreds of years of jurisprudence into a few pages. In doing so I emphasize the role of courts as *dispute resolvers*, as *coordinators*, and as *interpreters of rules*.

Dispute Resolution

So much of the productive activity that occurs within families, among friends and associates, even between absolute strangers takes place because the participants do not have to devote substantial resources to protecting themselves and their property or monitoring compliance with agreements.[4] For any potential violation of person or property, or defection from an agreement, all parties know in advance that an aggrieved party may take an alleged violator to court. The court, in turn, serves as a venue in which the facts of a case are established, punishment meted out to violators, and compensation awarded to victims. The court, therefore, is an institution that engages in fact finding and judgment.

Many disputes are between private parties, so the court

[3] The term *justice* is reserved for members of the U.S. Supreme Court. All other judges are called "judges," although some judges low in the pecking order are referred to as "magistrates." (However, entirely inconsistent with this nomenclature, one of the lowest categories of judges is "justice of the peace.") Throughout we will simply call all of them, with due respect, judges.
[4] Naturally, some resources are devoted to protection and monitoring. However, if extraordinary resources had to be devoted, then their rising cost would cause the frequency of the productive activities alluded to in the text to decline, according to elementary economic theory. Indeed, since the costs of negotiating, monitoring, and enforcing agreements (what we political economists call *transaction costs*) can be very high, they are a serious impediment to social interaction and productive activities of all sorts. Economizing on them—by providing the services of courts and judges, for example—is one of the great contributions of the modern state to social welfare.

serves principally to determine whether claims of violation can be substantiated. An employee, for example, may sue her employer for allegedly violating the terms of a privately negotiated employment contract. Or a consumer may sue a producer for violating the terms of a product warranty. Or a tenant may sue a landlord for violating provisions of a lease. In all of these cases some issue between private parties is in dispute. The court system provides the service of dispute resolution.

The examples in the preceding paragraph involve *civil* disputes. An entirely separate category of dispute, one in which the courts also have a role to play, involves *criminal* violations. In these cases "the public" is a party to the dispute because the alleged violation concerns not (only) something involving private parties, but (also) a public law. This brings the public agencies of justice into play as parties to a dispute. When an individual embezzles funds from his partner, he not only violates a privately negotiated agreement between them (namely, a promise of honest dealings), he violates a public law prohibiting embezzlement generally. A court proceeding, in this case, determines not only whether a violation of a private arrangement has occurred but whether the alleged perpetrator is guilty or innocent of violating a public law.

In all of these instances, the judge is responsible for managing fact-finding and judgment phases of dispute resolution (sometimes in collaboration with a jury). Thus, a large part of the daily life of a judge involves the provision of an independent, experienced look at the facts, an assessment of whether the dispute involves a violation of a private agreement or a public law (or both), and finally a judgment—a determination of which party (if either) is liable and, if so, what compensation is in order (to the private party victimized and, if judged a criminal activity, to the larger public). Judging is a sophisticated blend of reading a mystery novel, solving a crossword puzzle, and providing wise counsel.

Coordination

Dispute resolution occurs after the fact—that is, after a dispute has taken place. In a manner of speaking, it represents a failure of the legal system, since one function of law and its judicial institutions is to discourage such disputes in the first instance. We may also think of courts and judges as before-the-fact *coordination mechanisms* inasmuch as the anticipation of what happens once their services are called upon allows private parties to form rational expectations and thereby coordinate their actions in advance of possible disputes. A prospective embezzler, estimating the odds of getting caught, prosecuted, and subsequently punished, may think twice (or even three or four times) about cheating his partner. Surely, *some* prospective embezzlers are deterred from their crimes by these prospects. Two acquaintances, therefore, may much more confidently entertain the possibility of going into business together because their partnership will flourish (or fail) "in the shadow of the law." The sword (or is it the scales?) of justice hangs over their collaboration.

In this sense, the court system (like the dog in Sir Arthur Conan Doyle's story "Silver Blaze") is as important for what it doesn't do as for what it does.[5] The system of courts and law coordinates private behavior by providing incentives and disincentives for specific actions. To the extent that these work, there are fewer disputes to resolve and thus less after-the-fact dispute resolution for courts and judges to engage in. What makes the incentives and disincentives work is their power (are the rewards and penalties big or small?), their clarity, and the consistency with which judges administer them. Bright-line incentives (clearly defined standards that leave little or no room for varying interpretation), consistently employed, pro-

[5] In this Sherlock Holmes adventure, the key to solving the mystery was that a certain dog did *not* bark.

vide powerful motivations for private parties to resolve disputes ahead of time. This sort of advanced coordination, encouraged by a properly functioning legal system, economizes
on the transaction costs that would diminish the frequency of,
and otherwise discourage, socially desirable activity.

Rule Interpretation

Dispute resolution and coordination tremendously affect private behavior and the daily lives of ordinary citizens. Judges,
however, are not entirely free agents (despite the fact that
some of them are tyrants in their courtrooms). In matching
the facts of a specific case to judicial principles and statutory
guidelines, judges must engage in *interpretive* activity. They
must determine what particular statutes or judicial principles
mean, which of them fit the facts of a particular case, and
then, having determined all this, the disposition of the case at
hand. Does the statute of 1926 regulating the electronic transmission of radio waves apply to television, cellular phones,
ship-to-shore radios, fax machines, or electronic mail? Does
the law governing the transportation of dangerous substances,
passed in 1937, apply to nuclear fuels, infected animals, or ar-
tificially created biological hazards? Often, the enacting legislative body has not been crystal clear about the scope of the
legislation it passes. Indeed, a legislature acting in 1926 or
1937 hardly could have anticipated technological developments a half century later. Nevertheless, cases come up on a
regular basis, and judges must make judgment calls, so to
speak, on highly complex issues.

   Interpreting the rules is probably the single most important activity in which higher courts engage. This is because the
court system is *hierarchical* in the sense that judgments by
higher courts constrain the discretion of judges in lower courts.
If the Supreme Court rules that nuclear fuels are covered
by the 1937 law on transporting dangerous substances, then

lower courts must render subsequent judgments in a manner consistent with this ruling. The judge in a civil or criminal trial concerning the shipment of nuclear isotopes from a laboratory to a commercial user, for example, must comply in his or her ruling with the legal interpretations passed down by the higher courts. Also, because of the federal principle by which the American polity is organized, federal law and interpretations thereof often trump state and local laws.

At the highest levels, courts and judges engage not only in *statutory interpretation*, but *constitutional interpretation* as well. Here they interpret the provisions of the U.S. Constitution or a state constitution, determining their scope and content. In determining, for example, whether the act of Congress regulating the transportation of dangerous substances from one state to another is constitutional, the justices of the Supreme Court might appeal to the commerce clause of the Constitution (allowing the federal government to regulate interstate commerce) to justify the constitutionality of that act. On the other hand, a Supreme Court majority might also rule that a shipment of spent fuel rods from a nuclear reactor in Kansas City to a nuclear waste facility outside of St. Louis is *not* covered by this law, since the shipment took place entirely within the boundaries of a single state and thus did not constitute interstate commerce.

In short, judges are continually engaged in elaborating, embellishing, even rewriting the rules by which private and public life are organized. In these interpretive acts they are conscious of the fact that their rulings will not only affect the participants in a specific case before them but will carry interpretive weight in all similar cases percolating up in the lower courts. Thus, statutory and constitutional interpretations have a precedential authority over subsequent deliberation (and, in turn, are themselves influenced by earlier interpretations).

However, all the elaboration and embellishment and "redrafting" of statutes that constitute the interpretive activity of judges and justices are themselves subject to review. Statutory interpretation, even that conducted by the highest court in the land, is exposed to legislative review. If Congress is unhappy with a specific statutory interpretation—for example, suppose the current Congress does not like the idea of federal regulation of e-mail that a federal court claimed to be permissible under the 1926 act on electronic transmission—then it may amend the legislation so as explicitly to reverse the court ruling. Of course, if the court makes a *constitutional* ruling, Congress cannot then abrogate that ruling through new legislation. Since the famous early nineteenth-century case *Marbury v. Madison*, the federal courts generally and the Supreme Court in particular have come to be regarded as the supreme interpreters of the Constitution. But Congress can commence the process of constitutional amendment, thereby effectively reversing judicial interpretations with which it disagrees.

From this brief discussion I hope the reader now appreciates that courts, judges, and the legal system of which they are a part serve to resolve disputes when they arise, to discourage disputes in the first place by providing before-the-fact coordination of expectations, and to interpret and reinterpret the fundamental rules of the game by which the members of the political community regulate and govern themselves. In both their statutory and constitutional interpretive modes, courts regulate interactions of ordinary citizens and constrain exercises of authority by political officials and institutions. In turn, they are subject to regulation by ordinary and extraordinary political processes. Although the regal attire of judges and the formality of judicial settings serve to intimidate and to inspire awe, there is no gainsaying that courts are political institutions and that judges are political players.

I now take up each of these last two facets separately.

First, I ask precisely how we should treat judges as political players. Then I discuss the political role of courts in the government arrangement of separation of powers in the United States.

WHO ARE THE JUDGES, AND WHAT DO THEY WANT?

Judge Richard Posner provides partial answers to both of these questions and, in the process, brings judges under the rubric of rational-choice theory. Judges, to Posner, are mostly "ordinary people." Just as for other ordinary people for whom rationality is a perfectly respectable behavioral hypothesis, it is appropriate to suppose that judges, too, are rational:

> Politics, personal friendships, ideology, and pure serendipity play too large a role in the appointment of federal judges to warrant treating the judiciary as a collection of genius-saints miraculously immune to the tug of self-interest. By treating judges and Justices as ordinary people, my approach makes them fit subjects for economic analysis; for economists have no theory of genius. It is fortunate for economic analysis, therefore, that most law is made not by the tiny handful of great judges but by the great mass of ordinary ones.[6]

The issue for Posner, then, is how to conceptualize judging and other judgelike behavior as rational responses to the legal and political environment. He suggests several "types" that capture different aspects of judicial behavior.

The Nonprofit Analogy

The first is the manager of a nonprofit enterprise. The legal system, Posner observes, is indeed a nonprofit enterprise. Except for private judges (like Judge Judy or Judge Joe Brown,

[6] *Supreme Court Economic Review* 3 (1993): 1–41. Quotation is on pages 3–4.

stars of the television courtroom shows), arbitrators, and me-
diators—all of whom sell their services in the marketplace
(and thus are driven by the same profit incentives that motivate other sellers of services)—judges in the official judiciary
draw fixed salaries and fringe benefits but may not pocket
fees, user charges, or other differences between receipts and
running costs. Moreover, their salaries and other benefits are
fixed independent of effort, quality of work, or any other
performance-based standard. They are salaried managers of a
nonprofit system. Posner opines that because judges cannot
claim a monetary residual like the owners of a for-profit enterprise, because they are not compensated in accord with the
quantity and quality of their work like other sellers of professional services, and because they have lifetime tenure, judges
should be expected on average not to work as hard as lawyers
of comparable age and talent. He qualifies this opinion by noting that federal judges are nominated by political authorities
and must undergo an often thorough confirmation process, so
that it is conceivable that these filters select for industrious-
ness and other manifestations of commitment to the job.

In highlighting the nonprofit aspect of the job of judging,
Posner is able to say what judges do *not* maximize—namely,
profits. But nonprofit managers are not an entirely unmoti-
vated lot of ne'er-do-wells. Posner alludes to several motivational elements of the utility function of the judge as nonprofit
manager—popularity among fellow judges, law clerks, and
other court personnel; prestige in the legal and larger political
community; reputation in the academic legal world; track
record (especially the desire not to be reversed by a higher
court or the legislature). No doubt all these elements have
an effect, but Posner is skeptical that these are the central
considerations of judging (and he speaks from personal experience).

I would give slightly greater weight than Posner to *ambition*. Nonprofit managers are, as Posner suggests, "ordinary

people" in the sense that they do their jobs with an eye at least partly on advancing in their world (however they conceive of it). The program manager at the Mellon Foundation hopes to become a vice president at the Rockefeller Foundation and, beyond that, perhaps the president of the Ford Foundation. The dean of students at a small liberal arts college may aspire to be dean of admissions at the state university and, beyond that, perhaps dean of undergraduate education at an Ivy League college or university. The local director of United Way may harbor ambitions to rise through that bureaucracy to regional and then national office. In this manner, "unter" judges hope some day to become "über" judges. Federal district judges hope for promotion to one of the Courts of Appeals, and "great mentioners" in Washington always have their list of appeals court judges as candidates for the Supreme Court (The recently confirmed Justice Sonia Sotomayor is an apt illustration.)

Ambition for advancement, then, substitutes as a standard for other forms of performance-based compensation. But, as Posner notes, ambition cannot be a tremendously strong motivation because the odds of advancement, even for the very highest performing judges, are remote. It is probably more likely that a dean of students at a high-quality midwestern liberal arts college can become admissions dean at an Ivy League institution than that a federal district judge will move up the judicial hierarchy to the Supreme Court. My view, then, is that individual judges, like other nonprofit professionals, rationalize the energy and commitment they invest in their jobs by their desire for popularity, prestige, and reputation. They value these things partly for their own sake because standing among one's peers and within one's community is part of the nature of all human beings, a perspective that goes back at least to Aristotle. But they also value them because they conceive of these things as necessary attributes for advancement, however remote the latter possibility might be. In their heart of hearts, I suspect, many judges probably exaggerate their own importance and, therefore, the likelihood of lightning striking.

The Voting Analogy

A second aspect of judicial behavior that Posner highlights derives from the fact that much of what a judge does may be conceived of as voting. Rendering judgment is, at least in part, the casting of a vote (for the plaintiff or defendant). As we saw in Chapter 9, voting in mass elections is, in fact, difficult to rationalize on instrumental grounds because no single voter is very likely to be decisive. Judges, however, are more akin to legislators or committtee chairs in the sense that their participation takes place in a small-group setting in which the chances of being pivotal to an outcome are much more likely. Indeed, some judges are committees of one (federal district judges), others are members of small panels (federal appeals judges typically sit in panels of three), and still others are members of moderate-sized panels (Supreme Court justices are one of, at most, nine). Consistent ideological outliers may rarely be pivotal in a small or moderate-sized panel, but most others have a substantial probability of being the vote that affects an outcome, at least some of the time. Since judges may not be certain exactly when they have a chance to make or break a majority as opposed to being a peripheral vote, they may have an incentive to try to get their decisions "right" in terms of their beliefs about the proper disposition of cases—this effort may have a payoff.

Even a prospectively pivotal judge may not be moved much by this prospect if what he or she is pivotal for is "small beer." A vote on the merits of a case—whether in behalf of the plaintiff or of the defendant—has a limited impact. One of the parties to the case wins and the other loses. No one else is affected by the decision, per se. But judges "vote" not only on *who* should win a given case but, through the opinions they draft, *why* one side or the other should win. Judges vote not only with ballots but also with ideas—ideas about the facts, about judicial principles, about legal reasoning, and about moral values. It is through the opinions they draft, rather than the ballots they cast, that judges may influence a wider collection of interests, since these opinions serve to constrain lower-court judges in similar cases in the future.[7]

The Spectator and Game-Player Analogies

Another type Posner explores is that of judge as *spectator*—someone sitting in a theater or sports arena, or just in a comfortable easy chair with a mystery novel on his or her lap. Posner does not have a passive viewer in mind here but rather someone actively engaged in the drama taking place, empathizing with one or more of the participants and puzzling through the moral ambiguities the drama presents. At a slightly more activist level than the spectator is the judge as *game player*—as an actual participant in an unfolding drama. As a legal case develops, according to this interpretation, the judge, as either of these types, seeks to puzzle through the facts on display and connect them to the morally appropriate legal principles (as determined by the judge's own moral compass). The judge derives pleasure, just like a bridge player, simply from playing the game.

So, What Do Judges Want?

By his consideration of the different ways to think about motivations of judges, and by his elimination of motivations (such as maximizing profits and ambition for reelection) that pro-

---

[7] Posner (1993: 19) goes on to suggest that judges, like authors and scholars, may derive intrinsic pleasure from the act of drafting opinions, displaying their prowess, and disseminating their views. Thus, even those judges who have realistic beliefs about the likelihood that they will rise through the court system on the basis of their present actions may nonetheless devote considerable energy to those actions for the sheer pleasure they bring.

vide leverage in theorizing about entrepreneurs and politicians, Posner provides ample confirmation of my claim that judges are enigmatic actors in political life.

Posner's important contribution, I believe, is his insight that judges are difficult to figure because any connection between their performance and their compensation has been attenuated by lifetime tenure and fixed income. The difficulty with Posner's analysis is that (to his credit) he considered the category of "judge" in all its splendorous variety. If, in models of elected politicians that I have covered in previous chapters, my net had been as broad, I would have had to lump presidents and senators together with county sheriffs, city assessors, and town dogcatchers. Undoubtedly any simple motivational hypothesis—like maximizing the probability of reelection—would have fared much more poorly than it does when we focus mainly on the professional politicians who dominate our national institutions. Likewise, I believe an appropriate starting point in trying to fathom the judiciary is to focus on those judges who *are* "players" in the larger political game precisely because they *do* have ambition, both for their careers and their ideas about the law. Just as our models of elected politicians are most apt for those who have reached the political pinnacle—representatives, senators, presidents, and those who want to become one of these—I want now to focus on judges of comparable stature. These judges, I believe, may be thought of, essentially, as *legislators in robes*.

Legislators in Robes

In many models of legislative politics, legislators are thought of as *policy oriented*. In the spatial model (as described in Chapter 5), for example, a legislator (or, in Chapter 16, a political party), is characterized by an *ideal policy* and preferences that decline as one moves spatially more distant from that ideal policy. It is often unnecessary for the purposes of the model to identify *why* the legislator possesses these particular preferences. But if one were to pull back the curtain, so to speak, and speculate about why legislators hold the preferences they do, there are usually two answers.

The first is that legislative politicians actually care about the role of government—about the policies government pursues, and about the politics that get you to those policies. That may well have been their motivation for becoming active in politics initially. Indeed, to the extent a legislative politician cares about policy because her philosophy of government is relatively well worked out, she may be described (nonpejoratively) as an *ideologue*, or at the very least a *thinker*.

The second rationale for legislator policy preferences is political ambition. According to this view, a legislator may not care much about policy per se but does care about protecting his political flank from attack by political opponents. To do this, he pursues policy objectives in behalf of constituents. He is the faithful agent, serving the policy interests either of his current constituency or of some broader constituency toward which his ambitions point him.

We may think of judges as having policy preferences just like legislators. To the degree that higher courts do not merely resolve disputes between the participants in a case but, more significantly, shape the legal context in which millions of private citizens interact and in which thousands of public officials exercise power, these courts are critical in the formation and implementation of public policy. Higher-court judges, therefore, have opportunities to affect the public condition. There is simply no way, for example, to deny the central role played by the federal courts in transforming post–World War II America into a considerably more integrated and equitable society in terms of race and gender.

Now surely not all courts cases have the momentous effects of the *Dred Scott* case just before the Civil War, or *Brown v. Board of Education* just before the civil rights revolution. But, within fairly broad limits, it can be claimed that big-impact cases are often difficult to discern in advance. So, at least as a first approximation, it may be hypothesized that judges with policy preferences treat each case as though it might have impact, either directly on national politics or indirectly through its effects on how constitutional or statutory law is subsequently interpreted.

This is a radical view of judges, one with which most sitting judges (or aspirants thereto in the broader legal community) would be uncomfortable. They would be uncomfortable, I believe, because this conception of judges makes them much like other politicians, a view judges seem intent on discouraging. This strikes me as a rather prissy attitude. Besides, it is no badge of dishonor to be associated with wanting to have impact on the political life of the community, whether for ideological or careerist reasons. At the end of the day, this view of judges becomes compelling if it leads to interesting insights about how politics works. I claim that the legislator-in-robes conception of judges has precisely this potential, a claim I elaborate in the next section.

CASE 15.1
THE BEST JUDGES MONEY CAN BUY?

Sir Francis Bacon, one of the great philosophers, scientists, and legal scholars in English history, was impeached after having attained the highest judicial position in England, Lord Chancellor. The House of Commons determined that he had accepted twenty-eight bribes. Bacon defended his position by claiming, "I usually accept bribes from both sides so that tainted money can never influence my decisions." The Parliament didn't buy it and sentenced him to the Tower of London, where he remained until King James pardoned him.

I present this little vignette only to add credibility to my claim that jurists should be thought of in the same terms as other politicians, with the same variety of motives (save electoral ambition) that we encounter when thinking about legislators, executives, and bureaucrats. Graft and corruption, things that do not shock or surprise us when we encounter them occasionally in the hurly-burly of real politics, is undoubtedly a factor in the lives of judicial politicians as well.

Nevertheless, legal ethics, judicial temperament, and the culture in which courts and judges find themselves, on the face of things, appear to mitigate the connection between judicial activity and self-interest. A perusal of the Canons of Judicial Ethics of the American Bar Association makes this easy. One canon, titled "Self-Interest," states: "A judge should abstain from performing or taking part in any judicial act in which his personal interests are involved." Another, titled "Independence," states, "A judge should not be swayed by partisan demands, public clamor or consideration of personal popularity or notoriety, nor be apprehensive of unjust criticism."

Do these canons of proper behavior do any good? The answer is, probably, yes, so judicial politicians are probably less venal and corrupt than their compatriots in the elected branches of government. The reason is that violations of the canons provide a basis for dismissal; judges ambitious to remain judges, therefore, will observe them, thereby assuring that the judiciary, as a group, maintains a stature and prestige in public opinion that other politicians do not enjoy. But these canons probably provide far weaker incentives to induce judges to park their respective ideologies outside the courtroom door. In this sense, they share with elected politicians both the motive and the opportunity to impart their own political beliefs into their official activity.

Courts and Intergovernmental Relations

In conceiving of judges as legislators in robes, I am effectively claiming that judges, like other politicians, have policy preferences they seek to implement. I needn't say much at this point about where these policy preferences come from, only that they exist and provide the motivation for judicial activity. (I will have a little more to say about their origins in the concluding section.)

At both the national and state level in the United States, courts and judges are "players" in the policy game because of the separation of powers. Essentially, this means that the legislative branch formulates policy (defined constitutionally and institutionally by a legislative process); that the executive branch implements policy (according to well-defined administrative procedures, and subject to initial approval by the president or the legislative override of his veto); and that the courts, when asked, rule on the faithfulness of the legislated and executed policy either to the substance of the statute or to the constitution itself. The courts, that is, may strike down an administrative action either because it exceeds the authority granted in the relevant statute (statutory rationale) or because the statute itself exceeds the authority granted the legislature by the constitution (constitutional rationale). As I noted earlier, if a decisive coalition in the legislature is unhappy with this judicial action, then it may either recraft the legislation (if the rationale for striking it down was statutory) or initiate a constitutional amendment that would enable the stricken-down policy to pass constitutional muster (if the rationale for originally striking it down was constitutional).

A number of recent scholarly works have sought to model the judiciary in the setting outlined above. In the next few paragraphs, I will briefly give the reader some flavor of this analysis that employs the one-dimensional spatial model described in Chapter 5. Some in the literature refer to this as *Marksist* analysis in honor of Brian Marks, the first to attempt to incorporate the judiciary in spatial models of policy choice.[8]

A number of simplifying assumptions are employed, mainly to make the presentation less complicated; most authors believe that additional complications would not change the basic thrust of the conclusions. To begin with, it is assumed that the policy options in any given setting may adequately be represented by a one-dimensional interval, say [0, 100], over which all actors—legislative, executive, and judicial—have single-peaked preferences. Thus, the nine Supreme Court justices have ideal points on this interval labeled $x_J^1, \ldots, x_J^9$, whereas the ideals of the 100 senators are given by $x_S^1, \ldots, x_S^{100}$, those of the 435 representatives by $x_H^1, \ldots, x_H^{435}$, and the president's executive agent by x_A. (I will ignore the complexities associated with the presidential veto and veto overrides.) For each of these actors, preferences are highest for their respective ideal policies and decline as policy moves away to the left or the right from this ideal. Those with ideals near 0 may be thought of as on the extreme liberal end of opinion, while those with ideals near 100 are at the extreme conservative end. Thus, to take a recent Supreme Court case involving minority representation in municipal police and fire departments, if the [0, 100] dimension were taken to characterize affirmative action policies, those judges, legislators, and administrators favoring the setting aside of earmarked positions and resources for minorities (set-asides, quotas) would have ideal points toward the zero end of the

[8] For a critical review, the reader may consult Jeffrey A. Segal, "Separation-of-Powers Games in the Positive Theory of Congres and Courts," *American Political Science Review* 91 (1997): 28–44. The original paper on which the preceding is based is Brian A. Marks, "A Model of Judicial Influence on Congressional Policymaking," Working Papers in Political Science, P-88-7, Hoover Institution, Stanford, Calif., 1988. Unfortunately, it has never been published.

continuum; those favoring outreach and other expand-the-pool-of-eligibles policies, as well as the use of race as an "adjustment" factor, would have ideal points somewhere in the center of the continuum; and those who opposed affirmative action would have ideal points clustered near the 100 endpoint.

Although each chamber of the legislature is, as we saw in previous chapters, organizationally complex, to make things tractable here we assume that they are simple majority–rule institutions.[9] Given single-peaked preferences, Black's Median-Voter Theorem (see Chapter 5) tells us that we can take the policy ideal and preferences of the median voter in the chamber to represent majority preferences there. We thus may suppress the details of preferences of all legislators and focus exclusively on x_H and x_S, the median-voter ideals in the House and Senate, respectively. By the same reasoning, to know how the court decides, given that it, too, is a majority-rule institution, we need only focus on x_J, the ideal of the median justice on the court. Finally, we need to take account of the fact that in the policy dimension in question, there is a status quo policy, x_Q. In this simple setting, then, we can see the impact of judicial oversight by focusing on x_Q, x_J, x_H, x_S, and x_A. These five "parameters" will determine the outcome of policy in any specific application once we know the sequence in which behavior unfolds.

I assume at the beginning of any play of the policy game that a status quo legislative choice, x_Q, is in place—the result of previous iterations of the game. The administrative agent, either the current president's aide or a bureaucrat with long

---

[9] The complexities produced by committees with gatekeeping and agenda-setting powers, or by a chair or speaker with powers of recognition, or by party caucuses with the power to appoint their members to committees can be, and have been, accommodated in this literature. To ease the presentation, I have suppressed these details, but not because they cannot be incorporated in principle.

DISPLAY 15.1		
Sequence of the Policy Game		
Step	**Player**	**Action**
0		x_Q in place
1	administrative agent	implements policy A
2	court	strikes A or lets it stand; if former, then it names the new policy J
3	legislature	if unhappy with policy in place, either A or J, then selects new policy, L

tenure, decides what policy to implement, given this legislative choice in place.[10] The court then decides whether to strike down the agent's actions. Although, as noted above, the court may employ either a statutory or a constitutional rationale, I will focus only on the former. If the court declares the administrative agent's act as outside the permissible bounds prescribed by the legislation, I suppose the court's majority opinion can declare whatever policy it wishes. In effect, the court can "legislate." Finally, if the House and Senate are jointly dissatisfied with the outcome of this process—either the original agent's act that the court lets stand or the new policy enunciated by the court, then they can propose new legislation. In principle, this last action sets the stage for a subsequent round of the game. In this way it is possible to study the long-term evolution of a policy. For my purposes here, however, this is an additional layer of complexity that I do not wish to embrace. So I assume that in step 3, if there is a new legislative policy, it is automatically implemented and the game ends. This sequence is given in Display 15.1.

[10] See the discussion of McNollgast's model in Chapter 13.

FIGURE 15.1

| 0 | x_A | x_H | x_Q | x_S | 100 |

Given this sequence, the distribution of parameters will determine the rational response at each step of the process. To see the model in action, consider the distribution given in Figure 15.1. Existing policy, x_Q, is in equilibrium, lying as it does between the median ideal of the House and Senate. If an administrative agent had no court to worry about, then it would implement policy $A = x_H$, since this is the policy closest to its ideal that will not trigger a legislative response, despite the bureaucratic drift.[11] But the presence of a court changes the calculations.

Suppose the median justice's ideal, x_J, were between 0 and x_A—as might have been true of the liberal Warren court on affirmative action issues. The court majority couldn't hope to improve on x_H, given its preferences, so it would let the implemented policy $A = x_H$ stand. So, too, would the legislature, as we've already seen. So, for any court to the left of the bureaucratic agent's ideal, the agent's action is unaffected. By the same logic, a more conservative court, with a median justice ideal in the interval $[x_A, x_H]$, would be similarly disposed; so once again the bureaucratic choice would be $A = x_H$. In each of these cases it would appear to an unsophisticated observer that the court is irrelevant. This, of course, would be an inappropriate inference, since the agent makes the choice she does

---

[11] Recall from the analysis of the McNollgast model in Chapter 13 that any point in the subinterval between x_H and x_S (including its endpoints) is an equilibrium in the sense that any movement away from one of these points will be opposed by either the House or the Senate (or both). Since a legislative reaction to an agency decision requires the assent of *both* the House and the Senate, these points constitute equilibria.

because she knows her preferences are sufficiently in line with those of the court that the justices will let her action stand.

What about x_J in the interval $[x_H, x_S]$? This is a circumstance in which, no matter what the bureaucratic choice, the court can strike down the action and name its ideal, $J = x_J$, as the new policy. Since this lies in the legislative equilibrium set, the legislature will not react with new legislation. If the bureaucratic agent doesn't like being reversed, then she will anticipate the court's move in advance and simply name $A = x_J$ as her policy. She can do no better. Thus, we see that the presence of a court with a median ideal inside the legislative equilibrium set is a check on bureaucratic drift. Once again, though, if the agent does, in fact, act on her anticipation of the court's preferences, it will appear as though the court is irrelevant since it will leave the agent's choice in place.

Finally, suppose x_J is to the right of the median senator—in the interval $[x_S, 100]$—as may well be the case on affirmative action issues for the Roberts court. Any action taken by the bureaucratic agent will be struck down by the court; it will declare the new policy as $J = x_S$. This is the best the median justice could hope for, since any policy closer to x_J will trigger a legislative response—some policy in the $[x_H, x_S]$ interval worse from the median justice's perspective than x_S. Of course, a fully anticipatory response from the bureaucrat would have her declare $A = x_S$, with the court allowing that policy to stand. Even if the bureaucrat were, for some odd reason, to implement a policy A to the right of x_S—*even at the ideal policy of the median justice*, the court would still strike it down and declare $J = x_S$. Why? If the court allowed this nominally more desirable policy to stand, then the legislature would get involved with corrective legislation, ultimately producing a policy less desirable to the court median than x_S.

This little example hardly does justice to the growing body of work that seeks to integrate the courts into the intergovernmental policy game.[12] What it nevertheless conveys is that the court's role may often be subtle and unobservable. The equilibrium policy of this game, as we have seen, is often sustained by anticipatory behavior. The bureaucratic agent implements a policy in the expectation that, should the court or the legislature see it as in their respective interests, either can act in a corrective fashion after the fact. If the agent fully takes this expectation on board in her own calculations, then she will make a choice that does not trigger these after-the-fact reactions. Consequently, in many policy areas the court will be inactive, not because it has no role to play but rather because other players in the game have already accommodated it. Where we ought to expect proactive involvement by the court, then, are those areas in which relevant parameters have changed but other players have failed to notice or to react appropriately to them.

Conclusion

The legislator-in-robes conception of judges is, I believe, an extremely plausible way to think about judicial actors in a separation-of-powers regime. For different configurations of preferences, we obtain provocative and often nonobvious implications about where and whether there will be observable judicial activity. In principle, these implications can be tested against the experiences of the real world. This, after all, is what social science is all about. The interested reader may wish to play with Figure 15.1 a bit, determining how adminis-

---

[12] A highly accessible discussion of this approach, with many citations from other related work, may be found in John Ferejohn and Barry Weingast, "Limitation of Statutes: Strategic Statutory Interpretation," *Georgetown Law Journal* 80 (1992): 565–83. Equally accessible, and especially good at playing out the McNollgast model as it applies to courts is McNollgast, "Politics and the Courts: A Positive Theory of Judicial Doctrine and the Rule of Law," *Southern California Law Review* 68 (1995): 1631–83.

trative agents, legislators, and judges will behave under alternative preference distributions.

Nevertheless, I cannot conclude without expressing at least some doubts about this conception of judges. Putting judges on a par with legislators as strategic players does not sit well with some students of judicial politics (see the citation to Segal in footnote 8). They view the typical judge of one of the higher courts as a professional jurist who renders opinions in line with a well-thought-out judicial philosophy. Legislators, presidents, and bureaucrats may strategize, but jurists do not. They sustain this view by pointing to a jurist's body of opinions, demonstrating that there is often a consistency to them that would seem to be at odds with a more strategic vision. While sharing some of these doubts, I should point out that there is no reason to believe the behavior just identified is necessarily at odds with a strategic vision. As we saw in the example in the previous section, when other actors, behaving strategically, internalize the potential response of the court, they often accommodate the court and thereby remove the need for justices to behave strategically. It is the *potential* for strategic intervention, and the belief by other politicians that judges *will* behave strategically if their preferences are not accommodated, that provides the basis for the strategic vision of judicial behavior I have developed here.

In sum, there is no gainsaying the fact that judges are shadowy characters in most rational-choice theories of policy making. The attenuation of incentives linking judicial politicians to constituencies to which other politicians are linked opens the door to a variety of alternative motivational hypotheses. I have reviewed several of them in this chapter, and developed one—legislator-in-robes hypothesis—in some detail. Regardless of where a reader stands on this question, I hope to have persuaded him or her that courts are essential political institutions in intergovernmental policy making.

CASE 15.2
LEGISLATORS IN ROBES REVISITED

In this chapter I have argued that judges are usefully thought of as legislators in robes, motivated by policy preferences and ideological goals just like other politicians. To evaluate the legislators-in-robes hypothesis, we can turn to the writings of judges themselves.

The hypothesis that judges make policy in addition to interpreting laws is controversial. Robert Jackson, Supreme Court Justice from 1941 to 1954, has written that "few accusations against the Supreme Court are made with more heat and answered [by Court members] with less candor than that it makes political decisions."* The lack of candor to which Jackson alludes in the responses of justices to this charge is, in my view, due to the presence of more politics than the justices would care to admit to. This claim is sustained by Dalin H. Oaks, Justice of the Utah Supreme Court, who observes that "the conventional wisdom holds that the legislature makes the law, the courts interpret it, and the executive enforces it. Like most conventional wisdom, this is only partly true. Judges also make law. They do so inevitably as they interpret statutes passed by the legislature, since interpretation can never be free from choices illuminated by the creative instinct and motivated by personal preference."† Federal Circuit Court of Appeals Judge Howard T. Markey adds, "All people have values of some sort, and judges are people. A person totally devoid of values

---

* Robert H. Jackson, "The Supreme Court as a Political Institution," in Alan F. Westin, ed., *An Autobiography of the Supreme Court* (New York: Macmillan, 1963), p. 360.
† Dalin H. Oaks, "When Judges Legislate," in Mark W. Cannon and David M. O'Brien, eds., *Views from the Bench: The Judiciary and Constitutional Politics* (Chatham, N.J.: Chatham House, 1985), p. 147.

would be a robot, an automaton." He continues, "It would be foolish to pretend that no single Federal judge has ever, even subconsciously, viewed his or her roles as one authorizing a personal policy-making function. The elements of office can lead to confusion of the terms 'appointed' and 'annointed.' The temptation to 'do good' can be strong."‡

I would only add that, precisely because it is inevitable, it is hardly something about which to be particularly ashamed. Indeed, I would further claim that legislatures often *delegate* this lawmaking function to courts. I noted in Chapter 13 that the growth of governmental responsibilities has led Congress to implement "fire extinguisher" forms of monitoring and enforcement. Accordingly, citizens and groups are given legal standing to work out legislative detail in courts, where judges are the ultimate arbiters. In effect, Congress knowingly gives judges substantial latitude in how the laws are to be implemented. In this sense, judges make policy and therefore are legislators in robes not only because they are "people with values" but because Congress has encouraged the courts to share their legislative burden in an increasingly complex policy-making environment.

‡ Howard T. Markey, "On the Cause and Treatment of Judicial Activism," in Cannon and O'Brien, *Views from the Bench*, pp. 285–88.

PROBLEMS AND DISCUSSION QUESTIONS

1. The Chief Justice of the United States, John Roberts, drew the following analogy—now oft-repeated by those who favor a conservative judiciary—in the opening statement of his confirmation hearings in front of the Senate Judiciary Committee in September 2005: "Judges are like umpires. Umpires don't

make the rules; they apply them. The role of an umpire and a judge is critical . . . but it is a limited role. . . . It's my job to call balls and strikes, and not to pitch or bat." Explain in your own words Roberts's vision of the role of courts. What judicial role was he emphasizing, and what others was he implicitly criticizing? Then, assess Justice Roberts's metaphor overall. Is it sufficient for a Supreme Court justice to just "call balls and strikes"?

2. The federal court system, as well as most higher state courts, grant judges lifetime terms, and judges cannot be removed from the bench unless they committ a serious crime. This suggests that the judiciary may be the site of an extreme form of the principal-agent problem. Explain why the principal-agent paradigm might be a valid description of the relationship between politicians and judges, and then describe any before-the-fact and after-the-fact means of limiting agent discretion employed by the political principals. Then, discuss some of the positive aspects of lifetime tenure, and explain why such a system has been so widely adopted in the United States.

3. Sandra Day O'Connor was a moderately conservative Supreme Court justice from 1981 to 2005 who frequently played the role of the court's median voter by joining the court's four other conservative justices as the deciding vote in 5–4 decisions. According to various witnesses, O'Connor expressed dismay on election night 2000 when Florida prematurely declared a Gore victory, and her husband is supposed to have explained that she did not feel she could retire if a Democratic president was in power.

Assume that Supreme Court justices care only about policy, and that their policy preferences can be represented by a one-dimensional issue space ranging from liberal to conservative. Also assume that any justice nominated by the president will be approved by the U.S. Senate. If one of the current justices were to retire, what would be the policy position of the new court if the current president is a liberal Democrat, to the left of the median justice? Consider three cases: retirement of the median justice, retirement of a justice to the left of the median, and retirement of a justice to the right of the median. Now answer the same question if the current president were a conservative Republican, to the right of the median justice.

Does your answer help explain Justice O'Connor's desire for a Bush election victory? How does your answer depend on O'Connor's ideal point relative to her immediate neighbors to the left and the right?[a]

4. The Judiciary Reorganization Bill of 1937 would have authorized the president to appoint an extra judge to any federal court for each sitting judge over the age of seventy. This bill came on the heels of a string of defeats of New Deal legislation by the Supreme Court (in everything from 5–4 votes up to unanimous opposition). With six justices over age seventy, this bill, if passed, would have permitted President Roosevelt to add up to six new justices. Assuming the justices' preferences can be represented with a unidimensional spatial model, would the "court-packing plan" have been sufficient to guarantee more preferable decisions in the future in all cases? Could FDR at least have guaranteed rulings more to his liking in some cases?

*5. Ferejohn and Weingast (1992)[b] made a novel argument about strict interpretations of congressional statutes using a

---

[a] For further elaboration on these questions, see David Rohde and Kenneth Shepsle, "Advising and Consenting in the 60-Vote Senate: Strategic Appointments to the Supreme Court," *Journal of Politics*, 69 (2008): 664–77.

[b] John Ferejohn and Barry Weingast, "A Positive Theory of Statutory Interpretation," *International Review of Law and Economics*, 12 (1992): 263–79.

one-dimensional spatial model. Assume that the median legislator in the two houses of Congress has ideal points at x_H and
x_S and $x_H < x_S$, and the Supreme Court is hearing an argument about some statute passed in a previous session of Congress, which is at x_Q. Suppose that the Supreme Court acts
first and can amend the statute via a ruling or leave it alone.
The Congress acts second and can replace x_Q with new legislation—if both houses approve—or do nothing. Assume also that
the median Supreme Court justice's ideal point is at x_Q. Would
the Supreme Court vote to alter the bill if $x_H < x_Q < x_S$? Why or
why not? What would occur if $x_Q < x_H$ or $x_Q > x_S$ and the
Supreme Court then decides not to alter the law through a
ruling? What would then be the optimal strategy to defend the
status quo when x_Q does not lie between the ideal points of the
two houses of Congress? Ferejohn and Weingast conclude that
"judges who care about statutes are well-advised to pay more
attention to political realities than to the words of statutes
themselves." Why do they reach this conclusion?

6. What motivates judges, both in the types of decisions they
make and in the amount of effort they devote to researching
and articulating their positions? Do motivations differ across
different courts—for example, between federal trial courts, appellate courts and the Supreme Court; or between elected
county judges and unelected state judges?

16

Cabinet Government and
Parliamentary Democracy

So much of the material in this volume may seem to revolve around political life in America. Whether in describing the private ways in which individuals organize themselves into clubs and organizations to pursue collective purposes or the public ways in which they constitute their official political institutions, I may have conveyed the impression that I have been doing no more than analyzing politics, American style. Problems of group choice, collective action, and institutional politics, however, are not unique to the American constitutional order. Americans have no monopoly on voting, agenda setting, or dividing and specializing political labor, and I can make this point quite forcefully by turning to the ways in which most of the rest of the democratic world organizes its public politics.

In this final chapter on institutions, I lead a quick tour of institutional arrangements in parliamentary democracies. Rather than separating power into distinct branches of government, each checking and balancing the others as is done in the United States, the world of parliamentary democracy is organized according to a principle that emphasizes the coordination and concentration of power. The textbooks refer to this as the "fusion of powers" in contrast to the American-style "separation of powers." The centerpieces of this arrangement are the supremacy of parliament and the accountability of the political executive—the cabinet, the government, or the administration—to it.

THE PARLIAMENTARY SETTING
Electoral Arrangements

The best place to begin is with electoral arrangements. American legislatures, both state and federal, are elected according to the first-past-the-post principle. Legislative candidates campaign for office in districts, with the one receiving a plurality of votes there elected as the district's representative. I noted in Chapter 7 that this arrangement, which is also followed in Great Britain and some other of its former colonies, encourages two-party or two-candidate competition in each electoral district (Duverger's Law). If it is the *same* two parties in each district, then one of them will end up with a legislative majority.

Although, as just noted, some parliamentary regimes like Great Britain elect legislators in this fashion, the vast bulk of such regimes, especially those in continental Europe (including the democracies that emerged in eastern Europe late in the twentieth century) elect legislators according to one of several proportional representation (PR) formulas.[1] There is tremendous variety in the specific PR details, but however they are implemented, these arrangements tend to produce parliaments in which *many* parties are represented.[2] Indeed, because parliamentary seats are distributed among many parties instead of just two, it is rare for any one party to command a majority in parliament. Thus, with the exception of

[1] Some parliamentary democracies, like those in Germany, Japan, and New Zealand, have a hybrid electoral system in which some legislators are elected from districts according to first-past-the-post, while others are determined by a PR formula.
[2] See Gary Cox, *Making Votes Count* (New York: Cambridge University Press, 1997).

Britain and a few other instances in which a single party captures a parliamentary majority, it is necessary in most parliamentary democracies to engage in multiparty negotiations in order to organize government.

Governmental Arrangements

In parliamentary regimes there is a division and specialization of labor. The House of Commons does not run British politics. Nor does the Dutch *Tweede Kamer*, the German *Bundestag*, the Japanese *Diet*, or the Norwegian *Storting* run the politics of the Netherlands, Germany, Japan, or Norway, respectively. Rather, each parliament "elects" a *government* to serve as the executive arm of the regime. I thus need to describe exactly what a "government" is on the one hand, and how a country's parliament "elects" one on the other.

The political executive in a parliamentary democracy is, with a few exceptions that I won't stop to consider here, chosen by parliament. This executive is called the *government*; it is also known as the *cabinet* or *council of ministers*. It is a collection of senior politicians each of whom is the head of a department or ministry of state. In nearly every parliamentary regime there is a finance minister, foreign minister, interior minister, defense minister, justice minister, education minister, environment minister, and so on.

Thus, there is a division and specialization of labor at two different levels. The first distinguishes between legislature and executive. The legislature selects the executive in the first place; keeps it in place or replaces it with a different one; and considers various pieces of legislation, the most important of which is the annual budget.[3] I will discuss these features mo-

---

[3] It should be noted that legislatures in parliamentary regimes are not the hyperactive lawmaking engines we encounter in the American setting. Typically, parliaments vote a few broad delegations of statutory authority which are then implemented by the government. In the United States, on the other hand, Congress and the various state legislatures legislate with much greater frequency and in a much more fine-grained fashion.

mentarily. The second level of division and specialization of labor is in the government itself. In a manner quite parallel to the arrangements involving committees in the U.S. Congress, each ministry of state has jurisdiction over specified dimensions of public policy, called a *ministerial portfolio*. In this domain the minister and his or her senior civil servants have considerable discretion to interpret statutory authority and implement public policy.

Another way to think about this arrangement is as a chain of principal-agent relationships. Parliament as principal delegates executive authority to a collective agent, the cabinet. The cabinet as principal, in turn, delegates discretionary authority in various policy jurisdictions to its agents, namely particular cabinet ministers. To control its agents, and coordinate their activities, the cabinet employs various before-the-fact and after-the-fact mechanisms; usually one member of the cabinet plays the role of policeman and maestro—the *prime minister*. Likewise, to control *its* agent, parliament, too, exercises before-the-fact and after-the fact authority. We refer to this authority as that of "making and breaking governments," since parliament votes a cabinet into office in the first place and, if it is unhappy with cabinet performance after the fact, may vote it out of office and replace it with an alternative cabinet.[4]

The Government Formation Process

A typical sequence of events in one cycle of parliamentary democracy begins with a triggering event like an election. When the new parliament convenes there are often a number of parties represented, no one of which commands a majority of votes on its own. Each party has an *endowment* consisting of

[4] These details are developed in Michael Laver and Kenneth A. Shepsle, *Making and Breaking Governments: Cabinets and Legislatures in Parliamentary Democracies* (New York: Cambridge University Press, 1996).

a certain number of seats under its control and a set of policy priorities and positions on which it has just conducted its electoral campaign.[5] Also at this time there will be a government in place—the cabinet that was running the country just before the election. The first order of business facing the new parliament is whether to retain the status quo cabinet or replace it with a new cabinet. If the political fortunes of the various parties have changed as a result of the election, it is highly likely that a new cabinet will be selected, one better reflecting the balance of political forces in the new parliament. But since no one party is a majority in its own right, the new government will have to reflect the preferences of a *coalition* of political parties. Government formation requires coalition building.

Anyone watching this process, at least that part of it that is not conducted behind closed doors, will know when it has reached its conclusion. This is when a parliamentary majority allows a new set of senior politicians to take over the reins of each of the ministries of state. This transition is normally accompanied by much fanfare, including a press conference in which the new ministers "meet the public" and announce their policy goals. In some parliamentary regimes, there must be a formal *vote of investiture* in which the new government is formally approved by a parliamentary majority. In others, the head of state (the king or queen or president) simply announces the new government. In all cases the new government survives at the pleasure of parliament. At any time,

---

[5] In effect, each party may be treated as a unitary actor. Unlike legislative parties in the United States, which contain within them a wide range of opinion and whose members are relatively free to pursue their own private objectives, parliamentary parties are far more homogeneous in terms of policy preferences, and their leaders have powerful mechanisms by which to control the rank and file. Parliamentary party leaders, of course, must keep their followers happy, as I argued more generally in Chapter 14, but they may proceed in a manner that is best for their party as a whole. In effect, then, we may think of the parliamentary party as acting as if it had well-defined preferences, as manifested in the beliefs and choices made by its leaders.

parliament may entertain a *motion of no confidence* in the government, usually moved by an opposition party politician; if this passes, then the government must resign and the government formation process starts up anew.[6] Alternatively, the government itself may introduce a *motion of confidence*, or attach such a motion to an important bill before the parliament. If that motion or bill should be defeated, then the government is obliged to resign.[7]

So, the government formation process ends with the creation of a new government—a new set of managers of the various departments of state. But what of its beginning? Ordinarily, when either a new parliament convenes, an old government is defeated in a confidence procedure, or the old government resigns for whatever reason, the head of state appoints a leading politician, called a *formateur*, to try to assemble a new government. In some countries either the constitution explicitly, or constitutional conventions implicitly, restrict the discretion of the head of state. He or she must, for example, allow the prime minister of the previous government first crack at forming a new government. Or he or she must allow the leader of the largest party in the new parliament first shot. In other cases, the head of state is free to choose whoever he or she wishes as *formateur*. (In some circumstances, the head of state appoints an *informateur*—a respected elder statesman with no personal ax to grind—to consult widely in the political community and then advise him or her on whom to appoint *formateur*.) The *formateur* negoti-

[6] Indeed, a vulnerable government normally can anticipate whether a parliamentary majority no longer has confidence in it; as a result the government will resign in advance of the motion-of-no-confidence procedure so that the latter is not carried out to its ignominious conclusion.

[7] Why would a government do this? The chief reason is to raise the stakes of defeating the bill to which the motion is attached. It is a power play, a showdown move, in which the government puts parliament on notice that if it should defeat the government's bill, the government will come crashing down around its ears.

ates with other parties in assembling a distribution of ministerial portfolios to political parties—a government—that a parliamentary majority is prepared to support. The parties receiving a seat at the cabinet table (by being assigned a ministerial portfolio) are said to be the *government parties*. Those not included in government are the *opposition parties* (though some of these may lend the government support in parliament). I examine this process shortly, as well as the motivations that drive it.

Once in place, the new government governs. Each minister attends to day-to-day administration with senior civil servants in his or her ministry and, together with other ministers, meets regularly in cabinet to formulate and coordinate overall governmental policy. This will entail not only the implementation of existing policy but also the formulation of new policy. And the latter means that the government will need to have firm control of parliamentary politics, setting parliament's agenda and making sure it toes the line. Thus, there is a political tension between government and parliament, with the former in the driver's seat because of its control over day-to-day management of political affairs; but since the latter "makes" the government in the first place, it also can "break" the government. In short, the government governs *subject to keeping the confidence of parliament*.

A MENAGERIE OF GOVERNMENTS

In the U.S. Congress, the House and Senate are organized by the party capturing a majority of seats in that chamber. It is always the case in the modern era for either the Democrats or Republicans to win a chamber majority (although it wasn't always this way, especially early in American constitutional experience). In contrast, the process of government formation in parliamentary democracies briefly described in the last few pages produces governments of quite a variety of sizes and shapes (Table 16.1).

The number of parties represented at the cabinet table can be one or many—in which case the executive is a single party or a coalition, respectively. The number of seats in parliament controlled by the government parties can constitute either a majority or a minority. Thus, there are four different types of government. Their relative frequencies in Europe since 1945 are given parenthetically in Table 16.1.

Unified governments, which arise in slightly more than one of every eight governments in the period of study, are formed by parties that win outright parliamentary majorities. This is a relatively rare event, which occurs frequently in Great Britain but only occasionally anywhere else in Europe. In this case the majority party votes itself all the cabinet portfolios. The only serious threat to these "juggernauts" is intraparty factionalism. One faction of the majority party, if sufficiently numerous, can bring the government down by deserting it on a key vote.[8]

Much more common, occurring about half the time in the postwar era, is a cabinet composed of several parties that jointly control a parliamentary majority. These *multiparty majority* governments need to control their rank and file in order to continue in office, but the ordinary tools of party discipline are typically sufficient for this task. A "backbencher" who threatens to stray off the reservation may find that his or her parliamentary career prospects suddenly become bleak, not to speak of the fact that the party organization will refuse to back him or her at the next election.

---

[8] In Great Britain in 1994, the Conservative government of Prime Minister John Major was a unified government, but only tenuously so. It had a bare majority in the House of Commons and thus was potentially vulnerable to factional blackmail from within its partisan ranks. In parliamentary votes on expanding the role of the European Union in the spring of 1994, so-called Euroskeptics inside the Conservative Party threatened to desert the government (which favored further European integration). Major called their bluff and won . . . that time.

TABLE 16.1

PARLIAMENTARY GOVERNMENT FORMS*

Government Parties in Parliament

		Majority	Minority
	Single Party	Unified (.134)	Single-party minority (.238)
Executive			
	Coalition	Multiparty majority (.500)	Multiparty minority (.128)

* Cell entries give the proportion of each type as determined by Strom for a sample of Western parliamentary democracies, 1945–1982.
SOURCE: Kaare Strom, *Minority Government and Majority Rule* (New York: Cambridge University Press, 1990), p. 61.

A more serious threat to these governments is that during their incumbency, one or more of the governing parties will become dissatisfied and resign, essentially uniting with the opposition to bring down the government.[9] Short of pulling out of a sitting government in order to defeat it, a governing party may insist on a reallocation of portfolios. If, for example, recent poll results suggested that one of the minor government parties was rising in popularity at the expense of one of the major government parties, the former could insist on a *cabinet reshuffle* in which it received more portfolios, or more important portfolios.

A *single-party minority* government sounds pretty strange to American ears (although I suggest shortly that the reader has more familiarity with it than he or she realizes). It is a government in which one party receives all cabinet portfolios,

---

[9] If one of the governing parties pulls out, then, as we noted earlier, an actual vote of no confidence need not occur. If the parties remaining in the government believe they no longer have the support of parliament, the government may simply resign, triggering a new round of government formation. Alternatively, the prime minister may petition the head of state to dissolve parliament and call for new elections.

but that party has less than a majority of parliamentary seats. It governs at the sufferance of an opposition that, in combination, controls a majority of parliamentary seats. How can this be? It is able to retain office, as I shortly demonstrate, because the opposition, even though a majority, cannot agree on an alternative that it prefers. Imagine a large social democratic party—slightly left of center—controlling, say, 40 percent of parliamentary seats, that faces a radical left-wing party, an extremist right-wing party, and a religious party, controlling roughly 20 percent of the seats each. It is quite likely that anything preferred to a social democratic minority government by the left-wingers is strongly opposed by the right-wingers and religious partisans, whereas anything preferred to the social democrats by the two more conservative parties is opposed by the left-wingers. The opposition majority simply cannot get its act together, allowing the social democrats to survive in office even though they comprise but a minority of the whole parliament. This is not at all an unusual scenario and, as the evidence reported in Table 16.1 suggests, something like it occurs nearly one-quarter of the time in Western parliamentary democracies.

To complete the picture, about one in every eight governments in the postwar Western experience is a coalition government whose partners control less than a parliamentary majority. Typically they will be center-left or center-right coalitions that, like the single-party minority governments described in the previous paragraph, split the opposition.

Before turning to an analysis of government formation, it is worth mentioning that Americans often get depressed over a phenomenon conventionally referred to as *divided government*. This is a condition in which one party, say the Republican Party, controls the White House, but the Democrats control one or both of the legislative chambers. After the 2006 elections, Republican George W. Bush occupied the White House, but the Democrats had captured both houses of Congress. It is alleged by inside-the-Beltway pundits that this is a formula for gridlock as partisan majorities in the different branches of government prevent anything from happening.[10] Such pundits often cast an alluring look across the Atlantic, touting the advantages of parliamentary government. Yet, the data of Table 16.1 suggest that parliamentary regimes are also highly prone to divided government. Multiparty majority coalition governments are those that control a parliamentary majority, but divided government occurs *within* the executive. Single-party minority governments have a unified executive but, lacking a majority in parliament, are divided in exactly the same way American governments often are—an executive whose party lacks a legislative majority. (Thus, despite sounding pretty strange to American ears, single-party minority governments are structurally identical to the divided governments with which Americans have had frequent experience.) Minority coalition governments are divided both within the executive and between executive and legislature. Indeed, European parliamentary experience suggests that governments are divided about seven-eighths of the time, a proportion roughly equal to the postwar American experience. Parliamentary government, in short, is no cure for divided government.

ANALYZING GOVERNMENT FORMATION

I now want to analyze how governments of various types actually are formed. Government formation in parliamentary democracies is a subject that has been studied analytically for

[10] This does not often comport well with the actual facts (though this never stopped a pundit worth his or her salt). President Reagan enjoyed enormous success in his first term despite the fact that the Republicans did not control a majority in the House of Representatives. Alternatively, both Jimmy Carter and Bill Clinton enjoyed (hardly the right word!) unified government (in 1977–81 and 1993–95, respectively), but each would undoubtedly have given his eye teeth for a record of accomplishments matching that of Reagan's first term.

more than forty years. Scholars have produced an immense literature and I shall not be able to explore every nook and cranny.[11] Instead, I develop an example in some detail. The example typifies many of the possibilities that are encountered in the real world, but it is hardly *typical*, since the real world contains an enormous amount of variation (as suggested in Table 16.1). My purpose, however, is not so much to present the reader with a full-blown model of government formation as it is to show how rational politicians think through all the many permutations of the government formation game in order to pursue their objectives effectively.

German Example: Basic Setup

In Germany throughout the last quarter century, four parties won seats in the German parliament, the *Bundestag*: the Christian Democrats (CD), the Social Democrats (SD), the Free Democrats (FD), and the Greens (G). The CDs are a classic center-conservative party—procapitalist on economic issues, proactive in foreign policy, and traditional on social issues. The SDs are a classic social democratic party—left-leaning on economic matters, pacifist in the foreign realm, and progressive on social issues. The FDs are a liberal party—free-market oriented on economic issues, moderate in foreign policy, and progressive on social issues. The Greens, finally, are more left-leaning than the Social Democrats on economic and foreign affairs and more progressive than the Free Democrats on social issues.

Although the seat totals for each party varied from year to year, the strategic structure in Germany did not. Specifically, rarely did a single party win an outright majority of seats. Second, the CDs were sufficiently numerous that they could

---

[11] The standard bibliographic reference surveying this field is Michael Laver and Norman Schofield, *Multiparty Government* (New York: Oxford University Press, 1980).

form a majority with *any* of the other three parties. Third, a majority excluding the CDs required that *all* of the remaining parties coalesce. Thus, the set of possible majority coalitions in the *Bundestag* during this period included

- CD–SD
- CD–FD
- CD–G
- SD–FD–G

as well as any of the above with an additional party added.

A *government* (or cabinet), recall, is a distribution of ministerial portfolios among the parties (more accurately, among senior party politicians). Suppose there were only two key cabinet ministries in the government—Finance (F) and Foreign Affairs (FA). Display 16.1 lists all the possible German governments involving these ministries. There are four ways to assign the Finance portfolio to a party and, for each of these, four ways to assign the Foreign Affairs portfolio, giving a total of sixteen possible governments.[12] In the case at hand, then, there are four possible majority coalitions in the *Bundestag* (listed above) and sixteen possible governments (given in Display 16.1).

[12] If, as is often the case in the real world, there are more than the four parties in the example (say, p in number), and more than two portfolios (say, q in number), then there are p^q possible ways to divvy the portfolios up among parties, and thus p^q possible governments. Even for moderate values of p and q, this number can grow rather large. With ten parties (as was approximately the case at various times in countries like Belgium or Italy) and fifteen government ministries, for instance, there are ten million billion different conceivable governments. We would have to harvest an entire forest to print a list like the one in Display 16.1!

DISPLAY 16.1		
POSSIBLE PORTFOLIO ALLOCATIONS IN THE *BUNDESTAG*		
	Party holding	
	Finance portfolio (F)	**Foreign Affairs portfolio (FA)**
1.	CD	CD
2.	CD	SD
3.	CD	FD
4.	CD	G
5.	SD	CD
6.	SD	SD
7.	SD	FD
8.	SD	G
9.	FD	CD
10.	FD	SD
11.	FD	FD
12.	FD	G
13.	G	CD
14.	G	SD
15.	G	FD
16.	G	G

German Example, Continued: Party Preferences and Majority Preferences

We now need to consider how each party (and ultimately how each parliamentary majority) assesses each of the sixteen governments in Display 16.1. There is no right answer to this matter, since a party's assessment of a particular government will depend on what the party cares about. In the literature on government formation, two motivational hypotheses have been seriously entertained.

DISPLAY 16.2

OFFICE-SEEKING PARTY PREFERENCES OVER ALTERNATIVE GERMAN GOVERNMENTS*

CD	SD	FD	G
{1}	{6}	{11}	{16}
{2, 3, 4}	{5, 7, 8}	{9, 10, 12}	{13, 14, 15}
{5, 9, 13}	{2, 10, 14}	{3, 7, 15}	{4, 8, 12}
{6, 7, 8, 10, 11, 12, 14, 15, 16}	{1, 3, 4, 9, 11, 12, 13, 15, 16}	{1, 2, 4, 5, 6, 8, 13, 14, 16}	{1, 2, 3, 5, 6, 7, 9, 10, 11}

* The numbers in each column refer to the goverments listed in Display 16.1. A party prefers higher-listed to lower-listed governments and is indifferent among bracketed governments.

OFFICE-SEEKING. The first, the office-seeking motivation, assumes that parties care only about getting into office. Thus, the CDs, in looking over the possibilities in Display 16.1, will most like government 1, giving them both portfolios. If they care more about financial matters than foreign affairs (and I will assume this, for the sake of argument, for all parties), they will next prefer governments 2, 3, and 4 (among which they are indifferent), giving them the Finance portfolio and some other party the Foreign Affairs portfolio. Next they will prefer governments 5, 9, and 13 in which they get the Foreign Affairs portfolio and some other party gets Finance; again, they are indifferent among these three governments. Finally, they least prefer (and are indifferent among) governments 6, 7, 8, 10, 11, 12, 14, 15, and 16, in which they are excluded from government altogether. Display 16.2 gives the office-seeking preferences of each of the four parties.

Since we know which combinations of parties constitute *Bundestag* majorities (the bulleted list above), we can compute majority preferences over the sixteen possible governments from these individual preferences. For example, the CD–FD majority prefers government 3 (CDs get Finance and FDs get Foreign Affairs) to government 6 (SDs get both portfolios), since 3 ranks ahead of 6 in both party preference orderings. It is a bit tedious, and not particularly enlightening in this particular example, to examine all sixteen governments to see how majorities rank them. It is tedious because there are 120 such comparisons to be checked (though a computer with even a modest amount of power could do this in the blink of an eye); it is unenlightening because, as Display 16.2 reveals, there is a substantial amount of indifference in party preferences, the latter because the only thing parties consider is whether they are in government or not. For these reasons I go no further in an analysis based on office-seeking, though the reader now can see how it could be carried out. (This is one of those proverbial "homework exercises" that the enterprising reader may wish to pursue.)

POLICY-SEEKING. The second motivational hypothesis, that of policy-seeking parties, is richer in its possibilities, and arguably a more realistic conjecture about party behavior as well, so I explore it somewhat more deeply. Needless to say, ambitious politicians love the prospect of advancing to high office. The ego boost of power, not to speak of the creature comforts of a commodious office, an army of deferential assistants, the services of a leather-upholstered limousine, and frequent travel to exciting world destinations, all contribute to the allure of office. There is no gainsaying the potency of the office-seeking motivation to explain the wishes of individual politicians. But parliamentary politicians are not entirely free agents. They are members of parties which have been elected to the parliament to accomplish things. Party leaders must check the acquisitive instincts and other private motives of their senior party members to ensure that these partisan purposes are not jeopardized.

In particular, I conjecture that a more compelling motivational consideration derives from the fact that parties serve external constituencies, delivering policies desired by those constituencies in exchange for electoral support. External constituencies don't really care whether a politician from the party is a cabinet minister or not. They *do* care about the policies produced by the government in power. Always attentive to electoral considerations and ever mindful of the fact that electoral constituencies are the principals for which the party is an agent, party leaders seek to install governments that are disposed toward policies preferred by these constituencies. This may mean pushing to get fellow party members appointed to the cabinet, but it may not. Thus, despite the individual politician's lust for office, the party system, electoral competition, and the principal-agent relationship between parliamentary parties and external constituencies check and constrain this motivation.[13]

To see what is involved in a policy-seeking analysis of government formation, we need to know what policies a party wants to pursue on the one hand, and what policies a party believes other parties are pursuing on the other. To facilitate this, I employ the by now familiar spatial model initially developed in Chapter 5. Based on our crude characterization of the German parties earlier in this section of the present chapter, we portray their policy preferences in a simplified, two-dimensional spatial map (Figure 16.1).

The horizontal dimension captures economic policy, with a left-wing radical positioned to the left and a right-wing conservative to the right. The vertical dimension describes foreign policy, with a more pacifist orientation at the bottom and a more activist international posture at the top. Thus, given the

---

[13] I also note that it doesn't matter for our purposes whether a party is "really" committed to the policies it pursues (ideological parties), or instead whether it does so only to secure electoral benefits from satisfied constituents (instrumental parties).

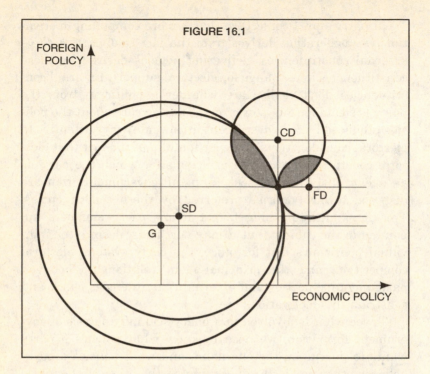

FIGURE 16.1

preferences of their electoral supporters, the CDs are the most activist party in the *Bundestag* on foreign policy issues and one of the more conservative on economic issues. The black dot next to their name locates the CD "ideal" policy on both dimensions. In a similar manner we locate the other three parties.

I assume that the horizontal dimension falls into the jurisdiction of the Finance Ministry and the vertical dimension is the responsibility of the Foreign Affairs Ministry. I also assume—and this is a strong assumption—that all parties in the *Bundestag* know that whichever party secures each of the ministries will push its ideal policy in that jurisdiction.[14]

---

[14] It is a strong assumption because it stipulates not only that a minister has a great deal of authority in his or her jurisdiction (something that any observer would accept), but also that other players on the parliamentary scene have virtually no influence over policy once the minister has been

I can now state precisely what is meant by policy seeking. A policy-seeking party will, if given the authority to do so, implement its ideal policy in the jurisdictions in which that authority applies. A party that obtains both portfolios, therefore, will implement its ideal point. A party that obtains one portfolio will implement the component of its ideal point that applies to the jurisdiction of that portfolio. Thus, if the CDs form a single-party minority government, they will implement the policies associated with their ideal point. If, on the other hand, the CDs and FDs form a multiparty majority government, with the CDs getting the Finance portfolio and the FDs the Foreign Affairs portfolio, then this government will implement the policies associated with the point identified by the intersection of the horizontal line through the FD ideal and the vertical line through the CD ideal. (It is the point from which the shaded petals originate—these will be described momentarily.) That is, the CD–FD government will implement the CD's ideal economic policy and the FD's ideal foreign policy.

German Example, Concluded: Equilibrium in Government Formation

In Figure 16.1 the four horizontal and the four vertical lines through each of the party ideal points define the foreign policy and the economic policy, respectively, that each of the four parties would implement if it secured the relevant cabinet portfolio. Thus, each of the sixteen possible governments (the ones listed in Display 16.1) is associated with one of the six-

---

designated. The only recourse for a parliamentary majority is to topple the government. As long as a minister does not cross that line, he or she is otherwise unconstrained. To say that this assumption is *strong* is effectively to say that it is very unrealistic. Models, as I hope I made clear way back in Chapter 1, are always unrealistic; the important issue is whether they are "close enough for government work" to permit some insight. This the reader must judge after thinking about the argument in its entirety.

teen points in Figure 16.1 defined by the intersection of one horizontal and one vertical line. For example, the point at the intersection of the vertical line through the CD ideal and the horizontal line through the FD ideal locates the policies of the CD–FD government in which the CDs get the Finance portfolio and the FDs the Foreign Affairs portfolio. I refer to these sixteen points so defined as the *lattice* of possible governments.

The ideal policies not only define what policies a party would implement if it were given the power to do so, but they also allow us to characterize party preferences over *other* policies. As in Chapter 5, I make the simplifying assumption that parties prefer policies closer to their ideal to those farther away from their ideal. With this assumption we can analyze the viability of alternative governments, each of which is judged by the various *Bundestag* parties in terms of the policies they are postulated to pursue.

Consider the CD–FD government just discussed. (Throughout this discussion, the first-named party obtains the Finance portfolio and the second-named the Foreign Affairs portfolio.) To determine how the CDs assess this government, draw a circle through the CD–FD point centered on the CD ideal (as shown in Figure 16.1). The CDs are indifferent among all the points on this circle and prefer any point inside it (because each point on the circle is exactly as far away from the CD ideal as is the CD–FD point, and all points inside the circle are closer to the CD ideal than the CD–FD point). The circle is an *indifference curve*, and the area inside it is a *preferred-to set* in the language of Chapter 5. Notice that the only *governments* the CDs prefer to the CD–FD government are the single-party minority government, in which the CDs get both portfolios enabling them to implement their ideal point, and the FD–CD government in which they swap portfolios.

The three other circles in Figure 16.1 reflect the preferences of the remaining parties regarding the CD–FD government. To see how parliamentary majorities feel about this gov-ernment, we look at relevant intersections of these circles. Re-call that there are four majority coalitions (the bulleted list given earlier). The shaded petal pointing northeast is the set of policies preferred by the CD–FD *Bundestag* majority to the policy that a CD–FD government would implement. While there are *policies* that this majority prefers, there is no *gov-ernment* (alternative allocation of portfolios as reflected in the various lattice points) that it prefers. There are two shaded petals pointing northwest (one is only slightly bigger than the other), reflecting the policies that the CD–SD and CD–G *Bun-destag* majorities prefer to the policies that would be imple-mented by the CD–FD government. Again, there are policies each of these majorities would rather see implemented, but no government (no lattice point) that would do it. Finally, only barely visible to the naked eye is a sliver of a shaded petal pointing almost due south—the policies preferred by the SD–FD–G *Bundestag* majority. Again, this majority prefers no government to CD–FD.

In short, *no other government is preferred by any of the bul-leted parliamentary majorities to the CD–FD government*. In the language of Chapter 5, this government has an *empty win-set* relative to the fifteen alternatives the *Bundestag* might consider. If this government were installed and set about im-plementing the CD ideal on economic policy and the FD ideal on foreign policy, then it would constitute an *equilibrium* of the government formation process. Any motion of no confi-dence would fail, since a *Bundestag* majority would not pass such a motion unless it had an alternative government in mind to replace the incumbent.[15]

It is actually rather remarkable that such an equilibrium exists, since typically in multidimensional spatial analysis

---

[15] In fact, this is actually the government that dominated German politics throughout the last quarter century (with occasional exceptions).

there is no majority-rule equilibrium (see Chapter 5). The reason there is one in this example is because we are considering only the sixteen lattice points, not the entire two-dimensional space of points. I have restricted focus to the points on the lattice because the government formation process chooses *governments*, not *policies*. If the *Bundestag* chose policies directly, then there would be no need for a government at all, since Germany would be run directly by its parliament. The fact is, however, that in Germany and every other parliamentary democracy, its parliament does *not* run the country; it chooses a government which does. So our focus on governments (the lattice of points) rather than policies (the entire space of points) is appropriate.

Let me conclude this brief equilibrium analysis by noting a couple of additional findings. First, although we did find an equilibrium in the German example—an empty-winset point from among those on the lattice—it does not always work out so nicely. Examples can be produced in which *no* lattice point is an equilibrium. In this case, majority preferences cycle over all the lattice points. However, systematic empirical work on the real world suggests that equilibrium is very likely.[16]

Second, an empty-winset lattice point may not be the only equilibrium. By this we do not mean that there can be more than one empty-winset point, for this is virtually impossible.[17] Rather, I am suggesting that there is a different way to think about equilibrium. We display this for our German example in Figure 16.2. There the analysis focuses on a CD single-party

---

[16] This evidence is found in Laver and Shepsle, *Making and Breaking Governments*, chapters 6–9.

[17] *Informal proof:* Suppose x and y are two lattice points. Logically, either x is preferred by some majority to y, or y is preferred by some majority to x (both cannot be true). Of course, a third possibility is that x and y tie in a vote between the two. If either of the first two scenarios holds, then the losing candidate does not have an empty winset, so that at most one of them does. Only in the third scenario is it possible for there to be more than one empty-winset lattice point.

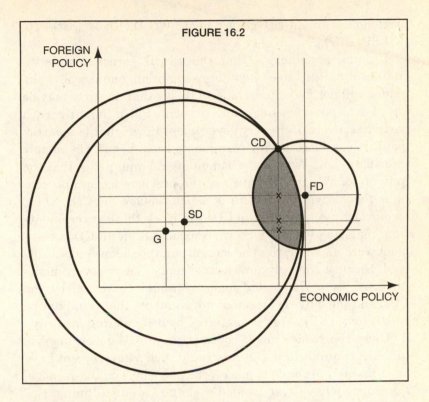

FIGURE 16.2

minority government in which the CDs receive both portfolios and implement their ideal policy. Clearly this is the best result for the CDs—they would certainly participate in no *Bundestag* majority trying to replace this government. The only majority which excludes the CDs is the SD–FD–G majority. Indifference curves through the CD ideal point for each of these three parties are shown in the figure, and their common intersection is shaded. This shaded area describes the winset, W(CD,CD), the set of policies that all three parties prefer to the one implemented by the CD government. Notice that there *are* three lattice points in this winset (indicated by *x*). Thus, a *Bundestag* majority prefers any government giving the CDs the Finance portfolio and any other party the Foreign Affairs portfolio to an all-CD government: W(CD,CD) = {(CD,FD), (CD,SD), (CD,G)}.

I claim, nonetheless, that the all-CD government is an equilibrium. But I need another assumption, one I believe the reader will not find offensive. And this is that no party may be forced into government against its will. Put differently, each party has a veto over every government in which it is a participant. It can block such governments from forming by simply refusing to join. With this assumption in hand, notice that the contents of W(CD, CD) given in the previous paragraph contains three governments, *all of which include the CDs*. Thus, by our last assumption, the CDs can block those governments from replacing (CD,CD). So we conclude: If an all-CD government were in power, then no motion of no confidence could succeed, because the only prospective replacement governments preferred by a *Bundestag* majority would be vetoed by the CDs, and the only replacement governments that could not be vetoed by the CDs are not preferred by a *Bundestag* majority.

Okay, the reader might concede, an all-CD government is indeed an equilibrium. But how could such a government have been selected in the first place? That is, why would a *Bundestag* majority have ever handed over the keys to all ministries to the CDs, especially if they appreciated the conclusion we just drew? This is a very good question, but I believe there is a good answer. Imagine that once upon a time the CDs were a *majority* party all by themselves. Naturally enough, they formed an all-CD government, since they had the votes in the *Bundestag* to do that. Now suppose there is a new election, and the CDs lose their majority. The new parliament convenes to form a government, *but the CDs are the incumbent sitting government and they stay in power until they are replaced by the new parliament*. In this situation, as Figure 16.2 graphically displays, the CDs can remain in power as a minority government because the new parliamentary majority is unable to replace it with something they prefer that is veto-proof.

I thus have derived two different kinds of government equilibrium. One, displayed in Figure 16.1, is an allocation of portfolios to which no other allocation is preferred, an empty-winset government. The second, displayed in Figure 16.2, is an allocation of portfolios to which other allocations are preferred, but these are vulnerable to veto.

CONCLUSION

This chapter has served as something of an antidote to the possible misimpression that rational behavior in institutional contexts is a distinctly American practice. In fact, institutional arrangements elsewhere, though they surely differ in fundamental ways, nonetheless serve some of the same purposes that I portrayed American institutions as serving in the other chapters of this part of the volume. Thus, political labor is divided and specialized; authority is delegated; and before-the-fact and after-the-fact control mechanisms are utilized. Rational actors in these political settings exercise sophistication and foresight in determining what actions will best serve their interests.

In the case of parliamentary behavior, in which the government (a specialized agent) is selected by a parliamentary majority (the principal), partisan political leaders calculate about government formation in terms of objectives they wish the selected government to serve. If office-seeking animates their behavior, then they will maneuver, whether in voting to bring a government down or to form one in the first place, to include their partisan colleagues at the cabinet table. If policy-seeking drives behavior, then the calculation will be in terms of which policies they prefer to see implemented. I have done no more than develop a specific example in detail. But I hope to have displayed how one might analyze politics, whatever the institutional context.

PROBLEMS AND DISCUSSION QUESTIONS

1. Like any complex institution, parliamentary democracies feature a division and specialization of labor, between the parliament and the government it elects on the one hand, and between the various cabinet portfolios or ministries within the government on the other. Discuss these arrangements in general terms. Which institutions are tasked with which activities? What purposes does this administrative setup serve? Is there any *delegation* involved, and if so, how do the principals keep their agents in line?

2. Mueller (2003)[a] provides an example of coalition formation in a one-dimensional setting to show that behavioral hypotheses strongly affect predictions of how coalition governments will form. Suppose some country with PR ends up with the following distribution of 100 parliamentary seats among five parties, ordered from left to right: $A(15) < B(28) < C(11) < D(33) < E(14)$. First, find all minimum winning coalitions (MWC)—that is, coalitions with greater than fifty votes but for which removal of any one party will make them a minority. Then, find the smallest minimum winning coalition. Then, find the MWC with the fewest members, which might be a plausible prediction if bargaining becomes more complex as the number of parties increases. Then, find all MWCs for which the parties are adjacent in the political space. Is one of these hypotheses more believable than the others? Does it depend on whether you think politicians are policy-seeking or office-seeking?

[a] See Dennis Mueller, Public Choice III (New York: Cambridge University Press, 2003), pp. 280–81.

3. Draw two sets of axes ranging from 0 to 10, with one dimension representing Finance and the other Defense, and suppose that there are three parties (A, B, and C) with ideal points (1, 2.5), (3.5, 1) and (9, 7). Any coalition of two parties (with one controlling each portfolio exclusively) is sufficient for a majority government, but no one party has an outright majority. What is the set of possible minority and majority governments? Is there a stable majority government coalition (i.e., with an empty winset)? Is there a minority government that is a stable equilbrium (if we assume that no party can be forced into a government against its will)? Illustrate all of your answers graphically and briefly explain your logic, taking special care to explain how minority governments come about.

4. In proportional representation systems it is almost always true that no single party wins an outright majority of votes. Using the logic of Downsian electoral competition, explain why this might be so.

5. After reading this chapter, what is your reasoned opinion about the merits of proportional representation within parliamentary democracies, relative to the U.S. system of single-member districts and presidential government? In your discussion, consider at least representation; divided government and gridlock; the government formation and breakdown process; and effective governance.

17

Final Lessons

To summarize this volume in all but the most superficial fashion is more than the reader is likely willing to tolerate. So I do so superficially. Part I provided the basic building blocks for political analysis—individuals, their preferences, and their beliefs. I emphasized there the importance of analysis and, with the rational choice paradigm, I nailed my colors to the mast by laying out an analytical approach.

Part II focused on group choice by voting. I demonstrated that groups, unlike individuals, could not always be treated as unitary because the aggregated preferences of group members did not always add up. Neither the method of majority rule nor, from Arrow's Theorem, any other "reasonable" method of preference aggregation can guarantee rational group preferences. This fact, in turn, means that individuals controlling motion making and other agenda mechanisms can strategically manipulate things to their advantage. Combine this with the fact that there are many ways in which to stage an election or structure a vote, and the bottom line is that the result of group deliberation is, in many respects, *artifactual*. It is dependent on the individual preferences and beliefs of group members, to be sure. But it also depends upon who makes motions, in what order motions are made, what the voting rule is, and many other features besides. One might well want the outcome of group choice to depend on individual preferences and beliefs. But it is considerably less clear that it is desirable for group choice to depend upon the many arbitrary features of the processes by which preferences and beliefs are aggregated.

Part III examined groups as ongoing entities, many of whose decisions and actions are taken by methods other than voting. I took the notion of "cooperation" as fundamental and built it up from two-person bargaining (over such things as whether or not to drain a marsh) to multiperson coordination and collective action problems. We saw that many of the difficulties facing modern societies are, in fact, manifestations of the inability of large groups to coordinate individual behavior in mutually profitable ways. Consequently, in equilibrium, life is not all sweetness and light: public goods are underproduced, while public "bads" are overproduced; there are too many negative externalities and too few positive externalities; common resources are mismanaged, overutilized, and poorly superintended. But this is only to observe that human societies are not utopias and that there is always room for improvement.

Part IV examined some of the ways in which human societies engage in such improvement. They invent institutions, some of which allow for more efficient performance (taking advantage of a division and specialization of labor) and others of which enhance coordination, standardization, and the "rationalization" of expectations. Some of these institutions are involved in the making of selections (legislatures and parliaments), others in the implementation of selected options (bureaucracies), while still others orchestrate (leadership institutions) and validate (courts and judges).

The methodology implicit in our various forays into "analyzing politics" is *portable*. You can take it with you, so to speak, to analyze novel political situations as they present themselves to you. So many of our life experiences take place in group settings, ranging from two-person emotional partnerships, to small-scale attachments (for example, rooming groups or families), to larger associations (like religious congregations or amateur sports leagues). Politics, as I endeavored to argue in the very first chapter, attaches to all such group interactions. To analyze these situations, you need to appreciate what it is the individuals want, what they believe, what actions are feasible for them, and what are the rules of interaction—the mechanisms by which individual actions (chosen for rational reasons) are transformed into outcomes. It is also often useful to know a bit of history—about what transpired to produce the circumstance you are now interested in analyzing; this history is often instructive as we seek to figure out what people want, what they believe, and what they think others want and believe.

Another lesson I hope the reader takes from this book is that the methodology of analysis I have described in these pages applies to the "small p" politics of private life as well as it does to the "big p" politics of public life. Politics attaches to *all* group phenomena. It doesn't just take place in forums of official deliberation. You don't need robes or uniforms or formal proceedings to have politics. The politics of the kitchen table is as interesting and complex as the politics of the cabinet table.

Finally, analyzing social life with the methodology of rational choice spans political science, sociology, economics, law, and philosophy and probably other subjects as well. Within political science, the rational choice approach is not limited to the study of American politics, though I drew many examples and illustrations from that arena. As Chapter 16 endeavored to illustrate, rational choice approaches to the study of parliamentary politics are well developed. So, too, are other aspects of comparative politics. International relations, whether in the study of national security, trade, or other forms of strategic interaction, is something that has been subjected to rational choice analysis for many decades now. Even political philosophy lends itself to the rational-choice approach. It is hard to imagine a complete examination of what is just, or good, or fair without repairing to a consideration of what is rational for those involved.

If you've taken some of these lessons away from a reading of this volume, then the enterprise of writing it has been worth it to me (and the enterprise of reading it has been worth it to you). If you haven't, then return to Chapter 1 and try it again! In either case, I encourage you to dip into the ever-growing literature on the subject, some of the more important contributions to which I have footnoted along the way. I believe the approach surveyed in these pages enriches the study of politics, but with this volume you have only scratched the surface.

Index